EUROPEAN
DEMOCRACIES

Meinem lieben

und interesanten

Freund Bill

Jan. 92   Stoy

Second Edition

EUROPEAN DEMOCRACIES

JÜRG STEINER

University of North Carolina at Chapel Hill
and
University of Bern
Switzerland

Longman
New York & London

European Democracies, Second Edition

Copyright © 1991 by Longman, Publishing Group

Longman, 95 Church Street, White Plains, N.Y. 10601

Associated companies:
Longman Group Ltd., London
Longman Cheshire Pty., Melbourne
Longman Paul Pty., Auckland
Copp Clark Pitman, Toronto

Senior editor: David J. Estrin
Production editors: Camilla T.K. Palmer and The Bookmakers, Incorporated
Cover design and illustration: Tony Alberts
Text art: J & R Services, Inc.
Production supervisor: Kathleen Ryan

Library of Congress Cataloging-in-Publication Data

Steiner, Jürg.
    European democracies/Jürg Steiner.—2nd ed.
        p.   cm.
    Includes bibliographical references and index.
    ISBN 0-8013-0406-7
    1. Europe—Politics and government—1945–   I. Title.
JN94.A2S74   1991
320.94—dc20
                                                                                90-40311
                                                                                CIP

ABCDEFGHIJ-DO-99 98 97 96 95 94 93 92 91 90

CONTENTS

PREFACE

This textbook, written by a European for American students, grew out of many years' teaching at both American and European universities. I am often struck by how little European and American students know about each other. Lack of communication between the academic youth on either side of the Atlantic is a real danger for the Atlantic partnership. The goal of this book is to help American students better understand the political situation in which their European peers grow up.

The accessibility of this text should be helped by four pedagogical principles. First, *the student should be led from known to unknown material.* This principle is violated if a text written for American students immediately begins with comparisons among European countries. This method creates difficulties, because comparisons are made among unknowns. This text, however, systematically compares the European to the American experience. For each topic, the text begins with the American situation and then asks how the European situation is both similar and different.

Given this method, the organization of the text must be by topics and not by countries. But how can information about the individual countries be presented in a topical framework? This is accomplished by following a second pedagogical principle, according to which learning is better helped by *in-depth analysis of a few carefully chosen illustrations* than by broad surveys. If a text tries to cover all European countries, the treatment of each country must necessarily be somewhat superficial. Limiting the discussion to the three or four largest European countries is also unsatisfactory, because some of the most exciting political questions arise in the smaller European countries. Rejecting both a broad survey of all European countries and a limitation to the larger countries, it seems best to proceed by carefully selected illustrations. In this selection, although I show a bias favoring the larger countries—because of their greater importance in world politics— quite often a point can be much better illustrated using some of the smaller countries. For example, Sweden in the 1970s provides an excellent introduction to the concept of a minority cabinet with the rule of the small Liberal party. This relatively simple example is used to explain the general circumstances under which a party lacking a legislative majority might form a cabinet and govern. When the students have mastered the Swedish case, they should also be able to understand the much more complex history of Italian minority cabinets. Generally speaking, our second pedagogical principle means that complete coverage of the individual countries is not sought in this text. Instead, the goal is that the students obtain a grasp of the major

concepts of European politics and an ability to compare them with the
United States. The text does not encourage students to memorize facts and
names but, rather, to understand the principles behind them.

As a third pedagogical principle, the text explicitly addresses the *"So
what?" question.* When the students have seen the many ways in which
Europeans handle politics differently from Americans, they may ask: "So
what? What does this mean for us? Should we do it like Europeans, or should
they do it like us?" The discussion of each topic ends with such normative
questions. The role of the monarchy in Europe can be used as an illustration
here. In highly industrialized democracies, a monarchy often serves as a
stabilizing national symbol and contributes to political stability. What institutions and symbols serve equivalent stabilizing functions in the United
States? What, if any, attributes of a monarchy does the American presidency
contain?

The text raises normative questions without trying to answer them in any
definitive way. Arguments that I have encountered while teaching on both
sides of the Atlantic are presented. It is striking how American and European
students have different answers for many normative political questions.
While students need not share the same values, they should become more
aware of how their values differ. In studying these normative questions,
students will ultimately learn more about themselves and their values. Thus,
our third pedagogical principle leads back to the first one: The study of
European politics should not only start at home but also should end at
home. Having seen how Europe is different, American students may change
some of their ideas about how a good democracy should function, while at
the same time some of their old ideas may be reinforced.

In organizing the chapters of this book, I have relied on a fourth pedagogical principle, *Proceeding from the easy to the more difficult.* In the first
chapter, the political parties are presented in a straightforward, descriptive
way. As the book progresses, the book becomes increasingly complex up to
the last chapter, where the European Community is discussed.

For her editorial help, I thank my wife, Ruth.

Jürg Steiner

EUROPEAN DEMOCRACIES

INTRODUCTION

Since the first edition of this book, dramatic changes have taken place in what is understood to be a European democracy. When the first edition was published in 1986, there was a clear understanding that the Iron Curtain delimited democratic from nondemocratic countries. However, even in the first edition I stressed that Europe was not only a geographical region but a cultural concept. Although strong variation exists among European countries, they are bound together by a common culture based on centuries of close interaction. This common culture also includes the countries behind the Iron Curtain, a highly artificial, political division of Europe.

That the Iron Curtain was highly artificial has been forcefully shown in the meantime. In the summer of 1989, the Hungarians tore down the barbed wire, and, while George Bush was visiting Budapest, he received as a symbolic gift a small part of the wire. Of even greater symbolic significance was the opening of the Berlin Wall on November 9, 1989. In the latter part of 1989 and the first half of 1990, a democratic process and freedom sped all over Eastern and Central Europe.

Here a discussion is in order about the terms Eastern and Central Europe (see map of European countries, page 2). During the Cold War, it became customary to classify Europe simply as Western and Eastern. This corresponded to the political reality of Europe. All the Communist countries were considered as Eastern Europe, all noncommunist countries as Western Europe. From a geographical view, this classification was not altogether correct, because there were some Communist territories more to the west than some noncommunist territories. Prague, for example, the capital of then Communist Czechoslovakia, is located more to the west than Vienna, the capital of Austria, a Western democracy since World War II. After the end of the Cold War, the division into Western and Eastern Europe became even more problematic. The old historical concept of Central Europe was then revived. Czechoslovakia, in particular, emphasized that historically and culturally it belonged to Central and not to Eastern Europe. Such classifications often have great symbolic value, speaking to deep-rooted identities of a country. During my visit to Czechslovakia in May 1990, I heard time and again that Eastern Europeans are people like Bulgarians and Romanians. This was always said in a pejorative way. The implication was that Prague is an old cultural center, not to be mixed up with the supposedly less cultured people living more to the East.

But what countries belong to Central Europe? Historically, Czechoslovakia, Austria, and Germany were considered to be at the core of Central

1

Figure 1. The European Countries.

Europe. It is more ambiguous whether Hungary and Poland belong to Central Europe or to Eastern Europe. When I visited Hungary in the summer of 1989, I heard hardly any references to Central or Eastern Europe. Hungarians like to insist that they are simply Europeans and contrast themselves with the Russians who are supposedly not Europeans. According to the predominant Hungarian view, Europe ends at the Hungarian-Russian border. But Mikhail Gorbachev often uses the metaphor of the common European house, which according to him also has space for the Soviet Union. But what parts of the Soviet Union? Gorbachev certainly means Russian cities like Leningrad and Moscow. Does he also mean non-Russian republics at the Soviet-Chinese border? This entire discussion shows that geographical terms may take on great political significance. In the course of this book, I will take account of the fact that terms like *Eastern Europe*, *Central Europe*, and for that matter *Europe* at large, may be defined in quite different ways. Such differing definitions will, for example, be important in the context of the European Community and its possible expansion to the east (Chapter 16).

Writing about "European Democracies," not only the term *Europe* has to be defined but the term *democracy* as well.

In a broad sense, we can define *democracy* as a regime in which citizens elect their leaders in regular and competitive elections and in which basic civil liberties are protected. Although this definition helps to distinguish countries that are clearly democratic from countries that are clearly undemocratic, we must also distinguish between different levels of democracy: Elections may give citizens more or less say in the political process, civil liberties may be more or less protected. Throughout this book, we will tackle the question of how democratic the European countries are, and how far the process of democratization has advanced in Central and Eastern Europe. Of particular interest to American students will be how the European countries fare in comparison with democracy as it is practiced in the United States.

None of the European countries has such a long and continuous history of democracy as the United States, although they are generally much older countries (see the photos on page 3 for a testimony to the historical and cultural heritage of Europe). France, as a result of its 1789 revolution, was the first European country to adopt a modern form of democracy. But that attempt ended in failure, and France suffered other setbacks, including the regime of Marshal Pétain in World War II. In West Germany and Italy, the current democratic institutions rose from the ashes of World War II and the

Testimony to the Historical and Cultural Heritage of Europe: In 1285, Edward I Founded Harlech Castle, *above*, in Wales. (Courtesy British Embassy, Bern, Switzerland.) *Right*, A Painting by Peter Paul Rubens (1577–1640). (Courtesy Belgian Embassy, Bern, Switzerland.)

dictatorships of Adolf Hitler and Benito Mussolini. Spain, Greece, and Portugal only reestablished democratic regimes in the mid-1970s, when they were able to overthrow right-wing dictatorships. Among the large European countries, Great Britain has the longest uninterrupted history of democracy. But, although some democratic notions can be traced as far back as medieval times, it took the British until the latter part of the nineteenth century to implement fully the basic democratic principle, "one man, one vote," and female suffrage was achieved only after World War I. Of all the European countries, Switzerland was the first (1848) to introduce the principle of "one man, one vote" on a continuous basis. But, as an important qualification, we must add that Swiss women only won the right to vote as recently as 1971. In this same context, Americans should acknowledge that, despite their proud history of more than 200 years of democracy, blacks and women for a long time had no political rights.

In Europe, the struggle for democracy took place in a very different context than in America. For Americans, the introduction of democracy went hand in hand with liberation from a colonial power. In Europe, the ideas of democracy had to overcome a highly stratified feudal system to which the notion that all human beings have equal rights was alien. Americans had a great advantage in building their democratic institutions from scratch, without the impediment of deep-seated feudal structures. Even today, the feudal heritage has an impact on European societies. This impact is not so much that the differences between rich and poor are any greater than in the United States; rather, the opposite is true. In Europe, although the rich have lost much of their wealth because of steep taxes, many of them retain a distinct life-style, differentiating them from the lower strata of society. Speech patterns, for example, tend to differ from the highest to the lowest levels of European societies. In France and Great Britain, in particular, it is easy to tell from the way someone speaks whether he or she belongs to a higher or a lower social stratum. For Americans, the importance Europeans attach to titles is also striking. There are still people in Great Britain who are addressed, "my Lord," or, "my Lady." In Germany, one of the leading politicians of the Free Democratic party uses the title *Graf* (duke), because he stems from an old family of nobility. Academic titles are also widely used, particularly in German-speaking areas. Not only medical doctors but also, for example, doctors of law or physics are commonly addressed as "Herr Doktor" or "Frau Doktor."

Besides speech mannerisms and titles, status differences are also stressed in European societies in the pursuit of leisure activities. Members of higher social strata rarely watch sporting events, which they consider more of a lower-class entertainment. In the United States, the situation is generally quite different: football, basketball, and baseball are eagerly followed, regardless of social status. The difference between European and American leisure cultures illustrates the importance of an egalitarian tradition in America, despite the very uneven distribution of wealth. In Europe, in contrast, differences are less with regard to material wealth but greater with regard to life-style. Social stratification is revealed more subtly in Europe than in the United States. For example, a Rolls-Royce salesman states that the top bankers in Zurich hardly ever buy his luxurious car—they do not like to display their wealth conspicuously. This does not mean that they are not conscious of their high social status but, rather, that they like to display it more subtly.

1

Political Parties

The years 1989 and 1990 brought great changes for communism in both Eastern and Western Europe, and it is not altogether clear what the future of communism will be in Europe. I will try to evaluate these prospects at the end of this section, but, first, let us go back to the intellectual roots of communism and discuss classical Marxism. Then I will describe how Neo-Marxists analyze the class structure of current industrialized societies. I will emphasize that we may very well agree with Neo-Marxist class analysis without necessarily subscribing to Marxist proposals for change. One strategy for Marxist change is terrorism; although the use of this strategy has subsided, I will describe how in the late 1970s and 1980s terrorism of the Left was important in countries like Italy, West Germany, and France. A very different strategy is used by the official Communist parties of Western Europe, which participate in the electoral process, and we will see that these parties have had some electoral success, in particular in Italy. Communism had a very different meaning in the countries of Eastern and Central Europe, and we will see exactly how these Communist regimes crumbled in 1989.

Classical Marxism

Who was Karl Marx, the man who to this day maintains a great influence on the entire European Left? A German philosopher, Marx was born in 1818 in Trier, in southwest Germany, and died in 1883 in exile in London. Among his famous publications are *Capital* and, together with Friedrich Engels, *The Communist Manifesto* (see Box 1.1). There is an extensive literature that has tried to interpret the writings of Marx. Specialists often disagree about what Marx said on particular points, and on some points Marx may have been ambivalent or may have changed his position during his life. European students are much more interested than their American peers in the intricacies of Marx's thought. His global explanations of world history appeal to their ideological inclinations. American students, on the other hand, are often too pragmatic to find much interest in the thinking style of Marx.

What is this style? It is a *deductive* way of arriving at conclusions. Marx starts with axioms, or assumptions, that are formulated at a very general and abstract level. From these axioms he then makes deductions about reality. Most American students are more accustomed to starting with observations of reality and moving from there to generalizations. This *inductive* style of

7

BOX 1.1

EXCERPTS FROM THE "COMMUNIST MANIFESTO"

The proletariat will use its political supremacy to wrest, by degrees, all capital from the bourgeoisie, to centralize all instruments of production in the hands of the State, i.e., of the proletariat organized as a ruling class; and to increase the total productive forces as rapidly as possible. . . .

The Communists disdain to conceal their views and aims. They openly declare that their ends can be attained only by the forcible overthrow of all existing social conditions. Let the ruling class tremble at a Communistic revolution. The proletarians have nothing to lose but their chains. They have a world to win.

Working men of all countries, unite!

Source: The World's Great Thinkers. Man and the State: The Political Philosophers (New York: Random House, 1947), pp. 509, 523. (Originally published in 1847 by Karl Marx and Friedrich Engels.)

---

thinking is in sharp contrast to the way Marx reasons. What are the assumptions on which the philosophy of Marx is based? The most basic axiom is that human thinking and behavior are determined by economic factors. Marx speaks of an economic infrastructure and a noneconomic superstructure. Therefore, all meaningful explanations must begin with the economy of a society—its infrastructure. Causality begins with the material aspects of human life. All other aspects, such as politics, religion, education, and the arts, belong to the superstructure. These superstructural aspects can be understood only on the basis of their economic infrastructure. Thus, in the Marxist view, religion has a primarily economic function; religious beliefs can be understood only on the basis of the society's economic infrastructure.

The economy is a broad concept, so which characteristics of economic life are of particular importance according to Marx? Here we come to a second basic assumption: The ownership of the means of production is the crucial factor. Marx distinguishes three means of production: land, capital, and labor. The basic distinction in society is whether someone owns land and capital or can offer only his or her labor. In industrial societies the former are *capitalists* and the latter, *proletarians*. During the early period of industrialization, when Marx wrote, many people could not clearly be classified as belonging to one of these two social classes. A baker, for example, who worked with his family and, perhaps, an apprentice, was neither a capitalist nor a proletarian. Marx predicted that such intermediate cases would become less and less frequent and that society would increasingly be divided into only the two classes of capitalists and proletarians. This prediction corresponded to what was to him a historical law, one he thought he had discovered in studying the industrialization of his time. With the increased costs of new technologies, companies needed to become bigger and bigger in order to survive. If the baker wanted to remain competitive, he had to transform his family bakery into a big factory. If he was not successful, he would become a laborer in such a factory. Land and capital accumulate in the hands of fewer and fewer capitalists, and these capitalists become richer and richer. But competition among capitalists remains fierce, and to finance their expansion they need money. The place where they can easily get this money is the proletariat. In this context, Marx coins the concept of *surplus value of labor*. This is the value of work done by the proletarians that is not returned to them in the form of wages but that is kept by the capitalists in the form of profits. According to Marx, this surplus value of labor will steadily increase so that less and less will remain for the proletarians, who will sink into poverty. This is what Marx means when he calls the capitalists exploiters and the proletarians exploitees.

Finally, Marx argues that the frustration of the proletariat will eventually lead to a revolution that will overthrow the capitalists and bring the proletariat to power. Following the historical laws that Marx thought he had discovered, this revolution will occur by necessity. The question is only where and when it will begin. According to Marx, it is also certain that the revolution ultimately will be successful. There is a broad Marxist literature about the exact circumstances of this revolution, concerning, for example, the role intellectuals must play in it. In our context, the most important point is that, at first, the proletariat establishes a dictatorship. Marx calls this the *Socialist phase*. This dictatorship is necessary in order to prevent a counterrevolution of the capitalists, who may also operate from foreign countries. Consequently, it is necessary to bring the proletarian revolution to the entire world. The capitalists, with their selfish profit orientation, must be defeated everywhere, and, until this is achieved, the proletariat must maintain its dictatorship.

The transition from the Socialist to the *Communist phase* can occur only when the capitalist mentality has been eliminated from the world. At this point, the dictatorship of the proletariat will no longer be necessary. All people will have been educated to think in an altruistic, unselfish way instead of their earlier egotistical way. With this new orientation, all people will take from society only what they need, and they will contribute everything that is in their capabilities. As a consequence, there will be no more scarcities, only a happy situation of plenty . Under these circumstances, the state—with its authority to regulate scarcity—becomes unnecessary, and it will fade away.

Within this plan of ultimate salvation, Marxism may be interpreted as a religion or, at least, as a substitute for a religion (see Box 1.2). This is the position taken, for example, by the famous French writer Albert Camus.[1] As with a religion, the promise of one day reaching a utopian land of no evil encourages people to sacrifice in the present. According to Camus, the uncertainties of the past and the present can be overcome by the certainties of the future.

Neo-Marxist Class Analysis

Marx presented a sociological class analysis that is logically separate from the promise of an ultimate classless society. One may agree with Marx's class analysis without agreeing with his promise of a classless society.

BOX 1.2

MARXISM AS RELIGION

What were the attractions of revolutionary Marxism that drew so many passionate intellectuals to its flag? What was the faith that, like that of the first-century Christian martyrs, summoned many to die for a cause? In one respect, the answer is simple: What once had appealed in the name of God crossed over to the banner of History. The belief remained in an eschatology that would end a divided consciousness, which placed men in a state of alienation. Marxism was a secular region.

Source: Daniel Bell, "The Fight for the 20th Century: Raymond Aron versus Jean-Paul Sartre," *New York Times Book Review*, February 18, 1990, p. 3.

At European universities, Marx's method of analyzing social classes has had a great influence on disciplines such as sociology, political science, economics, and history. This remains true even after the belief in Marx's utopia of an ultimate classless society has greatly faded. In order to communicate with their European peers, American students should be familiar with Marx's class analysis. This does not mean, of course, that they have to agree with the analysis, but they should be acquainted with the concepts used in Marxist class analysis.

Was Marx right in his belief that highly industrialized societies will become increasingly characterized by a two-class structure of capitalists and proletarians? American students always offer empirical arguments to refute Marx's class analysis. Their major contentions are:

1. Workers have not sunk into an impoverished proletarian situation. Instead, they are able to improve their standard of living, and today most of them enjoy a considerable wealth of consumer goods.
2. Stocks are not concentrated in the hands of a few individuals but are widely dispersed throughout the population.
3. Business decisions are not only influenced by those who own companies but also by a wide range of managers with special skills.
4. Class structure is flexible, and there are many people who, thanks to their energy and intelligence, move from the bottom to the top in their own lifetime.
5. There is a growing public sector of teachers, police, tax collectors, etc. For these occupations the distinction between capitalist and proletarian does not apply.
6. The democratic organization of elections gives everyone the same voting power without regard for ownership of land and capital.
7. Besides the difference between social classes, there are other important social distinctions; for example, those based on religion, race, language, and region.

All these arguments add up to a pluralistic view of society. This view does not deny the fact that some people are very rich while others are very poor. Most people, however, are somewhere in the middle class—some a little higher, others a little lower. How can anyone possibly claim that society is simply divided into capitalists and proletarians? Yet this is what modern-day Marxists do say. They are known as Neo-Marxists because they interpret the thinking of Marx in a new light. Their analyses often differ in details, but the conclusion is always the same: The highly industrialized countries of Western Europe and, incidentally, North America have basically a two-class structure, of capitalists and proletarians (on the power of capital see Box 1.3).

What do these Neo-Marxists have to say about each of the seven arguments just given? It is impossible to summarize here Neo-Marxist thinking in all its nuances, but their position is roughly as follows:

1. To give the workers access to consumer goods has a double advantage for the capitalists. First, it helps to pacify the workers. If they have cars for traveling and TV sets for watching sports, they lose their revolutionary zeal. But to possess consumer goods does not mean that the workers have gained any control over the important economic decisions in society; it only means that they forget that they have no real economic influence at all. The workers have moved into a state of *false class consciousness*. Blinded by the richness of consumer goods, they think subjectively that they are no longer exploited, whereas objectively they still are. Second, it gives consumer goods to the workers to keep the capitalist system going. Having carefully studied Marx, the capitalists are aware of the danger that an impoverished proletariat could not buy the increasing number of goods produced by the capitalist system. To prevent this danger, the capitalists are willing to increase the workers' wages. Although this marginally diminishes the profits of the capitalists in the short run, their profits will soar in the long run as a result of higher production levels. Therefore, giving consumer goods to the workers in no way threatens the powerful position of those who own land and capital.

2. But what about the argument that today many workers are themselves owners of stocks? Can't these workers exercise power in shareholders' annual meetings? Not

---

BOX 1.3

ON THE POWER OF CAPITAL

Though Marx's predictions about the immiseration of labor has proven quite inaccurate due to the astonishing productivity of capitalism, his description of the fundamental division between wage labor and capital is still descriptive of a considerable social reality. . . .

[O]nce this social division of labor has been established, so too is the political division of labor, regardless of procedural fairness, equal access to office, and rules about liberty. Productive enterprise is a society's lifeblood; those who legally control it—who monopolize both the authority and the power to set it in motion—have a special claim on the attention of the governing elite, even if the latter's members are not themselves capitalists or even morally sympathetic to the rule of private capital. People who are merely dispensable bodies have no claim at all, as such.

Source: Philip Green, "Equality Since Rawls: Objective Philosophers, Subjective Citizens, and Rational Choice," *Journal of Politics* 47 (August 1985): 982.

really, say Neo-Marxists. In order to have true power in a company, one must own a large block of its stocks, not just a token few. With 5 or 10 shares, workers get some dividends (and perhaps a nice meal at the shareholders' meeting) but have no real economic influence. The major effect is a reinforcement of their false class consciousness. With the possession of a few shares of stock, workers think of themselves as members of the middle class. Hoping to share in the profits, they now support the capitalist system. Thus, the dominant position of the capitalists is strengthened if they disperse stocks broadly among the population as long as they keep the majority of the stocks in their own hands, which of course they do.

3. How do Neo-Marxists handle the argument that many important business decisions are influenced, not by majority shareholders, but by managers, most of whom count themselves among the middle classes? A Neo-Marxist would respond that one must distinguish between the top managers, on the one hand, and the middle- and lower-level managers, on the other hand. The latter are merely useful tools in the hands of the capitalists. They help to control the workers, which does not mean that they have any broad-based economic power. Although they are not aware of it, these middle- and lower-level managers are just as exploited as the workers—in many ways even more so—because they have fewer opportunities to escape the pressures of work. The top managers, on the other hand, belong to the capitalist class, with which they share the same social background and values. Quite often, these top managers or their families also own a high percentage of the company's stock.

4. Aren't there top managers who have advanced their careers, not as a result of family ties, but through hard work and intelligence? Neo-Marxists do not deny the existence of such upward mobility, but they insist that such cases are rare and do not threaten the capitalist system. Before someone is allowed to reach the top level of a company, this person is carefully screened to make sure that he or she accepts the basic values of capitalism. Therefore, such upwardly mobile people constitute no threat to the existing class structure. Their success stories even help to reinforce this structure by giving it the appearance of flexibility. Here Neo-Marxists allude to the tendencies of the mass media to publicize the life stories of people who move from the bottom to the top. But these stories are always of a few rare cases, and the fact that the overwhelming majority of proletarians never has a chance to enter the capitalist class does not change. Yet, seeing others move up, proletarians begin to attribute their own failure to personal shortcomings instead of the objective characteristics of the existing class structure. Such a perception further diminishes the class consciousness of the proletariat.

5. How does the increasing number of public employees fit into the Neo-Marxist distinction between capitalists and proletarians? Just as in the private sector, a distinction is made between top public employees and the middle and lower levels. The top bureaucrats belong to the capitalist class, with which they share the same social background and values. Whenever a basic conflict between the social classes arises, the top bureaucrats always take the procapitalist position. Specifically, this means that the top bureaucrats always defend the concept of private property. Top bureaucrats only remain neutral in conflicts between two property rights; for example, between two automobile companies. Middle- and lower-level public employees are merely useful tools in the hands of the top bureaucrats. Teachers in the public schools help to socialize the children to the values of the capitalist system. In order to support this argument, Neo-Marxists refer to textbooks that teach children in subtle ways how the profit motive contributes to the betterment of society. Police help the capitalists to control the proletariat, and tax collectors extract money from the lower class. Although teachers,

police, tax collectors, and other public employees in similar positions are probably not aware of it, objectively they are in an exploited proletarian situation.

6. Isn't there a basic equality in Western democracies in the sense that every citizen has the same power to elect political leaders? Again, Neo-Marxists disagree. First, decisions made by politicians are relatively unimportant compared with the decisions made in the boardrooms of the big multinational corporations. The main function of the political game is to entertain the public while diverting its attention from the more important business decisions, which are made in secret. As a second point, to the extent that elections have any importance, they are manipulated by capitalist money. All the money goes to the major parties and, therefore, buys influence over nearly all candidates. To understand the outcome of elections, it is also important to know that newspapers, television, and radio are all directly or indirectly controlled by capital.

7. It may be true that there is an important social distinction between the superrich and everyone else. But aren't other social differences equally important? Not according to Neo-Marxists. These other distinctions either reinforce the class difference or are merely superficial. The former situation is found in the conflict between Protestants and Catholics in Northern Ireland, where the capitalist class is almost exclusively Protestant, while almost all Catholics have proletarian status. This does not mean that there are no Protestant proletarians, only that nearly all capitalists are Protestant. In the view of Neo-Marxists, this religious element helps to hide the real class structure. Capitalists are defended by proletarians of Protestant faiths who are not aware of their real class interest—which, objectively, would be with the proletarians, regardless of religious affiliation. Differences other than those based on social class can also be purely superficial, like the language divisions in Switzerland, where capitalists come from all three major linguistic areas. Large banks are located in German-speaking Zurich, French-speaking Geneva, and Italian-speaking Lugano. Objectively, the proletariat from all three linguistic groups has the same class interest. To play one linguistic group against another is merely a surface conflict that helps to divert attention from the real class conflict.

Looking at all seven arguments, we can see that the crucial point of Neo-Marxists is that false class consciousness prevents the present-day proletariat from recognizing its subordinate class status. American students traveling in Europe are always surprised that so many of their European peers are Neo-Marxists or at least have some sympathies for Marxist thinking. An extensive literature by a great variety of authors deals with nuances of Neo-Marxist class analysis. There is, for example, a heated debate among Neo-Marxists over exactly how to delimit the capitalist class in various Western countries. Pauline M. Rosenau stresses correctly that "(c)ontemporary Marxism is not a monolith, but rather constituted of different orientations with conflicting ideas. . . . Marxists do not have a single, unified, coherent set of philosophical and methodological assumptions about research any more than do non-Marxists."[2] European students are usually quite familiar with this literature and are surprised not to find the same familiarity among their American counterparts.

Can Neo-Marxists be convinced that Western societies are not simply divided into capitalists and proletarians? Or is Marxism like religious faith, which cannot be changed through rational argument? Do Marxists simply see what they wish to see? Perhaps. But this may be equally true of non-Marxists who see Western countries as pluralist middle-class societies.

Neo-Marxist class analysis of Western societies cannot be invalidated through reference to the rigid class structure of Soviet society. This is usually the first debating point that American students try to make. But a typical European Neo-Marxist would immediately agree that the Soviets have a rigid class structure, which should not be taken as a model for the West. Logically, an analysis of Western societies is separate from whatever one may find in the Soviet Union; therefore, a refutation of the Neo-Marxist class analysis of Western societies must stand on its own merits. The question remains: Why Neo-Marxist class analysis is so much more prevalent among European than among American students? Much has to do with differences in the educational system, which are covered in Chapter 9.

In the European population at large, Neo-Marxist class analysis is much less popular than it is among Europe's academic youth. The ordinary Communist voter is not very interested in the intellectual subtleties of Neo-Marxist class analysis. The unskilled workers of southern Italy, for example, have probably never read Marx. But from their own life experience they see society divided into a few rich and large masses of poor. This life experience makes them receptive to the Communist message—that a few capitalists exploit the helpless masses of the proletariat.

The Terrorist Left

Although Neo-Marxist factions agree that Western societies are divided basically into two classes—capitalists and proletarians—they disagree widely on how revolutionary change should be effected. There are heated debates among Neo-Marxists about exactly what Marx meant by the concept of revolution and how he would interpret this concept under current social and political conditions. The terrorist Left uses violence to overthrow the existing class system, while the official Communist parties hope to cause revolutionary change through democratic participation in the electoral process. The terrorist Left was particularly active in the 1970s and early 1980s. At that time, the viewer of American TV news heard quite a lot about Marxist terrorists in Europe. Estimates are difficult to make, but probably no more than a few thousand people in all of Western Europe were ever active in the terrorist Left. The European terrorist Left consists of no single organization but is split into a large number of groups that often are in fierce competition with one another. Well known among these groups are the Red Brigade in Italy, the Red Army Faction in West Germany, and Direct Action in France (see Boxes 1.4 and 1.5). Through kidnappings, assassinations, and other spectacular terrorist acts, these groups attract worldwide attention to their cause. Just what is this cause? What are they fighting for?

The terrorist Left of Europe believes that capitalism can only be overcome through violence. But because most proletarians have lost their true class consciousness, the violent overthrow of capitalism has become difficult. Before a successful revolution can take place, the proletariat must be

_____ **BOX 1.4** _____

A TOP ITALIAN LABOR ECONOMIST IS SHOT DEAD

A prominent economist for a labor federation was shot and killed here today, and the Red Brigades terrorist group claimed responsibility.

The police said Prof. Ezio Tarantelli, 43 years old, a leading advisor to the Roman Catholic-led union, the Italian Federation of Unionized Workers, was approached at noontime by two men in a university parking lot after he gave a lecture at Rome University.

They fired at him with a submachine gun and a revolver, the police said, and Professor Tarantelli was struck by at least 10 bullets. He died on arrival at a nearby university hospital. . . .

Source: New York Times, March 28, 1985.

stripped of its false consciousness so that it can recognize again the extent of its exploitation by the capitalists. How can this be demonstrated with sufficient clarity and vividness? Provoke the capitalists so that they are forced to show their real face. If you shoot them in the knees and kill a few, they will

_____ **BOX 1.5** _____

2 AMERICANS ARE KILLED AS CAR BOMB EXPLODES AT AIR BASE NEAR FRANKFURT

FRANKFURT (AP)—A bomb hidden in a parked car exploded Thursday morning outside the heavily guarded headquarters of the U.S. Rhein-Main Air Base, killing two persons and injuring 17, the authorities said.

In Washington, Larry Speakes, the White House spokesman, said that an American serviceman and a civilian American woman were killed in the blast. Of the injured, he said, 13 were U.S. servicemen, two were American civilians and two were foreign nationals.

No group claimed responsibility for the attack. The authorities suspect the leftist Red Army Faction.

The bomb went off at 7:15 A.M. in a parking lot near the headquarters building of the 435th Tactical Airlift Wing as many base personnel were reporting to duty. Investigators said the bomb was in a red Audi that had false American Forces license plates.

Security at the base, which adjoins Frankfurt Airport, is tight and all drivers are stopped at a checkpoint and asked to produce identification before entering the parking lot where the blast occurred.

Source: International Herald Tribune, August 9, 1985.

─────────────────────────── **BOX 1.6** ───────────────────────────

HEAD OF TOP WEST GERMAN BANK IS KILLED IN BOMBING BY TERRORISTS

BAD HOMBURG, West Germany—The head of West Germany's largest commercial bank was killed today when terrorists detonated a remote-control bomb, demolishing the automobile in which he was being driven to work.

Alfred Herrhausen, 59 years old, died instantly and his driver was seriously wounded in the blast at 8:34 this morning, the police said. The attack took place next to a popular thermal-bath spa on the Seedammweg, a busy, tree-lined street about three-quarters of a mile from Mr. Herrhausen's home in this fashionable suburb 12 miles north of Frankfurt.

Officials at the scene said a note was found nearby bearing the symbol of the Red Army Faction, a West German terrorist group that has taken responsibility for the killing. It was signed in the name of the Wolfgang Beer Commando.

Source: New York Times, November 31, 1989.

bring out their military and police forces, and the brutality of their regime will become visible. The eyes of the proletariat will be opened to the true class situation.

To date, this terrorist Left strategy has largely failed. The authorities have reacted to the waves of terrorism with moderation and within legal limits. Instead of turning against the authorities, the workers have turned against the terrorists. In Italy, for example, huge numbers of workers demonstrated several times against the terrorist Left. Yet, confronted with this failure, the terrorists' answer is simple: We have not provoked enough. The capitalist pigs are still hiding their fascist face—therefore, we must provoke even more!

Who are these terrorists? Are they the poorest of the poor in society, acting out of desperation? Not at all. Most terrorists come from affluent families and attended good schools. Women are heavily involved in the terrorist Left. Originally, many of these people had high ideals, a vision of a utopian classless society with happiness for all. But, once engaged in terrorist activity, they are so busy hiding, robbing, and acquiring weapons that they no longer have the time and leisure to reflect on the reality of this classless society. Consequently, the terrorist Left produces few ideas about what will happen *after* a successful proletarian revolution. With such a lack of clear ideas for the future, they have no chance of setting the European masses on fire. Their terror is, of course, real and often tragic, but it constitutes no major threat to the European democracies. In the late 1980s and early 1990s, terrorism by the Left diminished but there are still occurences (see Box 1.6).

_____ COMMUNIST PARTIES IN WESTERN EUROPE _____

Voter support for the Communist parties varies greatly among the Western European democracies, with Italy having by far the greatest Communist strength (see Table 1). American TV viewers may be tempted to identify the official Communist parties with the terrorist Left. But there is no surface connection between the two, although some people question whether there may be a level of secret collaboration, so that, ultimately, terrorist leftists and official Communists will band together.

First, let's look at public statements. The Communist parties in the various Western European democracies declare that they are not involved in any terrorist activities; their strategies are exclusively peaceful. They claim to respect basic democratic principles—in particular, the promise to accept the outcome of free elections. The Soviet Union is no longer used as a role model. On the contrary, for many years the Soviets were severely criticized, for example, over the invasion of Afghanistan and the existence of concentration camps. The Western European Communist parties say that they choose their own, European way.

What are their goals? In their election campaigns, they promise to bring more justice to European societies. They advocate stiffer taxes on the rich and more generous social programs for the poor. Would such policies ultimately lead to a classless society? This question is rarely discussed in their electoral campaigns, and it is irrelevant to the poor in Europe. The poor seek additional health care, education, old age insurance, and unemployment programs, and it is at this pragmatic and concrete level that the Communist parties in Western Europe are politically active. This does not mean that they have given up the Marxist goal of a classless society but rather that this goal is not of immediate concern in the daily lives of Communist leaders and voters. The Western European Communist parties consider the terrorist Left an unwelcome diversion because it endangers the Communists' progress to-

Table 1

Voter Support for Communist Parties in National Parliamentary
Elections (percentage, most recent year)

Austria	0.7	Italy	26.6
Belgium	0.8	Luxembourg	5.8
Denmark	0.9	Netherlands	0.6
Finland	9.7	Norway	0.2
France	11.3	Portugal	12.5
Federal Republic of Germany	0.1	Spain	5.7
Greece	11.7	Sweden	5.4
Ireland	0.0	Switzerland	0.8
		United Kingdom	0.0

Sources: European Journal of Political Research,: "General Elections in Western Nations," Vol. 14–17, 1986–89.

ward democratic respectability. For them, the terrorists are spoiled bourgeois youth "playing" at revolution; thus the Italian workers' demonstrations
against the terrorist Left. The workers seek immediate improvement in their
economic situation, not an elusive utopia.

On the other hand, the terrorist Left considers the official Communist
parties as traitors to the Marxist cause, co-opted by the capitalist system. By
taking part in meaningless elections and parliamentary debates, the Communist parties play right into the hands of the capitalist enemy. By accepting
its rules of the game, they help to reinforce and legitimize the existing system
of exploitation. In giving the false appearance that the working class has
some power, the Communist parties contribute to the false consciousness of
the proletariat. With such arguments, it is no surprise that official Communist party leaders themselves have also become targets of terrorist attacks
from the Left. How can the Communists in Europe prove their democratic
orientation? There are three useful indicators:

Exercise of Governmental Responsibility at the Local Level   Especially
in Italy and France, there are many local communities where the Communist
party is in power. How is this power exercised? Are basic civil liberties
curtailed? The answer is clearly no. A well-known example is the old Italian
city of Bologna, which has been ruled for many years by the Communists and
enjoys a relatively good administration. Do such examples prove that the
Communists have accepted basic democratic principles? Not necessarily.
Local communities are subordinated to the national authorities, which control the military. If local authorities were to deviate from basic democratic
principles, the national authorities could intervene militarily. Thus the fear
of such intervention may make the Communist party behave in a democratic
way at the local level.

Exercise of Governmental Responsibility at the National Level   During
a brief period following World War II, France had some Communist cabinet
ministers. More important, from 1981 to 1984 the French cabinet was formed
by Socialists and Communists. Did the Communist party misuse this power
to limit democratic freedoms? Again the answer is no. But, again, this is not
sufficient proof that the Communist party accepts democracy as a form of
government. It is important that the Communists were the junior partner in
the coalition with the Socialists, so that they were not in control of the
military. At one time or another, Communists also exercised executive power
in Finland, Portugal, and Greece but, like in France, only as junior partners,
so the question remains open as to how the Communist party would act if it
had control of the military.

Internal Party Debate   Whether a party is internally democratic should be
an indication of whether it accepts democracy as a general principle for
society at large. This is a severe test, because most non-Communist parties
also violate to some extent the principles of internal democracy. It is widely
documented that some internal debate takes place in the Italian Communist

_____ BOX 1.7 _____

MARIO BENEDETTI, ITALIAN AUTO MECHANIC

They say now that the Communist Party is in a state of crisis, but I don't feel at all crisis-ridden. My belief is firm. I have never had a moment of crisis in this sense. . . . They are talking a lot now about renewal. As far as I'm concerned, the Italian Communist Party has never been old.

First of all, it is a party that has never stolen. It has always fought for the interests of the community and for social causes. . . .

The Communist Party has always fought for causes like social justice.

Source: New York Times, January 23, 1989.

party; for example, over the question of whether the Communist party and the Socialists should work together. Skeptics may object that such debates are merely organized shows to project the image of internal democracy. Other Communist parties, like the French, tolerate much less internal debate than the Italian party.

From these three indicators no definite conclusion can be drawn about how Communists would behave if they got full political control in a European democracy. This uncertainty may have contributed to some recent electoral losses of the Communist party in various European countries. The downswing of the Communist party is also due to the fact that it is increasingly perceived as an old-fashioned party. Besides the social class issue, concerning which the Communists have their best arguments, other issues, such as the environment and feminism, have come to the forefront. As we will see in Chapter 9, for these newer issues the Communist party has hardly any convincing answers, so many citizens turn elsewhere, such as various social movements and the Green party.

_____ BOX 1.8 _____

JEAN-PIERRE QUILGARS, FRENCH FACTORY WORKER

Being a Communist has brought me many things. It has brought me friends, a way to reflect on both political and personal life. It has permitted me to have confidence in myself and believe in myself. I couldn't think of not being a Communist. It's my life. I don't make an effort to be a Communist. I live it. . . .

I AM PROUD to be a Communist and have always been proud to be a Communist. There were difficult times on the international front, Afghanistan, for example, but I was never embarrassed to call myself a Communist.

Source: New York Times, January 23, 1989.

But the Communist party is certainly not yet dead in Western Europe. It still has many faithful supporters, as illustrated in Boxes 1.7 and 1.8, in which an Italian auto mechanic and a French factory worker express their continuing belief in the Communist ideals. The fate of the Communists in Western Europe will depend very much on what will happen in the next few years in Eastern Europe and the Soviet Union.

COMMUNIST PARTIES IN EASTERN EUROPE

Nineteen eighty-nine was the memorable year when Communist parties crumbled in Eastern Europe. This was an important turning point, not only for these countries, but also for world politics at large. The Cold War, which had raged for over 40 years, came to an end. The dramatic events of 1989 came as a surprise to nearly everyone. There was always much speculation about the future of the Communist countries in Eastern Europe, but none of these speculations turned out to be correct.

Prior to 1989, there were two prominent predictions about what would happen in the future in Eastern Europe. One prediction, most notably identified with Jeane Kirkpatrick (1982), stated that in Communist totalitarian regimes no real internal changes would ever occur. The other prediction was based on a broad literature of interaction theories and claimed that increased contacts with the West would cause slow, gradual changes in the Eastern European countries.

Kirkpatrick argued in the early 1980s that "the history of this century provides no grounds for expecting that radical totalitarian regimes will transform themselves."[3] She contrasted radical totalitarian regimes with traditional autocratic regimes. Regarding the latter, she mentioned such countries as Chile, Argentina, Brazil, Taiwan, and South Korea. Although all were dictatorships at the time, these countries were said to be relatively open to internal change because they did not penetrate and control society as thoroughly as the totalitarian regimes do. For the Communist countries, Kirkpatrick claimed that their rulers "have not abandoned their efforts to stay in power and to exercise comprehensive control over society, culture, and personality."[4] Therefore, no Communist country has ever "produced either freedom or development. Not one has evolved into a democracy. Not one."[5] Although Kirkpatrick was correct in saying that autocratic regimes such as Chile and Argentina were open to democratic change, she was wrong in saying that Communist countries were not.

George Homans, one of the founders of interaction theory, argued that frequent interactions among people would gradually and slowly bring their value systems and behavior closer together.[6] Many exchange programs between countries, including Eastern European countries, were based on this theory. Politically, the theory became important for the Social Democrats in Western Europe, in particular for the West German SPD, for their policy towards Eastern Europe. Willy Brandt's *Ostpolitik* was based precisely on the expectation that more contacts with the West would slowly Westernize the Communist regimes. Interaction theories were correct in stating that increased contacts with the West would change the Communist countries of Eastern Europe, but the theories were incorrect in predicting that these changes would be slow and gradual.

Our task now is to describe what actually happened in Eastern Europe in the historic year of 1989. The starting point must be that for a long time these countries were not independent but occupied satellites of the Soviet Union. Therefore, it is impossible to say what would have happened if each of the Eastern European countries could have taken the Communist path on its own. Perhaps some countries would have been quite successful; perhaps all would have failed.

In this context, it is interesting to mention the Spring Movement of 1968 in Czechoslovakia, when the Communist party of the country, under the leadership of Alexander Dubcek, launched reforms that were meant to lead to Communism "with a human face." That spring was a time of great hope and excitement. The reform-minded Communist leaders saw the possibility that the ideas of Marx could finally be implemented in a true sense and not perverted, as in the Soviet Union. Social justice and democracy seemed possible in a Communist-run country. For a few months Czechoslovakia was in a fever. Freedom of speech existed, the arts blossomed, and there was a lively discussion about the exact nature of the reforms. But the experiment was stopped in August of the same year when the Soviet tanks rolled into Prague. The people tried to hold discussions with the Soviet soldiers, putting flowers into the guns of the soldiers, but in vain. The reformers were ousted, stripped of their influence; some of them even were arrested. Thus, it is impossible to say where the reforms would have led.

What we have, then, in Eastern Europe is a test of Soviet-style communism. And, as the events of 1989 revealed in an unambiguous way, the verdict of the Eastern European people was clearly negative. Soviet-style communism has failed dismally in the Eastern European countries. But, once again, this test does not speak about what would have happened if the Eastern European countries could have implemented communism on their own. One may argue that without Soviet interference these countries may not have turned to communism to begin with. Perhaps not, but perhaps some of them would have.

The revolutionary events of 1989 clearly were triggered by the decision of the Soviet Union and its leader, Mikhail Gorbachev, to let the Eastern European countries go their own way. This change in Soviet policy was made quite explicit. Thus, the Foreign Ministry spokesman coined the term "Sinatra doctrine," referring to a song sung by Frank Sinatra in which he says that he did it "my way." This doctrine replaced the old Brezhnev doctrine, according to which the Soviet Union had the right to intervene in a brotherly way in order to protect communism in the Eastern European countries. It was based on this doctrine that the Soviet tanks rolled into Czechoslovakia in 1968.

The reasons behind the Soviet decision to change its policy can be interpreted in many different ways. To discuss such interpretations, however, is outside the scope of this book; I refer the reader to textbooks about the Soviet Union. The focus here shall be on what happened in Eastern Europe, once the threat of Soviet military intervention had vanished. I wish to demonstrate that each country took a somewhat different path. To be sure, 1989 can be seen as one big revolution, but nevertheless there were interesting national differences. What is also important to stress is that each country was greatly influenced by what happened in the other countries. Thus, we have a complex sequence of events spread across all Eastern European countries. The leaders of the revolution in a temporal sense were Hungary and Poland, followed later by East Germany, Czechoslovakia, Bulgaria, and finally Romania and Yugoslavia. At first, I will simply outline the sequence of events, but at the end I will also attempt to give some explanations.

Hungary

Hungary's development was farthest away from Kirkpatrick's predictions and closest to the expectations of interaction theories. It was the Communist party itself that launched the reforms. At first, beginning in the 1970s, the reform process was very slow and gradual. Step by step, some free market elements were introduced into the planned economy. Politically, reforms were much slower to come. It was only in 1988 that some political liberalization began to occur. The great surprise then was how quickly this liberalization swept the country in 1989. During a visit to Hungary in July 1989, I witnessed this liberalization firsthand. Sitting in sidewalk cafes in Budapest, some Hungarians spoke freely to me about the situation in the country, not sparing critique of the Communist party. Asked whether such frankness at a public place was not dangerous, the reply was each and every time: "no more." Traveling by bicycle through the countryside, I found the same frankness among the rural population. A railroad worker told me that recently he had spoken openly with his superior, a Communist party member, and that only a year ago, such frankness would have put him in prison.

In contrast to other Eastern European countries, the Communists in Hungary were not forced by public demonstrations to grant the right to free speech. It was rather the reform wing within the party itself that pushed for such a basic and far-reaching change. The leading reformer was Imre Pozsgay, who, like Alexander Dubcek in 1968 in Czechoslovakia, claimed to fight for communism "with a human face." The Hungarian Communists recognized publicly that in the past they had made grave mistakes. The gravest mistake of all was their bloody crushing down, together with the Soviets, of the revolution in October 1956. This mistake was acknowledged in June 1989 when Imre Nagy, the leader of the 1956 revolution, was allowed a hero's reburial. The current Communist leadership was present, together with a huge crowd, for this very emotional event. During my visit, the bookstores were full of critical accounts of how the Communists had crushed the 1956 revolution.

In the spring of 1989, the Communist rulers tore down the barbed wire at its Western border, and Hungarians were free to travel to the West. Indeed, a farm family, whom I had met during my trip, did visit me in Switzerland a few weeks later, receiving the travel visa without any difficulties.

Further signs of a fundamental change occurred when the Communists were willing to take their symbol, the red star, from public buildings (see Box 1.9) and when freedom of religion was adopted (see Box 1.10). The most important element of political liberalization is, of course, free elections. Already in the summer of 1989, there were two by-elections for parliament that could be considered free; in both cases the Communist candidate lost. General elections for parliament took place in March 1990. The results of these elections will be discussed in Chapter 2.

Poland

In the early 1980s, developments in Poland seemed to support the claim of Jeane Kirkpatrick that Communist regimes never truly change. When Solidarity, the trade union led by the charismatic Lech Walesa (photograph, page 24), became too active and too popular among the Polish people, the Communist party cracked down hard. Solidarity was banned, many of its leaders were arrested, and a state of emergency was declared. Once again, as in 1968 in Czechoslovakia, 1956 in Hungary and Poland, and 1953 in East Germany, Communism had shown its iron fist. Despair and frustration spread among the Polish people. The stiff and grim-looking general Wojciech Jaruszelski, who headed the government, became the symbol for the apparent unchangeability of Communism. Soviet troops were at hand threatening intervention if the Polish Communists were not tough enough.

In 1989, the situation dramatically changed for the better in Poland. Solidarity, which had continued to be active underground, was legalized again, political prisoners were released, and the Communists began round-table discussions with Lech Walesa and his colleagues. What had happened? The country's economic situation had deteriorated so much and the malaise

---

BOX 1.9

HUNGARY TAKES RED STAR FROM PUBLIC BUILDINGS

BUDAPEST—The red star, the symbol of Communist rule in the Soviet bloc for four decades, will be removed from all public buildings in Hungary to reflect the country's move to a multiparty democracy.

A Government spokesman, Zsolt Bajnok, told reporters Friday that the time had come to replace the red star with the Hungarian coat of arms. . . .

The red star decorates all Hungarian public buildings, including Government ministries, radio and television, regional and local government buildings and factories.

Source: New York Times, September 24, 1989.

—————————————————— BOX 1.10 ——————————————————

HUNGARIANS FORMALLY ADOPT LEGAL
GUARANTEE ON RELIGION

BUDAPEST—The Hungarian Parliament formally buried the anti-religious practices of four decades of Communism today by adopting a law on freedom of conscience and religion.

The measure, passed 304 to 1 with 11 abstentions, says that freedom of conscience and religion is a fundamental liberty not granted by the state or any other authority.

Source: New York Times, January 25, 1990.

among the population was so deep that Poland was at the brink of collapse. Pushed to the wall, the Communist leaders could not think of any other way out than to begin a dialogue with the banned opposition. Thus, the course of events in Poland was very different from that in Hungary. Whereas the Hungarian Communists launched the reforms on their own, the Polish Communists were forced to change because of the desperate state of the country. Poland offers, therefore, a much less convincing case than Hungary that Communists are able to initiate changes on their own.

Lech Walesa. (Courtesy Polish Embassy, Bern, Switzerland.)

The talks between the Communists and Solidarity led to a complicated deal about a formula for elections to the Sejm, the Polish parliament. Solidarity was allowed to run candidates, but only one-third of the parliamentary seats would be open for competition. The Communist party, still insisting on keeping its leading role in the state, claimed the other two-thirds for itself. Therefore, it was guaranteed from the beginning that the Communists would keep their parliamentary majority. The elections took place on June 4, 1989. They brought a triumph for Solidarity, which swept all seats that were openly contested. But power was still in the hands of the Communists. They recognized, however, that they had to share this power somehow with Solidarity. Complicated negotiations began again. The result was a complex scheme of power sharing. Parliament elected Jaruszelski president and, in this capacity, head of state. In return, the Communists were willing to elect someone from Solidarity as prime minister. Lech Walesa declined the offer, and one of his close associates, Tadeusz Mazowiecki, became prime minister on August 24, 1989. A further twist in the arrangement was that, within the cabinet, the military and the state security apparatus remained in the hands of the Communists. Overall, the arrangement did not reflect at all that Solidarity had won all parliamentary seats that were open for competition. The Polish people clearly supported Solidarity, but the Communists were dragging their feet. Despite the verdict of the people, they were unwilling to yield power, wanting to keep control of the presidency and, above all, the military and security forces. Poland shows how difficult it was, even in 1989, to unsettle the Communists.

The first free elections for Poland, in which all seats could be freely contested, came in May 1990 at the local level. I will discuss the results in Chapter 2.

East Germany

Under Communist rule, East Germany called itself the "German Democratic Republic" (GDR). The word *Democratic* in the name is confusing; it was simply a propaganda plot of the Communists. In West Germany, there was hope that the *Democratic* in the name of the East German state would gradually become more meaningful as contacts between the two German states became more frequent. As we will see, this was, in particular, the position of the West German Social Democrats when, under Chancellor Willy Brandt, they opened more ties with East Germany. After 1982, when the Social Democrats were no longer in government in Bonn (see page 120), they continued as a party to have close contacts with the Communists in East Germany. But the hopes of the West German Social Democrats were greatly disappointed. The East German Communists were unwilling to liberalize at all. In the summer of 1989, when the Chinese Communists crushed down the student movement in a very brutal and bloody way, East Germany was the only Eastern European country that supported the Chinese action.

Yet 1989 brought dramatic changes to East Germany too. The crucial element was the demonstration effect of the developments in Hungary and

Poland. East Germans had easy access to West German television and were thus well informed about the reforms in the two countries. Watching how others moved forward made their own situation all the more unbearable. Without the demonstration effect of Hungary and Poland, it is highly unlikely that in 1989 any changes would have occurred in East Germany.

In September 1989, Hungary influenced the changes in East Germany, not only indirectly, but suddenly in a very direct way by allowing East Germans staying in Hungary to emigrate to the West (Box 1.11). Travel within the Communist countries of Eastern Europe was always relatively free, and many East Germans used to spend their summer vacations in Hungary, which was known for its tourist attractions. During my trip to Hungary in the summer of 1989, I saw many East German cars in Budapest and at the lake of Balaton. When in the spring of 1989 the Hungarians began to tear down the barbed wire at the Western border (see page 22), many East Germans exploited the situation to escape to the West. The entire situation became so chaotic, with hundreds of East Germans attempting the flight every night, that the Hungarian government finally and officially allowed the East Germans to travel to the West. This action was a breach of a treaty with East Germany, which infuriated the East German government. It was a big rift in the Eastern bloc for one country to let the citizens of another country to travel freely to the West.

When the East German government made it increasingly difficult for its citizens to go to Hungary, many went to neighboring Czechoslovakia, at the time still a hard-line Communist country. These East Germans sought refuge at the West German embassy in Prague. In front of the embassy, dramatic scenes occurred with the Czech police, who were trying to prevent East

---

BOX 1.11

HUNGARY ALLOWS EAST GERMANS TO EMIGRATE

BUDAPEST—Hungary announced today that more than 7,000 East Germans who have refused to return home can leave for West Germany, the final chapter in a summerlong exodus through the new Hungarian gap in the Communist frontier.

A Government declaration said that because of the "unbearable situation" created by the tide of East Germans trying to leave their country, Hungary has decided to temporarily suspend a 20-year-old agreement with East Germany and to allow the refugees free passage "to a country of their choice."

"It's like Christmas," said a young worker as he hugged his teary-eyed girlfriend in a flood of television lights. Next to them, a mother stood in silent embrace with three daughters. And all around, scores of children continued to romp among the tents, trailers and piles of knapsacks.

Source: New York Times, September 11, 1989.

Germans from climbing over the embassy fence. These scenes were shown on TV all over the world and could also be seen in East Germany on West German TV. Symbols are always important in politics, and here was a very powerful symbol of how eager and desperate thousands of East Germans were to leave their country. What made these scenes so damning for the East German regime was that most refugees were young people with children, who apparently saw no more future in their country.

The West German embassy in Prague became so overcrowded that the situation became untenable simply from a point of view of hygiene. Finally, the East German government gave in and allowed the refugees to travel by special trains to West Germany, ironically taking a route through East German territory. Again, pictures of great symbolic power flashed over the TV screens of the world, showing the refugees with tears of joy in their eyes arriving at West German railway stations. These pictures could, of course, also be seen in East Germany, and there were emotional moments when young refugees waved, with the help of the TV cameras, to their aging parents left at home.

According to economist Albert Hirschman, political dissatisfaction can be expressed either through exit or through voice.[7] The thousands of East Germans who escaped to the West chose the exit strategy. If this had been the only strategy used, it probably would not have been sufficient to topple the East German government. It ultimately was a combination of both an exit and a voice strategy that brought the government down. Thousands of other East Germans decided to stay in their country and to voice their dissatisfaction through demonstrations. In October and November 1989, more and more people went to the streets to demonstrate peacefully for reforms. How would the Communist leaders react? Having supported the Chinese crackdown earlier in the year, would they apply the same method in their own country? The 77-year-old party boss Erich Honecker seemed unyielding. Although he denies it, he is said to have given the order to the police to shoot at the demonstrators, but he was ousted and replaced by a younger man, Egon Krenz, who claimed to have revoked the shooting order.

In the hope of bringing the situation under control, Krenz made a spectacular move forward, opening the Berlin Wall on November 9, 1989; Box 1.12 and the photo on page 29 capture well the ecstasy resulting from this decision. At first it seemed that Krenz's gamble would pay off. Most East Germans who crossed the border were delighted to take a stroll in the West but returned back home. I mentioned several times the symbolic power of pictures, but the celebrations of East and West Berliners standing on the wall was the most powerful picture of all. These pictures symbolized for many the end of the Cold War. The Berlin Wall was the quintessential symbol of the division of the world. Many American presidents and other Western leaders had called for it to be torn down, and now it was open.

With the opening of the Wall in East Germany, it was discovered that the old leaders had lived in great luxury. They had maintained luxurious hunting lodges stuffed with Western goods. In Wandlitz, north of Berlin, they had an exclusive housing enclave protected day and night by the state's secret police. These revelations brought an outcry from the population, in particu-

_____ **BOX 1.12** _____

THE OPENING OF THE BERLIN WALL

East Germany on Thursday declared the end of restrictions on emigration or travel to the West, and within hours thousands of East Germans swarmed across the Berlin wall in a mass celebration of their newly won freedom. . . . The East German leadership announced permission to travel or emigrate would be granted quickly and without conditions. The leadership said East Germans would be allowed to move through any crossing into West Germany or West Berlin, including through the wall. . . .

"We know this need of citizens to travel or leave the country," said Günter Schabowski, a member of the Politburo who made the announcement at a news conference on Thursday evening. "Today the decision was made that makes it possible for all citizens to leave the country through East German crossing points."

A tentative trickle of East Germans testing the new regulations quickly turned into a swarm of ecstatic people, who were met in the middle of the crossings by crowds of flag-waving, cheering West Germans. Some West Berliners came in cars and offered to take those from the East on a tour, and others clambered on top of the wall, unbothered by border guards.

By 1 A.M. today, celebrating Berliners, East and West, had filled the celebrated Kurfürstendamm, blowing on trumpets, dancing, laughing and absorbing a glittering scene they had only glimpsed before on television.

Source: New York Times, November 10, 1989.

---

lar from Communist rank-and-file members, who felt betrayed by their leaders. Some of the top leaders, including Honecker himself, were expelled from the party. Later, Honecker and several other former high officials were arrested on charges of high treason (see Box 1.13). The indignation at Honecker and his regime increased still more when, in June 1990, it was discovered that leftist terrorists of West Germany had been offered refuge in Communist East Germany for many years.

Egon Krenz soon lost his leadership position and was even expelled from the party. Those who in the past had been too close to the power center fell in disgrace. Emerging as the new leader was Hans Modrow. He, too, was a Communist, but as party chief in the city of Dresden he had established a reputation as an advocate of change, and as such he was an outsider in the old regime. Despite his reform orientation, Modrow could not prevent the further deterioration of the situation. In early 1990, 2,000 to 3,000 East Germans left every day for West Germany. There were increasing demands for reunification of the two German states. To maintain some kind of order in the country, Modrow was forced to take into his government several representatives of opposition groups. The date of free elections was advanced from May to March 1990. The results will be discussed in Chapter 2. At the end of the

Berlin Wall, November 9, 1989. (Courtesy Embassy of the Federal Republic of Germany, Washington, D.C.)

book, in Chapter 16, I will discuss the question of German unification and put it into the broader context of European integration.

For the moment, it is important to stress once more that Honecker did not give up power voluntarily. It was an unusual set of circumstances that forced him out. It was also good luck that his shooting orders never came through, so that a bloodbath like the one in China could be prevented. For the West German Social Democrats, the 1989 events in East Germany were quite an embarrassment. They wished that they could swallow the flattering words about Honecker that they had used in their earlier visits to East Germany. Despite all hopes, these visits did not soften Honecker at all. He remained a dictator, exploiting his people, spying on them through the state secret police, all the while living in luxury and splendor.

---------- BOX 1.13 ----------

HONECKER ARRESTED

EAST BERLIN—East Germany's relentless pursuit of its former hard-line leaders finally reached Erich Honecker today. The ousted Communist Party chief was released from the hospital and immediately arrested.

The 77-year-old Mr. Honecker, who resigned on Oct. 19 under the pressure of public opposition, has been under treatment for cancer.

The state prosecutor general, Hans Jürgen Joseph, said Mr. Honecker would be tried for high treason. . . .

The East German television said Mr. Honecker was visited by his wife, Margot, a former Education Minister, and his daughter and granddaughter before leaving the hospital through the main entrance. He was taken to the Rummelsburg jail by plainclothes policemen. Mr. Honecker was shown on the television walking forward unassisted, his expression stern.

The press agency quoted a urologist, Dr. Peter Althaus, as saying that Mr. Honecker was dejected on parting with his family. "He finds it difficult to understand the events taking place," Dr. Althaus was quoted as saying.

Source: New York Times, January 30, 1990.

Czechoslovakia

After the movement in the spring of 1968 was brutally crushed by Soviet tanks, Czechoslovakia went through 21 sad and frigid years. Dubcek was not actually put into prison but was sent into exile in a province, where he had to earn his livelihood through odd jobs. The state secret police had him and his wife under constant surveillance. Whoever entered into contact with the Dubceks was afterwards watched too. This was a miserable life of nearly complete isolation.

Many other well-known dissenters were, in fact, put into prison and labor camps. Among them was Václav Havel, organizer of the human rights movement "Charta 77" (see photo on page 31). In 1979 he was sentenced to four and one-half years of labor camp, where he had to serve with ordinary criminals. By profession a playwright, Havel sent moving letters from the labor camp to his wife Olga.[8] These letters reveal him to be a very sensitive person who is concerned with the ultimate questions of life. He expressed to his wife his faith in the meaning of life. For him life is the constant search for meaning, and it is the tragedy of humans that this meaning can never be captured in any final way. Nevertheless, Havel believes in life and our responsibility to it. A fragile person, Havel suffered greatly in the labor camp, and he often reported to his wife about his deep depressions and physical illnesses. Reading his letters gives a very vivid impression of the cruel suffering that innocent and good people experience under Communism. In early 1989, Havel was again arrested for organizing a memorial service for Jan Palach, the

Václav Havel. (Courtesy Embassy of the Czech and Slovak Federative Republic, Bern, Switzerland.)

student who in January 1969 had burned himself to death to protest the Soviet crackdown. This time Havel was sentenced to nine months but was released after three months.

Seven months after his release, on December 29, 1989, Havel was elected president of the country by parliament! How was this possible? Certainly not without the demonstration effect of the reform developments in Hungary, Poland, and East Germany. Looking at the map (page 2), we can see that by November 1989 Czechoslovakia was, with the exception of the short border with the Soviet Union, completely surrounded by either reform-oriented Communist countries or Western-style democracies (Austria and West Germany). In this isolated position, the citizens of Czechoslovakia began to take courage, and they were able within a few short weeks, in the so-called "velvet" revolution, to bring about reforms that were the most far-reaching for any of the Eastern European countries at the time. With one big jump, Czechoslovakia turned from being a laggard into a leader of the reform movement.

When the first street demonstrations took place, the police intervened with brutal force. But this did not stop the demonstrations. Again, TV was important. When the scenes of police brutality were shown, an outrage overtook the population, and huge masses of hundreds of thousands of people went to the streets, not only in Prague, but in all the major cities. A general strike was declared, and the country came to a standstill. The people had seized power. Signs showing the names of the Communist leaders were waved, telling them: "It is over!" This was truly a popular revolution and a triumph for the people.

Confronted with this will of the people, the Communist leaders had no other choice but to yield; otherwise, the people would simply continue the general strike. Gustav Husak, who collaborated with the Soviets in 1968 and who was still president of the country, resigned on December 10, 1989. Alexander Dubcek and Václav Havel emerged as the new leaders. What a symbolic picture it was to see the two together addressing the people and everyone singing the national anthem and waving the national flag (Box 1.14). It quickly became evident that Havel enjoyed more popular support than Dubcek for the presidency. But, in a touching gesture, he refused to take the job if Dubcek did not simultaneously receive an important position. The solution was that Dubcek would become president of the parliament. It was then Dubcek who led Havel into the parliamentary meeting room to accept his election as president of the country.

The old, hard-line Communists were quickly removed from their positions and replaced with either Communist reformers or non-Communists. Jiri Dienstbier, like Havel a signer of "Charta 77" and also imprisoned, became foreign minister. Early in 1989, he had shoveled coal. At the Higher School of Economics in Prague, the Institute of Marxism-Leninism was abolished. This institute had taught the required courses in state ideology which were part of the curriculum in every field from law to music. Box 1.15 shows with what

---

BOX 1.14

DUBCEK AND HAVEL EMERGE AS LEADERS

PRAGUE—Alexander Dubcek, Czechoslovakia's symbol of change, returned tonight for the first time to Wenceslas Square, where 21 years ago Soviet tanks crushed the "Prague Spring" reform movement that he led. This time Dubcek drank champagne.

Dubcek, after a triumphant speech to 300,000 people jammed into the square, appeared at a press conference at the Magic Lantern Theater together with playwright and reform leader Václav Havel. As Dubcek spoke, Havel's brother suddenly ran in from the wings and whispered the news of the fall of the entire Communist Party leadership.

Havel threw his arms into the air. Dubcek, unaware, kept talking. Seconds later, Havel passed the word to Dubcek, and for the first time all evening, Dubcek's face broke into a broad smile. His expression immediately announced the news to the rest of the room.

Suddenly, glasses and champagne appeared. Havel hugged Dubcek, then stood up to give the victory toast: "Long live free Czechoslovakia!" Dubcek, vindicated after 20 years of political humiliation, downed his champagne in one long gulp.

Source: Washington Post, November 25, 1989.

BOX 1.15

NO MORE COURSES IN STATE IDEOLOGY

The professors conceded that the system required students and teachers to lie. "It was necessary that they knew positively the theory, even if they didn't believe it," said Professor Sojka.

Students agreed cheerfully that they lied in their exams. "You cram, you say what you don't believe, and you forget it immediately," said Hana Hornakova, a 19-year-old second-year student, in a corridor interview. "It's worthless, so why keep it in your memory?"

In an office of the strike committee of Civic Forum, the opposition movement, Dita Rozehnalova, said: "Naturally we all lied. You had to copy ideas from the textbooks that you don't agree with, and sometimes you even had to pretend that you agree with it."

Source: New York Times, December 14, 1989.

---

contempt and cynicism these courses were treated by the students in the past.

As president, Václav Havel worked quickly to reorient the position of his country in the world. In an address to the Polish parliament, he stated: "We want to belong to a Europe that is a friendly community of independent states, a stable Europe, a Europe that does not need protection from super-powers because it is capable of defending itself by constructing its own security system."[9]

Romania

Up to mid-December 1989, the revolution in Eastern Europe had been sur-prisingly peaceful. This changed when the Romanians tried to overthrow their leader, Nicolae Ceausescu. When demonstrations began in the western Romanian city of Timisoara on December 15, the demonstrators were bru-tally crushed down, and hundreds of people were killed. Nevertheless, the demonstrations spread to other areas, including the capital Bucharest. It was in Bucharest that the decisive battle was fought. Ceausescu tried to counteract the demonstrators, not only with force, but by mobilizing his loyal supporters for a demonstration of their own. After they had gathered in front of his palace, he addressed them in his usual way. But something unexpected happened: Suddenly there were boos from the crowd, and these boos became more and more vocal. Once again the TV cameras were crucial in the further development of events. The cameras captured a hesitant Ceausescu, unsure of himself, looking to his left and to his right for help but not getting any. This scene had a tremendous effect on the Romanian people. Having seen the weakness of Ceausescu, they had courage to take to the streets. As in East Germany and Czechoslovakia shortly before, huge demonstrations formed in Bucharest and other Romanian cities. The outcome was not a joyful festivity, as when the Berlin Wall was opened or when Dubcek and Havel had appeared on the balcony to greet the crowd. Instead, around Christmas, real street battles developed, which were followed in disbelief by millions of TV-watchers around the world. The revolutionary movement in Eastern Europe acquired a sad and tragic note. But the deaths were not in vain. On December 22, Ceausescu fled his presidential palace (see Box 1.16). The decisive element for the outcome of the battle was that the armed forces sided with the demonstrators. The corresponding announcement was made by the generals on live TV. It was crucial that at that time the demonstrators had gained control of the TV station, which then became the location of the fiercest battles. This showed once more in a very vivid way how important TV had become.

When the armed forces sided with the demonstrators, this did not mean the end of the fighting, because the well-equipped security forces remained loyal to Ceausescu, even when he was captured. They tried to liberate him, which explains why he and his politically active wife were quickly sentenced to death by a secret military tribunal and immediately executed. This may sound more like revenge than justice, but when a revolution turns bloody, extraordinary things are likely to happen. Eyewitnesses reported that Ceausescu and his wife were wildly running around in a courtyard trying to escape the firing squad. This was the somewhat surreal end of a brutal dictator. His dead body was displayed on TV, much like at the end of World War II when the dead body of Mussolini was displayed in the streets of Milan. Even after the death of Ceausescu, some security forces continued to fight for several more days.

Free elections took place in Romania in May 1990. As we will see in Chapter 2, these elections were strongly influenced by the fact that the revolution had caused so much bloodshed in the country.

***

_____ **BOX 1.16** _____

CEAUSESCU TOPPLED

BUCHAREST, Romania—Outraged Romanians and rebel soldiers toppled President Nicolae Ceausescu on Friday in fierce, daylong battles with troops loyal to the Soviet bloc's last dictator. Hundreds were reported killed in the fighting, which continued early today.

Army units joining with protesters were winning control of Bucharest from loyalist security forces in battles that continued after nightfall. . . . Mr. Ceausescu fled his presidential palace as hundreds of thousands of Romanians called for his death in retaliation for the massacre of their countrymen in a military crackdown unleashed a week ago.

Source: The News and Observer, Raleigh, N.C., December 23, 1989.

Bulgaria

The strong man in Bulgaria was Tador Zhivkov, in power since 1954. Without the events in other Eastern European countries, he certainly would not have lost his job in 1989. But, when the Bulgarians, encouraged by the events in the other countries, began to demonstrate, he was quickly ousted. There was no bloodshed in Bulgaria. After the ouster of Zhivkov, more moderate Communists took over and organized elections in June 1990 (see Chapter 2).

Yugoslavia

Yugoslavia was Communist, but it was not behind the Iron Curtain. The break with the Soviet Union was made in 1948 by the powerful Yugoslav leader Tito, war hero of the resistance against the German occupation. Under Tito, Yugoslavia developed its own brand of Communism, characterized by an emphasis on self-management of the workers at the plant level. Although the Communist party still claimed a monopoly of power, there was more freedom in Yugoslavia than in the Soviet satellite countries.

At first, the reform movement of 1989 left Yugoslavia untouched. But then it swept over to Yugoslavia too, and a broad discussion about the future of the country set in. Within this discussion, there were calls for more democracy and for change to a multiparty system. However, the really explosive issue quickly became the relations among the various Yugoslav republics and whether the country could stay together as a political entity. Political liberalization went hand in hand with a newly expressed awareness of the ethnic identity of each republic. For many Yugoslavs, freedom of speech meant placing greater emphasis on the values of one's ethnic group. A nationalism of the people of Serbia, Slovenia, Croatia, Macedonia, Montengro, and Bosnia/Herzegovina came to the forefront of the debate. Old mutual hatreds and prejudices were articulated. The Serbs, for example, boycotted merchandise from Slovenia (see Box 1.17). In many ways, the developments in Yugoslavia were similar to those in the Soviet Union, where more political freedom also helped to stir up old nationalisms in the various republics.

Chapter 13 will deal in a broader theoretical context with multiethnic countries. At that point, I will discuss the ethnic problems of Yugoslavia in greater detail.

Albania

Tiny Albania, located in a mountainous region between Yugoslavia and Greece, kept a hard-line Stalinist regime and did not follow any of the changes in the post-Stalinist Soviet Union, for example, during the Khrushchev era. It isolated itself to an extreme extent from the world, including the Communist world. Almost no foreigners, including journalists and tourists, were allowed into the country. In 1989, Albania was not touched by the reform movement, but in 1990 some timid reforms began to take shape.

_____ **BOX 1.17** _____

A SIGN OF BAD TIMES IN YUGOSLAVIA: TRADE WAR BETWEEN TWO REPUBLICS

BELGRADE—Shoppers in the "Beograd Woman" department store will find that the mention of certain brand names can make the staff snap as though a curse had just been directed at them.

A Gorenj television? "No, we are Serbs," two clerks said at once amid the fourth-floor appliances. Ljubljana cut glass? "This is Serbia," a matron at household goods said with a scowl.

The products touching such raw nerves are from Slovenia, a Yugoslav republic some 200 miles northwest of Serbia. They might as well be from enemy territory, for Serbia has declared a boycott of Slovene goods and broken cultural ties. The trade war, in its seventh week and growing, is the latest rumble in the unmelted pot called Yugoslavia.

Source: New York Times, January 28, 1990.

Explanations

How do we explain when and how exactly the various Eastern European countries joined the reform movement? The overall trigger for the 1989 developments in Eastern European countries was certainly the signal from the Soviet Union that it would not interfere militarily. Why the Soviets gave this signal in 1989 will be researched for many years to come, but it is not addressed here. I begin the analysis with the fact that the Soviets opened the gates for reforms. The question then is in what order and how exactly the individual countries came out of the gates. Figure 2 presents a simulation model, which is a first effort at such an explanation. (Yugoslavia is omitted because long before 1989 it was no longer under Soviet domination.)

Ideally, the construction of the simulation would come first and the data afterwards, so that actual predictions could be tested. For the 1989 events in Eastern Europe, I knew the outcome before I began to construct the simulation, so it should be no surprise that all cases fit. What I do is not a prediction, but a "postdiction." I try to find possible causal paths that fit the data. Other scholars will certainly come up with other explanations that will be equally plausible. Tests of competing explanations would only be possible if we could add more cases. In principle, this is not altogether impossible. To be sure, the 1989 sequence of events in Eastern Europe is historically unique. But, like the Soviet empire, there are other empires that have crumbled, for example the British empire. Thus, we could enlarge the scope of inquiry in studying when and how the various British colonies liberated themselves.

For the simulation techniques, the order in which the various factors are introduced matters a great deal. As can be seen in Figure 2, the first factor

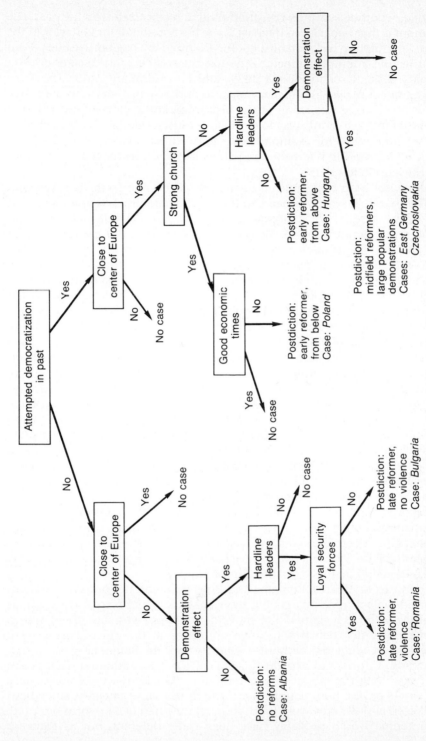

Figure 2. Simulation Model of 1989 Sequence of Events in Eastern Europe.

identifies whether a country had attempted democratization in the past. The argument is that behavior in the past is the best predictor for behavior in the future, a tendency well established, for example, by election studies. Four countries did attempt democratization in the past: Poland (1956 and 1981), Hungary (1956), Czechoslovakia (1968), and East Germany (1953). The three remaining countries—Romania, Bulgaria, and Albania—had no such history. While I place this factor at the beginning of the causal flow, I do not claim that this is the only way to model the causal sequence. Other scholars may wish to argue, for example, that the most basic factor was whether a country had good or bad economic times in 1989, a factor that I introduce into the simulation later.

The causal path that appears to the left of the first factor is somewhat simpler than that which appears to the right. Therefore, I examine first this part of the simulation. If Romania, Bulgaria, and Albania had never attempted democratization in the past, what factors could compensate for this? The model stipulates closeness to the center of Europe as the key variable. By this I mean not merely geographical but cultural closeness that allows for new ideas. None of these three countries was ever culturally close to the center of Europe; Bucharest, Sofia, and Tirana were always at the periphery. The three countries simply had no incentive to be early participants in the reform movement—neither from their past experience nor from the present influx of new ideas.

The only way participation in the reform movement could have been triggered in Romania, Bulgaria, and Albania was through the example of other countries, which I call a "demonstration effect." If this demonstration effect was absent, or at least very weak, as in Albania, the simulation postdicts no reforms. It should be noted that the model arrives at this conclusion through only three steps, whereas, for other postdictions, four or five steps are necessary. The reason is parsimony. If the researcher feels safe that a prediction, or in the present case a postdiction, can be made, the simulation process is stopped. For Albania, I think it is a sufficient explanation that it had no experience of democratization in the past, was isolated from the center of Europe, and that the media were so tightly controlled that the demonstration effect from other countries was very weak. Under these circumstances, I postdict no reforms, regardless of the strength of the church, the health of the economy, the type of leaders, and the loyalty of the security forces, the other factors contained in the model.

In contrast to Albania, Romania and Bulgaria could not prevent the demonstration effect from influencing their citizens, which explains why both countries ultimately joined the movement themselves. But there was a striking difference between the two countries in how the reforms were triggered—in Bulgaria without violence and in Romania with much bloodshed. In order to explain this difference, two additional factors are introduced into the model. First the model asks whether the leaders were hard-liners or not. Both countries are still in the same category, since both Ceausescu and Zhivkov were hard-liners. If they had been reform oriented, the outcome would probably have been quite different, but as Figure 2 shows, there was empirically no case. Since both Ceausescu and Zhivkov were hard-liners, the key distinguishing factor then was whether the security forces would remain loyal to them. In Bulgaria, they did not, and Zhivkov was ousted smoothly and quickly, whereas in Romania the violence was largely due to the resistance of the security forces loyal to Ceausescu.

We turn now to the right side of the simulation, which postdicts Poland, Hungary, East Germany, and Czechoslovakia. As Figure 2 shows, these countries had attempted democratization in the past, and they are also close to the center of Europe. Indeed, Czechoslovakia claims to have been historically at the very center of Europe (see page 1). As a consequence of both of these factors, the four countries had an excellent potential to start the reform movement, because they could profit from their past experiences and had an influx of new ideas in the present. This is also true for Poland, although it had no common border with a western country; since the 1970s, Poland had close cultural ties with the West, in particular with West Germany.

To have ideas for reforms is a necessary, but not yet sufficient, condition to start a reform movement. What is also needed is an organizational vehicle to launch the reforms. In the Eastern European countries, the societal control by the Communist party was so strong that, outside the party, hardly any societal organizations could flourish. Civil society was underdeveloped. The major exceptions were the churches, and here lies the main difference between Poland and the other three countries. The Polish Catholic church managed to remain a strong social force, and it was thanks to the church that Solidarity was able to organize so strongly in the early 1980s. When Solidarity was banned, it was again the church that helped the Solidarity leaders to continue their fight underground. But, to explain what happened in Poland in 1989, still another factor has to be introduced, namely the catastrophic economic situation. If economic times had been good, the Communists would have had little reason to begin round-table talks with Solidarity. Adding the bad economic situation to the model, we have now quite a plausible explanation for why Poland was at the forefront of the reform movement and why the reforms were pushed from below. Remembering 1956 and 1981, and with many cultural ties to the West, Poles had ideas for reforms. The Catholic church was allowed to organize these ideas, and when in 1989 the economy was at the brink of collapse, reforms could be forced to center stage from below.

Hungary, although also at the forefront of the reforms, took quite a different path. Its churches were quite weak, but its Communist leaders were reform oriented. This was already true to some extent for Janos Kadar. When he was ousted in 1988, there was an entire succession of new leaders, and each seemed more reform oriented than the previous one. Finally, Imre Pozsgay, a very strong reformer, took control of the party. As in Poland, then, there was an organizational vehicle for reforms, ironically the Communist party itself. This allowed Hungary to be a leader in the reform movement too, but here the reforms came from above. In the public discussion in 1989, Poland and Hungary were usually mentioned together. The present analysis shows that they were certainly similar in being the two leaders in the reform process, but they arrived there from very different paths.

East Germany and Czechoslovakia had in common a lack of organizational vehicles to launch reforms. To be sure, dissidents like Havel and Dienstbier in Czechoslovakia, and Protestant pastors in East Germany tried to organize, but repression by the hard-line leaders was too strong. I postdict that without the demonstration effect from Poland and Hungary, no reforms would have occurred in 1989. But, once the demonstration effect became strong, the necessary reform ideas were present, and, with the help of large demonstrations, the reform process proceeded very rapidly.

As an initial interpretation of the 1989 events in Eastern Europe, this simulation model will hopefully stimulate further interpretations of these events. More importantly, the model outlined here may be a contribution to a general theory of disintegration of empires. Although the disintegration of the Soviet empire is a unique historical event, many other empires have disintegrated too, so that work on a more general theory about the sequencing of such disintegration seems warranted.

PROSPECTS FOR COMMUNISM

After the crumbling of the old-guard Communist regimes in Eastern Europe, what are the prospects for communism in these countries? One conclusion is firm, namely, that communism in its Stalinist version is dead. There is no longer any support at all for the belief that the Communist party should have a monopoly on power. All the Communist parties in Eastern Europe have renounced their claim to a monopoly on power. They acknowledge now that they have to earn power through the electoral process. As we see in Chapter 2, the Communists were badly beaten in East Germany, Hungary, Poland, and Czechoslovakia. In Romania and Bulgaria, however, the Communists would stay in power, although under a different name; in Romania as the National Salvation Front, in Bulgaria as the Socialist Party. It still remains to be seen how the Communists will use the power gained through the electoral process. First indications, described in Chapter 3, show the possibility that the Communists will rule Romania and Bulgaria in a rather authoritarian way; although a return to the old Stalinist regime seems impossible. Too much has happened in these countries in the revolutionary year of 1989.

How about the prospects of terrorism on the Left? As a political force, it is as discredited as Stalinism. The romanticism of violence has vanished among young Europeans of the Left. This is also linked to the subsiding of Left terrorism in Central and South America. Fidel Castro, who wanted to spread his revolution through terrorist activities, is no longer the hero among the extreme Left in Europe, as he once was. The elimination of the terrorist Left as a viable political force in Europe does not preclude that some terrorists are still underground and will continue some occasional terrorist actions.

The political death of Stalinism and the terrorist Left does not mean that Karl Marx is dead as an intellectual force. After all, he was a philosopher of the nineteenth century, and it is not altogether clear how he would have reacted to the developments in the Soviet Union or the actions of such terrorist groups as the Red Brigade. One may very well argue that he would not have approved at all. As we have seen earlier in this chapter, Marx used the concept of *revolution* in a rather abstract form and left ambivalent whether violence should be part of the revolution. The contribution of Marx that will remain is his economic interpretation of society, and in this sense Marx will continue to have an intellectual influence in Europe. At the same time, it must also be said that the influence of Marx has diminished since the heydays of the 1960s and 1970s; for new issues, such as ecology and feminism, Marxism often is no longer seen as the appropriate way of analysis (see Chapter 11).

Although Marx will continue to have an influence, the Left should not be identified with Marxism alone. In the last 200 years, there was a great diversity of ideas of the Left, and this diversity will again become more apparent in the future. Thus, there was always a tradition of the Left warning against the dangers of too much centralization and demanding more autonomy for small groups, such as workers at their workplace or local communities. There was always also an anarchist tradition of the Left. How the Left will be organized in the coming years is an open question. One issue concerns the choice of labels. The Italian Communist party has already decided to give up its name, which it finds discredited by the practice of communism in such countries as the Soviet Union and the Republic of China. As of this writing, the Italian Communists have not yet decided what their new name shall be. In Eastern Europe, Reform-Communists tended to change their name to Socialist (see pages 88–106). Will there be in the future one big Socialist party in the European countries, or will the Left increasingly be divided into smaller parties? Is the emergence of the Greens the beginning of such increased division of the Left? Such questions naturally take us to the next section, in which we will explain what Socialists and Social Democrats stand for. Later in the chapter, we will also turn to the Greens. For a discussion of the Left, Chapter 11 is also relevant, in which we will deal with social movements, such as the environmental, peace, womens' and youth movements.

SOCIALISTS

In Western Europe at large, the Socialist parties are numerically much stronger than the Communist parties. Only in Italy do the Communists have consistently greater strength than the Socialists. In all other countries, the Socialists are the large force on the Left. In some countries, like Austria and Sweden, the Socialists usually win close to half the votes. Before we can discuss Socialist goals and strategies, we must first clarify tricky questions of terminology. This is particularly important in a book addressed to American readers, who may identify socialism with the Soviet Union, whose official name is indeed the Union of Soviet Socialist Republics. But there the term *socialism* refers to the first phase following the proletarian revolution, and the Soviets claim that they are still in this phase because capitalism has not yet been defeated worldwide. In European democracies, however, *socialism* has a very different meaning. The Socialist parties are firmly committed to democracy, and in Europe itself few people would identify them with the Soviet Union. In many ways, European Socialists correspond to liberal Democrats in the United States. Edward Kennedy, George McGovern, and probably even Michael Dukakis would easily fit into a European socialist party.

Is there a difference between a Socialist and a Social Democrat? Yes and no. The difference is certainly not in the sense that Social Democrats would support democracy while Socialists would not. To emphasize the point once more, the entire Socialist movement has a long democratic tradition, as demonstrated, for example, in its fight against Adolf Hitler. The precise party label depends on the country and is relatively accidental. In France the party is called Socialist and in West Germany, Social Democratic, but this difference in name does not mean that the French party does not support democratic principles. Particular national situations also explain why in Great Britain and the Netherlands, for example, the Socialists are called the Labour party.

Sometimes, however, the difference between Socialists and Social Democrats is significant. This is particularly true for countries where the Socialist movement has split into two parties, as in Italy, where the Social Democrats are the more moderate party, while the Socialists are more leftist. The same differentiation was made in Great Britain when moderate Labour members split and formed their own Social Democratic party. The distinction between Socialists and Social Democrats is sometimes also made in internal party discussions between leftists and moderates. In Spain, for example, leftists sometimes criticize the Socialist prime minister Felipe González for taking a Social Democratic route, by which they mean that he is too accommodating to the interests of the bourgeoisie. These questions of terminology are tedious but necessary to prevent misunderstanding. For the remainder of the book, the term *Socialist* will be used unless there is a need to make a differentiation.

What are the goals and the strategies of the Socialists? Marxist class analysis also has some influence on Socialists, although less than on Communists. The typical Socialist simply emphasizes that the gap between rich and poor is too great. The major goal of Socialist policy is to narrow this gap, but few Socialists expect ever to achieve a classless society.

According to Socialist thinking, the state must intervene if more economic equality in society is to be achieved. If market forces have free play, the gap between rich and poor will only widen. It is the state that has the authority to redistribute income from the rich to the poor. Is state intervention in the economy compatible with freedom and democracy? Isn't a free market economy a necessary precondition for democracy? This question is answered in the negative by Socialists, who argue that the fruits of democracy can only be enjoyed by people with a sufficient level of economic security. As the German novelist Bertolt Brecht (see photo below) wrote in the famous *Threepenny Opera*, people first must eat.[10] People who must constantly worry about what to eat, where to find shelter, and what to do in case of illness and in old age are not truly free. They are unable to participate in political life, which therefore tends to be dominated by the more affluent. In order to give this freedom to everyone, state intervention is necessary. For Socialists, state intervention in the economy is not an obstacle but rather a precondition for an effective democracy.

What we see here are fundamentally different definitions of *democracy*. From the perspective of a free market, a democracy should give everyone the freedom to profit from given opportunities. From a Socialist perspective, a democracy can only function if the state corrects the distribution of wealth arrived at by market forces. The latter perspective is, of course, also shared by most American liberals, bringing them close to European Socialists.

Although all Socialists agree on the necessity for the state to redistribute income, there is wide disagreement in the Socialist ranks on the specifics of this intervention. One option is to nationalize private companies. If business belonged to the state, the rich could not get richer through the accumulation of profits, which would go to the community as a whole. Nationalization was for a long time popular among French Socialists. When Socialist François Mitterrand became president of France in 1981, key sectors of the economy, including almost all banks and large pharmaceutical companies, were nationalized. These measures were less dramatic than they may appear to an American reader. First, there is a long tradition in France of state-owned companies. Thus, long before Mitterrand took office, some banks and, for example, the automobile company Renault belonged to the state. Second,

Bertolt Brecht: "Your prior obligation is to feed us." (Courtesy Embassy of the Federal Republic of Germany, Bern, Switzerland.)

the state did not take over small businesses like the corner bakery. The Socialists under Mitterrand always believed that the quality of the famous French bread would be better if a multitude of private bakers competed with one another. Socialists are not in principle against competition. In fact, part of their justification for nationalizing big companies was that competition could be increased, because the large multinational corporations often form cartels to keep prices at an artificially high level. The Socialist hope was that nationalized French companies could compete more successfully in the world market.

Today, many Socialists, also in France itself, express doubts whether this hope is justified. Socialist Helmut Schmidt, the former West German chancellor, never tried to implement a program of nationalization. Socialists like Schmidt prefer more indirect state intervention through tax laws, social programs, and so forth. They accept private ownership of big companies, as long as the power of this private money is checked through governmental regulations. In Sweden, where Socialists have been in power the longest, a large number of companies (for example, Volvo) are privately owned. In fact, Sweden has relatively little public ownership. Recently, the Socialist Swedish government even sold some state-owned companies to private interests.

Until recently, European Socialists agreed that economic growth was good, provided that the fruits of this growth were not unfairly distributed in society. The main controversy concerned the question of whether the state should directly intervene—through nationalization—or whether redistribution of income could better be achieved through more indirect state measures. Today, a more fundamental question is being discussed among Socialists, namely, whether the side effects of economic growth are so negative that, ultimately, they may place the survival of the human race in jeopardy. This debate has split the Socialists in a very severe manner. On one side are blue-collar workers who wish to profit through higher wages from continued economic growth. They tend to support, for example, the expansion of nuclear power to prevent energy shortages. On the other side is a new breed of more intellectually oriented Socialists. For them, limits must be imposed on economic growth; otherwise, our natural environment eventually will be destroyed. As a prime example they cite the death of the forests, caused by acid rain. They also point out that current economic life puts too much stress on working people, leading to all sorts of health problems. These Socialists see dangers not only in the free market but also in the large and often anonymous state bureaucracies. They advocate a much simpler life-style and a decentralized government with extensive self-administration. Instead of producing more cars to commute to increasingly distant workplaces, people should bicycle to work in their own relatively self-sustained, small communities.

Such an interpretation of Socialist thought leads to a search for new political allies. Traditionally, the Socialist parties were confronted only with the choice of alliances to the left or to the middle. They could try to forge a coalition with the Communists—the strategy chosen in France by Mitterrand from 1981 to 1984—or they could keep their distance from the Communists and seek partners from the middle of the party spectrum—which is what Schmidt and his predecessor, Willy Brandt, achieved through their coalition with the Free Democratic party, which is immediately to the right of the Socialists in the West German party system.

The new breed of Socialists sees political life less in terms of left and right than traditional Socialists have. For the new Socialists, the important questions are whether someone supports more economic growth and whether one is willing to reconsider the concept of growth and seek alternative life-styles. Here they find allies among environmentalists and, in particular, the Green party, which is described later in this chapter. Members of the women's movement, the youth movement, the peace movement, and oppressed minorities such as foreign workers and homosexuals are also seen as potential allies. With such a coalition, the Socialist party no longer fits neatly in the left–right continuum. Political life in Europe has become much too complex for the simple labels *left* and *right* to describe the various political parties.

At this point, it is important to recognize that European Socialists today have very divergent goals and strategies—vividly illustrated in a controversy over the expansion of the Frankfurt airport. The local Socialist governor, a former blue-collar worker, advocated the expansion in the interest of further economic growth for the region. He had to use police force against primarily Socialist demonstrators who fought against the expansion in the interest of a higher quality of life.

Generally speaking, Socialists become more moderate when they exercise executive power. This tendency can be nicely illustrated with the careers of French President François Mitterrand and Spanish Prime Minister Felipe González. As described in Box 1.18 Mitterrand downplayed the Socialist message when he sought reelection in 1988. Box 1.19 points out how González, who was quite a radical Socialist in the 1970s, became strongly concerned with efficient administration as he took over the prime ministership in the 1980s. In Sweden, the Social Democrats, after many years in power, acknowledge that they need to cut taxes (see Box 1.20).

Looking back over the first two sections of this chapter, we see a large

---

BOX 1.18

MITTERRAND DOWNPLAYS SOCIALIST MESSAGE

With a patriotic red, white and blue flag motif at his back rippling in an electrically generated wind, Mr. Mitterrand radiated a simple but forceful message: he is running as the President of the French Republic, not as a candidate of the Socialist Party. He did not mention the Socialists by name as he outlined his vision of "a united France, a France on the move."

Source: New York Times, April 12, 1988.

_____ **BOX 1.19** _____

ON HOW SOCIALISTS RUN SPAIN

(The Spanish Socialist) leaders view capitalist democracy as the only feasible and desirable political economic arrangement for Spain. They have thus endeavored to administer Spanish capitalism more efficiently and perhaps more equitably than their conservative and authoritarian predecessors. But Spanish Socialists no longer seek to alter capitalism fundamentally in the name of equality and economic democracy. The new emphasis on economic modernization, "efficient administration," and the desire to create "Things Well Done" (the PSOE campaign theme for the June 1987 elections) has replaced the old concern for equality and participatory democracy (*autogestión*). The PSOE has adopted a new image, based on its technocratic-administrative capability and the charisma of González, and it is rapidly shedding its social democratic skin.

Source: Donald Share, "Dilemmas of Social Democracy in the 1980's: The Spanish Socialist Workers Party in Comparative Perspective," *Comparative Political Studies* 21 (October 1988): 429.

variety of views, both among Communists and among Socialists, and no clear delimitation between the two groups. A radical Socialist may be very close to a moderate Communist but far apart from a moderate within his or her own party. With the new developments in Eastern Europe, a Communist in Hungary may have views quite similar to a Socialist in Sweden. The common

_____ **BOX 1.20** _____

SWEDEN'S SOCIAL DEMOCRATS VEER TOWARD FREE MARKET AND LOWER TAXES

STOCKHOLM—The governing Social Democrats, who have made Sweden a generous welfare state and the world's most highly taxed nation, have reached a crossroads and are taking a distinct turn toward the free market.

As they celebrate their 100th anniversary, the Social Democrats now not only admit that the public will not accept higher taxes, but they also plan to cut income taxes sharply. After decades of ignoring complaints that stratospheric taxes were encouraging people to work less, the Social Democrats have proposed reducing the top marginal tax rate from 72 percent to 55 percent.

"We have reached a tax ceiling," said Kjell-Olof Feldt, Sweden's Minister of Finance. "We don't believe we can get this economy to function if we increase the tax burden."

Source: New York Times, October 27, 1989.

bond among all kinds of Communists and Socialists is that they are at the left of the European party spectrum.

—————————————————— **LIBERALS** ——————————————————

It often surprises Americans to hear that in Europe Liberals espouse a free market philosophy. The term *Liberal* is derived from the Latin root word *libertas*, "freedom." Therefore, in some European countries the Liberals include the term *free* as part of their official name. In West Germany, for example, the Free Democrats are the Liberal party, and *Liberal* and *Free Democratic* are used interchangeably. Europeans find it both odd and confusing that in the United States *liberal* designates a position to the Left and *freedom* a position to the Right (for example, the conservative Young Americans for Freedom).

In Europe, Liberals and Free Democrats emphasize the importance of individual freedom in every aspect of life. Economically, this leads to a preference for the free market. But they advocate a "free market" for moral issues, too, in which individuals have the prime responsibility for their behavior. Liberals would leave the choice in issues such as abortion and divorce primarily to the individual. They don't like the state and its bureaucrats to intrude into the private life of citizens. The free and autonomous decisions of individuals are of crucial importance in Liberal thinking. Large organizations are viewed with skepticism because they tend to limit individual freedom. This danger extends past the organization of the state to include such organizations as trade unions and churches. (For the historical roots of European Liberalism see Box 1.21.)

If an American liberal Democrat roughly corresponds to a European Socialist, what does a European Liberal correspond to in the United States? The small Libertarian party places individual autonomy at the center of its philosophy, but it takes this idea much further than a typical European Liberal. Whereas an American Libertarian opts in a radical way for individual autonomy, a European Liberal is more moderate in recognizing that the state too has important tasks, both in the economy and in the regulation of moral behavior. Thus, Eurpean Liberals believe that the state is responsible for helping the unemployed, the handicapped, and the old, although Liberal social programs are more limited than those advocated by Socialists and Communists. Liberals in Europe also admit that certain regulations for moral behavior are necessary, in particular for adolescents. For example, they would support a fight by the state against drug abuse, although they might be willing to legalize "soft" drugs.

The exact role Liberals see for the state is a constant topic for internal discussion, and there are usually great differences between the left and right wings of the party. Internal differences are generally a major characteristic of European Liberals, which is understandable, given the heavy emphasis on individual autonomy. In parliamentary debates, the Liberals are usually the party with the least amount of voting discipline.

———————————— BOX 1.21 ————————————

HISTORICAL ROOTS OF EUROPEAN LIBERALISM

For the liberal, the individual is not merely separable from the community and his social roles, but specially valued precisely as such a distinctive, discrete individual. . . .

   This liberal view of man first arose and is structurally and culturally rooted in social changes that began to emerge in late medieval and early modern Europe, and which gained particular force in the eighteenth and nineteenth centuries. The "creation" of the private individual, man as *separate* from society, wanting and valuing a private life, is closely linked to the rise of a new, more complex division of labour. . . .

   The new division of labour in European commercial and industrial capitalism produced new, complex and changeable roles for individuals. Migration, urbanization and technological change opened a new range of occupational choice. These new opportunities, however, required new skills and capacities. The capacity to *achieve*, to perform new roles, acquired a value it had not had in the past. But achievement is an individual, not a group, characteristic. Thus the individual qua individual acquired a new importance, not only in an economic, but also in a moral sense.

Source: Rhoda Howard and Jack Donnelly, "Human Rights, Human Dignity, and Political Regimes: Liberal and Illiberal Societies and the Standard of Human Rights," Paper presented at the annual conference on the International Studies Association, Washington, D.C., March 1985.

Measured in voter strength, the Liberals or Free Democrats are relatively small parties in most European countries. Their support is usually only in the single digits; in the Federal Republic of Germany, for example, 9 percent, in Italy, merely 2 percent. An exception is Switzerland with a strong 23 percent for the Liberals. In some countries it is not easy to identify a Liberal party clearly. In France, for example, the Union for French Democracy (UDF) has many liberal aspects, but it is not a liberal party in a narrower sense. We will deal with the UDF in Chapters 2 and 3.

———— CONSERVATIVES AND CHRISTIAN DEMOCRATS ————

The meaning of European liberalism can be further clarified by comparing it to European conservatism. The term *Conservative* is derived from the term *conserve*, which according to the *Oxford English Dictionary* means "keep from decay or change or destruction." What do Conservatives wish to keep from decay, change, or destruction? The structure of authority in society. Conservatives believe that individuals are lost if they are not embedded in a firm structure of authority. Conservatives have a very different view of the individual from Liberals. According to Conservative thinking, individuals are basically weak and need guidance. If left alone, they are likely to mess up. They must be guided by authorities such as the state, the church, the family, and so forth. Conservatives worry that these authorities may decay. Therefore, it is the primary goal of Conservative policy to preserve the structure of authority in society. This does not mean that Conservatives object to all change, but change should not be sudden.

The major difference between Conservatives and Liberals concerns the extent to which moral decisions should be left to the individual. Unlike Liberals, Conservatives advocate relatively strict guidance in such matters as abortion and drug use. This guidance can come through governmental regulation as well as from the church and the family. Thus, it is only logical that Conservatives support measures to prevent a weakening of church and family.

Another difference between Conservatives and Liberals concerns attachment to symbols of the state. For Liberals, state symbols, such as the national flag and national anthem, are certainly accepted, but they do not have great emotional value. Liberals are too individualistic to enjoy marching with others behind a flag. They are sensitive to historical events when too much parading led to dictatorship. Conservatives take this danger less seriously. They claim that the state needs strong symbols to maintain its authority. According to Conservative thinking, the state must be based, not only on rational utility, but also on emotions. Therefore, Conservatives revere state symbols and are offended when others do not.

In economic questions, both parties share a preference for free market solutions and are therefore natural allies. If differences occur, it is usually because Liberals defend the principle of free competition more consistently than Conservatives. Such differences can be explained by the different way that Conservatives and Liberals justify the free market. For Liberals, free market competition encourages individuals to develop their potential to the fullest extent. Conservatives emphasize another aspect, related to the natural order of society. According to Conservative thinking, the hierarchical structure of society is a law of nature. Like animals, some human beings are naturally stronger and more successful than others. Conservatives applaud biologists like Konrad Lorenz, who have discovered that there are natural leaders in the animal world and that analogies can be made with the human race. To redistribute income with the goal of achieving economic equality in society would go against nature. From this perspective, Conservatives are less opposed to cartels than Liberals. Although in their rhetoric Conservatives tend to advocate free market mechanisms, if it happens that the strong in society band together in a cartel, Conservatives may not object, because they may see this as part of a natural order. For Liberals, preservation of an existing order is not in itself a valid goal, and they would always give priority to competition, even if it meant a shake-up of society. Conservatives, on the other hand, may be willing to limit competition if the existing order would otherwise be in danger. They may even support the idea of the state bailing out a private company if its bankruptcy could cause significant social upheaval.

If we think only in terms of a left–right continuum, it is difficult to understand how European Conservatives and Liberals differ. It becomes easier if
we introduce a second dimension, as illustrated in Figure 3. The dimension
from left to right should be understood in economic terms. The farther left
a party is located, the more that party supports state intervention to redistribute income from rich to poor. The farther right a party is located, the
more it supports free play for market forces. Figure 3 indicates a position
toward the right for both Liberals and Conservatives. Surprisingly, to Americans, Liberals support free economic competition more consistently than
Conservatives, for the reasons given above. However, the two ovals overlap
because some Conservatives are stronger proponents of the free market than
some Liberals, and vice versa.

The second dimension in Figure 3 is from authoritarian to individualistic
poles. An authoritarian position emphasizes the importance of authority in
society, whereas an individualistic position stresses individual autonomy.
Here Conservatives and Liberals are more clearly distinguished, although in
practice there is also some overlap in this dimension. Note that in this
second dimension neither party has an extreme position. As we have seen,
American Libertarians would be found much farther toward the individualistic extreme than European Liberals are. Conservatives are also relatively
moderate in their emphasis on authority in society. Here the extreme position is taken by the Neofascists, to whom we turn in the next section.

Great Britain is rather the exception, where the party with a conservative
orientation is simply called the Conservative party. In most European
countries, Conservatives carry other party labels. Prominent is the label
"Christian Democrats" used, for example, by Conservatives in the Federal
Republic of Germany and in Italy. To be sure, German and Italian Christian
Democrats have strong left wings emphasizing social programs on the basis
of Christian doctrines. But the existence of these left wings does not alter the
fact that these parties can be considered overall as conservative in orientation. There are also Christian Democratic parties, for example, in the Netherlands and Belgium, which stress social programs so much that they can
hardly be considered as conservative; rather, they are more centrist. If this
sounds confusing, it is indeed to some extent: Some Conservative parties are

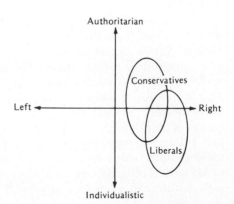

Figure 3. Location of Liberals and Conservatives on a Dimension from Left to
Right and a Dimension from Authoritarian
to Individualistic.

called Christian Democratic, but not all Christian Democratic parties can be called conservative.

There are still other labels used by the Conservative parties. In Austria, Conservatives are called the People's party; in Sweden, the Moderate Unity party; in Greece, New Democracy; in Spain, Popular Alliance. France is, again, as for the Liberals, a special case. The Rally for the Republic (RPR) may be considered a conservative party, but it is so much linked to its founder Charles de Gaulle that it has very unique characteristics. We will deal with the RPR in Chapters 2 and 3.

Why is there this variety among Conservatives from country to country? By their very nature, Conservatives stress the importance of national identity. As a consequence, each party has grown out from its specific national context without much international cooperation. Communists, Socialists and Liberals, on the other hand, have more universal messages, so that it was more natural for them to cooperate at an international level. The lack of international unity among Conservatives is shown in their difficulty to organize in the European parliament (see Chapter 16), whereas Communists, Socialists, and Liberals had no problem in forming their European-wide parliamentary groups. Conservatives, however, split in different factions, with the French Rally for the Republic and the Irish Fianna Fail, for example, forming together their own group.

NEOFASCISTS

Fascism was introduced by Benito Mussolini in Italy in the early 1920s. The term is derived from the Latin *fasces*, which means a bundle of sticks tightly held together—a symbol of strength in ancient Rome. In Germany, Adolf Hitler founded the National Socialist party, which is often referred to as a Fascist party because of its orientation was in many respects similar to Mussolini's party. The two dictators completely discredited the label fascism, so that today nobody would use it as a party name. Instead, political parties with a Fascist orientation have chosen other names: the National Front in Great Britain and France, the National Democrats and the Republicans in West Germany, the Italian Social Movement. Despite their official names, these parties are often called Neofascist. They are located in Figure 4 in the same dimensions as in Figure 3. The thick line from authoritarian to individuals should stem from services rendered to the larger good of the portant for the location of Neofascists than the left–right dimension. The position of Neofascists is at the authoritarian extreme because, for them, authority has the highest priority. The nation counts more than the individual, whose main task is to serve the fatherland. The true meaning in life for individuals should stem from the services rendered to the larger good of the country. In these services they find fulfillment. This Neofascist way of thinking attracts insecure people who are afraid to stand on their own and who only feel secure when they are part of a mass movement. To get this security, they are willing to subordinate themselves to strong leaders. This

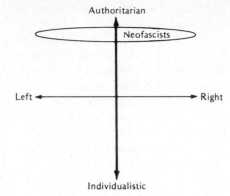

Figure 4. Location of Neofascists on a Dimension from Left to Right and on a Dimension from Authoritarian to Individualistic.

total identification with the nation has as a corollary the rejection of everything that does not "belong" to that nation. Under Hitler, this led to the effort to exterminate Jews in concentration camps. Other groups, like Gypsies, were also considered as un-German and suffered the same fate. Today, foreign workers are a convenient target of Neofascist hostility: Turks in Germany, Pakistanis in Great Britain, and North Africans in France, while Jews and Gypsies continue to have difficulties in many places (see Boxes 1.22 and 1.23).

Neofascists are often called extreme right-wingers, as in the newspaper clippings on pages 54–55. But this label is in many ways misleading, as

---

_____ BOX 1.22 _____

FOREIGN WORKERS IN WEST GERMANY

The obvious advantages of a foreign labor force that accepts the worst jobs and oldest housing and makes few costly demands are increasingly confounded by disadvantages, such as dependence on noncitizens by major industries and greater demands on social and educational programs. Perhaps more important, many now argue that the haste to define the question in economic terms is only a transparent effort to mask a deeper cultural hostility which, if not addressed more directly, could lead to serious social conflict nationally. . . .

. . . negative opinion is a predominant overall phenomenon. A generally exclusive attitude extends over the entire spectrum of the guestworkers' existence, from social habits to politics. Contrary to most official positions, negative opinion is not limited to the economic case in which jobs might be too scarce to meet the needs of both Germans and foreigners; nor is it limited to personal economic insecurity. If guestworkers are seen as intrusive, it is social and political as well as economic intrusion that Germans observe. As a result, there is no obvious support for promoting integration.

Source: Marilyn Hoskin, "Public Opinion and the Foreign Worker: Traditional and Nontraditional Bases in West Germany," *Comparative Politics* 17 (January 1985): 206–7.

BOX 1.23

JEW'S CORPSE MUTILATED, HORRIFYING THE FRENCH

CARPENTRAS, France—The body of a Jewish man was taken from its grave in southern France during the night and impaled by anti-Semitic marauders, police sources said Thursday.

Thirty-four graves were desecrated, their stones smashed or sprayed with anti-Semitic graffiti.

The corpse of the 81-year-old man, who had died about 15 days earlier, was exhumed at the Jewish graveyard in Carpentras near Avignon, mutilated with a beach umbrella and propped on a tombstone, the police sources said.

Reports of the desecration, discovered by two women, sent shock waves through France. Prime Minister Michel Rocard spoke of his horror and indignation; Jacques Chirac, the mayor of Paris, exhorted citizens to fight such "incitations of hatred," and President François Mitterrand said those who committed such "a cowardly act" must be found and punished.

Interior Minister Pierre Joxe, who expressed revulsion at the act, went to Carpentras. He said several of the tombs in the graveyard had been left "in conditions so abominable that one cannot describe them without embarrassment."

A police officer said the vandals had torn a Star of David from the disinterred coffin and placed it on the stomach of the corpse.

Jean Kahn, president of the Council of Jewish Institutions of France, deplored the incident, for which no one has claimed responsibility.

"This horrible crime comes right in the middle of a campaign of incitement to racial hatred in which the language of anti-Semitism has brutally returned to the lips of certain politicians," he said.

The far-right National Front issued a strong denial of involvement and condemned the act.

Source: International Herald Tribune, May 11, 1990.

---

shown in Figure 4. To be sure, they take extreme positions and they are not leftists, so it is understandable that many people see them at the extreme right. In everyday language, the terms *left* and *right* are so vague that they mean everything and nothing. If we define the position at the right as support for the free market, Neofascists are certainly not at the extreme right. They are, rather, spread all the way from the left to the right. This ambivalent attitude toward the free market could already be seen with Mussolini and Hitler. Mussolini was a militant Socialist before founding his Fascist movement, and Hitler included the term *Socialist* in the name of his party. The Fascist's main objection to the Left was its international orientation. Fascists found it unpatriotic that Communists and Socialists looked for allies in other countries. The call for proletarians of all countries to unite was diametrically opposed to Fascist thinking, which sees one's own nation as the sacred community to which all allegiance is owed. In this context, it is an interesting historical detail that Mussolini was expelled from the Socialist party because of his vehement support for the entry of Italy into World War I.

Rejecting Communists and Socialists for their lack of nationalistic feeling did not mean that Fascists had no reservations about the free market. The notion of competition was too disorderly for them. Fascists advocated a strong state that would show leadership in economic matters. Simply working for profits was too egotistical for Fascists, who deep down felt only disdain for the capitalist mentality. Hitler had a very stormy relationship with the business community. On the one hand, he needed its support, but, on the other hand, he hated the business world.

Neofascists today have a similarly ambivalent position on economic matters. They find support among small businessmen who complain about undesired intervention by the state, but they are also supported by workers for whom the parties of the Left are not tough enough on immigrants. These examples show that the economic dimension from left to right is not very useful in locating the Neofascist parties, which are mainly characterized by their extreme position on the authoritarian–individualistic continuum.

Is there any danger of a Neofascist revival in Europe? One hears many warnings in this regard, and the distinction must be made between the voting strength of Neofascist parties and more general Neofascist tendencies in society. In elections, neofascism has remained a minor factor since World War II. The atrocities of fascism are still so well remembered that the Neofascist parties have great difficulty in attracting voters. Usually, the support for these parties stays well below 10 percent, and it is sometimes practically nonexistent. In recent years, however, it has seemed to become more acceptable to vote for Neofascist parties. The biggest success up to now has been scored by the French National Front, whose leader, Jean-Marie Le Pen, received 14.4 percent of the votes in the 1988 presidential election. This is the man who belittles the gas chambers of World War II and is frightened that the influx of foreign workers will turn France into an Islamic republic (see Boxes 1.24 and 1.25).

BOX 1.24

FRENCH RIGHTIST BELITTLES GAS CHAMBERS

PARIS—Jean-Marie Le Pen, France's leading far-right politician and a candidate for the French presidency, has caused an uproar with a statement that the Nazi gas chambers were "a minor point" of history.

In a radio interview reprinted Monday in Le Monde, Mr. Le Pen said: "I am not saying that gas chambers did not exist. I couldn't see them myself. I haven't studied the question specially. But I believe that is a minor point in the history of World War II."

Source: New York Times, September 16, 1987.

_____ **BOX 1.25** _____

ON THE RIGHT, LE PEN TALKS OF DELUGE

AMIENS—Like the stand-up comic he sometimes resembles, Jean-Marie Le Pen, attired in a double-breasted blue blazer and gray slacks, strode the stage, a microphone pinned to his lapel. For two hours, without notes, he announced the apocalypse that awaits France if it does not reverse an "invasion" of third-world immigrants.

"This vanguard of millions of foreigners will turn itself into an army and then into a flood," warned the tribune of the ultra-right National Front. "France will become an Islamic republic!"

As Mr. Pen's silky, sarcastic oratory swept over a rapt audience of 1,200 or so that had paid $5 a seat, all of France's problems were revealed to be the fault of freeloading immigrants: unemployment, crime, housing shortages, an overburdened social security system, crowded hospitals and schools where too many children do not speak French.

"France," said the National Front's presidential candidate, bending down at the knees, twisting his face grotesquely and spreading his arms forlornly, "is like an old drunken lady whose purse is wide open and who gives money to whoever passes by." Laughter and applause exploded in appreciation for the gifted mimic on the stage.

Source: New York Times, March 29, 1988.

In West Germany, the National Democratic party has never won 5 percent of the vote, the minimum required for representation in parliament. But there is now a new development with the Republicans of Franz Schöhuber (no connection with Republicans in the United States). As can be seen in Box 1.26, Schönhuber is not ashamed of his service in the Waffen SS and pleads

_____ **BOX 1.26** _____

WEST GERMAN RIGHTIST BOASTS OF NAZI SERVICE

BONN—The head of a far-right party, flush with a strong showing in West Berlin, regaled an overflow rally in Bavaria today with his message of guilt-free nationalism, declaring in the process that he was not ashamed of his own service in the Waffen SS.

In a two-hour address to more than 6,000 supporters, the party leader, Franz Schönhuber of the Republicans, also criticised the head of the West German Jewish organization, American pop culture, foreign aid and resident foreigners, whose ouster is one of the foundations of the party program.

Source: New York Times, February 9, 1989.

for a guilt-free nationalism. He had some successes in local elections, gaining, for example, 7.5 percent in West Berlin.

It is not easy to determine who is Neofascist and who is not. Has a voter turned into a Neofascist who always voted for the Christian Democrats but has now switched to the Republicans? As the German political scientist Klaus von Beyme correctly points out, there is quite a large Neofascist potential in the existing democratic parties. This is particularly true for Conservative parties. Von Beyme argues that "(x)enophobia does not push the rigid nationalist potential into extremist parties" as long as Conservative leaders such as Thatcher and Kohl "offer an outlet for these feelings as part of the programmes of their dominant, moderate conservative parties."[11] The working of this mechanism could be seen when the charismatic Conservative Bavarian leader Franz Joseph Strauss died. According to the thesis of von Beyme, he could keep most voters with a Neofascist orientation in the ranks of his party. But after his death many of these voters felt lost and found a new home in the Republican party of Franz Schönhuber. Analyses of the Republican voters have also revealed that many crossed over from the Socialists, although not as many as from the Conservatives. Thus, there is also a Neofascist potential among Socialist voters, especially among working-class Socialists. They may be attracted by the simple language of someone like Schönhuber, given that many Socialist leaders tend to speak too much in an intellectual language. Sometimes, voting for a Neofascist party is simply a protest vote; for example, about housing conditions or the health care system.

There is also a Neofascist potential that is not expressed on the voting ballot. An increasing rowdyism among European soccer fans has attracted much attention (Box 1.27). Soccer is the most popular sport in Europe, but, unfortunately, international soccer games increasingly have become battlefields for nationalistic fanaticism. When Liverpool came to Rome to play the local team in a European Championship game, the police took great precautions to keep the fans apart. But all the carefully designed measures could not prevent bloody street battles after the game. Similar incidents occured in West Berlin during a game between German and Turkish teams, where all the prejudice and hatred against Turkish foreign workers was unleashed. Shock waves resounded throughout Germany when some soccer fans took up the habit of shouting Hitler slogans during games. The worst incident happened in May 1985, when rowdyism before a European championship game between Liverpool and Turin held in Brussels caused 38 deaths. Are such rowdies simply trying to provoke by whatever means they find, or do these actions have more serious political implications? Although the danger should not be exaggerated, this ugly nationalism on Europe's soccer fields is not harmless, either.

There is still another type of warning about Neofascist tendencies, of a more subtle nature, and many people do not agree that these warnings are justified and condemn them as hysterical. The warnings say that the state itself takes on Neofascist characteristics in its increasing control of the private lives of its citizens. This debate is particularly heated in West Ger-

_____ **BOX 1.27** _____

BRITISH SOCCER FANS RUN WILD IN STOCKHOLM

STOCKHOLM, Sweden—Police arrested about 100 British soccer fans who rampaged through downtown Stockholm on Wednesday before a World Cup qualifying match, the national TT news agency reported.

The hooligans, many drunk, ran through Stockholm's shopping district shouting, slapping passers-by and ripping clothing off sales racks outside stores. Police with riot shields chased and scuffled with them.

The news agency quoted a police duty officer as saying busloads of young Britons were taken into custody, but she did not know the exact number. "It could be 80, it could be 120," she said.

Most of them appeared to be teenagers.

Scattered incidents of brawling and vandalism were reported earlier from restaurants and on trains as some 2,000 visitors filtered through the city, waiting for Wednesday evening's game between Sweden and England.

The Swedes had braced for a display of British soccer hooliganism after one fan drowned Monday after he jumped into the North Sea from a ferry carrying hundreds of would-be spectators to Stockholm.

Source: The Daily Tar Heel, Chapel Hill N. C., September 5, 1989.

many, where the state is committed to the principle that all its employees give evidence that they support the basic democratic principles outlined in the West German constitution. The goal is to prevent undemocratic forces from infiltrating state institutions, and in order to pursue this goal, files are kept on potential applicants for state jobs, for example, student teachers. Although the Communist party is legally recognized, membership in that party may be included in the files. Participation in an antinuclear demonstration that turns violent may also be reported. Based on all the information in such a file, a judgment is made whether an applicant for a state position gives enough evidence through past behavior of future support for the basic democratic principles of the constitution.

Fair enough, because democracy must protect itself against its enemies? Not so, reply the critics, who argue that the clandestine collection of information for such files violates the most basic democratic principle of the right to privacy. If the needs of state authorities are held to be greater than the needs of the individual, the danger of a Neofascist state is present. In West Germany, such criticism led to promises that the state would be more restrictive in the compilation of files on its citizens. But the suspicion remains and is fed by other state actions. Thus, there were widespread protests against a too-detailed 1983 national census. It was feared that the data could be misused against the respondents by state authorities. By decision of the Constitutional court, the census was stopped and had to be rescheduled in a simplified form.

Looking at the entire picture presented in this section—from the voting record of Neofascist parties to nationalistic soccer fans and intrusions of state authorities into the private lives of its citizens—is there a Neofascist danger in European democracies? Probably no more and no less than in the United States, where there are similar fears that modern technology allows an unprecedented surveillance of the population by state authorities. Patriotism in America also sometimes turns into an unpleasant nationalism. It is probably only due to the great geographical distances that such nationalism is not expressed by American fans traveling to sports events in other countries. Finally, note too that the United States has such organizations as the Ku Klux Klan, the John Birch Society, and the Nazi party. That these groups play practically no role in elections can be explained by the particular American electoral system.

American TV networks render a disservice to their audience when they produce sensational shows about the dramatic rebirth of fascism in Europe, complete with the display of war veterans and youth wearing swastika signs. It makes good TV footage and may sound plausible, especially with German locations, which facilitate an appeal to memories of the Nazi past. But, in fact, Neofascist tendencies are no stronger in West Germany than in other European democracies and, for that matter, in the United States. This does not mean that we should underestimate the danger of neofascism in Western democracies. It is a complex phenomenon that needs to be carefully watched.

GREENS

With the Greens, a new party made its appearance on the European political scene in the late 1970s and early 1980s. The Green party is active in several countries, most prominently in West Germany. But even there, its voter support in the last general election was only 8.3 percent. The immediate public attention paid the party is not so much due to its electoral successes as to its newness in the existing party systems. The Greens cannot easily be located on the left–right continuum, and the dimension from authoritarian to individualistic is not of much help in clarifying this new party's position. A third dimension is necessary to define the political position of the Greens.

Several labels are possible to describe this third dimension, but we will use the terms *material* and *postmaterial* to designate the poles.[12] The material end of the dimension means a conventional support for economic growth. This position is based on the assumption that bigger is better: The more goods and services a society produces, the better off the members of that society are. At the postmaterial end of the dimension, limits to economic growth are advocated. This position was encountered earlier, in presenting a new style of thinking that has developed in a wing of the Socialist party, and the dimension from left to right was not sufficient for locating this type of Socialism either. Adding the material–postmaterial continuum allows us not only to situate the Green party but also to better understand the split in the Socialist party.

The main purpose of Figure 5 is to locate the Greens, so the line drawn vertical from material to postmaterial is thicker, to show its importance to the definition of the Green position. Postmaterialism indicates a developmental stage in society when material goods no longer have first priority and people seek fulfillment of their spiritual, ethical, and aesthetic needs instead. Self-actualization is the goal. Because this can only be accomplished in cooperation with others, communal life also is important. According to the Greens, it is time for Western societies to move from a material to a postmaterial orientation. This is the only way to save our souls and, also, our natural environment (see Box 1.28). The political implication of this thinking is a completely new orientation toward work.

In a postmaterial stage of society, we must again find fulfillment in our daily work. This is impossible for small wheels in large bureaucratic organizations, whether public or private. The desired situation is work in a small commune: Some people can bake bread, others can repair bikes, and positions can easily be exchanged. The Greens acknowledge that this is not the most efficient way to organize the economy, but they challenge the usual definition of economic efficiency measured in the annual increase of the Gross National Product. The GNP does not reflect, for example, stress on human beings and the destruction of nature. According to the Greens, the crucial criterion for work must be how much it contributes to the quality of life for human beings as well as for animals and plants. Nature must be brought back into an equilibrium. With this philosophy, the Greens have also developed a strong interest in world peace. A nuclear holocaust would be the ultimate disruption of the equilibrium of nature, and, according to the Greens, this catastrophe can only be prevented by rapid disarmament.

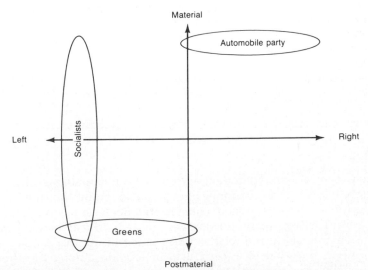

Figure 5. Location of Greens, Socialists, and Automobile party on a Dimension from Left to Right and on a Dimension from Material to Postmaterial.

——————————————————— **BOX 1.28** ———————————————————

SYMBOLIC PROTESTS AGAINST THE
DYING FORESTS IN WEST GERMANY

Nature lovers out for a Sunday afternoon stroll in the woods around Munich found newly-erected signs pointing out the various states of acid rain damage visible on the surrounding fir trees.

Hikers in a portion of the Black forest found a tree cemetery. Unknown environmentalists had painted white crosses on dozens of spruce and firs to symbolize the impending death of the trees.

Two dozen dead trees bearing skull-and-crossbones and the words "Help Us" written in lime stood near the Bavarian state parliament.

Local environmental groups have set up poster displays and information booths in the pedestrian precincts of every major city and town to distribute leaflets to Saturday shopping crowds. They have also arranged walking and bicycling tours of local woods with guides who teach citizens to recognize the danger signs of increasingly sickly trees. Bumper stickers proclaiming "I drive 100 [km/h] out of love for the forest" have begun to appear in the slow lanes of the Autobahn.

When Chancellor Helmut Kohl was sworn into office following the 1983 election, parliamentary deputies of the newly elected Green Party presented him with a bouquet of dead pine boughs.

Greenpeace activists attempting to demonstrate the shared responsibility of East and West Germany for each other's pollutants crossed the Berlin Wall in a hot air balloon. They were quickly arrested by East German police and escorted back across the line.

On the day the upper chamber of the Federal Parliament was scheduled to debate new restrictions on emissions from large stationary sources, one hundred members of an organization representing small farmers who own stands of forest land dragged a huge brown spruce tree through the inner city of Bonn. They proceeded to saw the tree into logs and erected a "monument" to officials in the Ministry of Food, Agriculture, and Forestry.

Source: Carolyn Watkins, "Action Strategies and Acid Rain: German Environmental Groups between Institutions and Indignation," Paper presented at the annual meeting of the Southwestern Political Science Association, Houston, Texas, 20–23 March 1985.

The Greens are united in their emphasis on postmaterial values, but they are more dispersed on economic questions. Generally, they tend toward the left, and many Greens, indeed, come from a Socialist or even a Communist background. Other Greens, however, see more merits in market mechanism. Disagreements about the relative importance of the free market and state intervention have led to a great deal of tension among the Greens and, occasionally, even to split into two separate parties, as in Switzerland.

Socialists are also included in Figure 5, to show the uneasy relationship they have with the Greens. The two parties share a common voter potential in the area of the figure where they overlap. There we find leftists with a postmaterial orientation, and for these voters there is a fierce competition between Socialists and Greens. In Chapter 3, we will see to what extent Socialists and Greens work together in practical politics.

Figure 5 also shows the position of the so-called Automobile party, which is the pure opposite of the Greens and helps clarify further the Green perspective.[13] The Automobile party was founded in Switzerland, but efforts are made to implant it also in other countries, particularly in West Germany. Although most political parties besides the Greens have quite a strong material orientation, the Automobile party takes this position to an extreme. The car is considered to be the ultimate material good, which has to be protected against government interventions by all means. A slogan of the Automobile party is "Unrestricted Driving for the Free Citizen." The supporters of the party protest whenever efforts are made to limit driving in the interest of the environment. Such measures include higher gasoline taxes, lower speed limits on highways, traffic-free streets in the inner cities, more stop lights, and less parking space. The Automobile party considers such measures to be unnecessary restraints on the enjoyment of driving a car. This view is diametrically opposed to what is dear to Green supporters. Emotions are high between the two sets of values, especially when they clash in a traffic situation in which a Green supporter is on a bike and a supporter of the Automobile party is in a fancy car. The thoughts and possibly the words that the two have for each other are not kind at all. Extreme materialism can be found in all European countries, although up to now it was only in Switzerland that a special party founded on this basis had some success (see Table 16 on page 123).

The Greens are unusual, not only because they do not fit the existing party systems of Europe, but also in the sense that they wish to be a completely different type of party. The Greens refuse to participate in the normal political game, which they consider undemocratic. According to their views, the leaders of other parties form an oligarchy that has lost touch with ordinary citizens. The Greens demand a fundamental democratization of political life and try to implement this principle first in their own ranks. Ideally, the Greens would like to have no leadership, but equal participation by all members. To move toward this ideal, the Greens have initially developed unusual party rules, particularly in West Germany. There, the Greens at first did not allow their members of parliament to have incomes higher than blue-collar workers; the surplus had to be contributed to the party. After two years in office, Green members of parliament were also expected to rotate their seats to others in the party. These rules have led to a great deal of acrimony in the German Green party, they have often been violated, and in the mean time many of these rules have been abolished or at least relaxed.

In Box 1.29 Herbert Kitschelt gives a concise summary characterization of the Greens. Kitschelt has also done an interesting study about the strength of

BOX 1.29

CHARACTERIZATION OF THE GREENS

Over the last two decades, New Left and libertarian parties in Scandinavia, the Netherlands, and France have made electoral inroads. Most recently, parties under the "green," "ecological," or "alternative" label have won significant electoral support in Austria, Belgium, Switzerland, and West Germany. Both types of party belong to a new cohort of left-libertarian parties. They share the traditional Left's concern for egalitarianism and political control of the economy, but they question centralized planning, a policy process dominated by small political elites, and the desirability of increased material affluence. Instead, they emphasize participatory democracy, political decentralization, and quality of life issues, such as environmental protection and more personalized social services. All left-libertarian parties share the same core constituencies: younger, educated, urban, secular members of the new middle classes who work overproportionally in the public service sector.

Source: Herbert Kitschelt, "Organization and Strategy of Belgian and German Ecology Parties," *Comparative Politics* 20(January 1988): p. 127.

the Greens in the various European countries.[14] He found that the party is strongest

- If the number of university students has strongly increased
- If the income per capita is high
- If social expenditures are high
- If the strike level is low
- If Socialists are strong in the executive

In the first edition of this book, I asked the question: "Will internal conflicts and inconsistencies kill the Green party, or is it here to stay?" In the meantime, chances have greatly increased that the party is here to stay. In Chapter 3, I will show how the Greens are increasingly willing to work with other parties. They are still an unusual party, but they are slowly fitting better into the overall political system.

REGIONAL PARTIES

In order to locate regional parties, we have to introduce still another dimension of party space, the center–periphery dimension. If we take a typical regional party, such as the Scottish National party, it is not possible to locate it on a left–right dimension, nor are the authoritarian–individualistic and material–postmaterial dimensions of much help. Regional parties defend the interests of a periphery against the interests of the center of a country.

Most political parties look at political life from the perspective of the capital, where they have their headquarters and the focus of their daily activities. From this perspective, the interests of peripheral regions are often neglected. It is against such neglect that regional parties try to fight. They look at politics from the vantage point of their regions.

In recent years, the importance of regional parties in Europe has increased rather than decreased. With more modernity, one may perhaps expect the opposite trend: With fewer people in farming, higher levels of education, more geographical mobility, more travel, and more exposure to mass media, one may think that the attachment to one's region may become less important. But there is obviously a need in the modern world for roots, and the region is for many an entity that gives roots to the past and a feeling of warm solidarity among people with similar traditions and values. I will deal with the question of regionalism in Chapter 6 in the section on federalism and in Chapter 11 in the section on social movements. At this point, I will simply give a few examples of regional parties.

The already mentioned Scottish National party gained three seats in the 1987 parliamentary election. In Wales, another peripheral region of the United Kingdom, Plaid Cymru, the party of the region, won also three seats. In Spain, regional parties had a combined vote of about 10 percent in the 1986 parliamentary election. These parties are representing in particular the Basque, Catalan, Andalusian, Galician, Aragonese, and Valencian regions. As a third example, I wish to mention Italy, where in the 1987 election the following regional parties were running candidates: Venetial League, South Tyrol People's party, Lombard League, Sardinian Action party, Piedmont, Val d'Aosta Union, and Friuli Movement. The combined national vote of these parties was, however, merely 3 percent.

Of all the European countries, Belgium has the strongest influence of regionalism on its party system. Not only are there special regional parties for the Flemish and Walloon regions; more importantly, some of the major parties have special organizations for the two regions. Thus, there is a Francophone Socialist party for Wallonia and a Flemish Socialist party. We will deal with the complex Belgian situation in Chapter 6.

MEMBERSHIP IN POLITICAL PARTIES

Membership in a European political party is quite different from party membership in the United States. Americans reveal their party identification by registering, voting in general elections, and answering opinion surveys, but they do not formally join a party as they would a professional association or service club—by paying annual dues and carrying a membership card. Europeans do precisely that when they join a political party: Membership in a political party is applied for, and the party has the right to reject applicants, although this happens rarely.

This may be a good time to say that since 1961 I have been a member of the Swiss Free Democratic party. A reader has the right to know with what possible bias a textbook was written. I have made an effort, of course, to describe the various party programs as objectively as possible. But, unconsciously my own party affiliation may still have influenced my writing, which is for the reader to judge.

Currently, my annual party fee, together with my wife's, is about $50. Whenever the local party in my Swiss home town has a meeting, I get an invitation by mail. It is at these meetings that the Free Democratic candidates for the local council are selected. It is also at the local party meetings that the selection process for higher offices begins, in the sense that the local party can send delegates to party gatherings at higher levels, which in turn select the candidates for higher offices.

My personal experience is fairly typical for ordinary members in European parties. There is usually no big rush in the general population to join a party. Figures vary strongly from country to country, but membership is usually below 20 percent of all citizens; in some countries, it is below 5 percent. That European parties are membership based is important to keep in mind when in the next chapter we turn to the question of how parliamentary elections are organized.

2

PARLIAMENTARY ELECTIONS

Americans are accustomed to very simple rules for parliamentary elections. For the U.S. Senate, whoever receives the most votes in his or her state is elected. The same rule applies to the U.S. House of Representatives: Whoever wins his or her Congressional district is elected. In Europe, this simple "winner-take-all" system is used only in Great Britain, where it is called "first-past-the-post." The other European countries use a wide variety of rules to elect their parliaments. In addition to Great Britain, I will describe the cases of the Netherlands, Switzerland, Ireland, France, and West Germany to illustrate this variety. Election rules are not interesting for their own sake, but because they influence the way the political game is played. To every American student, the connection between rules of the game and the game itself is well known from sports. Changes in the rules of a sport often influence the kinds of players who are able to make the team. As we will see in this chapter, the same holds true for politics. A politician who is successful under one set of rules may not be at all successful under another set of rules.

Most European democracies have an upper and a lower house of parliament, with the latter being usually the more important house. For the moment, we will focus on the election of the lower houses; thus, in Great Britain, we will focus on the House of Commons and not on the House of Lords. The function of the upper houses is addressed in Chapter 3.

GREAT BRITAIN: WINNER-TAKE-ALL

For elections to the British House of Commons (see photo page 66), the country is divided into as many electoral districts as there are parliamentary seats—650—and in each district the candidate who has the most votes wins the seat. As in the United States, there is no requirement that the winner must reach a majority; a mere plurality of the votes is sufficient. Thus, with three candidates in a district, the winner may have only 40 percent, with perhaps the two other candidates each getting 30 percent.

The winner-take-all system is strongly biased in favor of the two largest parties in a country. In the U.S. Congress, no third parties at all are currently represented. Is this due to the electoral system? Yes, most likely. But American third parties get so few votes in congressional elections that at first

Great Britain's Houses of Parliament, Westminster, London. (Courtesy British Embassy, Bern, Switzerland.)

glance it may not be clear how their lack of success could possibly be due to the electoral system. Is it simply the "natural" American way to have a two-party system? This chapter should make clear that under a different electoral system American third parties would at least have a better chance of representation in Congress.

In Great Britain, third parties are numerically stronger than in the United States. As a consequence, and paradoxically, it is easier to demonstrate with the British case how a winner-take-all system works against third parties. If third parties get a fair amount of voter support, it is easier to see how this support fails to translate into parliamentary representation. The discrimination against a third party can best be illustrated with the 1983 general election.

Comparing voter support and seats in the House of Commons in Table 2,

Table 2
Voter Support and Parliamentary Seats in 1983 General
Election to the British House of Commons

Party	Voter Support (%)	Seats (%)	N
Conservatives	42.4	61.1	397
Labour	27.6	32.3	209
Alliance of Liberals and Social Democrats	25.4	3.5	23
Others	4.6	3.2	21
Total	100.0	100.0	650

Source: European Journal of Political Research 12 (September 1984): 342.

we can make several points. First, with 42.4 percent voter support, the Conservatives won a plurality, but not a majority, of the electorate; this support, however, gave them a landslide 61.1 percent of parliamentary seats. This large victory was caused by the fact that the opposition was badly divided. We saw in Chapter 1 how moderate Labour members split from the party to form their own Social Democratic party (SDP). The SDP entered into the so-called Alliance with the Liberals, which meant that the two parties agreed to have only one candidate in each district—either a Social Democrat or a Liberal. Before the 1983 election, the Liberals were the perennial third party in British electoral history. They achieved sizable voter support but hardly any seats because they were "first past the post" in only a very few districts. In the October 1974 election, for example, the Liberals won a substantial share of voter support (18.6 percent) but managed to win only 13 seats (2.0 percent). Uniting their forces in 1983 in the Alliance, the Liberals and Social Democrats hoped to win not only voters but also districts. But this hope was disappointed; their voter support of 25.4 percent translated into a mere 3.5 percent of the seats. The Alliance was punished by an electoral system wherein only winning matters and a good showing—in second or third place—counts for nothing.

With only slightly higher voter support of 27.6 percent, Labour won nearly 10 times as many parliamentary seats (32.2 percent) as the Liberal-Social Democrat Alliance. The reason was that Labour voters were concentrated in working-class districts, where, in many cases, the party was able to come in first. The Alliance voters, in contrast, were spread more evenly over all districts. This distribution made for a good showing overall in the country but very few district victories. And with the winner-take-all system, only victories count.

In addition to Conservatives, Labour, and the Alliance, some smaller parties together won 3.2 percent of the seats, a surprisingly high number, given voter support of only 4.6 percent. But these were all local parties in Northern Ireland, Scotland, and Wales, where they were able to carry a few districts. Outside their region, they did not even have candidates.

In order to fully understand the winner-take-all system, we must also consider very strong anticipatory effects. Many voters do not like to "waste" their vote on a party that is expected to have no chance of victory. In the 1983 election, this mechanism worked strongly against the Liberal-Social Democrat Alliance. There were many voters who seriously considered voting for the Alliance but, according to surveys, eventually did not, because they anticipated that the Alliance candidate had no chance of winning their district.[15] This anticipatory effect also helps explain why the Communists and the Neofascist National Front won no parliamentary representation. It is not that these extremist forces are absent in Britain but only that their support is not translated into votes, because potential voters anticipate that these parties have no chance of winning any districts. In order not to waste their votes, such voters tend to vote for one of the larger parties— Communist sympathizers usually vote for Labour, and National Front sympathizers, for the Conservatives. Foreign observers of British politics are often surprised that the Labour party has a fairly strong Marxist wing. The explanation lies at least partly in the mechanisms of the electoral system just described. Under a proportional system, many Marxists who now vote Labour might very well switch their support to the Communist party. With proportionality, one might also expect a certain shift from Conservatives to the National Front.

Britain serves as a good illustration of how the electoral system influences the kind and strength of parties represented in Parliament. The British example should also help us understand that election rules are not simply a given but are an outcome of the political game. Because it was at a serious disadvantage under the winner-take-all system, the Alliance advocated a change to proportional representation. Conservatives and Labour, which both benefit greatly from the current system, were opposed to such a change that, given the distribution of seats in the House of Commons, had no chance to be accepted.

With the winner-take-all system continuing to prevail, it is no wonder that the fortunes of the Alliance went downhill after the 1983 election. Because it became clear that the Alliance had no chance of overcoming Labour for second place, voters increasingly feared that a vote for the Alliance was a wasted vote. As Table 3 shows, in the 1987 election the support for the Alliance dropped to 22.5 percent and its parliamentary representation to 22 seats. After this second, even more disappointing defeat, the Alliance went into complete disarray. Its support in opinion polls went even further down. In the hope of turning things around, the two parties of the Alliance attempted to fuse into a single party, but this made the situation only worse. The Social Democrats split over this issue. One faction of the party refused to unite with the Liberals and continued to operate under the old label, but only until June 1990, when the Social Democratic Party was dissolved. The other faction of the Social Democrats created, together with the Liberals, a new party called the Social and Liberal Democrats (SLD). This story tells vividly how difficult it is to be a third party under the winner-take-all system. Voters tend to vote either for the incumbent or for the candidate who has the greatest chance of unseating the incumbent. Although it is very difficult for a

Table 3
Voter Support and Parliamentary Seats in 1987 General
Election to the British House of Commons

Party	Voter Support (%)	Seats (%)	N
Conservatives	42.3	57.8	376
Labour	30.8	35.2	229
Alliance of Liberals and Social Democrats	22.5	3.4	22
Others	4.4	3.6	23
Total	100.0	100.0	650

Source: *European Journal of Political Research* 16 (September 1988): 584.

third party to become one of the two major parties, such a development is not entirely impossible. Early in this century, Labour became one of the two large parties, relegating the Liberals to third place.

With an understanding of the British case, we can now shed some new light on the American two-party system. American third parties are weak in congressional elections because of the anticipatory effect that they have no chance of winning anyway. This chance is only granted candidates of the two major parties—Democrats and Republicans.

A puzzling point is the absence of regional parties in the U.S. Congress when the United States is much larger than and geographically at least as diverse as Great Britain. If the Scottish National party has a chance of winning some districts in its own region, why should a Texan party, for example, not try to do the same? The answer is probably complex and would have to be dealt with in a text about American politics.

Until now, we have focused on the negative effects on smaller parties of the winner-take-all system. On a more positive note, we could also argue that this type of electoral system helps to prevent the fragmentation of Parliament and, in particular, to exclude extremist parties, thus making governance easier. The American and British cases seem to support this argument, since extremist parties are not represented in either country's legislature. This moderating effect, however, is likely to occur only for a unimodal distribution of voter preferences.

The United States and Great Britain have, by and large, unimodal distributions of voter preferences on most important dimensions, and therefore approach the situation depicted in Figure 6. Under these conditions, we would indeed expect a moderating effect, because, in order to win, the most rational strategy for a candidate is to advocate a middle-of-the-road position. Most voters, after all, are located in the middle. In Figure 7, representing a bimodal distribution of voter preferences, we can easily see that a moderate position in the middle has little appeal.

Let us assume that the voters at the left of our political dimension in Figure 7 are Catholics and those at the right are Protestants, with the two groups far

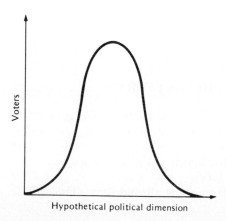

Figure 6. Unimodal Distribution of Voter Preferences on a Hypothetical Political Dimension.

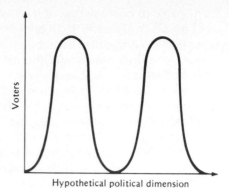

Figure 7. Bimodal Distribution of Voter Preferences on a Hypothetical Political Dimension.

apart on all important issues. With a winner-take-all system, one candidate is likely to appeal to Catholics; the other, to Protestants. The election then corresponds more to a census, in the sense that the size of the two groups is counted. The campaign will have a polarizing effect, because each candidate will do everything to mobilize the members of his or her group. This is basically the situation in Northern Ireland. The only difference between that situation and the situation represented in Figure 7 is that one group in Northern Ireland, the Protestants, is about twice the size of the Catholic group, which further exacerbates the problem, because Catholics have no chance of winning many districts. London is slowly beginning to recognize the unfairness of the winner-take-all system under these circumstances and has imposed proportionality rules for local elections in Northern Ireland and for elections from this region to the European parliament, although not for elections to the House of Commons.

The difficulties that the winner-take-all system encountered in Northern Ireland can also be seen in many Third World countries. If, for example, the electorate comprises two historically hostile ethnic groups, under a winner-take-all system each group will be highly motivated to use all legal—and, sometimes, illegal—means to turn out more voters than the other, and elections will tend to be polarizing.

THE NETHERLANDS: PARTY LIST PROPORTIONAL REPRESENTATION

The basic principle of party list proportional representation (hereafter PR) is quite simple: a party receives parliamentary seats in proportion to its share of the total vote. If a parliament has 100 members and a party wins 10 percent of the total vote, then that party will be awarded 10 parliamentary seats. If the party wins only 1 percent of the vote, it receives only 1 seat.

The Netherlands uses party list PR in its most simple form. The Dutch

Table 4
Voter Support and Parliamentary Seats in 1989 General
Election to the Parliament of the Netherlands

Party	Voter Support (%)	Seats (%)	Seats N
Christian Democratic Appeal	35.3	35.9	54
Labour Party	31.9	32.7	49
Liberals (People's Party for Freedom and Democracy)	14.6	14.7	22
Democrats '66	7.9	8.0	12
Green Left	4.1	4.0	6
Political Reformed Party	1.9	2.0	3
Reformed Political Union	1.2	1.3	2
Reformed Political Federation	1.0	0.7	1
Centre Democrats	0.9	0.7	1
Others	1.2	0.0	0
Total	100.0	100.0	150

Source: Royal Netherlands Embassy, Washington D. C.

parliament has 150 members, who are elected from a single nationwide electoral district. The political parties submit lists of their candidates, and the voters simply choose one of these lists.* The votes are tallied in a two-step process. First, the number of votes nationwide for each party is counted and is converted into a percentage of the total vote cast. In the 1989 election, for example, the Christian Democrats received the most votes (35.3 percent), the Labour party came in second (31.9 percent), and the Liberals finished third (14.6 percent). According to the PR system, the Christian Democrats were awarded 54 seats, the Labour party, 49, and the Liberals, 22. The other 25 seats were awarded to six smaller parties. The smallest party receiving parliamentary representation, the Centre Democrats, was awarded a single seat for its 0.9 percent of votes cast (Table 4). Careful readers will note that voter percentages can assign fractions of seats to parties. In order to deal with this situation, countries use different statistical formulas for distributing these fractions as whole seats.

We now know how the first step of the Dutch electoral system—the distribution of parliamentary seats to the political parties—works. The second step is to consider how the individual parties determine which of their candidates will be elected. Each party lists its candidates in the order in which they will be awarded any seats won by the party. For example, the Labour party's first 49 ranked candidates became its parliamentary repre-

---

* Parties submit different lists in different administrative districts. These lists are then linked at the national level.

sentatives; it had to disappoint all of its candidates listed 50th and below.*

This system of having the parties rank their candidates gives them an important means of controlling the behavior of party members. How is the ranking done? Who gets the favorable ranks at the top? Who would be so foolish as to enter the race last on a list? The ranking is done by the party organizations, without the help of primaries. A small group, such as the party's executive committee, usually prepares the party list. A party convention then approves the list, usually without making any major changes. A young party member beginning his or her career would feel honored just to be placed on the list, even if the actual rank gave absolutely no chance of election. By working hard for the party, a candidate expects to move up the list to finally receive a rank that assures him or her of election to a parliamentary seat. Prominent party leaders and successful members of parliament are usually given those places on the list that virtually guarantee reelection to parliament. This system strengthens the parties by giving them the opportunity to reward loyal party members with good rankings and to punish less loyal ones with bad rankings.

The Dutch system of party ranking is in sharp contrast to American practice. Members of the U.S. Congress depend on their party only to a very small degree for their own election and reelection. An American candidate need only receive the most votes in a district rather than demonstrate the party loyalty necessary for a good ranking on his or her party's list of candidates. This voter support often depends only slightly on the candidate's party loyalty, and it is sometimes even advantageous for an American candidate to demonstrate some independence from the official platform of his or her party.

The lack of party discipline of many U.S. congressional candidates can not, however, be due solely to the system of election, because Great Britain combines the same winner-take-all system with a fairly high party discipline. Although it is certainly true that party list PR as practiced in the Netherlands contributes to strong party discipline, it is obviously not true that strong party discipline is impossible under a winner-take-all system. Whether party discipline is strong or weak in a winner-take-all system also depends on other factors; in particular, on whether a country has a parliamentary system of government. As we will see in Chapter 3, Great Britain has a parliamentary system, and, in such systems, the vote of confidence in Parliament is very important. It is precisely this device—the vote of confidence—that necessitates party discipline. In the absence of a parliamentary system, the United States can afford low party discipline. Thus, the winner-take-all electoral system in combination with the absence of a parliamentary system explains to a large extent why American political parties have low party discipline.

In the Netherlands, party list PR has contributed to a diverse multiparty system, because small fringe parties have a chance of winning parliamentary

---

* The voters may change the parties' ranking by means of a preferential vote for a particular candidate, but it is extremely unusual for a candidate to be elected thanks to such preferential voting.

representation. With an electoral system similar to the Dutch one, any group receiving as little as 0.25 percent of votes cast would win a seat in the U.S. House of Representatives (one out of 435 seats). How many groups could receive this much support or even more? How many votes could a party stressing peace and environmental issues, like the West German Green party, win? Note in this context a letter to the editor of the chairman of the New York Green party (Box 2.1).

The introduction of party list PR in the United States might allow the election of representatives from many groups, such as the new right, the Right to Life movement, blacks, Hispanics, and others. Under such a system, congressional membership could more closely reflect the diversity of the American population, and many voters would find a party closer to their preferences than under the current two-party system of Democrats and Republicans.

What would be the major disadvantages of using a proportional representation system for American congressional elections? American students say that they would miss voting for a particular candidate who they could know personally and consider their own representative. This weakness can be remedied without abandoning the principle of proportionality. Party list PR

BOX 2.1

GREEN PARTY OF NEW YORK DEMANDS PROPORTIONAL REPRESENTATION

To the Editor:

As a minority party, what we most strongly urge is some form of proportional representation. In West Germany, for instance, once a political party has achieved 5 percent of the vote, it can designate an equal percentage in the Bundestag. Thus, though in perhaps no election district has a particular party achieved a majority, it will still be represented in an at-large seat.

While politically in the United States we are not used to such a concept, we do have, in that other most potent form of social organization in the Western world, the publicly held corporation, directors who are elected by minority shareholders and represent their interests.

Would proportional representation require a constitutional amendment? At a local level, not necessarily, depending on each state's own constitution, but it would appear to need one on the national level. So be it. The United States must take some fairly drastic steps if it is going to rearouse the electorate from the torpor that was reflected in the barely 50 percent turnout in the Presidential election of 1988.   PETER HIRSCH
                                                   Chairman, Green Party of N.Y.

Source: New York Times, February 2, 1989.

===================== **BOX 2.2** =====================

ARGUMENTS FOR THE WINNER-TAKE-ALL SYSTEM

. . . government by majority is government by persuasion. Members of a variety of ethnic, religious, economic, and other groups must be brought together. The result is civic education of the most effective kind. Members of minority groups, by cooperating, learn first of all to tolerate and then to appreciate each other. Their leaders must pursue policies acceptable to all.

*   *   *

The doctrinaire PR (proportional representation) advocates and the poll-takers have made us accustomed to thinking of an election as a means of obtaining a more or less accurate image of all of the opinions in a country—or even as a means of "photographing" these opinions. But democracy does not consist of assembling a parliament which is a small-sized model of the distribution of a nation's different spiritual families in all their diversity and nuances. Voters should not choose their doubles who must resemble them as closely as possible. They should choose governments with the capacity to make decisions. By dispersing the voters among numerous independent parties, PR prevents the citizens from expressing a clear choice for a governmental team. . . .

PR properly expresses the citizens' diverse preferences, but it does not allow them to choose a concrete set of policies and a team to execute them. In contrast with this representation of opinions, what may be called the representation of wills enables the voters to choose those who will lead them during the entire life of the legislature. . . .

What is the point of guaranteeing that each party's number of deputies will be exactly proportional to that of its voters, if it remains free to ally itself with whomever, whenever, and for whatever purpose it wishes, and to change partners at any moment? . . .

. . . PR generally weakens democracy and . . . plurality and majority systems strengthen it, which, in the final analysis, makes the latter more moral and just: The first duty in the development of morality and justice in political relationships consists of reinforcing democracy and weakening dictatorship.

Source: Ferdinand A. Hermens, "Representation and Proportional Representation," in Arend Lijphart and Bernard Grofman, eds., *Choosing an Electoral System: Issues and Alternatives* (New York: Praeger, 1984), p. 18; and Maurice Duverger, "Which Is the Best Electoral System?" ibid., pp. 32–35.

as practiced in the Netherlands is not the only way to implement the principle of proportionality. More personalized forms of proportionality are also feasible. We turn next to Switzerland as an illustration of a more personalized system of proportional representation. (For arguments on the merits of winner-take-all and proportional representation, see also Boxes 2.2 and 2.3).

BOX 2.3

ARGUMENTS FOR PROPORTIONAL REPRESENTATION

There is growing dislike of the unpleasant atmosphere of British politics, of the tendency to think in terms of party warfare rather than of government in the interests of the whole nation. That again is encouraged by the majority system of election. In each constituency, only one candidate can win; he must strive to "kill" his opponents. Where he has only to take his fair share of several seats, hostility is likely to be less. The British elector has to vote as if he thought candidate X was perfect and all others abominable. . . . Multimember constituencies . . . have an additional advantage: they give a fair chance of election to categories of people who now, under a single-member system, find great difficulty in becoming candidates for a winnable seat. The most conspicuous of such groups are the female majority and ethnic minorities. . . . It is for this reason that all countries with single-member systems have about the same low percentage of women MPs as Britain has, while, with the solitary exception of Malta, all countries with proportional systems have more—usually far more.

Source: Enid Lakeman, "The Case for Proportional Representation," in Arend Lijphart and Bernard Grofman, eds., *Choosing an Electoral System: Issues and Alternatives* (New York: Praeger, 1984), pp. 48–50.

SWITZERLAND: PERSONALIZED PROPORTIONAL REPRESENTATION

For the election of the National Council, the lower house of Parliament, the Swiss modify party list PR in two important ways. Both modifications have the consequence of personalizing relations between voters and candidates. The first Swiss modification is that, rather than a single national electoral district, they have 26 electoral districts, corresponding to the 26 Swiss cantons. The 200 National Council seats are divided among the cantons according to population. The largest canton, Zurich, elects 35 representatives, and the smallest districts, only one. The parties submit candidate lists in each canton containing the names of their candidates for that canton's seats. The results are counted separately for each canton.

This modification of having 26 electoral districts instead of a single national district works against the smaller parties. If Switzerland were treated as a single electoral district, only one-half of 1 percent of the vote would be needed to win one of the 200 National Council seats. With election taking place in 26 separate districts, however, a higher percentage of votes is needed to win. In Zurich, a party must win about 3 percent of the vote to win one of the canton's 35 seats. In a canton with 10 seats, 10 percent is necessary to receive one seat. In the small cantons with only one seat, the party with the most votes wins the seat, which means that these cantons use the winner-take-all system.

Applied to the United States, the 50 states could be the electoral districts, and within each state the congressional delegation would be elected according to proportional representation. In this way, some of the disadvantages of pure proportional representation could be alleviated. Very small parties would only be able to win seats in the largest states, such as California and New York.

The second Swiss modification is that the voters, not the parties, rank the candidates. The parties merely submit a list of names without rank, usually in alphabetical order. The number of names cannot be more than the number of seats to be filled from each respective canton. Voters can modify this by writing some names twice and removing others. The overall number of names still cannot be greater than the number of seats to be elected from each canton, and no name may be listed more than twice. A voter can also decide to make no changes in the party list he or she has selected. In this case, no preference is given to any of the candidates, but the ballot counts for the number of seats attributed to the party.

Voters may further complicate their list by writing in candidates from other parties. Thus, a Socialist voter may put a Communist candidate on his or her list, either once or twice. The only condition is that a corresponding number of names is crossed off the list. With this write-in possibility, computation of the results becomes very complicated. In the above example, the Communist write-in would count for the Communist party and detract from the Socialist party strength; the voter would have split his or her vote between the two parties. Voters can go even further to write in candidates from as many parties as they wish, but, again, the total number of names is not allowed to exceed the number of seats in the district.

The computation of the results proceeds in principle in the same manner as in the Netherlands. First, for each canton, the number of seats each party receives is determined. Second, candidates win these seats in order of their ranking. This ranking is based on the number of times a candidate's name appears on all the lists, including write-ins on other parties' lists.

The freedom of choice that the Swiss system permits the voter obviously weakens the party's control over its candidates, and thus party discipline may be as low as in the United States. While a Swiss party still controls whether or not a candidate gets listed, it cannot determine a candidate's chances of election through rank on the list. Once candidates are listed, they are on their own and must try to get a maximum number of voters to write them in twice, and a minimum to cross them out. While this system seems to give great power to the electorate, it also increases the influence of special interest groups. These groups inform their members about the candidates who favor their interests and for whom two votes should be cast as well as candidates who should be crossed out because they do not favor the group's interests. A teachers' group, for example, will inform its members which candidates are sympathetic to teachers' needs and which are not. Letters are sent out by a large number of groups ranging from businesspeople to fishermen. Candidates depend on political parties only for getting listed on the ballot; in order to be elected, they must obtain the support of a large number of different interest groups.

With this electoral system, the Swiss currently have 14 parties in the

200-member National Council. The Free Democrats have 51 seats, the Christian Democrats 42, the Social Democrats 41. The remaining 66 go to all other parties combined (for detailed figures, see Table 16 in Chapter 3).

The Swiss still vote for party lists, but their electoral system allows them to express preferences for and against particular candidates. The election also takes place in relatively small districts, where voters feel more at home than in a single national district. These factors together personalize the relations between voters and candidates.

IRELAND: SINGLE TRANSFERABLE VOTE

Personalized proportional representation can also be attained through the single transferable vote system (STV), as practiced in the Republic of Ireland. The system was introduced in Northern Ireland with the hope of alleviating its civil strike (see Chapter 11). Other than in Northern Ireland, it is only on the small Mediterranean island of Malta that STV is used within Europe. Outside Europe, Australia is the only country to use STV at the national level for the election of its upper house.

The reason that this electoral system is called single transferable vote should become clear as we proceed by using the example of Ireland to explain it. Ireland's Parliament, with a total of 166 seats, is elected from 41 districts, with the number of seats per district ranging from 3 to 5. In each district, voters indicate on their ballot their first-choice candidate. Voters may also indicate their second choice, third choice, and so on.

To be elected, a candidate needs a quota of the total votes according to the so-called Droop formula:

$$\frac{\text{total valid votes}}{\text{seats} + 1} + 1$$

At first, only the first choice on each ballot is considered. If a district has 100,000 valid votes and five seats to be elected, the quota is 100,000 divided by $6 + 1 = 16,667$. Whoever reaches this quota is elected. A little arithmetic shows that it is impossible for more than five candidates to attain the quota. Let us assume that two candidates attain the quota: candidate A with 20,000 votes and candidate B with 17,000 votes. Thus, candidate A has 3,333 votes that he or she does not need, and candidate B has 333 such superfluous votes. Now the single transferable vote comes into play. The ballots not needed by the two top candidates are transferred by the counting officials to the candidates who appear as second choices on these ballots. Let us assume that candidate C received 16,000 first votes, 667 short of the quota. Now there are 700 ballots that have either candidate A or B at the top, but candidate C ranked as number two. These ballots are transferred to candidate C, who therefore crosses the quota and is also declared elected. He has even 33 superfluous votes that are transferred to the third-ranked candidates on these ballots. In this way, all extra ballots are transferred. This may allow also candidate D, who had 15,800 first choices, to reach the quota thanks to such transferred votes. But no other candidate attains the quota. At this point, the counting officials begin from the bottom defeating the candidate with the least votes. This may be candidate Z with only 500 votes, first and transferred votes together. These ballots are now transferred to the next-ranked candidates. If these candidates are A, B, C, or D, they do not need more votes, so they are transferred to the candidates one rank lower. Candidate Y is the second lowest with 1,000 votes. The counting officials declare him or her next as defeated, and his or her votes are also transferred. This may now allow candidate E to reach the quota that would be the end of the computation process, since all five seats are filled. The system works like runoffs, in which voters are called to the ballot a second time. With STV, however, voters make their choices in a single ballot, hence the term *single transferable vote*.

One problem still remains open: How exactly do the counting officials decide which ballots to keep in the quota and which others to transfer? There is obviously a potential for abuse. Complex rules exist to prevent such abuse in making the system work as randomly as possible. As Table 5 shows, STV has a proportional effect on the distribution of seats in the Irish parliament. The smaller parties—Progressive Democrats, the Labour party, and the Workers' party—get also roughly their proportionate representation. The two large parties—Fianna Fáil and Fine Gael—have both grown out of the Irish struggle for independence.

Although the single transferable vote is used in few places, it has strong supporters. One of them, Enid Lakeman, states, "STV will force [the voter] to recognize that there are degrees of excellence among the candidates of his preferred party and will further invite him to consider candidates of other parties and indicate any with whom he has a measure of agreement."[16] With regard to the United States, experts on electoral systems agree that a change from the current winner-take-all system to the principle of proportionality would only be possible if the new system were based not on party lists but on the single transferable vote. An advocate of STV for America, George H. Hallett, Jr., argues that "it can transform our legislative elections from contests to win all the spoils of victory for one group and keep other people out

Table 5
Voter Support and Parliamentary Seats in 1987 General
Election to the Irish Parliament (Dáil)

Party	Voter Support (%)	Seats %	Seats N
Fianna Fáil	44.2	48.9	81
Fine Gael	27.1	30.7	51
Progressive Democrats	11.9	8.4	14
Labour Party	6.4	7.2	12
Workers' Party	3.8	2.4	4
Others	6.6	2.4	4
Total	100.0	100.0	166

Source: European Journal of Political Research, 16 (September 1988): 579.

———————————— BOX 2.4 ————————————

SINGLE TRANSFERABLE VOTE IN CAMBRIDGE, MASSACHUSETTS

CAMBRIDGE, Mass.—By the time the votes from Tuesday's City Council and School Committee elections are counted, many voters may have long since lost track of which candidates they voted for. For Cambridge, a city known for the intellectual giants of Harvard University and Massachusetts Institute of Technology, uses a controversial voting system that challenges even the strongest intellect.

"Probably five people in the city understand it from A to Z," said Kevin P. Crane, a former city councilor whose father was a four-term Mayor under the system. . . .

First promoted at the beginning of the century by the progressive "good government" movement, P.R. is designed to insure the representation of political and racial minorities in Cambridge's case, Italians, Irish, Jews and blacks.

"It's the reason Cambridge didn't burn during the years of the demonstrations, the reason desegregation of the schools was achieved without any significant community disruption," said Glenn S. Koocher, a former School Committee member.

Under P.R., all candidates run at-large. Voters number the candidates according to their preferences, omitting any candidate they oppose.

Source: New York Times, November 4, 1987.

to invitations to all citizens to come in and take part in a great cooperative democracy."[17] Hallet even expects that STV may eventually be required by the courts in the United States because it gives adequate representation to such minorities as Hispanics and blacks.

The STV system is not unknown in the United States. In New York City, the local school boards are elected according to this system; in Cambridge, Massachusetts, the City Council. A story in the *New York Times* (see Box 2.4) makes fun of the complicated nature of the system, but it refers also to its beneficial effects.

———————————— **FRANCE: DOUBLE-BALLOT SYSTEM** ————————————

In 1985, the French changed their double-ballot system to the principle of proportionality, but in 1986 they changed back to the double-ballot system. These two changes illustrate that political rules are not given but are the result of the political game.

France practiced proportional representation under its Fourth Republic. With the change to the Fifth Republic in 1958, Charles de Gaulle and his supporters introduced a system whose most visible feature is that two separate ballots take place a week apart. For the purpose of parliamentary elections, France is divided into the same number of electoral districts as there are seats in the National Assembly—the lower house of the French parliament. To be elected on the first ballot, a candidate has to receive an absolute majority (50 percent plus one) of votes cast in a district. In addition, a candidate's share of the vote has to constitute no less than one-fourth of registered voters. Because the first ballot usually lists candidates from several parties, there are relatively few districts where a candidate receives the votes necessary to win election at that point. In the 1988 election, for example, there were only 120 such districts out of a total of 577 districts. In the other 457 districts, a second ballot was necessary, and then a plurality (the greatest number but less than a majority) of the vote was sufficient for election. Only candidates who appear on the first ballot can be listed on the second ballot, and all candidates who receive less than 12.5 percent of the first ballot are eliminated.

In addition to these formal methods of reducing the number of candidates for the second ballot, the French parties informally practice voluntary withdrawals. To understand this practice, we must add some details to our previous discussion of political parties in France. French political parties are basically either of the right or of the left, and the strength of these two large divisions is much the same. The main parties of the left are the Communists and the Socialists, and the parties of the right are the Union for French Democracy (UDF) and the Rally for the Republic (RPR). The two parties of the right are specific to France and must be understood as part of the combined presidential-parliamentary system of the Fifth Republic (see Chapter 3).

In the first ballot in most districts, candidates from all four major parties— and, usually, also from some minor parties—enter the competition. Besides the few districts where a candidate actually wins at this point, the main function of the first ballot is to check the voting strength of each individual party. Thus, the first ballot functions in some ways like an American primary. The main competition occurs within each side of the political spectrum. At the left, the question is whether the Communist or the Socialist candidate receives more votes. Similarly, UDF and RPR candidates compete among each other for the first place on the right.

For the second ballot, the usual situation is that the weaker candidate at both the left and the right withdraws. The purpose of withdrawing is to increase the chance of winning of one's own side. If, for example, the UDF candidate in a district receives 30 percent of the first ballot and the RPR candidate, 25 percent, the winning chance of the Right can be increased if their forces are combined so that only the stronger candidate remains in competition. If the Right unites behind the UDF candidate, it would be suicidal for the Left to continue the race with both a Communist and a Socialist candidate. The logic of the electoral system is for the Left, too, to withdraw its weaker candidate.

This device of voluntary withdrawal works best if in the country as a whole both parties on either side have about equal strength. Thus, if the RPR candidate withdraws in the above example, this could easily be compensated for by the withdrawal of a UDF candidate in another district. The situation is more complicated when one party is clearly stronger than the other party of the same side.

In recent years, this was the situation of the Socialists vis-à-vis the Communists. In the 1981 parliamentary election, for example, the Socialists received nationally 37.8 percent voter support in the first ballot; the Communists, merely 16.1 percent. If the Communist candidate was required to withdraw in every district where the Socialist candidate was stronger on the first ballot, there would have been very few districts where the Communist candidate could have represented the Left on the second ballot. Recognizing this difficulty, and in an effort to ensure maximum Communist voter turnout on the second ballot, the Socialists withdrew some of their own first ballot candidates, even though they ran ahead of the Communist candidates. With the support of the Socialist voters, the Communist candidates in these districts then had a chance to win the second ballot. Which candidate withdrew in a particular district was decided in negotiations between national and local party headquarters. The goal of this political maneuvering was to ensure that both sides got parliamentary seats in approximately the same proportion as their national strength on the first ballot. Sometimes, however, this goal is not attained because voters do not follow the recommendations of their party leaders.

This is especially a problem for the Communist party, which is considered by many Socialist voters as not sufficiently democratically oriented. As a consequence, such voters often do not follow their party leaders' recommendations and abstain in the second ballot or vote for the candidate of the right. This mechanism can be demonstrated by comparing the seats received by the Communist party in the 1981 election with its voter support. Although the voter support was 16.1 percent, the party received only 9.1 percent of the seats. For the political scientist Domenico Fisichella, "the general conclusion that emerges from the French experience is that its Communist party is always—and almost always to a marked extent—underrepresented under the double-ballot system."[18] The Socialists, on the other hand, profited from the Communist support in the second ballot and received 59.3 percent of the seats, although their voter support in the first ballot was "only" 37.8 percent (see Table 6).

This discussion shows that the French double-ballot system demands a great amount of skill on the part of the political parties and their leaders. The game has to be played very differently in the two ballots. In the first ballot, the main competition is within the coalition of the left and within the coalition of the right; in the second ballot, the competition changes to the battle between the left and the right. As political scientist George Tsebelis explains in Box 2.5, political parties must make sure that in the first ballot competition within their coalition is not too fierce if the coalition as a whole wants to win in the decisive second ballot.

Why did the French change in 1985 from the double-ballot system to proportionality? It was the Socialist party—in particular its leader, François Mitterrand—who pushed for the change. With the Socialists in control of the National Assembly, this move was guaranteed success. Why did the Social-

Table 6
Voter Support and Parliamentary Seats in the 1981
Election for the French National Assembly

		Seats	
Parties	Voter Support (%)	%	N
Socialists	37.8	59.3	281
Communists	16.1	9.1	43
Rally for the Republic (RPR)	20.8	16.9	80
Union for French Democracy (UDF)	19.3	13.3	63
Others	6.0	1.4	7
Total	100.0	100.0	474

Source: European Journal of Political Research 10 (1982): 334.

ists replace an electoral system from which they so obviously had benefited? The electoral situation had changed since 1981, and the Socialists feared that they would be hurt by the double-ballot system in the 1986 election. Opinion surveys and local elections had revealed such a loss of voter support for both Socialists and Communists that the parties of the right were expected to take over control of the National Assembly. This situation would be difficult for Mitterrand, whose mandate as president did not end until 1988. As we will

―――――――――――― **BOX 2.5** ――――――――――――

STRATEGIC CONSIDERATIONS IN THE FRENCH
DOUBLE-BALLOT SYSTEM

In France, each party has to do two things: It must affirm its own political line (otherwise it will lose its supporters in the first round), but in the second round it has to promote the coalition. . . . If the two partners of a coalition go too far criticizing each other in the first round, they will not have the time to change their strategies in the second round, even if they wish to. The votes of the loser within each coalition will not be transferred to the winner, and, therefore, in the decisive second round the coalition might lose because it has been too competitive in the first round. On the other hand, if a party is not critical enough towards its partner in the first round, it might lose the crucial votes which would make it the frontrunner in that round and thereby give it the right to represent the coalition in the decisive second round (and maybe win the seat).

Source: George Tsebelis, "Nested Games: The Cohesion of French Electoral Coalitions," *British Journal of Political Science* 18(April 1988): 148.

Table 7
Voter Support and Parliamentary Seats in the 1986
Election for the French National Assembly

Parties	Voter Support (%)	Seats	
		%	N
Socialists	31.4	36.6	211
Communists	9.8	6.1	35
Rally for the Republic (RPR)			
Union for French Democracy (UDF)	41.0	48.0	277
National Front	9.7	6.1	35
Others	8.1	3.2	19
Total	100.0	100.0	577

Source: *European Journal of Political Research* 15 (1987): 719.

Note: Besides RPR lists and UDF lists, there were also joint RPR–UDF lists.

see in Chapter 3, a French president under the Fifth Republic has much power, and Mitterrand used this power to ram this change in the electoral system through parliament. Mitterrand hoped that proportional representation would increase the number of parties in the National Assembly, thus making the parliamentary situation more fluid and allowing him more room to maneuver. This is exactly what happened in the March 1986 election. Splinter parties of the Right distracted so much voter strength from the RPR and the UDF that the two parties' combined seats fell short of an absolute majority in the National Assembly. The two parties were particularly hurt by the entry of the Neofascist National Front, which received 35 seats in the 577-member parliament. Dividing the opposition with the new electoral system helped the Socialists to remain the largest party in parliament, although their voter support dropped from 38 to 31 percent (Table 7).

Immediately after the 1986 election, the newly elected parliament changed the electoral rules back to the double-ballot system. This time, the push came from the RPR and the UDF. They did not like the fact that the National Front could challenge them at the extreme right. Returning to the double-ballot system would weaken the National Front, which indeed it did. When, after the 1988 presidential election, early parliamentary elections were called (see page 142), the National Front virtually disappeared from parliament, although in voter strength it still reached 9.6 percent (Table 8).

Are such changes in the rules of the game democratic? What is the meaning of *democratic* in this context? Who should decide about rule changes? A simple majority of parliament as in France? In the United States, basic changes of the rules are much more difficult to obtain. Most changes would need a constitutional amendment, which in the American context is very difficult to obtain, and certainly not by a simple majority in Congress.

Table 8
Voter Support and Parliamentary Seats in the 1988
Election for the French National Assembly

Parties	Voter Support (%)	Seats	
		%	N
Socialists	37.6	48.5	280
Communists	11.3	4.7	27
Rally for the Republic (RPR)	19.2	22.2	128
Union for French Democracy (UDF)	18.5	22.4	129
National Front	9.6	0.2	1
Others	3.8	2.0	12
Total	100.0	100.0	577

Source: *European Journal of Political Research* 17 (1989): 749.

FEDERAL REPUBLIC OF GERMANY: TWO VOTES FOR EACH VOTER

The Federal Republic of Germany uses a very complex electoral system. Its main feature is that each voter has two votes on his or her ballot, the so-called first and second votes. Surveys indicate that most West German voters do not fully understand how their complicated electoral system operates. Whether or not it is understood, however, the system's results have been reasonable compared to the extreme party fragmentation of the pre-Hitler Weimar Republic. West Germany's political system includes two major parties—the Christian Democrats* (CDU/CSU) and the Social Democrats (SPD)—and two minor parties—the Free Democrats (FDP) and the Greens—which have representation in the Bundestag, the lower house of the West German parliament. The fringe parties—such as the Communists and the Neofascists—have no parliamentary representation.

When the new West German constitution was written in 1949, The Western powers, especially Great Britain and the United States, urged the adoption of a winner-take-all system that they hoped would prevent severe party fragmentation. Many West German leaders recognized, however, that a winner-take-all system could not adequately represent the political diversity of West Germany. The innovative solution was to elect one half of the lower house by the winner-take-all system and the other half by proportional representation.

There are 496 members in the Bundestag. The winner-take-all system is used to elect 248 members, and the other 248 are elected by proportional representation. Each voter votes twice, once in the winner-take-all election and once in the proportional representation election. The former is called the voter's first vote; the latter, their second. Both votes are cast the same day,

* Called Christian Social Union (CSU) in Bavaria and Christian Democratic Union (CDU) in the rest of the country.

on the same ballot. For the first, or winner-take-all, vote, the country is divided into 248 electoral districts, and in each district the candidate with the most votes is elected. Only the two largest parties generally win these seats. In the 1987 election, in fact, they won all the seats: the CDU/CSU, 169 and the SPD, the remaining 79. The smaller parties, however, are able to win seats on the second, or proportional representation, vote. The specific system is party list PR, with the candidate ranking done by the parties. The electoral districts are the 10 West German states (*Laender*), such as Hamburg and Bavaria. Up to German unification, West Berlin was excluded from participation in general elections because of its four-power status and was represented in the Bundestag by 22 nonvoting members elected by the West Berlin state parliament.

Voters are allowed to split their two votes. In the winner-take-all election, they may vote for one party and in the party list PR election, for another. This provision creates the opportunity for some highly sophisticated voting behavior. Members of the FDP might cast their first vote for the CDU/CSU candidate knowing that their own party has virtually no chance of winning the winner-take-all election, and their second vote for their own FDP party list, since every vote cast for the list helps increase FDP representation in the Bundestag. Candidates may run in both parts of the election, further complicating the situation. Important party leaders, like Helmut Kohl of the CDU, will run both in a single district and as the head of the party list in a state. If they win their single district, they give up their place on the party list.

The most difficult task for the voter is to understand how the results are actually computed. According to political scientist Max Kaase, "surveys have repeatedly shown that even at the height of any given campaign, less than half of the voters know the precise meaning of the two ballots. . . . Shortly after an election, even this percentage drops, to roughly one-fifth of the voting population."[19]

The crucial point of the system is that only the second vote determines the number of seats a party gets in parliament. Each party receives the same proportion of seats as its nationwide proportion of second votes. With the first vote, the voters merely determine which specific candidate should represent their district; how many candidates from the various parties enter the Bundestag is determined solely by the second vote.

The 1987 election results help to illustrate with figures how the system operates. The SPD won 37.0 percent of the second vote, giving them 186 Bundestag seats. At the same time, based on the first vote, 79 SPD candidates, as mentioned above, won in their single districts. These 79 candidates were declared elected from the onset, and their number was subtracted from the 186 total number of seats won by the SPD. This left 107 seats to be filled from the top of the SPD party lists.

The results for the CDU/CSU contain a complication. The party received 44.3 percent of the second vote, entitling them to 222 seats. As already mentioned, 169 CDU/CSU candidates won in their single districts. Therefore, an additional 53 candidates were elected from the top of the CDU/CSU party lists. But as Table 9 indicates, the CDU/CSU won a total of 223 seats. Where does the extra seat come from? It is a so-called surplus seat, which the party

Table 9

Voter Support and Parliamentary Seats in the 1987 General Election
to the Bundestag of the Federal Republic of Germany

Party	Voter Support (%)	Seats	
		%	N
Christian Democratic Union/Christian Social Union (CDU/CSU)	44.3	44.9	223
Social Democratic Party (SPD)	37.0	37.4	186
Free Democratic Party (FDP)	9.1	9.3	46
Greens	8.3	8.5	42
Others	1.4	0,0	0
Total	100.0	100.0	497

Source: *European Journal of Political Research* 16 (September 1988): 577.

won in the state of Baden-Württemburg. The reason for this was that in this state the number of single districts won by the party was higher by one district than the proportional share won by the party based on the party lists. In such cases, the strict principle of proportionality is broken, in the sense that the party can keep as surplus mandate the additional seat(s) won in single district(s). With the surplus seat, the CDU/CSU increased its overall number of seats to 223, giving the Bundestag a total membership of 497.

In the electoral history of West Germany, the number of surplus mandates has ranged from one to five, so the issue may appear to be a technicality with little significance. Kaase, however, makes the interesting comment that "if two parties in a coalition advise their supporters to strategically split their ballots between the two partners, or if one large party were to formally split into two parties, then a large number of surplus mandates could be artificially created." He mentions that the percentage of split voting has increased from 4.1 percent in 1961 to 10.9 percent in 1983. For Kaase, the issue of surplus seats "points to a definite deficiency, a fault in the present electoral system that could be used for a manipulation of the electoral outcome because it allows for different weights of individual voters."[20]

We now turn to the smaller parties. Both the FDP, which won 9.1 percent of the second vote and 46 parliamentary seats, and the Green party, which won 8.3 percent of the second vote and 42 seats, did not win any single districts and thus had to fill all their seats from the top of their party lists.

The West German system also contains a provision for a threshold against small parties. This threshold denies parliamentary representation to parties that win less than 5 percent of the second vote and are also unable to win three single districts. To get parliamentary seats, at least one of these two criteria must be met. The threshold is defended on the grounds that parties failing to cross it have no real parliamentary legitimacy. The Communist party (DKP) and the Neofascist party (NPD) were excluded from the 1983 Bundestag on the basis of the threshold. The actual electoral disadvantage for small parties is even greater, because most voters do not expect them to cross the threshold and therefore tend to vote for other parties that they know will win seats. Such anticipatory effects were discussed earlier with regard to Great Britain.

The writers of the West German constitution tried to set up an electoral system that would lead to greater political stability than Germany had in the Weimar Republic. So far, their complicated system seems to provide stable, democratic government. It remains to be seen how the system will fare after German unification.

VOTER TURNOUT

Table 10 shows the voter turnout of European democracies in parliamentary elections. Overall, the results are much better than in the United States, where in 1988 only 50 percent of all eligible voters turned out to vote in the presidential election. In off-year elections, when only congressional seats are at stake, turnout is even lower; in 1986, for example, it was merely 33 percent.

Why is there so much more interest in elections in Europe than in the United States? Many factors may come into play, such as differences in the system for voter registration or in the size of countries. In the context of the present chapter, it is interesting for us to discuss the possible influence of electoral rules on voter turnout. Generally speaking, electoral rules as used in Europe give the voter more influence on the outcome than in the United States. In most U.S. congressional districts, the incumbent is so firmly estab-

Table 10
Voter Turnout for Parliamentary
Elections (Most Recent Available Data)

Austria	89%
Belgium	87%
Denmark	86%
Finland	72%
France	64%
Federal Republic of Germany	84%
Greece	83%
Ireland	73%
Italy	85%
Netherlands	86%
Norway	84%
Portugal	71%
Spain	69%
Sweden	89%
Switzerland	46%
United Kingdom	75%

Source: European Journal of Political Research,
Section "General Elections in Western Nations,"
Vol. 14–17, 1986–1989.

lished that a challenger has very little chance. Usually, competition only works when there is no incumbent or when the incumbent is just a freshman. Even if a district is truly contested, voters with somewhat unusual views may feel left out because both the Democratic and Republican candidates tend to run on a platform that is somewhere in the middle. If a voter has a Green preference, for example, the voter may not feel represented by either candidate and may stay home. With some modifications, the same arguments apply also to senatorial elections.

In parliamentary elections in Europe, it is not so unrealistic that a single vote may make a difference. In a proportional election system, just one more vote may secure an additional seat for a party. It is important that voters belonging to a marginal group enjoy this potential impact. Our argument also helps to explain the notable European exception of Switzerland, which has a much lower turnout than all of the other countries. As we will see in Chapter 7, the most important issues are decided in a referendum. Therefore, it is less important who sits in parliament. Furthermore, all major parties are represented in the seven-member executive, according to the principle of power sharing (page 123) which also diminishes the importance of parliamentary elections. Whatever the exact election outcome, the composition of the executive council will not change greatly.

Let us return to the case of Great Britain. Why do the British have a much higher turnout than the Americans, although both practice the winner-take-all system? The British case helps us to make the transition to the next chapter. Contrary to the United States, Great Britain has a parliamentary, not a presidential, system for selecting its executive. In the United States, the president does not depend on a vote of confidence in Congress to keep his job. Therefore, the party composition of Congress is of less importance. As President George Bush currently demonstrates, an American president can easily survive if Congress is dominated by the opposition party. This would not be true in a parliamentary system as practiced in Great Britain. There, political parties are crucially important. Political competition is much more a battle between political parties than in the United States. As a consequence, party discipline is strong in Great Britain, which in turn helps to mobilize voters on election day. The conclusion is that it is a winner-take-all electoral system, combined with a presidential system, that contributes to the low voter turnout in the United States. Rules are not neutral but help to shape how the game is played. In Europe, rules generally are an incentive for voters to go to the polls.

ELECTIONS IN EASTERN EUROPE

East Germany

On March 18, 1990, East Germany was the first Communist country in Eastern Europe to hold completely free elections. In the context of this chapter, it is interesting to note that the East Germans used a much simpler election system than did West Germany. For the election of the 400-member parliament, East Germany was divided into 15 electoral districts. Thus, on the average there were 27 members of parliament to be elected per district. Each party submitted per district a rank-ordered list of candidates. The voter simply had to make a choice among the party lists submitted in his or her district. Contrary to the system used in Switzerland, for example, the voter had no influence on the rank order of the candidates. The results were computed according to the strict principle of proportionality, and candidates were declared elected beginning at the top of the list in each district. This is party list proportionality in its simplest form. As expected, this electoral system translated percentage voter support nearly exactly into percentage of parliamentary seats. It also allowed very small parties to enter parliament (see Table 11).

The electoral campaign was nearly exclusively focused on the issue of German unification. (For a general discussion of the unification issue, see Chapter 16.) Even the Communist party recognized the mood in the population and supported unification, although at a slower pace than the other parties. As already described in Chapter 1, the Communists ousted their old hard-line leaders, in particular Erich Honecker. Their new leaders, prime minister Hans Modrow and party head Gregor Gysi, stressed in the campaign that deep reforms were necessary in the direction of more democracy and more market elements in the economy. In order to underscore their willingness for reforms, the Communists gave themselves a new name: Party of Democratic Socialism (PDS). Under this new name, the party tried to change its old grey image by using much color in the campaign, for example, by

Table 11
Voter Support and Parliamentary Seats in 1990 Election
to the East German Parliament (Volkskammer)

Party	Voter Support (%)	Seats %	Seats N
Christian Democratic Union	40.6	41.0	163
Social Democratic Party	21.8	21.8	88
Party of Democratic Socialism	16.3	16.3	66
German Social Union	6.3	6.3	25
Alliance of Free Democrats	5.3	5.3	21
Alliance 90	2.9	3.0	12
Democratic Peasant Party	2.2	2.2	9
Green Party and Independent Women's Association	2.0	2.0	8
Democratic Awakening	0.9	1.0	4
National Democratic Party	0.4	0.5	2
Democratic Women's League	0.3	0.2	1
Action Alliance United Left	0.2	0.2	1
Others	0.8	—	—
Total	100.0		400

Source: Frankfurter Allgemeine Zeitung, March 24, 1990.

putting bright colors on the outside of their headquarters. The new strategy paid off, because they received 16 percent of the vote, which was a respectable result for a party that was thought to have been totally discredited. There were apparently still many East Germans who certainly had no more respect for the Honecker regime but who were still willing to give reform communism a chance.

The Social Democrats (SPD) received 22 percent of the votes, which was a big disappointment for them, since early in the campaign they were the clear front-runners. They were hurt in several respects. For one thing, they had difficulty in differentiating themselves sufficiently from the Communists. When, after World War II, the Communists took over in East Germany, they integrated by force the Social Democrats into their own ranks and called themselves the Socialist Unitary party (SED). Although, in everyday language, the party was often called the Communist party, the official name still contained the word *Socialist*. With this historical background, it was easy for the conservative parties in the electoral campaign to condemn socialism in general, lumping PDS and SPD together. This could be done all the more successfully because, following Willy Brandt's *Ostpolitik*, the West Germany SPD often had cozy contacts with the Honecker regime (Chapter 16). Not surprisingly, the conservative parties missed no chance for exploiting this somewhat embarrassing history of the Social Democrats, who were further hurt on the issue of German unification. To be sure, they also supported unification but warned against too much haste. To many East Germans, this position appeared too cautious. Thus, although Willy Brandt had coined the often quoted phrase, "What belongs together, will grow together," the Social Democrats lost on the key issue of unification. For the Social Democrats, the bad election results were all the more frustrating because, before the dictatorships of the Communists and the Nazis, they had particular strongholds in the industrial centers of East Germany.

The Christian Democrats were the big winners with 41 percent of the votes, yet they had entered the campaign with a big handicap, because in the past they had acted as junior partners of the Communists. This needs some explanation. In order to give the appearance of democracy, the East German Communists always put some candidates from other parties on their own election lists. But these so-called bloc parties, among them the Christian Democrats, were merely puppets under complete control of the Communists. Elections remained a farce, because the voters had no choice but a single list. That this list contained some names of candidates who were formally not Communists did not change anything. Given this tainted name of the East German Christian Democrats, the West German Christian Democrats were at first quite hesitant to support them. After revamping the party and its leadership, the West German Christian Democrats supported the East German Christian Democrats as a sister party. Despite the handicap of their past history, the Christian Democrats were the big winners in the East German election, which indicates how powerful their message was that Germany should proceed with unification as soon as possible.

In the election campaign, the Christian Democrats worked together with two other parties, the German Social Union and Democratic Awakening, in a so-called Alliance for Germany. This Alliance received 192 seats at large, just short of a majority in the 400-member parliament. The German Social Union is a sister party of the Bavarian Christian Social Union (page 84), whereas Democratic Awakening grew out of the East German reform process. Five percent of the votes went to the Alliance of Free Democrats, which had the support of the West German Free Democrats.

In a democratic transition, it is always interesting to watch what political parties emerge at the first free election. In this respect, East Germany is a very special case, because for almost all voters the first free elections were also seen as the last elections for East Germany as a political entity; the East Germans wished to join with the West Germans to share in their economic wealth. Under these conditions, it was natural for the East Germans to orient themselves to the West German party system. And the West German parties, in turn, were eager to influence the election campaign. Indeed, all the important West German party leaders, such as Helmut Kohl, Willy Brandt, and Hans-Dietrich Genscher, actively campaigned in the East German election. The result was that the two major parties in West Germany, the Christian Democrats and the Social Democrats, also emerged as the two biggest parties in East Germany. Given the strong influence of the West German parties, newly founded parties in East Germany had hardly a chance. This was particularly true for New Forum, which in the fall of 1989 was the leading dissident movement in the fight to overthrow the Honecker regime. In the election, New Forum campaigned together with other dissident groups as Alliance 90. But this new party simply did not have the necessary organizational and financial means to compete with the parties supported from West Germany. It was remarkable that the Greens did so poorly, because East Germany has very severe environmental problems. In this election, however, voters were mainly concerned with their bad economic situation and they saw that the only real hope of relief would be in unifying with West Germany. In the forefront were the blue-collar industrial workers who voted heavily for the Christian Democrats and thus for quick unification. It is an irony of history that, in the supposed "workers' paradise" of East Germany, the Communists were abandoned in particularly high numbers by the workers themselves. Voter turnout was 93 percent, which gave a high degree of democratic legitimacy to the newly elected parliament. This legitimacy could be transferred to the new cabinet appointed by parliament. How the cabinet was formed will be discussed in Chapter 3.

Hungary

On March 25, 1990, one week after East Germany, Hungary held its first free election. Whereas the East German election was a very special case because of the issue of German unification, in Hungary there were no such special circumstances. Therefore, it would be the first true test case to see what political parties would emerge in the transition from one-party communism to multiparty democracy. Although there was some influence from Western European parties, Hungarians basically fought the election among themselves. Given the poverty of the country and the newness of competitive elections, raising campaign funds was difficult, as vividly described in Box 2.6. The campaign did not have the professional smoothness that appears in established democracies. Many things went wrong: microphones did not work, computers broke down, and so on. But these were mere technical flaws. What really mattered was that the campaign and the election itself occurred with very few irregularities. There were no incidents of violence and no intimidation of voters. According to the general consensus of voters and observers, the election took place in an atmosphere of freedom.

The election rules were rather complicated, leading to some confusion among the voters. As in West Germany, each voter had two votes: one for a candidate in a single district and one for a party list at the county level. Overall there were 386 parliamentary seats to be filled. From this total number, 176 seats were filled in single districts according to the winner-take-all system. In addition to the 176 single districts, Hungary was also divided into 20 larger districts, which corresponded to its 20 counties. At the county level, the remaining 210 seats were filled according to party list proportionality. Thus, each voter could vote for a candidate in a relatively small district and for a party list in a larger district. This combination of winner-take-all and party list proportionality favored the larger parties but still gave the smaller parties some chance. This conclusion can easily be derived from the earlier discussion in this chapter of the two pure election systems. Whereas the East Germans simply chose pure party list proportionality, the Hungarians wished to mix in some elements of the winner-take-all system. The two systems can be mixed in very different ways, and it happens that Hungary chose to have 210 parliament members elected by proportionality and 176 by

--------------------------------- BOX 2.6 ---------------------------------

CASH-STARVED PARTIES INTRODUCE VOTERS
IN HUNGARY TO THE FUND-RAISER

BUDAPEST—Democracy has its price, as Hungary's new political parties are learning now that they must pay the bill for the posters, leaflets, 30-second television spots, lapel pins, cigarette lighters, helicopters, hot-air balloons and other props of this country's first full-fledged electoral campaign in 40 years.

To come up with money to get their message across, the parties are looking for help at home and abroad to supplement the fixed sum they get from the Government. Like-minded foreign political parties have been tapped for contributions in cash and in kind, and Hungary's aspiring entrepreneurial class is being wooed from all sides.

But fund-raising, in the style that Americans are used to, is still an undeveloped art in Hungary. "It doesn't work here," said Anna Petrosovits, president of the Social Democratic Party of Hungary. "We tried to invite people to coffees and teas, but there was no—how shall I put it—outcome."

Source: New York Times, March 14, 1990.

winner-take-all. This was simply the outcome of the bargaining about the details of the electoral law. The Hungarian case helps to reinforce the point made earlier in this chapter that electoral rules are hand-made and that there are many options from which to choose.

The headline in the Western media concerning the Hungarian election was about the big defeat of the Communists. This result may seem surprising, because, as we have seen in Chapter 1, Hungary was the only Eastern European country where reforms were pushed by the Communists themselves. But they received very little credit from the voters on election day. Only 11 percent voted for the party list of the Socialist Party, the new name chosen by the Communists. Most Hungarians had had enough of the Communists, however reform oriented they were. It should be noted that, to the credit of the Communists, they gave up power graciously. Their party chairman declared: "We will be an opposition party. This, to use a religious term, will be penance for the party." Along the same gracious line, the outgoing Communist prime minister stated: "I will hand over the reins head high and with a clear conscience. I don't have bitterness in my heart but satisfaction."[21] Who would have thought that one day Communists would yield power in this way?

When in 1989 the Communists embarked on a course of reform, the more Marxist-oriented wing split from the party and founded their own Socialist Workers party. But it fared much worse than the Reform-Communists, getting less than 4 percent for their party list, the minimum required to be seated as a party in parliament. This minimum threshold was also not reached by the Social Democratic party, which had the support of its sister parties in Western Europe. Thus, altogether the parties of the left did very poorly in Hungary, even more so than in East Germany, where the commentators already talked about a big defeat of the Left. Hungary clearly wished a break with the Left.

Who were the winners? Because of the complicated election system, we will look first at only the results for the party lists and turn later to the election of candidates in the single districts. The two top vote-getters for the party lists were the Democratic Forum with 24 percent of the vote and the Free Democrats with 21 percent. The Democratic Forum roughly corresponds to the Conservatives in Western Europe, as described in Chapter 1. It is a center-right party favoring a transition to a free market economy. The Democratic Forum also displays a Christian image, and its overall message has rather strong nationalist overtones. The Free Democrats more or less correspond to their sister parties in Western Europe. They stress even more than the Democratic Forum a quick transition to a free market economy, which is in line with the general distinction between Conservatives and Free Democrats (page 50). According to our general discussion in Chapter 1, the Hungarian Free Democrats are also individualistic, not putting as much emphasis on church and nation as the Democratic Forum.

With 12 percent of the party lists, the Independent Smallholders' party came in in third place. Before the Communist regime, it was the largest party in Hungary. Its major campaign plank was that all land should go back to those who owned it in 1947, before Communists took over. As we will see in

Chapter 3, it is not unusual for agrarian interests to be organized in a special political party.

We turn now to the election results in the 176 single districts. The electoral rules specified that, in order to be elected, a candidate had to receive more than 50 percent of the votes. If no candidate reached this threshold, a second round of elections would be organized two weeks later on April 8, 1990. In order to compete in this second round, a candidate had to receive at least 15 percent of the votes in the first round. Candidates were so numerous that there were only 5 districts where a candidate could be declared elected in the first round. Thus, there were 171 seats to be contested in the second round. For both rounds together, the Democratic Forum was the big winner, taking 114 of the districts; the Free Democrats were far behind, winning in only 35 districts. The Smallholders' party won in 11 districts, and the Reform-Communists won in only 1 district. The remaining 15 districts went to several small parties and some independent candidates. Thus, as expected, the winner-take-all part of the election favored the largest party. As the British say of the winner-take-all system, what counts is who is first past the post. Having come out as the front-runner in the first round, the Democratic Forum had the necessary momentum to capture so many districts. In the winner-take-all system, nothing is as successful as anticipated success, since supporters of smaller parties do not like to waste their votes and therefore cast their votes for a candidate with a real winning chance.

Table 12 gives the total results, adding the seats won in the districts and those won from the party lists.

Voter turnout in Hungary was much lower than in East Germany: 63 percent in the first round and 45 percent in the second round. This was still a good result, given that the Hungarian election campaign had no overriding issue like unification in East Germany. It should also be noted that the Hungarian voters had to choose from a very high number of parties (not less than 58) using a very complicated election system. The election was able to weed out most of these parties and to limit the political game to relatively few viable parties. (For the process of cabinet formation, see Chapter 3.)

Table 12

Parliamentary Seats in 1990 Election to Hungarian Parliament

Party	Absolute	%
Hungarian Democratic Forum	165	42.7
Alliance of Free Democrats	92	23.8
Independent Smallholders' Party	43	11.1
Socialist Party	33	8.5
Federation of Young Democrats	21	5.4
Christian Democratic People's Party	21	5.4
Other Parties and Independents	11	3.1
Total	386	100.0

Source: *Frankfurter Allgemeine Zeitung*, April 10, 1990.

Romania

Romania was the third country to hold elections; they were held on May 20, 1990. In contrast to the preceding elections in East Germany and Hungary, the Romanian elections were marred by many irregularities. This should come as no surprise, because in Romania much violence occurred before the democratic reform process was launched (page 33–34). Violence also continued after Communist dictator Nicolae Ceausescu was ousted. So much hatred had been built up in the country that it was very difficult for the emerging political parties to establish a climate of mutual trust among themselves.

There was so much hostility against Communism that no Communist party ran in the election, not even under a new name, as it did in East Germany and in Hungary. All former Communist party members participating in the election tried to distance themselves as much as possible from their past. This was in particular true for Ion Iliescu who, as head of the National Salvation Front, led the government after the overthrow of Ceausescu (page 34). Iliescu had served in high positions under Ceausescu but had fallen in disgrace under the former dictator. Iliescu now claimed that his National Salvation Front was a center-left party with a Social Democratic orientation. Not everyone believed him. Many Romanians saw in Iliescu a Communist who tried to continue the old regime in a new form. There were protest demonstrations and hunger strikes against Iliescu. At one time, as described in Box 2.7, a jeering crowd seized the offices of Iliescu, shouting that he had stolen the revolution from the people.

Iliescu spoke of his political adversaries as counterrevolutionaries, thereby using the old ideological jargon of the Communists. This manner of speaking reinforced the perception that he was still a Communist. There were also

---

BOX 2.7

JEERING ROMANIANS SEIZE OFFICES TO DEMAND GOVERNMENT'S OUSTER

BUCHAREST, Romania—Protesters demanding the ouster of President Ion Iliescu took over the provisional government's headquarters this evening, roughly handling one of the new leaders, tossing red-bound party manuals to the crowd below and shouting for a complete end to Communism.

Soldiers on the steps moved aside as hundreds of demonstrators swarmed into the ornate Foreign Ministry building after hours of window smashing, rock throwing, and chanting protests. Many were shouting that the violent revolution that overthrew the dictator Nicolae Ceausescu in December had been "stolen."

Source: New York Times, February 19, 1990.

————————————— BOX 2.8 —————————————

PROTESTERS BESIEGE PARTY OFFICES

Shouting menacing slogans, crowds of demonstrators today massed in front of the headquarters of the Peasants' Party and the Liberal Party in downtown Bucharest and demanded the dissolution of both. While the police stood by, protesters broke into the offices of the Liberal Party, forcing its leaders to flee.

Source: New York Times, January 30, 1990.

many incidents of intimidation on the part of the National Salvation Front. A typical incident is reported in Box 2.8, in which supporters of the Front broke into the offices of another party, forcing their leaders to flee.

Up to election day, incidents such as the ones reported resulted in hundreds of injuries and even a few deaths. Conditions were too precarious for truly free elections to be held. The United States was so worried about all the electoral irregularities that shortly before the election it recalled the U.S. ambassador as a sign of its concern (see Box 2.9). Was Romania not yet ready for democracy? Doubts certainly come up for segments of society. Thus, the *New York Times* quoted a factory worker as saying: "Those parties don't know anything about us. They come from abroad and want to buy us. Before, we had one party. Now every party has an opinion. That is what worries me. People want to make politics rather than work." This is an attitude that is intolerant of a pluralism of opinions needed for a true democracy. Romanians such as this factory worker were eager to vote for Iliescu because he is a strong father figure. When Iliescu appeared in the remote villages of the country, indeed many called him "father."

————————————— BOX 2.9 —————————————

ROMANIA VOTE WORRIES U.S.

WASHINGTON—The United States said Thursday it was recalling its ambassador from Romania for consultations as a sign of its concern that national elections scheduled for May 20 might not be fair.

The State Department spokesman, Margaret D. Tutwiler, said the decision to recall Ambassador Alan Green was made "in light of the reports of irregularities in the Romanian electoral process which raise questions about whether those elections will be free and fair."

Source: International Herald Tribune, May 11, 1990.

In addition to a widespread lack of democratic culture, Romania was plagued by ethnic strife, in particular, between native Romanians and ethnic Hungarians. The newly found freedom of expression was used by many to express hatred against other ethnic groups. This could even lead to brutal physical attacks, as reported in Box 2.10, which describes a deadly street battle in the Transylvanian town of Tirgu Mures.

On election day, Romanians had to elect both a president and a parliament. Voter turnout was 86 percent. Both elections were an overwhelming victory for the National Salvation Front. Iliescu, as head of the Front and interim president, won the presidential race with 85 percent of the votes. There were two other candidates—one from the National Liberal party and the other from the National Peasants party. The former received 11 percent of the votes; the latter, 4 percent. Parliament was elected according to party list proportionality, as in East Germany. There were two chambers to be elected—the National Assembly with 387 seats and the Senate with 119 seats. More than 80 parties participated in the election process. Jokingly, most of these parties were called "bench parties" because their supporters seemed to be able to sit on a single bench.

Indeed, for most of these parties, the election results were dismal. Table 13 gives the results for the National Assembly. (For the Senate, the distribution of the votes was basically the same.)

Why was it such a triumph for the National Salvation Front, and why were the results so weak for all the other parties? One answer has to do with

---

BOX 2.10

ROMANIANS AND ETHNIC HUNGARIANS ATTACK EACH OTHER

TIRGU MURES, Romania—About 2,000 Romanians armed with scythes and clubs attacked 5,000 ethnic Hungarian protesters today in the Transylvanian town of Tirgu Mures, killing one man and injuring about 60, a hospital spokesman said.

The Romanians charged the Hungarians and drove them from the central square, where they had occupied the town hall.

Witnesses saw Hungarians being clubbed to the ground, and Arad Kovacs, an official of the Hungarian Democratic Union, a political party, said: "I am afraid this is going to be a horrible night."

As night fell, seven army tanks formed a barricade between the rival groups.

The Hungarians had gathered this morning to protest a Romanian attack on the Hungarian Democratic Union headquarters in Tirgu Mures the night before.

The Hungarian Government has protested to Romania against "grave atrocities" and said the ethnic Hungarians have been subjected to "pogromlike" attacks.

Source: New York Times, March 21, 1990.

Table 13
Voter Support and Parliamentary Seats in 1990
Election to the Romanian National Assembly

Party	Voter Support (%)	Seats %	Seats N
National Salvation Front	66.3	60.2	233
Democratic Union of Hungarians in Romania	7.2	7.5	29
National Liberal Party	6.3	7.5	29
Green Party	2.6	3.1	12
National Peasants Party	2.5	3.1	12
Alliance for the Unity of Romania	2.1	2.6	10
Other Parties and Independent Candidates	13.0	16.0	62
Total	100.0	100.0	387

Source: *Neue Zürcher Zeitung*, May 28, 1990.

organization. As head of the incumbent government, the National Salvation Front had many organizational advantages, in particular, better access to TV and radio. In addition, the Front had at its disposal the still more or less intact apparatus of the old Communist party. After the election, the opposition parties complained bitterly about the misuse of power by the Front, and they demanded the invalidation of the election. About 500 international observers also had a lot of criticism for the Front, in particular, the incidents of intimidation and ballot-box stuffing. But, despite all this criticism, it seems also to be true that Iliescu and his National Salvation Front had the support of the majority of the people. Iliescu was seen, rightly or wrongly, as the man who had liberated the country from the hated Ceausescu. Romanians were also happy that, under Iliescu as interim president, there was more food on their tables and more lights in the streets.

Under these conditions, the opposition parties never had any real chance. The National Liberal party and the National Peasants party are old historical parties, dating back to the time before the Communists took over. Most of their leaders came back from exile. But, in the short few weeks before the election, they were unable to do the necessary organizational work and to present to the voters coherent programs. Confronted with a very uncertain future, the Romanians decided to stick with the government that they had, which was at least better than the preceding Ceausescu regime. Noteworthy was the strong showing of the party that represents the interests of the Hungarians living in Romania, showing how strongly ethnic Hungarians feel about their identity.

Poland

In 1989, Poland was the first Communist country to make an important step toward free elections. As we have seen in Chapter 1, these elections were not entirely free. The Communist Party reserved two thirds of the parliamentary seats for itself and allowed free competition for the remaining third only. This free part of the election brought triumph to Solidarity which swept all contested seats. The first completely free election with all seats open for competition took place May 27, 1990 at the local level.

The results were a big victory for Solidarity and a total defeat for the Communists. The latter had tried to save themselves by confessing to all their mistakes in the past. Box 2.11 shows the self-criticism of the first secretary of the Communist party at the party congress in January 1990. He acknowledged "the abandonment of political democracy" as the main failing. The party went so far as to dissolve itself and to create a new party with the label Social Democratic. As seen in Box 2.12, the Communists tried to distance themselves from their past. But all these efforts were in vain, and even as a new party with a new name the Communists received merely 0.2 percent of the votes in the local elections of May 27, 1990. Indeed a catastrophic result!

In the councils of the big cities, Solidarity won the overwhelming number of seats: in Warsaw 301 of 345, in Gdansk 56 of 60, in Cracow 72 of 75. In the villages, the story was different, because many candidates won who ran as independents. For the entire country, Solidarity received 41 percent of the votes. Where had all the other votes gone? The votes went to independent candidates, and to a large number of small parties. The most striking result of the election was that none of the newly created parties could really catch on. The Peasants' party received 6 percent of the votes, which was by far the best result. All other parties stayed below 2 percent. The conclusion is that Poland has not yet crossed the threshold to a multi-party system. Instead of dominance by the Communists, we now see a dominance by Solidarity. This does not mean that basic changes in the direction of democracy have not taken place. The local elections were indeed completely free, and Poland now enjoys all the basic civil liberties, like freedom of speech and freedom of religion. But a country needs more than one strong party for a functioning

---

BOX 2.11

SELF-CRITICISM OF RAKOWSKI, FIRST SECRETARY OF POLISH COMMUNIST PARTY

Mr. Rakowski's hourlong speech opening up the congress was a rare concession by a party leader about the mistakes made during Communist rule. He said Marxist socialism had "caused the slowdown of economic development, the disappearance of incentives for innovation and effective work, and the formation of a strong bureaucracy."

He added that "the main weakness of the Communist movement and the source of all its failings was the abandonment of political democracy."

Source: New York Times, January 28, 1990

—————————— **BOX 2.12** ——————————

CALLING PARTY TOO WEAK TO GO ON, POLISH COMMUNISTS ACT TO DISBAND

WARSAW—Many of the 1,600 delegates at a Communist Party congress severely criticized their party today and moved toward dissolving it and replacing it with a new left-of-center political grouping.

Party leaders acknowledged that the party had become too weak to run in free elections.

"The Communist Party's sources of strength and ability to regain popular trust have dwindled to the point of exhaustion," the party's leadership said in a declaration.

"The new party must not be in any way a continuation of the Communist Party, which had adopted the mentality of the Stalinist era," said Mieczyslaw F. Rakowski, a former Prime Minister, who is now head of the party.

As the delegates met in Warsaw's Palace of Culture, an intimidating Gothic skyscraper built by the Soviet Union in the 1950s, about 500 youths protested outside, with some of them throwing rocks. The police pushed them away as they yelled "Down with the Communists!"

Source: New York Times, January 28, 1990.

democracy. Within Solidarity, there are various tendencies with different political outlooks. Sooner or later these tendencies will emerge as independent parties. But at the local elections, this process has not yet taken place. This has contributed to the relatively low voter turnout of 42 percent. Many Poles were confused by the large number of parties and independent candidates, therefore, they tended to vote for the organization they knew— Solidarity. It remains to be seen what will happen to Solidarity. Perhaps it will not participate directly in elections, but go back to its original function as a trade union. Perhaps it will emerge as a regular party among others in Polish politics. For the time being, Solidarity forms a big roof, below which many politicians and voters seek shelter for lack of a better alternative.

Czechoslovakia

In Czechoslovakia, the first free elections took place June 8 and 9, 1990. There were two chambers to be elected; the Chamber of the People and the Chamber of Nationalities, each with 150 seats. In the former, Czechs and Slovaks are represented according to population figures, in the latter the Czech Republic and the Slovak Republic each have 75 representatives. The election system was party list proportionality with a 5 percent threshold against smaller parties, like in the Federal Republic of Germany. The voters were allowed to make changes in the candidate ranking by the political parties.

Voter turnout reached 96 percent, indicating a vivid interest in the election. I witnessed this interest firsthand, when I visited Czechoslovakia during the campaign. At the famous Wenceslas Square in Prague, I encountered a festive atmosphere with many people gathering for political discussions. Although posters were not made professionally, they had clear messages (see photo below). A little poster simply said "Havel = Democracy," referring to the dissident playwright turned president. Another poster contrasted two sets of names; under the heading "dictators" one could read the names of Stalin, Breznew, Gottwald, and Husak; under the heading of "patriots" those of Masaryk, Dubcek, Svehla, and Havel (see photo page 102). A clear message could also be seen in a poster with a lion with a foot on a red star, the lion being a national symbol for Czechoslovakia and the red star standing for Communism.

There were some complaints from all sides about dirty campaign tricks, and a week before the election a bomb went off in the old city of Prague. But overall, the elections were marred by only a few irregularities. Table 14 shows the results for the Chamber of the People (the results for the Chamber of Nationalities are similar). The clear winner was Civic Forum, which is called Public Against Violence in Slovakia. Thus, the party which led the fight against the Communists in the Revolution of November and December 1989 (page 30–33) was rewarded. The election was also a personal victory for Václav Havel, one of the principle founders of Civic Forum. It is noteworthy that Alexander Dubcek, the Reform-Communist of 1968, had joined the Civic Forum.

With 14 percent of the votes, the Communists did relatively well. They were the only party in Eastern and Central Europe still running under the old party label. But they had recognized their mistakes; in their party program, they spoke of "the mistakes, errors and injustices our party had committed in the past," and they asked bluntly: "Why has the Communist Party of Czechoslovakia failed to accomplish their goals and objectives and

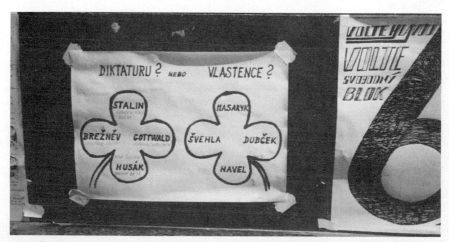

Election posters at Wenceslas Square in Prague. (Courtesy Ruth Steiner.)

Election posters at Wenceslas Square in Prague. (Courtesy Ruth Steiner.)

not succeeded to put them into effect in the period when it acted as the leading force of our society?" Their answer was to present "the program of the revitalized Communist Party of Czechoslovakia, the program of a party of labour and democratic socialism seeking to establish its new identity and new position in society." The Communists did not use the red star, but two morello cherries as a symbol in the election campaign. Jokingly, the official spokesman of the Communist Party told me that morello cherries are red only at the outside, and white in the inside, implying that at their core the Communists are not red anymore. With this reform message, the Communists managed to attract a fair number of voters. Thus, the sarcastic black-

Table 14

Voter Support and Parliamentary Seats in 1990 Election to the First Chamber (Chamber of the People) of the Parliament of Czechoslovakia

Party	Voter Support (%)	Seats	
		%	N
Civic Forum	46.6	58.0	87
Communists	13.6	15.4	23
Christian Democrats	12.0	13.3	20
Movement for Morovia and Silesia	5.4	6.0	9
Slovak National Party	3.5	4.0	6
Ethnic Hungarians	2.8	3.3	5
Others	16.1	0.0	0
Total	100.0	100.0	150

Source: Neue Zürcher Zeitung, June 12 and June 15, 1990.

framed campaign poster announcing in solemn words the death of the Communist Party at the age of only 41 years was premature, but still witty. After the election, the Communist Party chairman announced that "we will be playing the role of left-wing opposition—not opposition to the democratic system."

The Christian Democrats emerged as the third largest party, a rather disappointing result, given that they were heavily supported by Christian Democratic and Conservative parties in Western Europe. The Christian Democrats were hurt by a revelation shortly before the elections that one of their leaders had worked for many years for the secret state police.

As we will see in Chapter 13, ethnicity is an important issue in Czechoslovakia. This was also revealed in the election results in the sense that three ethnically based parties made it to parliament. The Movement for Morovia and Silesia gained 5.4 percent of the votes. To understand this movement, one must know that the Czech Republic consists of the regions of Bohemia, Morovia, and Silesia. Bohemia is strongest with Prague as its center so that Morovians and Silesians often feel neglected. During my visit in Brno, the center of Morovia, I heard many complaints so that I was not surprised that the Movement received the support of every third voter in Brno. Ethnicity is even more a force in the Slovak Republic where the Slovak National Party advocates much more autonomy for Slovakia. Some of its supporters are even demanding a separate nation state. For the country as a whole, the Slovak National Party reached 3.5 percent of the votes which would have kept it below the threshold to enter parliament; thanks to a special clause in the election law it still made it. It is sufficient to reach 5 percent in only one of the two republics, and the Slovak National Party crossed this hurdle easily with more than 10 percent support in Slovakia. As a third ethnically based party, the ethnic Hungarians, who live mainly in Slovakia, also were elected to the national parliament.

Many parties stayed below the threshold of 5 percent, perhaps most notably the Social Democrats although they were heavily supported by their sister parties in the West. But the Social Democrats were not able to differentiate themselves clearly from the popular Civic Forum. The Greens' hope to enter parliament was not fulfilled, either, although Czechoslovakia suffers severely from environmental damage. The pull of Civic Forum was simply too great for most of the smaller parties to survive electoral competition.

What was this pull exactly? Mainly, the fact that it had been at the forefront of the Revolution. Otherwise, there was not much of a common program holding Civic Forum together. The Forum considers itself not a party, but a movement, a point stressed heavily at its headquarters in Prague. There, I talked with a man who introduced himself as one of the leaders of "Civic Democratic Alliance," a subgroup of the Forum. He told me that his Alliance belongs to the Civic Forum only for electoral purposes and that as soon as possible it plans to become its own independent party. This man told me also that he takes the free-market approach of Margaret Thatcher as model. But within Civic Forum, there are also subgroups with strong leftist and environmentalist orientations. Thus, the situation of Civic Forum is comparable to the Polish Solidarity, and it is likely that Civic Forum too will soon break apart. The emerging of a party system is more advanced in Czechoslovakia than in Poland, but it still remains to be seen what will happen in the next few years to Civic Forum.

Bulgaria

As the last of the former Soviet satellite countries, Bulgaria held free elections June 10 and 17, 1990. Four hundred members were to be elected to a single chamber of parliament. Like Hungary, Bulgaria combined the winner-take-all system with party list proportionality. Two hundred members of parliament were elected in single districts with an absolute majority of the votes being required for election in the first ballot. If no candidate fulfilled this requirement, a run-off a week later was necessary with a simple plurality being sufficient at that time. The other 200 members of parliament were elected on party lists in 28 electoral districts. Like Czechoslovakia, Bulgaria also had a threshold against smaller parties, but of 4 rather than 5 percent.

As we saw in Chapter 1, at the end of 1989 the Bulgarian hard-line Communists were swept from power. But the Communist Party kept control of the country, although it changed its name to Socialist Party. With its party apparatus still in full operation, the Communists had a big electoral advantage, and they won the election easily. In the proportionality part of the election, they won 47 percent of the votes against 36 percent for the main opposition party, the Union of Democratic Forces. The opposition suffered not only from the organizational strength of the Communists, but also from its internal weakness. The Union of Democratic Forces was merely a loose electoral alliance of 16 parties with very different political goals. There were two other parties crossing the 4 percent threshold, the Agrarian National Union with 8 percent of the votes and the party representing ethnic Turks with 6 percent. More than 30 other parties stayed below the threshold of 4 percent and thus did not make it to parliament.

With 83 percent voter turnout was high. According to international observers, the elections were relatively correct, although there were several violent incidents during the campaign. The Communists certainly made the best of their organizational strength, and quite a number of Bulgarians wished to keep the party in power. The leadership of the Communists was rewarded for having kicked out the old hard-line guard under Zhivkov and for making relatively free elections possible. Especially in the rural parts of the country, the support for the Communists was strong and also quite genuine. The situation was different in the capital Sofia, where the Union of Democratic Forces clearly outscored the Communists with 55 against 36 percent of the votes. It was also in Sofia that on the day after the first ballot, a large Anti-Communist rally took place with chantings of "We are not going to work for the Reds" (Box 2.13).

For the winner-take-all part of the election, run-offs were necessary in 81 of the 200 districts. As we have seen several times in this chapter, the winner-take-all electoral system tends to favor the largest party, and Bulgaria was no exception. Thanks to the winner-take-all part, the Communists reached an

—————————————— BOX 2.13 ——————————————

100,000 ANTI-COMMUNISTS RALLY IN SOFIA

SOFIA—Tens of thousands of supporters of Bulgaria's largest opposition group, angered by predictions of a victory by former Communists in the country's first free elections in four decades, demonstrated Monday in central Sofia.

The crowd, waving blue flags of the opposition Union of Democratic Forces, thronged a square outside the National Palace of Culture, where results of Sunday's election were to be announced.

Witnesses said the marchers swelled to around 100,000 as thousands of people poured in from side streets to join the rally, chanting "We are not going to work for the Reds" and "Victory UDF."

Source: International Herald Tribune, June 12, 1990.

absolute majority in parliament, with a total of 211 seats for both election systems combined. For the Union of Democratic Forces the total was 144 seats, for the Ethnic Turks 23 seats, and for the Agrarian National Union 16 seats; the remaining 6 seats went to independent candidates.

How Much Has Changed Through Elections?

With all the former Soviet satellite countries in Eastern and Central Europe having had free elections in the first half of 1990, the question is how much change was brought about by these elections. The answer is much more change in Hungary, Poland, Czechoslovakia, and East Germany than in Romania and Bulgaria. Why this difference? The explanation may relate to the simulation model I developed in Chapter 1. I asked when and how the reform process was launched in the individual countries, and I argued that Poland and Hungary had good cultural preconditions for reforms. These two countries had, in addition, organizational vehicles to launch reforms—in Poland the Catholic Church and Solidarity, in Hungary a reform-minded Communist party, thus explaning why these two countries were the first to launch the reform process. These same arguments also explain why Hungary and Poland underwent rapid change once reforms were launched. Czechoslovakia and East Germany also had good cultural preconditions for reforms, but they lacked efficient organizational vehicles. Therefore, the reform process was triggered only through the example given by Hungary and Poland. But once launched, the reform process proceeded rapidly because it had the necessary cultural basis. It was relatively easy to establish organizational forms to carry the reform process forward. Consequently, Czechoslovakia and East Germany, with Hungary and Poland, are in the same category of great change.

Romania and Bulgaria to a large extent lacked the necessary culture for reforms. According to my simulation model, in these two countries the reform process was largely due to the example provided by other countries. Therefore, Romania and Bulgaria were not only late to engage in reforms, they now also have great difficulties sustaining the reform process. Once the worst abuses of Ceausescu and Zhivkov had been eliminated, many Romanians and Bulgarians were content to support the old order—in Romania the National Salvation Front, in Bulgaria the renamed Communist party. But, as we will see in Chapter 3, severe abuses still continue in these two countries.

3

CABINET FORMATION

Having described various systems of electing the legislative branch of government, we turn now to the executive branch. In the United States, the relationship between the two branches is characterized by a system of checks and balances. The president, as chief executive, is elected not by Congress but directly by the people, if we disregard the aspect of the electoral college. Congress cannot oust the president with a vote of no-confidence. The only exception, impeachment, is very different from a vote of no-confidence. On the other hand, the president cannot dissolve Congress and call for early elections.

Most European democracies have a parliamentary system with rules fundamentally different from the American presidential system. The major exception is France, which combines a presidential with a parliamentary system under the constitution of the Fifth Republic.

The most important characteristic of the parliamentary system is that the executive is selected by parliament and depends on the confidence of parliament for survival. The voters elect their parliament, which is therefore the sole body that can claim to represent the will of the people in a direct way. The ways in which presidential and parliamentary systems relate voters to the legislative and executive branches of government are presented in Figure 8.

As mentioned in Chapter 2, most European democracies have two chambers of parliament—an upper and a lower house. In some countries, the upper house is also involved in the selection of the executive. We will deal with this issue when we examine the individual countries.

The executive branch in a European parliamentary system is the cabinet, which is headed by a prime minister whose role is very different from that of the U.S. president. In the United States, cabinet members are appointed by the president, and serve at his pleasure. In a parliamentary system, the prime minister is merely the first member of a team. With rare exceptions, cabinet members are chosen from parliament. The rule is that they retain their seats in parliament while serving in the cabinet, but there are a few exceptions to this rule. In Switzerland, Norway, and the Netherlands, cabinet members are required to give up their parliamentary seats. The size of a cabinet may vary a great deal but is usually around 15 to 25. Within any particular cabinet, the prime minister's role may be stronger or weaker, depending on the individual's personality and the overall political circumstances. Legal authority also plays a role. In West Germany, for example, the prime minister, or chancellor, is particularly strong because he has the legal authority to give directives to

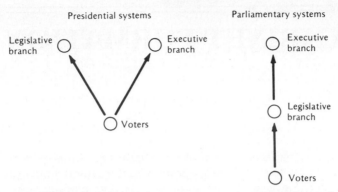

Figure 8. Relations between Voters and the Legislative and Executive Branches of Government in Presidential and Parliamentary Systems.

other cabinet members. This authority is not available in many other countries, where the prime minister must rely on other means to exert influence.

To select a new cabinet, a vote of confidence takes place in parliament. The cabinet needs a majority of the votes. We must add that, technically, in some countries an explicit vote of confidence is not necessary. In such cases, the cabinet is formally appointed by the head of state—for example, by the queen in Great Britain—and it is assumed that the cabinet has the confidence of parliament unless the latter explicitly expresses its lack of confidence. But this technicality does not change the basic fact that the cabinet depends on the confidence of parliament. Whether the vote of confidence occurs explicitly or implicitly, it is important to note that members of parliament cannot make individual choices. Party discipline is imposed, so that parties act as blocs. If a member of parliament breaks party discipline in a vote of confidence, this is likely to lead to severe sanctions and, in some cases, even to expulsion from the party. To understand the vote of confidence, we must understand that the relevant actors are not individual members of parliament, but the parties. The question is not how individual X, but how party X, will vote.

Just as parliament gives its confidence to the cabinet, it may withdraw this confidence at any time. The only formality required is a vote of no confidence. Such a vote does not imply that the cabinet has done something improper or illegal; it merely confirms that parliament is no longer satisfied with the policies pursued by the cabinet. Thus, a vote of no confidence is very different from impeachment in the United States. An impeached U.S. president leaves political life in disgrace, whereas a prime minister whose cabinet loses a vote of no confidence usually stays on as a member of parliament. He or she may even continue to play a leadership role, most likely as head of the opposition.

How parliament handles votes of confidence and no confidence varies greatly from country to country. The most influential factor is whether a single party controls a majority in parliament.

GREAT BRITAIN: ONE-PARTY MAJORITY IN PARLIAMENT

Among European democracies, Great Britain is the classical case of one-party majority in Parliament, especially for the period since World War II. General elections usually give an absolute majority of seats in the House of Commons to either the Labour or the Conservative party. Since 1945, there have been only two exceptions to this rule, both in the 1970s. In the March 1974 election, Labour received the most seats but fell short of reaching a majority. New elections were held in October of the same year, and that time Labour won a narrow majority, but the majority soon eroded as a result of defections and by-election defeats. We will deal with these two episodes later in this chapter, when we address situations in which no party controls a majority in parliament (page 128–129). For now, we turn our attention to the normal British situation, in which one of the two large parties enjoys a majority in the House of Commons.

The upper house of Parliament, the House of Lords, can be disregarded in the process of cabinet formation. The House of Lords consists mainly of members of the hereditary nobility and some members who receive titles in their own lifetime. Over the centuries, the power of the House of Lords has diminished more and more, and today its power is limited to delaying fiscal bills for up to one month and other bills for up to one year.

If one party has a majority in the House of Commons, cabinet formation is straightforward: The majority party simply forms a cabinet. This happened in 1987, for example, when the Conservatives won 376 of the 650 seats (see

Margaret Thatcher. (Courtesy British Embassy, Washington, D.C.)

Table 3 in Chapter 2). After this victory, it was clear that the Conservatives would form a cabinet. Who would be the prime minister and the other cabinet members? We must first distinguish between two situations: Either the winning party was already in power before the election, or it was in opposition. In 1987, the Conservatives had already been the majority party since 1979. In accordance with the idea of never changing a winning team, most members of the old cabinet, including Prime Minister Margaret Thatcher (see photo on page 109), retained their positions. The second situation was illustrated in 1979, when the Conservatives won the elections as the opposition party. In such cases, the concept of a *shadow cabinet* is important. During the period of opposition, a party announces the names of its members who would fill the various cabinet positions in the case of electoral victory. This cabinet-in-waiting is called the shadow cabinet. Its members act as spokespersons of their party in parliamentary debates. The shadow foreign minister, for example, confronts the actual foreign minister in debates on foreign affairs. This is a good training ground, giving the shadow foreign minister some experience in foreign affairs should his or her party win the next election.

This raises the question of how a member of parliament can advance in the party to become a member of the cabinet. Because the House of Commons is very large—650 members—there will always be many more ordinary members than leaders. The leaders, incidentally, sit on the front benches at either side of the aisle in the House of Commons—the government on one side, the opposition on the other. The nonleaders have to sit at the back and are therefore called back-benchers. How do back-benchers become parliamentary leaders? They must prove their competence to their peers in Parliament. If this is done successfully, they may one day rise to a cabinet position and, ultimately, to the prime ministership. A good summary of these career paths is contained in Box 3.1, in which political scientist Donald D. Searing aptly describes how ministerial aspirants learn to think and act like ministers.

If we compare the career path of a British prime minister with the usual path to the American White House, the differences are striking. Both Jimmy Carter and Ronald Reagan became presidents without any prior Washington, D.C., experience. Both, in fact, made use of the argument that they were not part of the capital government establishment. In contrast, British prime ministers complete a long apprenticeship in the House of Commons before entering office. Which career path is preferable? An American president who comes from outside may have the advantage of bringing a fresh "wind" and a new outlook, but this advantage is countered by a lack of experience, which can be seen as a real disadvantage. As former West German Chancellor Helmut Schmidt notes: "It remains a pity that the process of nominating and electing a [American] President does not pay any attention to their foreign political expertise or experience or ability. They have never been tested in it, whereas in a parliamentary system, people who make it to the top have been tested first."[22]

Schmidt said this in 1984. In the meantime, George Bush became president, and he certainly had plenty of foreign policy experience prior to

_____ **BOX 3.1** _____

MINISTERIAL ASPIRANTS IN THE HOUSE OF COMMONS

Ministerial Aspirants are concerned above all with advancement and strategies for achieving it. They must study strategy carefully because their apprentice-ship is so haphazard and its prescriptions so unclear. They try to make regular, though not frequent, speeches in the House attacking political enemies rather than allies. With colleagues, they try to be convivial; with colleagues who are superiors they try to impress with their competence and diligence in commit-tees. To appear serious they also specialize; but just as they must not seem too serious, so they must not seem too specialized, for this might stereotype them as men of narrow vision. . . .

Aspirants prepare themselves to be Ministers by "taking the role," by trying out characteristic attitudes and beginning to think about it as a role of "Me" rather than only for "Them." This orientation takes time to develop; and many never learn very much about horses till they are themselves in the saddle. Yet some quickly cut through the cliches to understand the significance of style in debate and the utility of sensitivity to the moods of the House. They also begin to think like Ministers, or, as they suppose Ministers must think: Machiavellian enough to avoid moralizing and to be convincing when cases are weak; con-trolled enough to develop the clever manner of the accomplished actor; real-istic enough to work, as necessary, with opponents from the other side of the House and to control one's civil servants and one's department.

Source: Donald D. Searing, "Ministerial Aspirants," forthcoming.

becoming president. Have Americans become concerned about electing a Washington outsider as president? Has the complaint of Helmut Schmidt and similar critics been taken seriously? Was it the lack of foreign-policy experience that contributed to the defeat of Michael Dukakis? In a parlia-mentary system, it would certainly be someone like George Bush, rather than someone like Reagan, Carter, or Dukakis, who would become prime minister.

Differences between Great Britain and the United States are also striking with regard to the role of the opposition. In Great Britain, as long as the government party does not lose its majority through defections or by-election losses, it can pursue whatever policies it chooses. In the Falkland Islands crisis of 1982, for example, the Labour party had no means of imped-ing the policy of the governing Conservatives. Under the British system, the majority party governs with an absolute mandate. The prime minister's main task is to keep control of his or her own party. This is forcefully expressed in Box 3.2.

In this context, the function of a vote of no confidence demanded by the opposition needs clarification. As long as the governing party controls a majority of the parliamentary seats, a no-confidence vote has no chance of

_____ BOX 3.2 _____

ON THE BRITISH PRIME MINISTER

One distinctive feature of a Prime Minister's job in Britain is the importance of party management. The party in Parliament elects the Prime Minister. . . . As long as the Prime Minister can dominate the party in fact as well as name, then his or her position is secure. Doing this is a continuing and imperative task.

Because of the dominance of the executive over Parliament, a Prime Minister need have little concern about losing votes on legislation in the House of Commons. Unlike votes in the U.S. House of Representatives, votes in the Commons can usually be taken for granted. Managing Parliament is not so much a matter of legislation as it is a party task. It means maintaining good relations with backbenchers whose confidence is important for the Prime Minister's successful presentation of self.

Source: Richard Rose, "British Government: The Job at the Top," in Richard Rose and Ezra N. Suleiman, eds., *Presidents and Prime Ministers* (Washington, D.C.; American Enterprise Institute, 1980), pp. 47–48.

success. But this is not the purpose, as everyone knows. The purpose is to give the opposition the chance to say what it finds wrong with the policies of the government and what it would do instead. In this way, the voters can see what the alternative to the governing party would be. On election day, the choices are thus clear: The voters can either opt for a continuation of the existing policies or for a change to the policies advocated by the opposition.

In the United States, the distinction between governing and opposition parties is much less clear. In the 1988 presidential election campaign, the Democrats criticized the Republicans for the huge budget deficit of the Reagan administration. The Republicans replied that the Democrats in Congress opposed many of the cuts proposed in the Reagan budgets. In Great Britain, such ambivalence could not occur. In the next election, particularly after three terms in office, Margaret Thatcher and her Conservative party must take full responsibility for all government policies. As a consequence, the voter will have a clear choice: Continue with the Conservatives or oust them. Americans prefer to check and balance governmental power. They may vote for a Republican president, but they are not unhappy when a Congress dominated by the Democrats opposes him. The penalty of the U.S. system is that it is never quite clear who is responsible for a particular policy. David Broder, one of the most respected American columnists, applauds the British system for allowing the opposition party to formulate a clear alternative to the policies of the party in power (Box 3.3).

Although the executive branch in Great Britain, when compared to the United States, has much more leeway to pursue long-term policies, its power should not be exaggerated. It must contend with powerful interest groups.

_____ **BOX 3.3** _____

DAVID BRODER APPLAUDS THE BRITISH SYSTEM

The lack of a policy voice is one of the chronic problems for the out-party in America. In a parliamentary system like Great Britain's, the opposition party has a "shadow Cabinet," whose members not only sit on the front bench in Parliament and debate policy with their Cabinet opposites, but turn up constantly on the radio and TV talk shows telling the public where their party stands.

When Britain's Labor Party lost for the third straight time in 1987, its leader, Neil Kinnock, invited party officials at all levels to review Labor's message. The process has led Labor to dump some damaging policies like its advocacy of unilateral disarmament and has won the party new credibility with the voters.

The Democrats have lost three in a row, too. But they have no machinery for asking themselves where they went wrong or figuring out what they might say differently. They do not even have a policy voice.

Source: David Broder, "The Democrats Have Lost Their Collective Voice," *The News and Observer,* Raleigh, N.C., September 25, 1989.

The British cabinet must also consider the wishes of its own party's back-benchers; otherwise it might suddenly be faced with internal party rebellion, as illustrated in Boxes 3.4 and 3.5. Between elections, a prime minister is safe from the opposition but not from being overthrown within his or her own party.

_____ **BOX 3.4** _____

32 CONSERVATIVES FORM A GROUP TO OPPOSE THATCHER

LONDON (Reuters)—More than 30 Conservative Party members of Parliament announced Sunday that they have formed a group to oppose the policies of Prime Minister Margaret Thatcher, the party leader.

Francis Pym, a former foreign secretary, and 31 parliamentary colleagues said they have set up an organization called Conservative Center Forward to fight for a more liberal form of conservatism.

The MPs, who have been meeting secretly for several weeks under Mr. Pym's chairmanship, said they would vote as a block against the government in Parliament when they believed such action was justified.

Source: International Herald Tribune, May 13, 1985.

——————————————————— BOX 3.5 ———————————————————

INTERNAL PARTY CHALLENGE TO MARGARET THATCHER

Prime Minister Margaret Thatcher . . . met the first direct challenge to her
leadership of the Conservative Party in 14 years. Sir Anthony Meyer, a little-
known Conservative, put up his candidacy for leader of the party to rally
opposition to Mrs. Thatcher's handling of the economy and her reluctance to
integrate Britain deeper into the European Community.

Sixty of the 374 Conservative members of Parliament did not vote for her; 33
supported Sir Anthony, 24 deliberately cast invalid ballot papers and 3 did not
cast votes at all. The result, with 314 members of Parliament supporting the
Prime Minister, was generally viewed as a setback to her, but not a fatal one. She
described the result as "splendid."

Source: New York Times, December 6, 1989.

How are cabinet decisions made? What is the role of the prime minister?
As political scientist Thomas A. Baylis argues in Box 3.6 the British cabinet is
characterized by a mixture of collegial and monocratic decision making.
Typically, there is an open and frank discussion, in which every cabinet
member is heard, but the prime minister has the right to sum up the
discussion. Votes are virtually never taken. Patrick Gordon Walker, a former
member of the cabinet, describes an imaginary cabinet meeting. After a
lengthy discussion, the prime minister sums up and concludes as follows:
"Is the cabinet agreed with my summing up and the additional points made

——————————————————— BOX 3.6 ———————————————————

DECISION MAKING IN THE BRITISH CABINET

The British executive, then, is characterized by a mixture of collegial decision-
making with monocratic leadership. The prime minister often initiates action,
and may be able to persuade, manipulate, and occasionally circumvent collegial authority. But she is not in a position to ignore it, and if she seeks to do so,
as even Mrs. Thatcher has discovered, she is likely to provoke a storm of
controversy.

Source: Thomas A. Baylis, *Governing by Committee* (Albany: State University of New York
Press, 1989), p. 60.

—————————————————— **BOX 3.7** ——————————————————

THATCHER ACCUSED OF AUTOCRACY

LONDON—One of Prime Minister Margaret Thatcher's longest-serving ministers, Chancellor of the Exchequer Nigel Lawson, angrily resigned tonight in a dispute over who was in charge of British economic policy—the Chancellor or Mrs. Thatcher's economic adviser at 10 Downing Street. . .

Admiration for her ability to denounce Britain's and her own detractors has turned, in many minds, to a feeling that she has become arrogant and autocratic, publicly humiliating her ministers and driving them out of the Government if they stand up to her.

Accepting her Chancellor's resignation, Mrs. Thatcher pointedly wrote, "It is a matter of particular regret that you should decide to leave before your task is complete."

Source: The New York Times, October 27, 1989.

by the chancellor? (Silence, with a few muttered 'agreeds.')"[23] This summing up gives quite a bit of power to the prime minister. Richard Crossman, another former cabinet member, argues that the summation by the prime minister "may not represent the discussion at all. . . . The Prime Minister can define the consensus as being what he thinks fit. Even though a majority of the opinions expressed were against him, that would not necessarily prevent him from deciding as he wishes—if he can get away with it."[24]

Margaret Thatcher has tried to get away with too much. In this sense, she is not a typical prime minister, and there are indeed many complaints that her leadership style is too autocratic, as illustrated in Box 3.7. This autocratic style is increasingly hurting Margaret Thatcher and her Conservative party. They are also hurt by the strengthening of the Labour party. As we have seen in Chapter 2, Thatcher never received a majority of the popular vote. It was only because there was a severe split in the opposition that Thatcher could translate a popular support of 42–43 percent into an overwhelming majority in the House of Commons. This is likely to change now. As explained in Chapter 2, to establish with the Alliance a strong party in the middle turned out to be a failure. This helped Labour, which under the leadership of Neil Kinnock (photo, page 116) made the electorally smart move to change more to the middle (Box 3.8). Therefore, the Conservatives will be confronted in the next election with a much more formidable adversary. Many of the votes of the opposition may go to Labour. Even if the Conservatives could keep their popular support, it will be much more difficult for them to be "first past the post" in as many districts as they were in the three previous elections.

Neil Kinnock. (Courtesy British Embassy, Washington D.C.)

_____ BOX 3.8 _____

BRITAIN'S LABOR PARTY TRANSFORMING ITSELF

LONDON—Discarding its once-sacrosanct policy of unilateral nuclear disarmament, Britain's opposition Labor Party completed a transformation at its annual convention this week.

From rambunctious, radical and noisily left-wing, the socialist movement has shifted center, spruced up its image, dumped its old working-class rallying cries and borrowed some of Conservative Prime Minister Margaret Thatcher's clothes.

The reward has been Labor's most commanding and consistent lead in polls since the party lost power to Mrs. Thatcher a decade ago.

The price, dismayed Labor leftists complain, has been the party's soul.

"They (the Labor leaders) aim to win by detaching the Labor Party as a whole," former energy secretary Tony Benn, doyen of the Labor left, complained during the week-long party conference in Brighton.

Source: Chapel Hill Newspaper, October 8, 1989.

FEDERAL REPUBLIC OF GERMANY:
———— MINIMAL-WINNING-SIZED COALITIONS ————

In a parliamentary system, when no party controls a majority in parliament, the process of cabinet formation is very different from the one in Great Britain. Americans often think that under these conditions instability and even chaos will necessarily result. As an example, they may refer to Italy, which has had nearly 50 cabinets since World War II. We will deal with the frequent cabinet crises in Italy at the end of this chapter.

In fact, parliamentary systems can be quite stable, even when no party has a majority in parliament. Our first example is the Federal Republic of Germany, which has had only six chancellors (Konrad Adenauer [see photo below], Ludwig Erhard, Kurt Kiesinger, Willy Brandt, Helmut Schmidt, and Helmut Kohl) since its foundation in 1949.

Besides the Bundestag—the lower house of parliament—West Germany also has an upper house—the Bundesrat. Its members are not elected by the voters but are appointed by the state (*Laender*) governments. Federal bills

Konrad Adenauer, First Chancellor of the Federal Republic of Germany. (Courtesy Embassy of the Federal Republic of Germany, Bern, Switzerland.)

that have an impact on state matters must also pass the Bundesrat. All other parliamentary decisions, particularly selection of the cabinet, are solely in the sphere of the Bundestag. As you will recall from Chapter 2, the 1987 election led to the following distribution of seats in the Bundestag:

Christian Democrats (CDU/CSU)	223
Social Democrats (SPD)	186
Free Democrats (FDP)	46
Greens	42
Total	497

With this distribution of seats, the preconditions for the formation of the cabinet were fundamentally different from those in Britain in the same year (as discussed above). In West Germany, no party had achieved a majority so that it alone could form the cabinet. Given a total of 497 seats in the Bundestag, at least 249 votes were needed for a cabinet to win a vote of confidence. The CDU/CSU, as the largest party, fell 26 seats short of the required majority. Thus, the only way to achieve a majority was for a sufficient number of parties to enter a coalition. Several winning coalitions for cabinet formation would have been numerically feasible. The coalition that actually emerged consisted of the CDU/CSU and the FDP, headed by Chancellor Helmut Kohl (see photo below). Together the two parties controlled 269 votes in the Bundestag, a sufficient number to win a vote of confidence. The

Helmut Kohl. (Courtesy Embassy of the Federal Republic of Germany, Bern, Switzerland.)

coalition was of a minimal winning size with regard to number of parties because it had just enough parties to win but not more.

Should we expect all coalitions to be of a minimal winning size? What would be a rational motive for adding more parties than are necessary to win?[25] Why include a third party in a coalition if two parties have enough votes for a majority in parliament? This can and does occur. As we will see in the case of Switzerland, oversized coalitions that include more parties than needed to win are formed under certain circumstances.

In West Germany, minimal-winning-sized coalitions are the rule, and only in the 1950s did a few exceptions to this rule occur. Since the early 1960s, no coalitions have been formed with more parties than necessary to win. In this context, a comment is called for regarding the CDU/CSU-SPD coalition from 1966 to 1969 (see Table 15). It was minimal-winning-sized in the sense that one party alone would not have had enough votes to win, so that a coalition of both parties was necessary to achieve a majority. But *minimal-winning-sized* could also be defined in the narrower sense of applying not only to the number of parties but also to the number of individual members of parliament. At that time, CDU/CSU and SPD together had 447 seats, and the FDP, as the only party in opposition, had a mere 49 seats. Taking into account not only the number of parties but also the number of individuals, the CDU/CSU-SPD coalition was clearly oversized, which led to a lot of criticism. The argument was made that the opposition has a vital function in a democracy, and the opposition is too weak if the two largest parties together form the cabinet. In terms of their own self-interest, too, the two largest parties generally have little incentive to enter into a coalition, because in such a coalition each must settle for fewer cabinet ministries than in any other type of coalition. Following the 1966–1969 experience, there has been great reluctance to form another coalition between the two largest West German parties, and there is a more or less informal rule against such a coalition.

At least two other informal rules have developed that guide the process of cabinet formation in the Federal Republic today. One of these rules emerged after the 1969 coalition formation. That election resulted in the following distribution of seats in the Bundestag:

CDU/CSU	242
SPD	224
FDP	30
Total	496

Table 15
West German Cabinets Since 1966

Years	Coalition	Chancellor
1966–1969	CDU/CSU-SPD	Kurt Georg Kiesinger
1969–1974	SPD-FDP	Willy Brandt
1974–1982	SPD-FDP	Helmut Schmidt
1982–present	CDU/CSU-FDP	Helmut Kohl

The Christian Democrats felt that they had won the election, and they pondered the question of whether they should continue their coalition with the Social Democrats or return to their earlier coalition with the Free Democrats. They were shocked when, late in the election night, SPD and FDP announced that they had made a deal. With a combined 254 seats, they were just above the necessary majority of 249, so that they could indeed win a vote of confidence in parliament. Legally, everything was in order, but a big public debate began over whether the procedure was in accordance with the spirit of basic democratic principles.

The question was raised whether excluding the party with the most votes from the cabinet violated the will of the electorate. The counterargument was that more voters had supported SPD and FDP together than CDU/CSU alone, so that the new cabinet was in fact based on the majority will of the people. What emerged from this debate was the "rule" that the voters should be informed of the coalition intentions of the various parties before the election. It should not be left to a few leaders to decide after the election what coalition was to be formed. In all West German elections after 1969, the parties have announced their coalition intentions beforehand. In 1987, for example, the voters knew before the election that CDU/CSU and FDP would form a coalition if together they received a majority vote. Thus, the voters no longer remained in the dark about what kind of cabinet they were supporting with their vote. Voting for the FDP in 1987 meant supporting CDU/CSU leader Helmut Kohl as chancellor. The rule of announcing coalition intentions before the election is considered to be more democratic and has gained broad support in the West German political milieu.

Another informal rule regarding cabinet formation developed from an episode in the fall of 1982. The 1980 election resulted in a continuation of the 11-year-old coalition between Social Democrats and Free Democrats, but there were increasing strains between the two coalition partners, especially over economic matters. Under the strong influence of its economics minister, FDP advocated more free market solutions and, in the fall of 1982, broke its coalition with SPD and entered into a coalition with CDU/CSU. Social Democrat Helmut Schmidt was thus replaced as chancellor by Christian Democrat Helmut Kohl. The reason Schmidt was ousted was not unpopularity; on the contrary, opinion surveys indicated that Schmidt was more popular than Kohl at that time. The reason was that the FDP wished to change coalition partners. A public debate began as to whether a small party should have the power to replace the chancellor in this way. After all, the Free Democrats had campaigned in 1980 with the promise to continue their coalition with the Social Democrats. Was this promise valid for the entire legislative period? Was it a betrayal of the voters to change coalitions midcourse? The argument was again made that a cabinet had been formed without due input by the voters. Early elections were demanded for such situations so that the voters could decide. Kohl took this demand seriously, and in the spring of 1983, early elections took place. The coalition of CDU/CSU and FDP won, now with a clear mandate from the voters. It seems likely that in the future changes of coalitions will no longer occur without a prior election.

The development of a set of widely accepted, informal rules for the process of cabinet formation is important for the stability of West German democracy. This contrasts with the Weimar Republic, before Hitler's takeover, when deep disagreements existed about the very rules for cabinet formation. Today, the political elites by and large agree how the game should be played.

The small Free Democratic party seems to have a very strong position in the coalition game as played in West Germany. We saw, for example, how in 1982 the FDP ousted the SPD and brought in the CDU/CSU. Although the FDP was often the pivotal party in the coalition game, another aspect of the game is less pleasant for the party. Changing coalitions usually has high costs. The FDP learned this in 1969, when it allied itself with the SPD instead of returning to its former coalition with the CDU/CSU. This change in coalitions cost the FDP many of its right-wing voters who refused to support a party in alliance with the SPD. These voters then turned to the CDU/CSU. In 1969, the FDP lost not only many of its conservative voters but also some leaders with a conservative orientation, including, for example, a former party chairperson. After 1969, the Free Democrats had to rebuild the party more to the left on the West German party spectrum. The switch back to the CDU/CSU in 1982 brought new disruptions to the party. This time, it lost voters as well as some leaders from its left wing. The lesson is that a party changing coalitions may be perceived as unprincipled and opportunistic, causing it severe image problems.

The Greens, which entered the Bundestag only in 1983, did not yet participate in any government coalition. Initially, it seemed as if the Greens were unwilling to participate in any coalition games. They claimed that the game played by the three established parties was corrupt, and they said that they would refuse to enter any "deals." The purity of their ideals seemed more important to the Greens than any gains from parliamentary maneuvers. More recently, many Greens seem to accept that a systematic refusal to

---

_____ **BOX 3.9** _____

LEFTISTS FORM COALITION TO RULE WEST BERLIN

BERLIN—The leftist Social Democrats and West Berlin's equivalent of the anti-NATO Greens formed a government Friday that pledged to reduce Allied military control of the city and curb police action against street protests. . . .

Voters gave the Christian Democrats and Social Democrats 55 seats each in the 138-member legislature, and the Alternative List got 17. The far-right Republican Party won the other 11.

Chancellor Helmut Kohl's Christian Democrats have been slipping in opinion polls, and the so-called "Red-Green" government in West Berlin will be a major test of whether such a coalition can work nationally.

Source: The News and Observer, Raleigh, N.C., March 11, 1989.

participate in any agreements with other parties would be irresponsible and could ultimately hurt the goals of the party. According to this view, the Greens have to cooperate to some extent with other parties if they wish to achieve at least some of their goals. After much heated internal debate, this view slowly seems to prevail. At the local level, there have been some prominent cases, for example, in West Berlin (see Box 3.9), where the Greens entered a coalition with the SPD. Another "Red-Green" coalition formed in June 1990 in Lower Saxony. As mentioned in the box, such "Red-Green" cabinets are "a major test of whether such coalitions can work nationally."

SWITZERLAND: GRAND COALITIONS

We have seen how the game of cabinet formation is played in a competitive way in the Federal Republic of Germany; usually it leads to cabinets of a minimal winning size with regard to the number of participating parties. In Switzerland, on the other hand, the normal pattern is oversized cabinets with more parties included than necessary to win a majority in parliament (so-called grand coalitions). Do the Swiss therefore play the game of cabinet formation in a cooperative rather than in a competitive way; and if so, what would be their motives? Before answering this question, let us examine the most recent parliamentary election to see how the cabinet was formed.

In 1987, a basically proportional electoral system led to the results shown in Table 16 for the National Council, Switzerland's lower house of parliament. Some of the smaller parties listed in the table are specific to Switzerland and require brief comments. The Swiss People's party split from the Free Democrats after World War I and is mainly geared to the interests of farmers and small business, while the Independents are oriented to consumer interests. The National Action is known for its fight to reduce the number of foreign workers and foreign influence in general (In June 1990 the party was renamed Swiss Democrats). The Progressives are an extreme leftist party but, unlike the Communists, without ties to Moscow. The Liberals belong to the Free Democrat "family" but stress the importance of the free market even more. And the Evangelicals represent Protestant sects outside the Protestant state church. The remaining parties are covered in Chapter 1, on political parties in Europe at large. Note the split among the Greens in Switzerland.

Table 16 shows how, by and large, the electoral system translates voter strength proportionally into parliamentary seats. The resulting number of parties in parliament is very high, which may lead to the expectation of a very complicated process of cabinet formation. However, the opposite is true. The cabinet is elected in a joint session of both houses. The upper house, or Council of States, has only 46 members, two from each canton.* The relative

---

* Three cantons split in the past, resulting in 6 half cantons. Each of these half cantons has only one representative in the Council of States, which explains why the total number of 26 full and half cantons results in 46 instead of 52 members in the upper house.

Table 16
Voter Support and Parliamentary Seats in 1987
Election for the Swiss National Council

Party	Voter Support (%)	Seats	
		%	N
Free Democrats	22.9	25.5	51
Christian Democrats	20.0	21.0	42
Social Democrats	18.4	20.5	41
Swiss People's Party	11.0	12.5	25
Green Party	5.0	4.5	9
Independents	4.2	4.5	9
National Action	3.2	1.5	3
Liberal Party[1]	2.7	4.5	9
Automobile Party	2.6	1.0	2
Green Federation	2.3	0.5	1
Progressives	1.3	1.5	3
Communists	0.8	0.5	1
Autonomous Socialist Party	0.6	0.5	1
Alternative Greens	0.5	0.5	1
Others	4.5	1.0	2
Total	100.0	100.0	200

Source: European Journal of Political Research 16 (September 1988): 583.

[1] The relatively high number of seats received by the Liberals is due to the concentration of their votes in only a few districts.

strengths of the various parties are not very different in the joint session from those in the lower house shown in Table 16.

The size of the Swiss cabinet—seven members—is unusually small. That size was fixed by the Swiss constitution. Another specifically Swiss feature is that all seven cabinet members are of equal rank, and no one carries the title of prime minister. After the 1987 election, the party composition of the cabinet seats was as follows:

Free Democrats	2
Social Democrats	2
Christian Democrats	2
Swiss People's party	1
Total	7

This distribution corresponds exactly to party strengths in parliament. The Free Democrats, Social Democrats, and Christian Democrats are the three largest parties, with roughly equal strength. Each got two cabinet seats. The seventh seat went to the Swiss People's party, which has about half the strength of the three largest parties. None of the smaller parties received a cabinet seat. Thus, the principle of proportionality was applied: Each party was awarded cabinet seats in proportion to its parliamentary strength. This principle limits competition among parties. To be sure, they try to win as many parliamentary seats as possible. But, once parliament is elected, it is mutually agreed that each party will receive its fair share of cabinet seats, with *fair* being defined as proportionate.

In this way, cabinet formation is indeed simple. Once the results of the parliamentary election are known, it is a question of pure arithmetic as to how the cabinet seats will be distributed among the parties. No complicated maneuvers are made to change coalitions, and, unlike the situation in West Germany, small parties are unable to play a pivotal role. In Switzerland, the process of cabinet formation does not lead to clear winners and losers. Swiss cabinet formation seems dull as a spectator sport because it lacks the spirit of true competition.

Are the Swiss by nature more cooperative than others? This hypothesis must be rejected, because there was a time when the Swiss played the game of cabinet formation very competitively. For many centuries after its foundation in 1291, Switzerland was a loose federation of independent cantons. The country lacked a common executive at the national level. In the first half of the nineteenth century, Switzerland experienced a bitter fight over the issue of centralization of power. The Free Democrats advocated more centralization, while the Christian Democrats—at that time called Conservatives—fought any attempt to create a central executive. This conflict led as far as a short civil war in 1847, won by the Free Democrats. As the winners, the Free Democrats established a constitution in 1848 that provided for a national executive—the seven-member cabinet. For parliamentary elections, the winner-take-all system was chosen. In the 1848 election, the Free Democrats received a parliamentary majority and used this majority to form a cabinet consisting only of members from their own party. Election after election, greatly helped by the winner-take-all system, they renewed their majority in parliament and each time filled the cabinet posts with their own people.

A turning point came only in 1891, after nearly a half-century, when the Free Democrats still had a majority in parliament but offered one of the seven seats to the Conservatives. In 1918, the Conservatives received a second seat, with the Free Democrats still controlling the other five seats. In the same year, the winner-take-all system for parliamentary elections was changed to the current system of proportionality. The same development—from confrontation to cooperation—happened with regard to the Social Democrats, who began to gain parliamentary strength early in the twentieth century. Initially, the Social Democrats had been treated as outcasts. When they organized a general strike in 1918, the cabinet intervened with troops. This resulted in bloody clashes, and on several subsequent occasions parliament refused to accept any Social Democrats in the cabinet. The turning point came during World War II, when the first Social Democrat was allowed to join the cabinet. In 1959, the Social Democrats received a second seat, and since then the principle of proportionality has been fully implemented. The current formula of two Free Democrats, two Social Democrats, two Christian Democrats and one representative from the Swiss People's party came into effect in 1959 and has yet to be changed. A major shift in voter support would be required in order for the proportionality principle to lead to a different distribution of the seven cabinet seats.

The principle of proportionality is applied not only to political parties but also to the various linguistic and religious groups in Switzerland. The country has four official languages, with about 70 percent of the people speaking German, 20 percent, French, 10 percent, Italian, and less than 1 percent, Romansh. The three minority linguistic groups combined always have two or three seats in the cabinet, corresponding to their proportion in the population. Religiously, Switzerland is about half Protestant and half Catholic, and again the principle of proportionality is applied, with each group usually getting at least three cabinet seats.

This method of cabinet formation is not unique to Switzerland. Among the European democracies, proportional cabinet formation has also been practiced at one time or another in Austria, the Netherlands, and Belgium. Even Great Britain, the classic example of a competitive democracy, went through a period of proportionality when, during World War II, Conservatives, Labour, and Liberals together formed the cabinet. A recent example is Greece (Box 3.10), where two consecutive parliamentary elections in June and November 1989 did not lead to conclusive results. Neither of the three major parties—Conservatives, Socialists, and Communists—reached a majority of the seats in parliament. It was also impossible to form a coalition between any two of the three parties. Faced with this complete deadlock and not hoping that still another election would bring very different results, they decided that the only viable solution was a grand coalition of all three parties. However, with Greece not having a tradition of rule by grand coalition, the experiment soon came to an end. A third election within 10 months was inevitable. This time, the Conservatives won 150 of the 300 parliamentary seats, and with the help of the single deputy of a small center-right party they formed a cabinet of their own, April 1990.

_____ **BOX 3.10** _____

GRAND COALITION IN GREECE

ATHENS—Ending a two-week political crisis, the three main political parties set aside their differences today and agreed to a coalition government that will rule Greece until new elections are held in April.

After four days of difficult negotiations, the Conservatives, Socialists and Communists issued statements saying that compromise was needed to address pressing economic problems and to avoid a new election immediately. Elections have been held twice since June, and no party gained a parliamentary majority in either.

Source: New York Times, November 22, 1989.

Different terms are used when cabinet formation is based on the principle of proportionality. *Power sharing* is perhaps most widely used and has become an often discussed concept for many trouble spots around the world; for example, Lebanon, South Africa, and Northern Ireland. The argument is made that power sharing is the only hope for these countries to reach some kind of democratic stability in spite of their deep cultural divisions. Switzerland is often presented as a good model, because there the practice of power sharing seems to have allowed diverse cultural groups to live together peacefully within a single country. Could the same principle be applied to such troubled countries?

To answer that question, we must know how power sharing translates into the actual political game. Are policy outcomes in Swiss politics changed if the linguistic minorities or the Socialist party are represented in the executive cabinet? Do they have any real influence, or are they outvoted most of the time? Is power sharing merely a subtle means of repression that silences minorities? To answer these questions, we must wait for Chapter 13, where we will see how the rules described in the present chapter translate into actual decision making. For the moment, consider that power sharing offers not only benefits but also costs that might not be apparent at first glance.

SWEDEN: MINORITY CABINETS

We speak of minority cabinets when the party (or parties) forming the cabinet do not control a majority of the seats in parliament. Sweden is a good example of why minority cabinets form and how they operate. With the 1988 election, Sweden has again a minority cabinet that I will discuss in a moment. But first, I wish to turn to an episode in the late 1970s that is particularly helpful in explaining the concept of a minority cabinet.

Sweden has no upper house of parliament and is thus unicameral. The results of the 1976 elections are shown in Table 17. The distribution of seats allowed the Center, Liberal, and Conservative parties to form a winning coalition of the right together with 51.6 percent of the seats. But strain quickly developed among the three coalition partners, in particular, over the further development of nuclear power. The Conservatives advocated expansion, whereas the Center demanded a phaseout program. The Center is a specifically Swedish party that grew out of the old Agrarian party and now attracts many environmentalists. The Liberals took a middle position in this coalition conflict. The tensions between the Conservatives and the Center became so great in the fall of 1978 that the two parties came to the conclusion that they could no longer work together in the same coalition. This coalition breakup opened the possibility for a Social Democrat return to power. Because the Social Democrats took a somewhat antinuclear position, a coalition with the Center, and perhaps also with the Liberals, seemed feasible. But

Table 17
Voter Support and Parliamentary Seats in 1976
Election for the Swedish Parliament

Party	Voter Support (%)	Seats	
		%	N
Social Democrats	42.7	43.5	152
Center Party	24.0	24.6	86
Conservatives[1]	15.6	15.8	55
Liberals	11.1	11.2	39
Communists	4.8	4.9	17
Others	1.8	0.0	0
Total	100.0	100.0	349

Source: *European Journal of Political Research* 5 (September 1977): 324.

[1] Formally known as Moderate Unity Party.

the Social Democrats refused to assume governmental responsibilities, which might at first appear to be not very rational behavior.

Why would a party prefer to stay in opposition if it has the option of becoming part of the cabinet? To understand the behavior of the Social Democrats, it is important to know that the breakup of the coalition occurred only one year before the next scheduled parliamentary election (in the fall of 1979). The Social Democrats felt that their chances of winning the election would be better if they ran as an opposition, rather than as a governmental, party. The rationale for this was that the Social Democrats wished to demonstrate to the voters that the three parties of the right were unable to maintain a stable coalition. The Social Democrats would then present themselves as the only party able to govern the country in a responsible and stable way. Thus, a rational electoral strategy was behind the Social Democrats' decision to refuse any coalition arrangements before the election.

For the last year prior to the election, the Liberals formed the cabinet alone. The other parties tolerated this solution, allowing the Liberals to survive, although they were far from controlling a majority in parliament. Such a minority cabinet allows the day-to-day business of a country to continue, but no major new initiatives are possible. The term *caretaker government* expresses this situation well.

The electoral calculations of the Social Democrats were disappointed, and the three parties of the right once again won a majority in the fall 1979 election. They renewed their coalition and neutralized the nuclear issue by letting the people decide in a popular referendum. (The result of this referendum was a long-term phaseout program.) In the 1982 election, the three parties of the right lost their majority, but the Social Democrats did not get a majority either, because the Communists also got some seats.

Seats in Parliament
After 1982 Election

Social Democrats	166
Conservatives	86
Center party	56
Liberals	21
Communists	20
Total	349

As in 1978, a minority cabinet was formed, this time by the Social Democrats. They were the largest party, but with 166 seats they still were a minority in the 349-member parliament. For governing, they depended on the support, partly of the Communists, partly of the two parties in the middle. In this way, they were really able to govern and to make important decisions. Thus, they were not merely a caretaker cabinet, as was the Liberal cabinet in the year prior to the 1979 election. The Social Democratic cabinet also endured the entire legislative period until the election of 1985. This election brought only minor changes in the distribution of parliamentary seats, and the Social Democrats continued to govern as a minority cabinet for another three years. The 1988 election brought the following results:

Seats in Parliament
After 1988 Election

Social Democrats	156
Conservatives	66
Liberals	44
Center party	42
Communists	21
Greens	20
Total	349

Although the Greens made their entry into parliament, the overall parliamentary situation remained basically the same, and the Social Democrats continued to govern as a minority cabinet. If we overlook Swedish history since 1976, there were only five years (1976–1978, 1979–1982) during which the country did not have a minority cabinet, yet there was no great instability in the governing process. This does not mean that a minority cabinet may not run into difficulties in parliament and possibly collapse. Exactly this happened to the Social Democrats in February 1990, when all five opposition parties from the Communists to the Conservatives united against an economic austerity plan of the cabinet. Consequently, the cabinet had to resign; since there was no alternative cabinet feasible, the Social Democrats were able, within the same month, to form still another minority cabinet.

Minority cabinets are not unique to Sweden. In the next section we will encounter minority cabinets in Italy in a much more complex context. Even Great Britain, where normally one party wins a majority and forms the cabinet, occasionally has minority cabinets—for example, during the two periods in the mid-1970s described earlier in this chapter. When Labour won the most, but not a majority of, seats in parliament in the spring of 1974, it formed a minority cabinet until new elections were held in the fall of the same year. Labour received a narrow majority in that fall election but soon lost it again through defections and by-election defeats. Labour then entered into a pact with the Liberals, the so-called Lib-Lab pact. Under this arrangement, the two parties agreed on selected broad policy matters, and the Liberals agreed to support the cabinet in votes of confidence but held no cabinet positions.

It should be clear by now that chaos will not necessarily result if a majority coalition cannot be formed in a parliamentary system. With the formation of a minority cabinet, governmental life can continue in an orderly way for quite a while. The toleration of minority cabinets can take very different forms, ranging from tacit abstentions from votes of confidence to more formal arrangements like the British Lib-Lab pact.

ITALY: FREQUENT CABINET CRISES

We have now discussed four European democracies in which the executive cabinet is selected by parliament: Great Britain, West Germany, Switzerland, and Sweden. In each of these countries different rules govern the process of cabinet formation, yet all four countries have relatively stable executives. This finding should lead us to reject the hypothesis that selection of the executive by parliament necessarily leads to instability. Indeed, it seems that stability is possible under widely differing circumstances. By the same token, there is no guarantee that a parliamentary system leads to cabinet stability. In Europe today, Italy offers the prototypical example of high cabinet instability under a parliamentary system.

Italy has had about 50 cabinets since World War II. Two other classical cases of unstable parliamentary systems belong to the past: the Weimar Republic in Germany, which was overthrown in 1933 by the Nazis, and the Fourth Republic in France, which ended in 1958 when Charles de Gaulle established the Fifth Republic. How much longer can the parliamentary system in Italy survive? It has often been declared dead, yet it continues to limp along and may do so for a long time to come. Let us begin our analysis of Italy by looking at the parties represented in the Chamber of Deputies after the 1987 election (Table 18).

Italy uses a proportional electoral system (party list PR), so that voter strength is fairly accurately translated into parliamentary seats. The party labels generally conform to those used in the other European democracies. In Italy, however, the Socialist movement is split into two parties—the Socialists and the Social Democrats. The Italian Social Movement is patterned on Mussolini's fascist movement. The Republicans fought the monarchy when it was still an issue and simply kept the old name when the monarchy was abolished after World War II. The Radicals are an extreme

Table 18
Voter Support and Parliamentary Seats in 1987
Election to the Italian Chamber of Deputies

Party	Voter Support (%)	Seats %	Seats N
Christian Democrats	34.3	37.0	234
Communists	26.6	28.1	177
Socialists	14.3	14.9	94
Italian Social Movement	5.9	5.6	35
Republicans	3.7	3.3	21
Social Democrats	3.0	2.7	17
Radicals	2.6	2.1	13
Greens	2.5	2.1	13
Liberals	2.1	1.7	11
Proletarian Democracy	1.7	1.3	8
Venetian League	0.8	0.0	0
South Tirol People's Party	0.5	0.5	3
Lombard League	0.5	0.2	1
Sardinian Action Party	0.4	0.3	2
Piedmont Regional Autonomy	0.2	0.0	0
Piedmont	0.2	0.0	0
Val d'Aosta Union	0.1	0.2	1
Others	0.6	0.0	0
Total	100.0	100.0	630

Source: European Journal of Political Research 16 (September 1988): 580.

leftist party with a strong Green element. As seen in Chapter 1, Italy has also several regional parties.

Besides the Chamber of Deputies as the lower house of parliament, Italy also has an upper house—the Senate. The cabinet needs a separate vote of confidence in both chambers. This double vote is usually not a problem, because the party composition of the two houses tends to be very similar, with both houses elected according to the proportionality principle, although with slightly different rules. Our figures here always refer to the Chamber of Deputies but would not be very different for the Senate.

The Italian parliament has a large number of parties, but so does the Swiss parliament, and we have seen how much cabinet stability Switzerland enjoys. In contrast to Switzerland, however, Italy has strong parties at the extremes. The Neofascist Italian Social Movement has 5.6 percent of the seats in parliament. More important, the Communists get 28.1 percent of the seats. These two parties have always been excluded from cabinet positions. The argument for their exclusion is that they do not accept basic democratic principles. The game of cabinet formation, therefore, has always been limited to the moderate parties in the middle: the Christian Democrats, Liberals,

Republicans, Social Democrats, and Socialists. At first it was easy to form a majority cabinet from among this set of parties. Immediately after World War II, the Christian Democrats had close to, and at one time even slightly above, a majority in parliament. They developed into *the* governing party: Without their participation, no cabinet could be formed. The prime minister and other key ministers were always selected from the ranks of the Christian Democrats, the largest party in the cabinet.

The dominant position of the Christian Democrats turned out to be a basic weakness of the system. In a democracy, the voters should have a realistic possibility of ousting a party from power.* But in Italy, there was simply no numerical alternative to a cabinet led by the Christian Democrats, because participation in the cabinet of the Communists and Neofascists was out of the question. Whatever the election results, the prime minister was always a Christian Democrat.

It might be expected that the dominant position of the Christian Democrats would at least have the advantage of leading to cabinet stability, but the opposite was true. Cabinets were usually short-lived, and Christian Democratic prime ministers succeeded each other at brief intervals. This occurred in part because the Christian Democratic party is in fact a loose federation of several independent factions. Each faction is identified with a particular Christian Democratic leader and has a strong organization of its own. During the time of Christian Democratic dominance, cabinet formation was mainly a result of infighting among these various factions. If a faction was excluded from important cabinet posts, it maneuvered to overthrow the cabinet and replace it with a cabinet dominated by its own people. As a consequence, Italy had frequent cabinet crises despite the fact that the prime minister was always a Christian Democrat.

The composition of the cabinet changed all the time, but the game was always played among the same few leaders. These leaders were mostly Christian Democrats, but they also included some members of the smaller parties of the middle. Thus, a key actor might be prime minister in one cabinet, absent from the next one, then foreign minister, and prime minister again in still another cabinet. Depending on who prevailed in the Christian Democratic party at a particular moment, coalition partners were sought either more at the right or more at the left. The Socialists, for example, were sometimes included in the cabinet, sometimes not.

The voters eventually tired of all the cabinet changes because nothing basic really changed. Corruption also developed within the governing parties, especially the all-powerful Christian Democrats, who naturally became the scapegoat for whatever went wrong in the country. So it is not surprising that the Christian Democrats increasingly lost voter support until the prevailing system of cabinet formation broke down in 1976, when the Communists received almost as many parliamentary seats as the Christian Democrats. The distribution of seats was as follows:

---

* A functional equivalent is a strongly developed referendum like that practiced in Switzerland, where the voters have the possibility of turning down government proposals.

Christian Democrats	262	(41.6%)
Communists	228	(36.2%)
Socialists	57	(9.0%)
Italian Social Movement	35	(5.6%)
Social Democrats	15	(2.4%)
Republicans	14	(2.2%)
Liberals	5	(0.8%)
Others	14	(2.2%)
Total	630	(100.0%)

A coalition of the five center parties was numerically still possible, but the Socialists refused any further governmental participation. They were losing more and more of their voters to the Communists and felt that they could stop this defection only by changing to a position of opposition. Without the participation of the Socialists, however, there was no majority in the middle of the party spectrum. The remaining four parties—the Christian Democrats, Social Democrats, Republicans, and Liberals—did not control a majority, their combined total being only 296 seats—20 less than the necessary majority of 316. A coalition of the left involving the Communists and Socialists would have had even fewer seats and was, therefore, also not a viable alternative.

Many observers thought in 1976 that Italy's parliamentary system had come to an end. There were rumors of a possible military coup from the right. In this desperate situation, the Communists proposed the so-called historical compromise, by which they meant a grand coalition between the two largest Italian forces—the Christian Democrats and themselves. They declared that in this national emergency they were primarily Italian patriots. They also insisted that they accepted basic democratic principles.

Some factions in the Christian Democratic party were willing to accept the Communist offer. Other factions, however, claimed that the Communists could not be trusted and that any deal with them would be dangerous for Italian democracy. Finally, the historical compromise was implemented in an informal rather than formal way. The next cabinet consisted only of Christian Democrats, but it received the tacit, and later even the open, support of the Communists. The formula was similar to the Lib-Lab pact in Great Britain, which was discussed earlier in this chapter.

In return for their support, the Communists received some important chairs on parliamentary committees. More important, an ad hoc steering committee in which all important policy matters were discussed and decided was formed between Christian Democrats and Communists. Although this committee met in the parliament building, it had an informal character and lacked legal decision-making power. Decisions were still formally made in the cabinet, but the Christian Democratic cabinet ministers promised to adopt decisions reached in the steering committee.

This arrangement continued for three years, until 1979. Initially, it worked quite well, but increasingly cases arose in which the Communists complained that steering-committee decisions were changed in the course of implementation by the cabinet. As a result, the Communists demanded formal representation in the cabinet, and the Christian Democrats refused once again. The Communists at that point ended the historical compromise by returning to a position of opposition.

Again there were warnings that the parliamentary system in Italy was at its end, but a new solution was found when the Socialists were lured back to the cabinet. The Socialists demanded the prime ministership as a "prize" for their renewed participation in the cabinet. At first, the Christian Democrats refused, arguing that as the largest party they alone had the right to the prime ministership. The Socialists maneuvered skillfully, for a short time conceding the prime ministership to the Christian Democrats. Then, as an intermediate step, they accepted a decision that the prime minister be neither a Christian Democrat nor a Socialist but a member of the tiny Republican party. After the 1983 election, the Socialists finally reached their goal: Socialist Bettino Craxi gained the prime ministership. His tenure was unusually long for Italy, but his cabinet was always based on a very plastic equilibrium. This unstable situation was revealed in October 1985 during the *Achille Lauro* affair described in Box 3.11. This case illustrates nicely the usual, complicated, and hectic maneuvering during an Italian

---

BOX 3.11

ITALIAN GOVERNMENT COLLAPSES OVER THE ACHILLE LAURO AFFAIR

ROME—The coalition Government of Prime Minister Bettino Craxi collapsed Wednesday night, and Mr. Craxi was expected to resign today.

A political crisis developed earlier Wednesday when the small Republican Party of Defense Minister Giovanni Spadolini withdrew from the five-party coalition to protest the Government's handling of the hijacking of the cruise liner Achille Lauro and the release of a Palestinian leader sought by the United States.

Mr. Spadolini, the Republican Party leader, announced Wednesday afternoon that he and the two other Republicans in the Cabinet had submitted their resignations to Mr. Craxi, a Socialist.

Mr. Spadolini's party, which is generally sympathetic to both American and Israeli policies, holds 29 seats in the 630-seat Parliament. Besides the defense portfolio, it also held the Finance Ministry and the Ministry on Relations With Parliament.

Mr. Spadolini's announcement set off a storm of reaction and late-night meetings among the major coalition partners. Besides the Republicans and the Socialists, the Cabinet consists of the Christian Democrats, Italy's largest party, and the small Liberal and Social Democratic Parties. In theory, the Government would command a small majority in Parliament without the Republicans, but it seemed unlikely that the coalition could carry on in its current form.

Source: New York Times October 17, 1985.

cabinet crisis. In this particular instance, Craxi succeeded himself as prime minister. After his resignation, no alternative was in sight, and Craxi formed a new cabinet with exactly the same five parties as before. But several months later, in the summer of 1986, Craxi had to resign again, because he lost a vote of confidence—some Christian Democrats had voted with the opposition parties. Once again, however, Craxi succeeded himself, but this time he had to concede that in March 1987 he would turn over the prime ministership to a Christian Democrat.

As might be expected in Italian politics, in March 1987 the transition from Craxi to a Christian Democrat did not go smoothly at all. Craxi found excuses for considering the accord of the previous summer as not binding. Unwilling to yield but having lost the support of the Christian Democrats, Craxi could block the system so that there would be no alternative but to have early parliamentary elections. Craxi's calculation was to profit as early as possible from the popularity he gained as prime minister. And, indeed, when early elections were held in June 1987 (Table 18), the Socialists of Bettino Craxi increased their parliamentary seats from 73 to 95. Having reached this goal, the Socialists were now willing to support a Christian Democrat, Giovanni Goria, as prime minister. He formed a cabinet with the same five parties as Craxi before him.

By November of the same year, however, Goria resigned, because the Liberals left the cabinet over a budget issue (Box 3.12). As can be seen from

---

_____ **BOX 3.12** _____

ITALY CABINET FALLS AS SMALL PARTY QUITS COALITION OVER DEFICIT ISSUE

ROME—The 15-week-old Government of Prime Minister Giovanni Goria resigned today after the small Liberal Party withdrew from the governing coalition in a dispute over measures to reduce the huge budget deficit.

Senior politicians said it was unclear whether a quick solution would be found by forming a new government without the Liberals or whether Italy faced a long political crisis that would produce major leadership changes.

The Goria Government collapsed just as it was trying to contend with a looming economic crisis, a wave of labor unrest and the establishment of an Italian naval presence in the Persian Gulf.

The Liberals, who won only 2.1 percent of the vote in national elections in June . . . announced on Friday night that they would withdraw from the five-party coalition. The decision followed a week of negotiations aimed at resolving differences over the Government's finance bill.

At issue was a revision of the bill that eliminated a proposed income tax cut to help lower the Government's deficit. The Liberals maintained that the coalition's basic agreement on policy envisioned deficit reduction through cutting spending rather than increasing revenues.

Source: New York Times, November 15, 1987.

_____ **BOX 3.13** _____

ITALIAN COALITION REVIVED WITH LIMITED MANDATE

ROME—Greeted by applause mingled with cries of "Shame, shame," Italy's 47th postwar government was resurrected Thursday night with a limited mandate.

Parliament gave Prime Minister Giovanni Goria's five-party coalition a 364-208 vote of confidence although Goria, 44, had told the chamber, "We all know it would have been more convenient for me and my ministers to step down."

Source: The News and Observer, Raleigh, N.C., February 19, 1988.

Table 18, Goria would still have mastered a majority in parliament without the small Liberal Party, but he nevertheless preferred to resign. A few days later, he was able to put together another cabinet, again with the same five parties. The Liberals, having gained some concessions, were willing to reenter the cabinet. Three months later, in February 1988, Goria resigned over still another issue but could again revive the old coalition (Box 3.13). However, a month later Goria had to resign a third time (Box 3.14); this time he was succeeded by another Christian Democrat, Ciriaco De Mita, who was still ruling with the same five parties. De Mita endured more than a year without a cabinet crisis, but on May 19, 1989, his cabinet collapsed too. After a government crisis of 64 days, Giulio Andreotti, another Christian Democrat, was sworn in as the 49th prime minister, still heading a coalition of the same five parties. Andreotti, 70 years old, had already been prime minister five times before. He illustrates well that in Italian cabinet formation, the more things change, the more they remain the same. As political scientist Sabino Cassese states in Box 3.15, the Italian system of cabinet formation is so fluid that it could "be written on water": Despite all the changes of the water, the water itself always remains the same. This is particularily true of the partici-

_____ **BOX 3.14** _____

YOUNG ITALIAN PREMIER RESIGNS FOR A THIRD TIME

ROME—Premier Giovanni Goria announced his resignation Friday as the leader of Italy's 47th postwar government, a shaky coalition battered by seven months of political infighting.

It was the third time since taking office in August that Goria, a Christian Democrat, had announced that he was quitting.

Source: The News and Observer, Raleigh, N.C., March 12, 1988.

_____ **BOX 3.15** _____

ITALY'S SYSTEM OF GOVERNMENT

Italy's system of government can be said to be written on water, for it is a highly fluid system. . . .

The system has obvious weaknesses, the first of which derives from the fact that the leadership exercised is more the result of mediation among factions, pressure groups, and parties, than the result of elaboration, promotion, and planning by responsible and expert ministry officials. . . . The Italian system is more suited to reaching agreement about problems as they gradually emerge than to ensuring positive guidance and direction. Consequently, coordination has been replaced by institutionalized political bargaining.

Source: Sabino Cassese, "Is There a Government in Italy? Politics and Administration at the Top," in Richard Rose and Ezra N. Suleiman, eds., *Presidents and Prime Ministers* (Washington, D.C.: American Enterprise Institute, 1980), p. 201.

pation of the Christian Democrats in the cabinet for which there has not been a single exception since World War II. The Christian Democrats will stay in office as long as there is no viable alternative. Thus, Italy continues a stalemate in which it is impossible to push the Christian Democrats out of office. The only scenario that would allow a real turnover in office involves a cabinet of the Left. After the 1987 election, the Communists and the Socialists together have obtained 43.0 percent of the seats in parliament. If one adds the smaller parties of the Left, such as the Radicals and the Greens, a coalition of the Left would come quite close to 50 percent.

Would the United States tolerate a Communist prime minister in Italy? In the past they did not and exercised heavy pressure that such an event would not occur. With the new developments in the Soviet Union and Eastern Europe, all this may change in the future.

_____ **FRANCE: DUAL EXECUTIVE** _____

The present French constitution of the Fifth Republic was established in 1958 by Charles de Gaulle, one of the dominant figures in modern French history (photo, page 137). The preceding Fourth Republic had a parliamentary form of government, with the parliament electing the prime minister and the cabinet. Much like Italy today, the Fourth Republic was very unstable and had frequent cabinet crises. The country also suffered from internal conflict over its involvement in colonial wars in Indochina and Algeria. In 1958, the turmoil was so great that it was no longer possible to form a viable cabinet. De Gaulle stepped in. In 1940, he had escaped the German occupa-

Charles de Gaulle. (Courtesy Embassy of France, Bern, Switzerland.)

tion to London, where he organized the Resistance movement. Returning to France in triumph in 1944, he served briefly as head of the government, but soon, disgusted by the bickering among the many parties, he retreated to his small hometown, Colombey-les-Deux-Eglises, to await the hour when he could emerge as the savior of France.

Unlike other strong leaders in French history, de Gaulle did not establish a dictatorship. However, he changed the political institutions so much that his coming to power in 1958 was counted as the beginning of the Fifth Republic. He built a government that was between a presidential and a parliamentary system, with both a president and a prime minister. De Gaulle thought that such a dual executive would serve him well. Since the retirement of de Gaulle, the relation between president and prime minister has greatly changed, but now let us see what the relation was under de Gaulle himself. As president, he liked to handle the big questions, leaving the routine day-to-day work to the prime minister. The president was elected by an electoral college and, after 1962, directly by the people. To be popularly elected corresponded to de Gaulle's leadership style. He did not want to depend on party politicians in parliament, whom he detested for their lack of vision. De Gaulle liked to enter into a dialogue directly with the French people, who in his view had more common sense than ordinary politicians. De Gaulle saw himself as France's father figure, looking after his countrymen. If he explained what had to be done in the higher national interest to the men and women of France, he was sure they would trust and follow him. De Gaulle believed strongly that his special personal mission was to restore the past greatness of France.

De Gaulle held office from 1958 to 1969, and, during those years, he acted in many ways like a powerful monarch. Many important decisions were made by him alone, and some critics raised the question whether France was still a democracy. A bothersome issue was (and still remains) the fact that the president is elected for a very long term—seven years—and can run for reelection as many times as he wishes. Is seven years too long a period for a president to govern without any opportunity for the people to hold him accountable?

Another distinguishing characteristic of the early years of the Fifth Republic was the importance attached to the popular referendum. At first sight, this might seem to increase the democratic quality of the regime. In Chapter 7, we will indeed see how in some European countries the referendum is used to strengthen the political role of the people. But, under the rules of the Fifth Republic, the referendum primarily strengthens the presidency. De Gaulle used this instrument several times to bypass parliament and appeal directly to the citizens. Critical observers made comparisons with Napoleon I and Napoleon III, who had both used the referendum to strengthen their personal power. In their cases, the plebiscitary nature of their regimes was spoken of negatively. Is it democratic if a leader seeks legitimacy for a decision by getting approval in a plebiscite? Or is there a danger of demagogy in the sense that the leader can manipulate the people?

Another issue that raised questions about the democratic nature of the Fifth Republic was that in its early years parliament had virtually no power. In contrast to the Fourth Republic, the prime minister was not selected by parliament but was appointed by the president. Under de Gaulle, the prime minister served completely at the pleasure of the president, who could dismiss him at any time. The role of parliament was very limited. Sometimes a new cabinet sought the approval of parliament, but such approval was not necessary. Under de Gaulle, parliament also had few legislative powers, because the president often ruled by executive decrees requiring no parliamentary approval. With regard to the relationship between the president and the prime minister, all essential power lay with the former. The prime minister had to do whatever the president did not wish to do himself. This system was tailored to the personal needs of de Gaulle, who saw himself as a world leader and liked to concentrate his attention on the big questions of foreign policy and defense. He left the day-to-day business, and especially contact with parliament, to the prime minister.

In the first years of the Fifth Republic, de Gaulle was very popular and much admired. The French people were grateful that he saved the country from the chaos of the Fourth Republic and restored order. De Gaulle fulfilled the longing for a strong leader, as Napoleon I had after the French Revolution; Napoleon III, after the revolution of 1848; and Marshal Pétain, after France's defeat in 1940. But unlike his predecessors, de Gaulle was not a true dictator. To be sure, he eliminated many checks and balances from the system. Ultimately, he was responsible only to the people. Some feared that this was empty rhetoric and that de Gaulle would secure his reelection by manipulation, but this fear was unjustified. When his first term was over, de Gaulle sought reelection in a free and open competition. His main adversary was Socialist François Mitterrand, the current president of France (see photo

François Mitterrand. (Courtesy Embassy of
France, Bern, Switzerland.)

above). Mitterrand and several other candidates forced de Gaulle into a
runoff, which de Gaulle won with 54.5 percent against 45.5 percent for
Mitterrand.

This margin was much less than the one de Gaulle had received in 1959,
when he was awarded almost 80 percent of the vote in the electoral college
(which consisted of about 80,000 delegates, mainly local councilmen). In the
referenda before 1965, support for de Gaulle's proposals had varied between
60 and 90 percent. But, by the election of 1965, many Frenchmen felt that de
Gaulle had restored order and thus fulfilled his role. After his narrow victory
in 1965, much of de Gaulle's charismatic attraction was lost. In May 1968, he
was openly challenged by a massive student revolt in Paris. In the following
year, he tried to restore his prestige with a referendum on regional reform
and reorganization of the Senate, the upper house of parliament. De Gaulle
hoped that these reforms would be popular and that an overwhelming
approval by the people would again enhance the legitimacy of his regime.
But he was disappointed when the referendum was defeated by a majority of
53.2 percent. De Gaulle had seen enough and, although he was legally not
required to do so, he resigned from the presidency and retired to his small
hometown, deeply hurt.

Can the Fifth Republic survive without de Gaulle, or is its constitution
tailored too much to its founder and first president? Since 1969, France has

had three presidents, and the Fifth Republic is still intact. The presidency is still the most powerful institution in France, although not as much as in the early years of de Gaulle. But, since de Gaulle, other institutions—in particular parliament and the prime ministership—have been strengthened, so that today the system has more checks and balances than when de Gaulle was at the height of his power.

The long, seven-year term of the presidency has remained the same. There have been some discussions about reducing the length of the presidential term, but these have gone nowhere. It is noteworthy that the current president, Socialist François Mitterrand, sharply opposed the notion of a strong presidency when he was in opposition; but in office himself now, Mitterrand has not seriously pursued the idea of weakening the presidency and, in particular, reducing the term of office. He obviously enjoys the ceremonial trappings and substantive power of the office, and at times he himself is criticized for being a quasi-monarchical president.

What *has* been reduced since the time of de Gaulle is the plebiscitary nature of the presidency. The last referendum was organized by de Gaulle's immediate successor, Georges Pompidou, in 1972. Since that time, no president has thus appealed directly to the people. In 1984, Mitterrand attempted unsuccessfully to use the referendum when the issue of public subsidies to Catholic schools was blocked in parliamentary maneuvers. But he gave up the idea of the referendum when he realized that he lacked the necessary charismatic appeal to guarantee its outcome. In the end, he chose to work out a compromise with parliament. This episode indicates that the French president is no longer in a class by himself, far above ordinary politicians, as de Gaulle was. He has become one among several top leaders, although still holding the most powerful office.

That the president has been brought down to earth can also be seen in his relationship with the prime minister. Unlike under de Gaulle, it is no longer one of master and servant. The prime minister enjoys a reputation in his own right.

The most ambivalent feature of the Fifth Republic is the relationship between prime minister and parliament. What happens if parliament is of a different political orientation than the president? It was only in 1986 that such a situation actually occurred. Before, parliament was always of the same political orientation as the president. Up to 1986, there were four parties in parliament: the Socialists, the Communists, the Rally for the Republic (RPR), and the Union for French Democracy (UDF). The latter two parties are specific to France and need explanation. The RPR was founded by de Gaulle and is still often called the Gaullist party. It has changed its name several times and was originally Rally for the French People. As we have seen, de Gaulle was in principle opposed to the notion of political parties, which he considered divisive, but he had to establish a party organization in order to compete in elections. He hoped to rally all Frenchmen of goodwill to his party, to which he gave the most general label possible. Who would not stand for the ''French People''? De Gaulle was indeed successful in bringing together most people who had supported the many parties of the right in the

Fourth Republic. The program of the Gaullist party was always vague: The party was held together by its leader's charisma, and in the RPR today the heritage and mythos of de Gaulle are still of great importance.

The UDF was founded in the 1970s by the second president after de Gaulle, Valéry Giscard d'Estaing, and its supporters are therefore often called Giscardists. Giscard d'Estaing was a supporter of de Gaulle but later felt the need for his own party organization in order not to be too constrained by de Gaulle's heritage. Compared to the RPR, the UDF is generally located more to the middle.

Up to 1981, RPR and UDF had together a majority in the National Assembly, the lower house of parliament.* Therefore, the selection of the prime minister by the president—at the time always from the political right—did not encounter any serious opposition in parliament.

With the 1981 election, the parties of the right lost the majority in parliament for the first time in the history of the Fifth Republic (see Table 6 in Chapter 2). A few weeks before, Mitterrand had won the popular election to the presidency. Confronted with a parliament dominated by the Right, he immediately called early parliamentary elections, which the Left won. It was no problem, therefore, for Mitterrand to appoint Pierre Mauroy, a trusted Socialist friend, as prime minister. In order to demonstrate the unity of the Left, the Socialists also invited the Communists to participate in the cabinet, although such participation was not necessary numerically to establish a parliamentary majority. The Communists accepted the invitation and received four relatively unimportant ministries.

Three years later, in 1984, two important changes occurred in the cabinet. Mitterrand replaced Mauroy, who seemed exhausted, with another Socialist, Laurent Fabius, an energetic young man still in his thirties. The other change was that the Communists decided to leave the cabinet because they were unwilling to support the Socialists' policy of economic austerity. This move by the Communists did not change the fact that the Socialists still had a majority in parliament.

But this Socialist dominance changed with the parliamentary election of March 1986. Although still the largest party in parliament, the Socialists lost their absolute majority. The combined strength of the two parties of the Right—the RPR and the UDF—was also short of an absolute majority. The new element in 1986, as we have seen in Chapter 2, was the entry of the Neofascist National Front to parliament with 6 percent of the seats. Since neither the Left nor the Right was willing to enter a coalition with the National Front, parliament was nearly deadlocked. But RPR and UDF managed to gain the support of some regional splinter parties and thus gained a shaky majority in parliament. Confronted with this situation, Mitterrand chose to invite Jacques Chirac, leader of the RPR, to form the new cabinet.

---

* The French Senate as the upper house of the National Assembly merely has a delaying power. It is elected by an electoral college in which small communities are heavily overrepresented. The Senate plays no role in the selection of the prime minister.

This was the first time in the history of the Fifth Republic that the president and the prime minister had come from opposite ends of the party spectrum.

This system of a president of the Left and a prime minister of the Right was called *cohabitation*. Although there were fears of a constitutional crisis and even of a breakdown of the Fifth Republic, cohabitation worked relatively smoothly. It came to an end in 1988, when Mitterrand was reelected to a second seven-year term as president. He immediately called early parliamentary elections, which brought to the RPR and the UDF and its small allies the loss of the parliamentary majority (see Table 8 in Chapter 2). The Socialists could increase their parliamentary representation, even if they did not reach a majority. Mitterrand selected Socialist Michel Rocard as prime minister, who formed a minority cabinet, finding support partly from the Communists and partly from members of the UDF. Support from the latter side was facilitated by an internal crisis of the UDF, in which factional splits developed. One of these factions even created its own parliamentary group, the Christian Democratic Union of the Center. It remains unclear which exactly will be the parties of the Right entering the next parliamentary election.

In conclusion, we can say that the dual executive, which was so much tailored to the needs of de Gaulle, survived its creator remarkably well. The Fifth Republic is here to stay for some time. Its institutions have been able to adapt to the socioeconomic modernization and the value changes in French society.

CABINET FORMATION IN EASTERN EUROPE

East Germany

About a month after the East German parliamentary election—a relatively short period of time—parliament convened and was able to select a cabinet. It consisted of a coalition of five parties: the Christian Democratic Union, the Social Democratic Party, the German Social Union, the Alliance of Free Democrats, and Democratic Awakening. The ministerial positions were distributed pretty much according to the numerical strength of the individual parties in parliament (see Table 11 on page 89). The Christian Democrats as the largest party received 11 seats, including the prime ministership, which went to Lothar de Maizière. The Social Democrats as the second largest party could fill 7 ministerial positions, including the foreign ministry. Three ministries went to the Free Democrats, two to the German Social Union, and one ministry to Democratic Awakening. This five-party coalition was broadly based, having the support of 301 of the 400-member parliament. According to the terms used earlier in the chapter, this was a grand coalition, containing more parties than necessary to win. Remarkably absent from the coalition were the Communists, who now called themselves the Party of Democratic Socialism. From the beginning of the coalition negotiations, it was clear that no other party was willing to enter a coalition with the Communists; everyone tried to keep a safe distance from the old rulers.

Besides the Communists, the theme of the coalition negotiations was inclusion and not exlusion. On the eve of the election, the Christian Democrats invited the Social Democrats to participate in the cabinet, yet such participation would not have been necessary from a numerical point of view. The Christian Democrats, together with the German Social Union and Democratic Awakening, with whom they worked together in the election campaign (see page 90–91), would have had 192 seats. Adding the Free Democrats, with whom the Christian Democrats had a coalition in Bonn (see page 117–122), would have resulted in a comfortable majority of 213 seats.

Why then did the Christian Democrats reach out to the Social Democrats? Why did they attempt to enter into a grand coalition and not a minimal winning coalition? The explanation can be nicely derived from what we said earlier in the chapter and from what will follow in Chapter 13. Attempts to share power are most likely to occur in crisis situations—for example, in Great Britain during World War II. In a crisis situation, governing means imposing burdens on the population, and East Germany in the spring of 1990 was certainly in an economic crisis situation. Although unification with West Germany promised hope, massive problems like sudden high unemployment had to be anticipated. Under these conditions, it was rational for the Christian Democrats to share the burdens of governing with the Social Democrats as the second largest party. Why were the Social Democrats willing to cooperate and to share in the costs of governing? A refusal on their part would have meant even higher costs, because the voters would have labeled them spoilers who were unwilling to shoulder their responsibilities in hard times.

In addition to this general argument, there is also a more technical argument for the formation of a grand coalition, namely the requirement of a two-third majority for constitutional changes. Such changes were necessary for the process of German unification. Yet, it would have been perfectly possible for the Social Democrats to stay outside the cabinet and still to vote in parliament for the constitutional changes. However, preference was given to include the Social Democrats already in the cabinet. Overall, East Germany is a good example of how politicians in a crisis situation see the need for a grand coalition. For East Germany, the political scene had completely changed between the fall of 1989 and the spring of 1990. Whereas in the fall of 1989 the two dominant forces were the Communists and the dissident movement, New Forum, six months later political parties that were inspired and often directly guided by their West German counterparts dominated the scene. The steps toward German unification taken by the new East German cabinet will be discussed in Chapter 16.

Hungary

Whereas in East Germany the cabinet was formed with the purpose of making itself redundant as soon as possible in the process of German unification, Hungary needed a cabinet to govern the country on a permanent basis. These were more normal circumstances, and, as a consequence, the cabinet was also formed in a more normal way. As we have seen in Chapter 2,

Democratic Forum won the most seats, with 165 out of a total 386. This was not enough to form the cabinet alone, but, as is customary in a parliamentary system, Democratic Forum as the biggest party was allowed to put together a coalition. Not surprisingly, Democratic Forum allied itself with the Independent Smallholders' party and the Christian Democratic People's party, which are both ideologically close to the Democratic Forum (see pages 91–94). Together the three parties had a 59 percent majority in parliament. This coalition was slightly oversized, because even without the Christian Democrats the two other parties would have had enough votes to win the vote of confidence in parliament. Apparently, however, there was a desire to have a comfortable majority.

Why was there not a grand coalition, as in East Germany? This possibility was considered in Hungary, too, but ultimately it was decided that the Free Democrats as the second largest party should play the role of a strong opposition. However, the Free Democrats were not excluded from power altogether; as a gesture of goodwill, the governing parties were willing to elect a Free Democrat as president of parliament. They chose Arpad Göncz, a respected writer, who had severely suffered under the Communists. In return for this election, the Free Democrats pledged to cooperate from the opposition benches on a series of laws that required a two-thirds parliamentary majority. Later, parliament elected Göncz to the ceremonial position of president of the country. All in all, transition of power from the Communists to the new government was practically without flaws. The Socialist party, as the Communists were now called, yielded power without major problems and began to play the role of opposition in parliament.

Romania

With the overwhelming election victory of Ion Iliescu and his National Salvation Front (page 95–98), no coalition negotiations were necessary to form a cabinet. Iliescu and his government simply stayed in power. They were now greatly strengthened because they had a popular mandate, and this was in spite of all the irregularities in the election. Had Romania become a true democracy? This is less certain. It was still basically a one-party country, and there were no opposition parties of any strength. This was partly due to the intimidation tactics of the National Salvation Front. But it must also be recognized that the political culture of the country was not ready to accept a true multiparty system. Most Romanians still liked a single strong leader, although a more benign one than the ousted Ceausescu. Iliescu seemed to correspond to such an image. It remains to be seen how he will use his power, especially considering his Communist past.

The first indications are that Iliescu will not have much tolerance for dissenters. When, in protest against his regime, students occupied the university square, Iliescu chased away the students with brutal methods. In addition to the police and the military, Iliescu called in miners who were particularily crushing against the demonstrators (see Box 3.16).

BOX 3.16

ROMANIAN MINERS, CALLED BY ILIESCU,
ATTACK PROTESTERS

BUCHAREST—Thousands of coal miners responded to a call for help in putting down anti-government protests by streaming into Bucharest on Thursday, clubbing people and ransacking opposition party offices.

The miners flocked to the capital in response to an appeal from President Ion Iliescu for support in crushing anti-government violence.

Carrying clubs and wearing helmets with their lamps lighted, the miners surged at dawn into Magheru Boulevard, the main area of anti-government protests and street fighting on Wednesday.

The miners, estimated to number 10,000, took over central Bucharest, hunting for anti-government protesters, checking identities and manhandling people they suspected. Onlookers saw them beat up several people and march them to police stations.

Health Ministry officials said that five persons had been killed and 277 wounded in the violence, which began on Wednesday. The clashes were the worst in Romania since the revolution in December that toppled the Communist dictator, Nicolae Ceausescu.

Source: International Herald Tribune, June 15, 1990.

Poland

As we saw in Chaper 1, Poland was the first country in Eastern and Central Europe to have a non-Communist prime minister—Tadeusz Mazowiecki of the Solidarity movement, who took office in the summer of 1989. But the Communists kept some important power, in particular the presidency under Wojciech Jaruzelski. This arrangement was the outcome of complex negotiations between the Communists and Solidarity. During 1990, Poland fell behind other countries in the process of democratization. Its first completely free parliamentary elections are not scheduled until 1993; thus, the parliament elected in 1989 remains in office. As we have seen, the 1989 elections were only partly free, because the Communists reserved two-thirds of the seats for themselves. That Solidarity won all remaining seats was a big moral victory but did not allow control of parliament. This situation at the national level did not change when completely free elections took place in May 1990 at the local level, with a big victory for Solidarity and catastrophic results for the Communists (see Chapter 2).

Poland is extremely difficult to govern in this lingering period of transition, especially given its bad economic situation. It is unclear who exactly has a mandate to exercise power. Does president Jaruzelski still have any power, and what is the basis of such power after the total defeat of the Communists in the local elections? What is the power base of Prime Minister Mazowiecki?

––––––––––––––––––––––––––––– BOX 3.17 –––––––––––––––––––––––––––––

SPLIT IN SOLIDARITY

A result of the split in Solidarity can be seen most afternoons on the floor of the Sejm, or parliament. There, a centerpiece of the government's renewal effort—a bill on privatization of state industry—is being amended again and again. Twelve times, at last count.

The government's economists want to sell off state property to anyone, including foreigners, on a first-come, first-served basis. But a powerful left-leaning wing in the Solidarity parliamentary caucus insists on giving factory workers the first crack at owning their plants.

Source: International Herald Tribune, June 1, 1990.

His Solidarity movement is badly split, in particular over economic issues, as vividly illustrated in Box 3.17. While key government economists try to give the country a free-market shock therapy, a more leftist wing in Solidarity wishes to proceed more cautiously. The founder of Solidarity, Lech Walesa, seems to support this leftist wing and emphasizes that a main goal of Solidarity is the protection of the workers. In May 1990, when the railroad workers organized a general strike, Walesa declared their wage demands "just." Thus, Poland had an ironic situation wherein workers struck against a government headed by their own trade union. Walesa decided to stay out of government, not even taking a seat in parliament. As head of Solidarity, he has his own power base, and it is not yet clear for what purpose he wishes to use it. At one time, he called for early parliamentary and presidential elections and hinted at the possibility that he might be a candidate for the presidency. But immediately afterward he denied any such intentions. It would probably benefit Poland if free national elections took place as soon as possible, to clarify the overall power situation. For the time being, Poland remains in a difficult transitional period.

Czechoslovakia

In Czechoslovakia, cabinet formation was easy because Civic Forum (and its counterpart in Slovakia) had gained 58 percent of the parliamentary seats (see Table 14, page 102). Although Civic Forum could have formed the cabinet alone, it entered a coalition with the Christian Democrats. Left outside the cabinet were the Communists and the three ethnically based parties. Václav Havel was confirmed by parliament as president, the ceremonial head of state. Having received 82 percent of the votes, Havel said, "I would not have felt at ease if I would have been elected like my predecossors with 100 percent of the votes." With this statement, Havel aptly stressed that his country had entered the normalcy of democracy.

Bulgaria

In contrast to Czechoslovakia, Bulgaria is still far from the normalcy of democracy. Like Romania, Bulgaria has great difficulties in establishing a legitimate government. As we have seen in Chapter 2, the two countries have something in common: the Communists could stay in power, although under new name—in Romania as the National Salvation Front, in Bulgaria as the Socialist party. Many Bulgarians are not willing to accept the election results, and there are frequent clashes between demonstrators and police. In August 1990, the crisis went so far that the headquarters of the Socialist party were stormed and set on fire.

In one respect, the Socialists have yielded to the main opposition party, the Union of Democratic Forces, in the election by parliament of the president, the ceremonial head of state. A two-thirds majority is necessary for election. The Socialists, lacking such a majority, were willing, after much maneuvering, to accept Schelju Scheleff, a man of the opposition. But this election does not change the fact that the Socialists control parliament and therefore still have all essential power.

Little Attraction for Westminster Model

The British tend to consider their Westminster model (pages 109–116) as the classical form of democracy. It is interesting to note that this model had little attraction in the early phase of democratization in Central and Eastern Europe. In no country has a governing system emerged with one large party in government and another large party in opposition; nor can one expect a regular rotation in government between these two large parties in any country. It is more likely that the Central and Eastern European countries will develop democracies with a multitude of parties that must form coalitions. Some of these coalitions may be of a minimal winning size, but there are indications that oversized coalitions may also frequently occur. A fascinating new field for students of cabinet formation!

4

JUDICIAL REVIEW

Judicial review means that the courts, as the third branch of government, have the right to overturn as unconstitutional decisions of the two other branches of government. In the United States, judicial review has generally greater importance than in Europe. There are even some European countries where the courts have no rights of judicial review at all; for example, Great Britain and Switzerland. In Britain it is parliament and in Switzerland, the people that decide whether a law or act corresponds to constitutional requirements. We will deal with these two countries first, and the Federal Republic of Germany will serve as a European example of a strongly developed judicial review.

With regard to the courts, the issue of judicial review has the greatest political importance. As with judicial review, other aspects of the court system, too, vary greatly among European democracies. The court system in Great Britain, for example, is based on common law, whereas in continental European countries code law prevails. With common law, traditions have high importance and judges continually reinterpret old precedents in the light of new circumstances. Code law derives from the Roman legal tradition and is characterized by complex bodies of categories and subcategories. With very specific codes, the courts have limited discretion in handling particular cases. Under common law the legal profession is considered more as an art; under code law, as a science.

Looking even more specifically into the court systems, the variation within Europe is enormous. Whether and how much juries are used, for example, depends on the country, and in federal countries such as Switzerland, even on the regional units. The same is true for the appointment and election of judges, their length of tenure, the rights of defendants, and so on. In the present context, we cannot address such specific variations. Instead, we shall focus on the key political issue of judicial review.

GREAT BRITAIN

Some American readers will be surprised to learn that the British have no written constitution in the sense of a single document. British political institutions, practices, and civil liberties have evolved over many centuries. Some of the resulting rules are codified; others exist only as unwritten customs and conventions. Even the most fundamental laws have no special status and can therefore be changed by Parliament just like any other laws. Great Britain is said, therefore, to have an unwritten constitution.

In their daily work, the courts apply the law to specific cases, but they have no right to say whether a law is constitutional or not. Questions of constitutionality rest in the hands of parliament. Does this lack of judicial review by the courts lead to an arbitrary regime? Is there a danger that the majority in Parliament will abuse its power to rewrite and reinterpret the constitutional rules according to its own selfish interests? Where are the checks and balances in this system? These are troublesome questions for someone accustomed to the American system.

The British system is based on a very different philosophy of government. In Great Britain, the main task of the voters is to elect Parliament, which alone has the legitimate right to express the will of the people. Since the people give full power to Parliament, it would be illogical according to British tradition for a high court to check the actions of Parliament. These checks are made by the people in the next election. If the majority in Parliament interprets the constitution against the wishes of the people, the voters can replace the governing party with the party in opposition.

Does this system run the risk that one day a governing party might restrict democratic freedoms or even cancel future elections? In other words, what prevents a governing party from establishing a dictatorship? The answer is not a supreme court but a commonly accepted political culture. The British system is based on the assumption that everyone accepts certain basic rules of the game. One such rule is that free elections take place at regular intervals. There are also many commonly accepted rules concerning the protection of individual freedoms, some of which go back to medieval times. The British assume that no governing party will ever dare to touch these fundamental rules. Thus, the stability of the system is ultimately based on an element of fair play.

Given the fact that some basic rules will never be changed, it is up to Parliament to take whatever actions it sees fit. Thus, Parliament could establish the death penalty or nationalize key industries, and no court could intervene with the argument that these measures violate the constitution. Parliament is sovereign, and it alone can say what is constitutional. For many American observers, this lack of judicial review is appalling, as witnessed by the report of the *New York Times* correspondent in Box 4.1. To be sure, the report deals with an extreme case—the unrest in Northern Ireland—but the correspondent is correct in believing that even in such an extreme case an American president could not curtail civil liberties as Margaret Thatcher did. It is also interesting to note that the British are not as concerned as the American correspondent was, and a distinguished British jurist apparently told the American visitor that Great Britain " 'is a bloody free country indeed.' "

Which is the better system? One could argue that the voters have greater influence in Great Britain, because they can replace the governing party with the opposition, thereby hoping to reverse earlier decisions of Parliament. Such reversals took place with regard to the nationalization of certain indus-

BOX 4.1

AMERICAN JOURNALIST APPALLED BY LACK OF JUDICIAL REVIEW IN BRITAIN

If they had occurred in the United States, measures taken by the Government in recent weeks to deal with violence and terrorism in Northern Ireland and revise the Official Secrets Act would have provoked a major confrontation with the Supreme Court or required a constitutional convention.

But there is no such threat on the horizon for Prime Minister Margaret Thatcher, whose Government has had a parliamentary majority of about 100 seats since the 1987 election. Under the unwritten British constitution, there is virtually no limit on what a government with a strong majority in Parliament can do. . . .

In Britain, no Fifth Amendment protects a defendant from being compelled "to be a witness against himself." So earlier in the fall, the Thatcher Government could simply decree that in Northern Ireland, the courts may take a negative view of any defendant who chooses not to cooperate with the police or take the stand in his own defense, not just in terrorism cases but in all criminal trials. . . .

No First Amendment prohibits Parliament from "abridging the freedom of speech or of the press." The Thatcher Government has prohibited taped or broadcast interviews not only with members of the I.R.A. and other banned terrorist groups, but also with Sinn Fein, which supports the I.R.A., from the British airwaves. And on Nov. 30 it introduced legislation revising the Official Secrets Act of 1911, forbidding any present or former member of the British security or intelligence services to disclose anything at all about them without authorization. . . .

Many Britons who think about constitutional issues at all view their own flexible, unwritten system as being more up-to-date than the American Constitution, written in the 18th century to guard against dangers they feel no longer exist. And, as one distinguished jurist said this week, "It is a bloody free country indeed."

Source: New York Times, December 11, 1988.

tries nationalized by Labour only to be denationalized by the Conservatives. With this system, the will of the majority of the people can be quickly translated into political action. In the United States, Supreme Court decisions are less open to the influence of the voters. Voters in the United States can only vote for a particular presidential candidate in the hope that, if elected, he will have the chance to appoint new judges. But sometimes the composition of the Supreme Court does not change very much over many years. Under such circumstances, the Court may be unresponsive to the immediate wishes of the people. On the other hand, although this system appears less democratic, it has the advantage of giving more continuity to the law of the land. Who then should be watchdog for the constitution: parliament, which is directly accountable to the people, or judges, who are more detached and insulated from popular pressures?

SWITZERLAND

In contrast to Great Britain, Switzerland does have a single document that serves as its constitution, but, like Britain, Swiss courts do not have the right to determine whether a particular law is constitutional or not. In the Swiss case, this decision is ultimately made by the people in a referendum. Thus, the Swiss go a step further than the British in giving authority over constitutional questions, not merely to the representatives of the people, but to the people themselves. Most Swiss believe that in a true democracy the most vital decisions must be made not by judges or members of parliament but by citizens. Are the voters mature and legally educated enough to decide complex constitutional issues? Switzerland is an ideal case for examining this question.

How is the Swiss government organized so that the voters can decide questions of constitutionality? First, voters have the right to call for a popular referendum on every bill decided by parliament. The only requirement is that 50,000 signatures be obtained, which is relatively easy, even in a small country of 6 million inhabitants. There are many motives for calling a referendum on a particular bill, but one possible reason is that some voters may feel that the bill violates the constitution. It is then up to the majority of all voters to decide whether this is so. A bill is enacted into law only if no referendum is called or if it is accepted in the popular vote.

The voters also have the final say on constitutional amendments. All constitutional amendments decided by parliament must be submitted to the voters; in this case, no signatures are required for a referendum to take place. If, on the other hand, a group of voters collects 100,000 signatures, they can submit a constitutional amendment of their own, which will first be debated by parliament but finally decided in a popular referendum. This instrument, the popular constitutional initiative, is widely used and can be applied to whatever question the people wish to decide. If the voters wish to amend the constitution in a particular way, neither parliament nor the courts has the power to intervene. Recently, a constitutional initiative was launched to establish a system of hiking trails throughout the country. Constitutional lawyers might argue that this issue is not important enough to be included in the constitution and that it should be dealt with by a law. But the people decided otherwise, so the Swiss constitution now contains an article about hiking trails.

From the perspective of a clear and systematic separation between the constitution, on the one hand, and laws derived from the constitution, on the other hand, it is bothersome that sometimes the voters approve constitutional amendments that may not be important enough to be included at this level. A far greater problem arises if the voters add an article to the constitution that contradicts other parts of the constitution. Such an extreme case occurred early in this century, when a constitutional initiative was accepted prohibiting the killing of animals according to Jewish kosher rites. On the surface, the proposal was presented as an animal protection measure, but its real intent was clearly anti-Semitic. The referendum allowed anti-Semitic feelings to be expressed in the secrecy of the voting booth. Did such an amendment contradict the religious freedom guaranteed by the constitution? One would assume so. However, if the people themselves decide that the two parts of the constitution are compatible, so be it. The people interpret what is constitutional, and no court can overrule their decision, because the people are the highest authority in the land—the sovereign, as the Swiss like to say.

The example of the kosher rites shows the dangers of giving ultimate power over the most basic constitutional questions to the people. Unlike judges, voters may be less concerned with the logical consistency of their decisions. Because most voters have had little, if any, legal training, there is a risk that they will follow their emotions and prejudices. Thus, the people may act like a whimsical dictator. On the other hand, participation in referenda may help educate the voters, making them more responsible and consistent in their judgments. Should the notion of democracy be carried so far that the people of a country become the final judges of their fate? We will come back to this question in Chapter 7, which is devoted entirely to the referendum.

FEDERAL REPUBLIC OF GERMANY

In addition to Great Britain and Switzerland, some other European democracies, including Belgium, the Netherlands, and Finland, have no judicial review. But courts in other countries, in particular the three largest continental democracies—France, Italy, and the Federal Republic of Germany—do have established powers of judicial review. The most interesting case is the Federal Republic of Germany, which tried to learn from the manner in which Hitler overthrew the Weimar Republic. Hitler based his power in many respects on newly written laws. The courts at that time possessed only a very weak tradition of judicial review and were therefore hesitant to strike down these laws as unconstitutional. As a consequence, Hitler was able to argue that he had acted within legal limits. When the constitution of the Federal Republic was written, great care was given to avoid the possibility of a dictatorship being established by seemingly legal means. The key responsibility for this endeavor was given to the Federal Constitutional Court. The structure of this court was heavily influenced by the American occupation authorities, who used the U.S. Supreme Court as a model.

The Constitutional Court has 16 members who are elected by parliament. The court is administratively independent; it has its own budget and the right to hire and fire its employees. In the brief history of the Federal Republic, the court has established its moral and political authority as watchdog of the constitution. Like the Supreme Court in the United States, the Constitutional Court in West Germany has played an important role in the abortion issue. When the government coalition of Social Democrats and Free Democrats liberalized the abortion law in 1974, Christian Democrats brought the issue to the court, which declared the new law unconstitutional. The judges argued that the right to life guaranteed by the constitution also applied in principle to the unborn child. Following this decision, parliament enacted a less liberal law. It is noteworthy that the right to life was included in the constitution in order to prevent atrocities such as those committed under Hitler. The hope was that the constitutional court would remain strong enough to strike down any act violating the constitutionally guaranteed right to life.

In Chapter 1, we discussed the case wherein the Constitutional Court disallowed the planned census because it included questions that the court found interfered with the constitutional guaranteed sphere of privacy of the citizens. In Chapter 8, we will discuss still another case in which a law allowing worker participation in the decision making of private companies was brought before the Constitutional Court.

FRANCE AND ITALY

Generally, there is a tendency in Europe to give more importance to judicial review. France and Italy are good examples of this tendency. Political scientist Paul Furlong summarizes his study on the constitutional court in Italian politics as follows:

> Despite the difficulties inherent in its role, the constitutional court appears to be one of the few institutional successes in the development of the Italian Republic. Although politicians of all colours are willing to take a tilt at individual decisions, in its general structure and mode of operation it attracts an almost unique degree of consent.[26]

For France, political scientist Alec Stone comes to a similar positive conclusion with regard to the Constitutional Council:

> The study shows, not least, that the Council's impact on the legislative process is extensive, significant and multi-dimensional. Polemics aside, there is some basis for the view that the institution does function as a kind of third legislative chamber within parliamentary space, and an umpire in the political "game." One simply cannot understand the French legislative process today without an understanding of the role, direct and indirect, of the Council.[27]

5

HEADS OF STATE

In the United States, the president is both the head of state and the chief executive. This dual role becomes especially evident when he travels abroad, to Great Britain for example. There the president is greeted by the queen in his role as head of state, while the prime minister talks with him about political matters. In most European democracies, the roles of head of state and chief executive are played by two different people. In this chapter, we will discuss the European head of state and the functions that he or she exercises. In some countries, the head of state is a monarch, and, in others, the head of state is an elected president.

MONARCHICAL HEAD OF STATE

Great Britain probably best illustrates the functions of a monarch in a modern European democracy. The reigning monarch is, of course, Queen Elizabeth. How does she spend her days? We have already seen in Chapter 3 that she appoints the prime minister but that this appointment is a pure formality. Who becomes prime minister depends solely on the results of elections for the House of Commons. There is also, however, an important symbolic aspect to politics, and it makes for a nice ceremony when the queen invites the leader of the winning party to come to Buckingham Palace and asks him or her to form Her Majesty's next government. The losing party is called Her Majesty's oppositon. An even grander ceremony takes place when the queen opens the first session of Parliament with a speech. To be sure, the speech is written, not by the queen, but by the prime minister, who uses it to announce the new government's program (see Box 5.1 and photo on page 156).

In former centuries, the symbolic trappings of the monarch also had substance. The king or queen was an important political actor who, for example, had a great say in the appointment and dismissal of the prime minister. Together with other institutions, such as the House of Commons and the House of Lords, the monarch ruled the country. But, in a slow and long process, the monarchy lost its substantive power. Today, the saying is that the queen reigns and the prime minister rules. Only the trappings of the queen's power remain, but these trappings have great symbolic value for the British people. The popularity of the monarchy is even increasing, and there is always great public interest in the royal family. In our bureaucratic and anonymous world, the public seems to have a great need for colorful images.

BOX 5.1

QUEEN OPENS SESSION OF PARLIAMENT

LONDON—As prescribed by the British Constitution, Queen Elizabeth II, all but immobilized by crown, robe and official ceremony, told Parliament today what her Government plans to do over the next year. . . .

Borne in a horse-drawn Australian carriage to the neo-Gothic House of Lords entrance on Parliament Square this morning, she was given a silver satchel containing the speech prepared for her by Prime Minister Margaret Thatcher's Government, and read it verbatim, as she must.

Source: New York Times, November 23, 1988.

This need is not well fulfilled by modern-day politicians who, at best, give the impression of being efficient managers of huge government programs. At worst, they appear power-hungry, inefficient, and sometimes even corrupt. In contrast, the royal family does not have to run for office, and its members cannot be held accountable for what goes wrong in the government. Thus, in an ironic way, the absence of political power contributes to the popularity of the monarchy.

Of course, popularity has no great value in itself; movie stars and top athletes are also popular. Is the British queen simply a celebrity? By reading

Queen Opens Session of Parliament. (Courtesy British Embassy, Washington, D.C.)

certain newspapers and magazines, one could arrive at that impression. But there is definitely more to the British monarchy, in the sense that its popularity is used for a higher national purpose. The queen is a symbol that helps hold the British nation together. The national flag and the national anthem are also symbols, but the queen has the advantage of being flesh and blood— a human being who represents the British nation. British citizens can look up to their queen; they can admire her; they can identify with her. They find a bond with the past in the royal family, because this same family has been identified with the fate of Great Britain for many centuries. The need to find historical roots is fulfilled by the existence of a monarchy.

Financially minded people may ask whether it is perhaps not too costly for a country to have a monarchy. Only a very small share of the government budget is spent for this purpose, and this money can be considered well invested because it triggers tourist revenues that Britain would not have otherwise. For example, the changing of the guard at Buckingham Palace is a world-renowned tourist attraction. More important, the monarchy has value for the stability of the country that cannot be expressed in financial terms. Occasionally, a member of the House of Commons demands the abolishment of the monarchy, but such proposals have no chance of acceptance in the foreseeable future.

Although the queen never speaks up on controversial political matters, her heir, Prince Charles, increasingly does so, as illustrated in Box 5.2. It remains to be seen whether he will retain this frankness if one day he becomes king. This could cause problems for the monarchy as an institution whose high prestige depends very much on its staying above politics.

—————————————— **BOX 5.2** ——————————————

PRINCE CHARLES SPEAKS UP

LONDON—Prince Charles says that Britain's educational establishment is murdering the Queen's English. It is being taught "so bloody badly" in the schools that he cannot get a letter written properly.

"All the letters sent from my office, I have to correct myself," the heir to the throne said here Wednesday. "And that is because English is taught so bloody badly."

The royal complaint was taken in stride by his office staff, but it drew a quick rebuke from a teachers' union official, who said that the prince "probably doesn't pay enough to attract the right quality of staff to write his letters."

Britons have become accustomed to hearing Queen Elizabeth II's oldest son, now 40, speak his mind, especially on environmental and architectural issues. He has, on occasion, not shied away from criticizing government policy, as when he urged energy conservation measures instead of nuclear power development.

Source: New York Times, June 29, 1989.

Although Americans may be most familiar with the British monarchy, several other European democracies also have monarchs. These countries include Belgium, Denmark, Luxembourg, the Netherlands, Norway, Spain, and Sweden, as well as the tiny countries of Liechtenstein and Monaco (see Box 5.3). In some of these countries, the monarchical trappings are not quite as splendid as in Great Britain. The extreme case of a stripped-down monarchy is found in Sweden. According to a 1974 constitutional amendment, the king is not even symbolically allowed to appoint the prime minister or open parliament. The Swedish king has become more of a citizen like everyone else (see photo on page 159). He does not even get special parking permits (Box 5.4). The main task of the Swedish king is to cut ribbons, open museums, and make state visits. It remains to be seen how well the Swedish monarchy can survive in this modernized form.

There are two European countries in which the monarch still has political significance: Belgium and Spain. Belgium is plagued by a conflict between its two major linguistic communities, Dutch-speaking Flanders and French-speaking Wallonia. The king makes a great effort to be impartial in this conflict, speaking with equal frequency in both languages. If the linguistic conflict in Belgium were to develop into a real national emergency, the possibility exists that the king could step in as a political mediator.

The position of the Belgian king was weakened in the spring of 1990 over the abortion issue. The king declared that in good conscience as a Roman Catholic he could not sign a new law permitting abortion. Normally, his signature on a new law is a formality. To circumvent the unexpected difficulty, the cabinet temporarily suspended the king and promulgated the law on its own power. Afterward, the parliament was called into a special session to reinstate the king. This bizarre episode shows the delicate position of European monarchs.

Another bizarre episode concerning a king occurred in Romania in the spring of 1990. King Michael, who was forced by the Communists to abdicate

---

BOX 5.3

EUROPEAN MONARCHS

Belgium	His Majesty King Baudouin
Denmark	Her Majesty Queen Margrethe II
Liechtenstein	His Serene Highness Prince Franz Josef II
Luxembourg	His Royal Highness Grand Duke Jean
Monaco	His Serene Highness Prince Rainier III
Netherlands	Her Majesty Queen Beatrix
Norway	His Majesty King Olav V
Spain	His Majesty King Juan Carlos I
Sweden	His Majesty King Carl XVI Gustaf
United Kingdom	Her Majesty Queen Elizabeth II

Sweden's King Carl XVI Gustaf and Queen Silvia. (Courtesy Swedish Embassy, Washington, D.C.)

_____ **BOX 5.4** _____

FOR THE SWEDISH KING, IT'S STILL NO PARKING

STOCKHOLM—King Carl Gustaf's request for a special parking permit to speed the collection of his dry cleaning and groceries has been rejected by the city.

The Swedish court applied for six permits, saying special parking dispensation was necessary for collection of washing, groceries and presents and for other errands for the King, Queen Silvia and other members of the royal family.

The city parking office turned down the request, saying it would create a precedent.

Source: New York Times, October 6, 1988.

in 1947 and lived a middle-class life in Switzerland, gave hints that he would be willing to serve again as Romanian king. Although he did not gather much support for his plan, the Romanian government was sufficiently worried to withdraw the exiled monarch's visa when he tried to visit his native country.

Spain was a dictatorship until the death of Francisco Franco in 1975. Afterward, the monarchy was reestablished with Juan Carlos I as king. Instead of trying to keep dictatorial powers for himself, he led his country to a democratic form of government. But for some time the Spanish democracy was still frail, primarily because Franco supporters remained in the armed forces and the police. At one point, these groups even attempted a coup to overthrow the democratic government. Some officers holding weapons in their hands entered parliament and began shooting in the air. They had hoped to get the support of the king, but Juan Carlos acted forcefully in the defense of a democratic form of government. In normal times, he wishes to be merely the symbolic figurehead of his country, but if new threats to the stability of the Spanish democracy should occur, King Juan Carlos can be expected to step in again and to exercise a political role.

ELECTED HEAD OF STATE

Those European democracies without a monarch have elected presidents as head of state. The only exception to this rule is Switzerland, which has neither a monarch nor an elected head of state. When the Swiss speak of the sovereign, they mean the people, who often decide political issues in popular referenda (see Chapter 7). When the verdict of a referendum is in, the media tend to use the expression, "the sovereign has spoken." The Swiss example indicates that a country can survive without any head of state.

But the other nonmonarchical countries all have an elected head of state, who is a symbol of national unity. The Federal Republic of Germany serves as a good illustration. In the long history of Germany, emperors and kings have played significant roles. After Germany's defeat in World War I, however, Germany sent its last emperor—Wilhelm II—into exile. When the Federal Republic was established in 1949, its constitution—the Basic Law— provided for the office of federal president, whose current occupant is Richard von Weizsaecker (photo page 161). Helmut Kohl is the chancellor and as such the chief executive, whereas von Weizsaecker is head of state. How is the president elected, and what are his functions? Is he as politically powerless as the typical European monarch?

The German president is elected by a special assembly that consists of all members of the lower house of the federal parliament (the Bundestag) and an equal number of deputies from the various state parliaments. Successful candidates must have a reputation that transcends party lines. Thus far, the federal president has been a leading politician who no longer seemed likely to become chancellor. Von Weizsaecker is a typical case: Before his election, he held the important position of mayor of West Berlin and had had a long

Richard von Weizsaecker (left) with violinist Yehudi Menuhin. (Courtesy the German Information Center, New York.)

and distinguished political career; already in his sixties, however, he had practically no chance of becoming chancellor.

The role of president has been interpreted very differently by the six men who have filled the office. The first president, Theodor Heuss, played the role of political philosopher, often speaking out forcefully on fundamental questions of the democratic order. He instructed the German people on the value of democracy in a critical period of their history. When Heuss retired in 1959, Chancellor Konrad Adenauer announced his intention to follow him. Adenauer, however, soon realized the limits of the office with regard to the exercise of power, and at the last minute he decided to stay on as chancellor. A new candidate had to be found quickly. He turned out to be Heinrich Luebke, minister of agriculture. Unfortunately, he was not quite up to the job and soon began to show some signs of senility. During his time in office, many Luebke jokes began to circulate. His election demonstrates the risk that a man, who really belongs in retirement, takes when he becomes president. It is not easy to find an outstanding candidate who is willing to retreat from the vibrant excitement of day-to-day politics to the calmer, dignified sphere of the presidency.

Fortunately, the next president, former Minister of Justice Gustav Heinemann, was able to restore the reputation of the office. He was a citizen-president, seeking contact with ordinary men and women, visiting them in their private homes. A deeply religious man and modest in his personal life-style, Heinemann spoke up on the great moral issues of the day. He was followed by Walter Scheel, the leader of the Free Democratic party, who was the key actor along with Social Democrat Willy Brandt when their two parties formed a coalition in 1969. In that SPD/FDP coalition, Scheel was vice chancellor and foreign minister, but as a member of a small party he had no chance of ever becoming chancellor. Under those circumstances, he decided to run for the presidency when Heinemann retired in 1974. Scheel brought great elegance to the presidency and sponsored many splendid performances by artists at the presidential palace. His successor, Karl Carstens, speaker of the Bundestag, was a cooler and less flamboyant personality than Scheel. But he also became quite popular, especially as a result of his efforts to get in touch with the people through long hiking tours across the country.

These brief descriptions indicate that West German presidents tend to be distinguished leaders who bring high prestige to the office. Based on this prestige, a president can also exercise a certain amount of power, not in day-to-day politics, but in more fundamental questions. When von Weizsaecker was elected president in 1984, he quickly made it clear that he wanted to have a voice in the great questions confronting the country. For example, using his experience as a former mayor of West Berlin, he gave speeches in which he called for closer cooperation between East and West Germany. But he treated the topic only in general terms, avoiding the specifics of ongoing negotiations. When on May 8, 1985 West Germany commemorated 40 years since the end of World War II, von Weizsaecker gave the keynote speech in the Bundestag. He reminded Germany that its defeat in 1945 had as its real cause Hitler's 1933 takeover.

Compared to a typical European monarch, the West German head of state exercises more political power and leadership but also runs the risk of crossing the fine line where he or she might suddenly become too political. Walter Scheel had such an experience at the beginning of his term when he was rebuked by Chancellor Helmut Schmidt, who told him in no uncertain terms that it was not the business of the president to run the foreign policy of the country. This episode shows the delicate nature of the role played by the German president. Unlike a monarch, whose prestige is assured by a royal background, the German president must earn his prestige through public statements that must be neither trivial nor too overtly political.

In most other countries with an elected president as head of state, the situation is basically the same as in the Federal Republic of Germany, although there is some variation with regard to methods of election and the amount of power exercised by the president. The only real exception is France, where the president is not only head of state but also exercises strong executive power (Chapter 3). The president has also a relatively strong role in Finland. A special remark is in order with regard to Austria: Its president, Kurt Waldheim, was severely criticized for his actions as an officer in World War II, which prevents him to a large extent from fulfilling the role of a true head of state. Instead of being a symbol of national unity, he has become a symbol of national shame and controversy.

What implications might this chapter have for the United States? Clearly, the introduction of a monarch into the American system is out of the question, because the necessary historical tradition is missing. But perhaps the two roles of head of state and chief executive could be more strongly differentiated. The fact that the American president is simultaneously head of state and chief executive has led to two sorts of complaints. One is the complaint that the president misuses his prestige as head of state to impose his policies as chief executive. In this context, the danger of an imperial presidency is cited. The other complaint is that the president is overburdened with ceremonial tasks as head of state, so that he doesn't have enough time for his duties as chief executive. Although the vice president often helps with ceremonial tasks, the president himself must appear on important occasions.

A possible change could be to give the title of prime minister to the chief of staff of the White House. The chief of staff already has great coordinating responsibilities in the daily operations of the American government. These responsibilities could be made more visible with a strong title. Such a system, with the president still as the chief executive, would draw heavily on the French experience.

Another change, based on the German experience, could be to have a president as ceremonial head of state and a prime minister as chief executive. In the American context, this would not necessarily mean a change to a parliamentary system. The ceremonial president could be elected by a joint session of Congress, while the politically more important prime minister could be elected by the people.

Finally, the United States could follow the Swiss example by eliminating the office of head of state altogether. Shouldn't the people themselves symbolize the unity of the nation? Could Americans make the argument, as the Swiss do, that the people are the sovereign? What works for a small country may not work for a large one, of course. Having gone through the various alternatives, many American readers may decide that they wish to stick with the current system, in which the president is simultaneously head of state and chief executive.

6

FEDERALISM

The United States has a *federal* system of government. The Latin root word, *foedus*, means tie, or bond. A federal system of government consists of autonomous units that are tied together within one country. In the United States, these units are, of course, the 50 states tied together by the union, the United States of America. In a federal government, the individual units are not simply bureaucratic districts of the central government; instead, they have their own independent power, which is constitutionally guaranteed. In other words, under federalism government activities are divided and sometimes shared between one central and several regional governments. The opposite of a federal government is a unitary government, in which regional units are merely bureaucratic in nature. In the United States, efforts are being made to transfer more power from the central government in Washington to the state governments. In most European democracies as well, similar efforts are being made to decentralize power.

FEDERAL TREND

The most dramatic change from a unitary to a federal government occurred in Germany after the defeat of the Nazis. Under Hitler, Germany was a unitary state, with all political power concentrated at the center. This government structure was seen as a major factor in Hitler's ability to take such total control of his country. After his defeat in 1945, the occupying powers were eager to dismantle Germany's centralized government structure. The French even suggested breaking Germany down into several independent countries, so that the military might of the German people would be broken forever. The division of Germany into Eastern and Western parts should be seen in this same context. Although the Western powers certainly were not happy that the Soviet Union had established a Communist state—the German Democratic Republic—in East Germany, they were not too unhappy that Germany was thus divided into two countries. For many years, the official policy of the Western allies was that Germany should be reunited, but beneath the surface there were still fears, especially in France, about the potential strength of a reunited Germany. (We will discuss German reunification further in Chapter 16).

The effort to decentralize power in Germany was also apparent in 1949, when a democratic government was established in the three Western zones.

The structure of that government, in accordance with the wishes of the United States, Great Britain, and France—the occupying powers—was federal in nature. The importance of this was reflected in the new country's name, the Federal Republic of Germany. Like the United States, the Federal Republic was divided into states (*Laender*). There were 10 *Laender* within the Federal Republic proper, with Western Berlin being an eleventh and special state. Some *Laender*, Bavaria, for example, have a long tradition of autonomy, and even independence, in German history. (With German unification, five or more *Laender* will be added [see Chapter 16].)

Like the American states, the German *Laender* have areas for which they are solely or mostly responsible, such as education. As noted in Chapter 3, the federal parliament has a second chamber, the Bundesrat, in addition to the Bundestag. The government of each German state sends representatives to the Bundesrat, where all federal bills that impact on *Laender* affairs must be passed. Politically, German *Laender* are not quite as strong as American states. Even so, federalism has helped to decentralize power in West Germany. Important decisions are made not only in the federal capital, Bonn, but also in the state capitals. There are always some *Laender* that have different parties in power than at the federal level. The negative side to this system is that government responsibilities are sometimes blurred, leading to a certain lack of leadership. Despite this drawback, federalism has become firmly established in the West German political culture.

Like Hitler in Germany, Mussolini established a strongly centralized structure of government in Italy. But, when democracy was restored, Italy remained a unitary state. The need to divide power was felt less acutely in Italy than in Germany, because Mussolini's abuses of power seemed less excessive than Hitler's. Also, there were no occupying forces in Italy to influence the drafting of the new constitution, as there were in West Germany. After the war, Italy had a unitary form of government except that limited autonomy was given to five peripheral regions, such as the island of Sardinia. The argument for this was that these regions had special needs that could not all be taken care of by the remote capital of Rome.

In 1970, regionalization was extended to the entire country, and Italy is now divided into 20 regions, each of which has a regional parliament and a regional cabinet. Why did this federal development occur in Italy? Interestingly enough, the main reason is not that the central government in Rome had too much power but, on the contrary, that it had too little. For many centuries, Italy had a cultural and geographic but not a political unity. Only in the second half of the nineteenth century was the country united politically, and its historically rooted political diversity is still felt today. The people of Naples, for example, have not forgotten that they had their own kingdom for centuries. Given the different historical traditions of the various regions of Italy, it is often difficult for the central government to exercise its authority today. Add to this a certain level of bureaucratic sloppiness and corruption, and it is easy to see why the central government in Rome is often inefficient. The impetus behind regionalization is the hope that, by bringing government closer to the people, its efficiency will increase. This is the same argument made for transferring more power from Washington, D.C., to the states.

It remains to be seen how successful regionalization will be in Italy. Preliminary research has shown that some regions have been much more successful than others in establishing themselves as autonomous political units pursuing their own independent policies.[28] Can Italy's government now be classified federal? Compared with the American states and the West German *Laender*, the Italian regions are weak. The fact that almost all their revenues come from taxes collected by the central government and not by the regions is especially detrimental to their autonomy. On the other hand, regional authorities are elected by regional voters, not appointed by the central government. Thus, whether Italy today is classified as a unitary or a federal government depends on the criteria used. Political scientist Arend Lijphart is probably correct when he classifies Italy as still unitary because the autonomy of the regions is not yet sufficiently guaranteed by the constitution.[29]

Spain is another country with a strong federal trend. Francisco Franco, like his fascist friends Hitler and Mussolini, established a strongly centralized government. When democracy was restored after Franco's death in 1975, the central authorities were immediately confronted with demands for regional autonomy. These demands, which were suppressed under Franco, could be articulated under a democratic form of government. The demand for more autonomy is particularly intense—and sometimes even violent—in the Basque province, which has a cultural tradition distinct from the rest of Spain. The Basque problem is further complicated by the fact that Basques also live across the French border. Other Spanish provinces, such as Catalonia and Andalusia, also seek more autonomy, although the Basques most often make news headlines. (For the importance of regional parties in Spanish politics, see Chapter 1.)

In Great Britain, too, the central government is confronted today with vigorous demands from regional movements. These demands come mainly from the Scots, the Welsh, and the Irish Catholics in Northern Ireland (see Chapter 11). Although Great Britain's official name is the United Kingdom of Great Britain and Northern Ireland, it remains to be seen how united the country can remain. The Irish Catholics are clearly fighting for independence from Great Britain and unification with the Republic of Ireland. In Scotland and Wales, although the main demand is for more autonomy, some people seek complete independence. The cases of Spain and Great Britain show that a federal trend can in fact become so strong that separation becomes an option. This issue, of course, was raised in the United States in the Civil War, when North and South fought over the Confederacy's right to secede from the Union.

Traditionally, the most unitary state in Europe has been France, the "one and indivisible nation." The basis for its unitary government structure was established in the time of absolutism of the Bourbon kings and was later reinforced by the regimes of Napoleon I and Napoleon III. As a result of these historical developments, Paris dominates the country like no other capital in Europe. Paris is not only the political but also the artistic, intellectual, and economic center of France, to an overwhelming extent. Nearly every fourth French person lives in metropolitan Paris. From a Parisian view, the rest of France is often considered in a condescending way, as provincial.

The departments into which France is divided are established as bureaucratic districts of the central government, not as means for local self-expression. Government buildings throughout France display no regional flags, only the national blue-, white-, and red-striped flag. But, even in France, regional movements have begun to demand more local autonomy—in Britany and on the island of Corsica, for example. You might expect a Socialist government to have no sympathy for demands for decentralization, because central planning was always a key to Socialist thinking. French Socialists, however, when in office, came out in favor of some decentralization in order to stimulate citizen participation in a less bureaucratic environment. Despite all efforts, however, France remains a very unitary country.

All five major European democracies display evidence of a federal trend, although the motives are somewhat different from country to country. Among the smaller European democracies, the federal trend is most apparent in Belgium, which was formerly a strictly unitary country. The delicate language situation, which will be described in Chapter 11, is behind this change in structure. Belgium is now divided into three regions: French-speaking Wallonia, Dutch-speaking Flanders, and bilingual Brussels. In addition to these three regions, its governmental structure contains two so-called cultural communities: French speakers and Dutch speakers. This dual federalism of regions and communities has led to a very complicated division of responsibilities among the central government, the three regions, and the two cultural communities. Furthermore, the tiny German-speaking minority of Belgium also has government institutions supporting its integrity.

--------------- **SWITZERLAND AS A FEDERAL MODEL** ---------------

Switzerland is culturally very diverse. It has four official languages: 70 percent of Swiss speak German; 20 percent, French; 10 percent, Italian; and less than 1 percent, Romansh (an independent Swiss language). Approximately half of the Swiss are Protestant, and half, Catholic. Switzerland's regional differences range from mountain valleys to cosmopolitan cities like Zurich and Geneva. All this diversity occurs in a population of only 6 million, crowded into a relatively small area. Yet Switzerland has survived as a political unit for many centuries, enjoying prosperity and stability.

A major reason for Switzerland's success is its extensive federalist structure. The country is divided into 26 highly autonomous cantons, some of which proudly call themselves republics. The official name for the canton of Geneva, for example, is Republic of Geneva. Swiss federalism may be a useful model for other European countries trying to decentralize. Switzerland, however, is unique in Europe in terms of the development of its federal structure, so it is not easy for other countries to learn from it. Swiss federalism developed on its own, in the sense that the cantons existed before the Swiss Confederation. The cantons built up a *foedus,* or bond, holding them together within a single political system. Thus, federalism in Switzerland can be compared to federalism in the United States, where the states also existed before the Union.

To understand Swiss federalism, it is important to emphasize that the cantons, not the linguistic communities, are the building blocks. All but four of the cantons are linguistically homogeneous—recognizing only one language within their territory. In the canton of Geneva, for example, French is the sole official language, and public school students are taught only in French. French speakers control educational matters in Geneva and can organize their schools according to their own cultural preferences. Leaving educational and cultural matters to the linguistically homogeneous cantons alleviates a thorny problem for the multilingual country; for instance, the Swiss do not have to fight at the national level over which textbooks should be used in the schools.

There is always the possibility that blocs of cantons could form along linguistic lines, so that the language differential might still have great political importance. This happened recently when the French-speaking cantons bitterly complained that representatives of the German-speaking cantons in the federal parliament favored the Zurich airport over the one in Geneva for subsidies. Such head-on confrontations between French- and German-speaking cantons, however, are relatively rare. One reason is that the border between French- and German-speaking Switzerland occurs in three bilingual cantons, blurring the distinction between linguistically based blocs of cantons. More important, neither the German-speaking nor the French-speaking parts of Switzerland are internally very homogeneous. Important differences cut across the linguistic borders, and on certain issues German speakers may have more in common with French speakers than they do with other German speakers. This is often true from an economic perspective: The tourist industry, for example, is located in all four linguistic areas, leading to close cooperation among them. It would be very different if the tourist industry was, say, concentrated in the French-speaking area. In that case, economic and linguistic interests would reinforce each other. Many other industries, such as the manufacture of watches and cheese, are also located in at least the two largest language areas. Thus, the interests of those industries are not represented by a single language group.

It is also significant for Swiss federalism that the Catholic-Protestant division cuts across the border between German and French speakers. Some German-speaking cantons are predominantly Catholic; others, Protestant, and the same division can be found among the French-speaking cantons. If the religious and linguistic areas were the same, it would be much more likely that coherent blocs of cantons would confront one another. But with linguistic, economic, and religious regions cutting across one another in a very complex way, Swiss politics is characterized by constantly shifting coalitions. A German-speaking mountain farmer of the Catholic faith may have interests in common with other German speakers on one issue, with other Catholics—irrespective of language—on another issue, and with other mountain farmers—irrespective of language and religion—on still a third issue. Due to these shifting coalitions, no single group is a permanent majority; each group risks being in the minority on at least some issues.

The absence of coherent language blocs also has the consequence that language is not always of prime importance. To be sure, in some issues in Swiss politics, like the aforementioned subsidies to the airports of Zurich and Geneva, language affiliation becomes a key consideration. But other identities, like canton, religion, or occupation, are more important at other times. In addition, German speakers in Switzerland have a great number of distinctive dialects, and identification with a dialect may also be very significant. Given all this complexity, German speakers rarely function as a unified and dominant bloc in Swiss politics, despite their majority.

Elsewhere in Europe where attempts are made to introduce federalism, the building blocks are linguistic or other cultural units. Belgium runs the risk of frequent head-on confrontations between French and Dutch speakers. Could Belgium have chosen the Swiss solution of a large number of units within each language group and a few units cutting across the language border? Probably not, because the Belgian provinces have not historically developed the strong local identities of the Swiss cantons. A Belgian federalism based on provinces would be artificial and lacking sufficient historical roots.

Unlike Belgium, Switzerland has no dominant capital, another factor that has helped make federalism work. If a country has a very strong center, like Brussels in Belgium, Paris in France, or London in Great Britain, it is difficult to decentralize power, not only in form, but also in fact. The Swiss federal authorities are located in the capital, Bern, but the Swiss supreme court, for example, is located in French-speaking Lausanne, and the Swiss National Accident Insurance Institute is in Lucerne. Bern is only the fourth largest city in Switzerland: Zurich, Basel, and Geneva each has more inhabitants. Bern is also not Switzerland's business or cultural center. Banking, for example, is concentrated in the larger cities.

In recent years, Zurich's economic importance has begun to be a problem for the complex and subtle balances in Swiss society. Representatives of other cantons complain that more and more of the largest companies are moving their headquarters to Zurich. Nearly one-sixth of the population already lives in the Zurich canton.

To counterbalance the might of the stronger cantons, Swiss federalism gives special weight to the weaker cantons. As in the United States, parliament in Switzerland has a second chamber in which each canton holds two seats regardless of population.[30] In the popular referendum, a constitutional amendment requires not only a majority of the voters but also a majority of the cantons, further strengthening the small cantons. Another important aspect of Swiss federalism is that the cantons are regularly consulted about the drafting of federal legislation. Although this involvement again seems to give a strong voice to the small cantons, a growing weakness of Swiss federalism in fact becomes apparent in this process of cantonal consultation. As a highly industrialized country, Switzerland is increasingly confronted with very complex issues, such as nuclear power, that require specialized expertise. This development puts the smaller cantons at a disadvantage, because they often lack the necessary staff to prepare well-researched answers for the federal authorities. Generally speaking, this raises the question of how far decentralization can be taken in our complex world without endangering the problem-solving capacity of countries.

Problems like acid rain transcend the borders of a Swiss canton or a German *Land* or, often, even national borders. Thus, it is not surprising that Europe is encountering a trend not only toward federalism but also toward supranational integration. In Chapter 16, we will see that the two tendencies are not necessarily mutually exclusive. They may instead complement each other, in the sense that certain tasks demand decentralization, from a national to a local level, while other tasks might be better transferred from a national to a European level. It is noteworthy that many citizens who advocate federalism also favor European integration.

POPULAR REFERENDUM

Basically, we can distinguish between a representative and a direct form of democracy. If a democracy is of the representative type, the citizens elect their representatives, who then make the substantive decisions. In a direct democracy, substantive matters are decided by the citizens themselves. Using these definitions, the United States is a representative democracy at the national level, whereas at the state and local levels it tends to combine both representative and direct elements.

In Switzerland, the referendum is used extensively. Of all the national referenda held in Western democracies since World War II, more than two-thirds were held in Switzerland.[31] The Swiss are strong believers in the referendum, and they have developed a broad justification for its frequent use. Great Britain provides the classic example of a representative democracy. The British argue that decisions are best made in Parliament.

SWITZERLAND

The notion of direct citizen involvement in actual decision making has deep roots in Swiss history. In medieval times, the pastures high in the mountains were communal property; thus, decisions about these pastures were made communally. All cow owners assembled under the open sky and decided, for example, on what day the cows should be brought down to the valley in order not to be trapped by the first snow. When modern Switzerland was established with the constitution of 1848, its founders drew on these ancient traditions. In a mystical way, the Swiss spoke of reviving the old democratic freedoms in the nineteenth century. They certainly remembered Old Switzerland too nostalgically, however. For example, they forgot that there were many serfs, who did not share in the communal property of the pastures. But however imperfect the historical reality of medieval times, it was crucially important that the nineteenth-century founders of modern Switzerland could cite democratic traditions that they were trying to restore. Combined with the revolutionary ideas of the Enlightenment, these old democratic traditions led the Swiss to incorporate the popular referendum in the constitution of 1848.

In the beginning, the referendum was limited to constitutional amendments proposed by parliament. Later in the nineteenth century, the people themselves received the right to propose constitutional amendments. The voters also got the right to call for a referendum on legislative bills at that time. In Chapter 4, we described how many signatures must be collected for a referendum to be held.

When the referendum was introduced, it was expected that its effect would be innovative. The founders of modern Switzerland wished to overcome the inaction of the old regime and its dominance by a few ruling families. They anticipated that the voters would be open to change, but in fact the opposite was true and the referendum has often had a delaying effect. The best example is probably the introduction of female suffrage. Parliament was prepared much earlier than male voters to grant women the right to vote. Several amendments to the constitution that would have established female suffrage were defeated in referenda. The margin of defeat, however, got smaller each time until, finally, in 1971, women were given the right to vote. This example is typical in the sense that it shows how it often takes a long time to convince people to accept a new idea.

Of course, it's not always undesirable to delay a decision. Delay can prevent precipitous decisions that are regretted in retrospect. As time goes by, there have been quite a few cases in which the people were wise not to move as fast as their leaders desired. In the 1970s, for example, some referenda outcomes prevented Switzerland from expanding its system of higher education as quickly as countries such as West Germany had done. Today there is general agreement that these votes had the positive result that fewer Swiss university graduates are unemployed.

Although the referendum generally has had a delaying effect, on some occasions new ideas have been brought into public debate as a result of a referendum. After the Arab oil embargo in 1973, some students had the original idea of making one Sunday every month traffic-free on Swiss roads. This not only would have saved energy but also would have brought some calm to everyday life. Once a month, the highways would have been opened to strollers and bicyclists. The students collected enough signatures so that the proposal had to be submitted to a referendum as a constitutional amendment. Although some exceptions, such as for ambulances, were planned, all major parties and special interest groups found the idea well intentioned but impractical. The students received broad popular support, but their proposal was still narrowly defeated. Despite this ultimate defeat, this is a good illustration of how the referendum can help to bring unorthodox ideas to public attention.

Another good example of how the referendum can introduce fresh ideas into public debate, is the popular initiative signed by 111,300 citizens to abolish the Swiss army. Although the initiative was defeated on November 26, 1989, by a margin of two to one, it allowed the Swiss people to reflect seriously on whether a small neutral country such as theirs really needed an army (see Box 7.1).

How self-centered are Swiss voters when they participate in a referendum? Is there a danger that they simply will vote for their own narrow interests? Is there, in particular, a threat that the interests of minorities will be neglected? There is always the possibility of a tyranny of the majority. And yes, there are

BOX 7.1

SWISS REJECT PLAN TO SCRAP ARMY

GENEVA—Switzerland today voted to keep its army as the best way of maintaining its neutrality. An initiative to abolish the army was turned down by a margin of almost two to one.

"A majority of the states rejected it," a Government spokesman said. Only in Geneva and Jura did the majority vote in favor of the proposal.

The initiative, forced by a petition signed by 111,300 citizens, set off a fierce national debate on the usefulness of an army in a small neutral country.

Source: New York Times, November 27, 1989.

cases in Swiss history when minorities suffered from the results of a referendum.

In Chapter 4, we described how a constitutional amendment prohibiting the slaughter of animals according to kosher rites was approved. Another conflict over minority rights concerns conscientious objectors. Parliament would be willing to allow them to serve the country outside the army, but all attempts to change the constitution in this direction have failed in the referendum. Such examples show the worst side of the referendum. But in many other cases the referendum has revealed great consideration for minority rights. Illustrative are several referenda on the issue of foreign workers in the 1970s.

During the economic boom of the 1960s, Switzerland admitted so many foreign workers that they came to number more than 1 million in a total population of 6 million. This foreign presence was felt in many segments of Swiss society: In some school classes foreign children outnumbered Swiss children, and railway stations became gathering places for foreigners in the evening and on weekends. Many Swiss no longer felt at home in their own country and began to refer to the "foreignization" of Switzerland. Politically, an antialien movement developed, demanding a severe reduction in the number of foreigners allowed in Switzerland. This movement launched several constitutional initiatives that would have forced hundreds of thousands of foreigners to leave the country almost immediately. There was a great temptation for Swiss voters to accept these constitutional initiatives. Not only was the economic boom over, but Switzerland also gave the impression of being overcrowded, with too much traffic on the highways and a severe housing shortage. To be sure, all major political parties and special interest groups recommended rejection of the constitutional amendments proposed by the antialien movement, because they felt it would be morally wrong to treat a defenseless minority in such a harsh way. But there was the obvious danger that frustrated voters would vent their antiforeigner prejudices. No rational justification was necessary, only a mark on a secret ballot.

The constitutional amendments received broad popular support but were defeated each time, although sometimes quite narrowly. The leading newspapers printed editorials applauding the maturity of Swiss voters. It must indeed be recognized that, in these referenda, a majority of Swiss voters were willing to protect the rights of a weak minority. However, the federal government itself took some vigorous steps to limit the number of foreigners in Switzerland. Thus, the majority of the voters preferred the milder policy of the government to the harsher measures of the antialien movement.

The foreign worker issue was a very difficult test for the notion that a direct democracy is able to protect minorities. When the minorities are not as marginal to Swiss society as foreign workers, Jews, and conscientious objectors, they usually have a good chance of having their special rights protected. It may even be a popular argument in a referendum that a proposal would benefit small minorities like Italian speakers in southern Switzerland or mountain farmers.

How does the Swiss voter make his or her decision in a referendum? Is the Swiss citizen a wise sovereign who is well informed and carefully weighs all arguments for and against a proposal? The referendum has certainly had an educating effect and has raised the level of political knowledge, but the Swiss citizen should not be viewed too idealistically. Propaganda is an important feature in referendum campaigns. Even more than in elections, the views of citizens can be molded in referenda. In elections, most voters have some long-standing party loyalty that is difficult to change. But, in a referendum, voters may be very unfamiliar with the issue and consequently much more open to propaganda effects. Money and organization are therefore important weapons in referenda. However, a costly campaign can backfire by creating sympathy for the financially weaker side.

Voter turnout in referenda is often shamefully low. This problem is of great concern because the trend has continued downward since the 1950s. There are today many referenda in which voter turnout is between 30 and 40 percent. There are exceptions, however, like the referendum on the army, which was considered to be such an important issue that 69 percent of the people voted.* Many explanations for the generally low turnout have been offered by scholars and other commentators. Might four times a year (on average) be too often to call on voters to cast their ballot? Have the issues become too complicated? Are the causes deeper, for example, a selfish retreat into private lives, or a general distrust of politics? In fact, the explanation of declining voter turnout probably lies in a combination of these and many other factors.

Probably the greatest weakness of the referendum as practiced in Switzerland is that unconventional minorities may not be sufficiently protected. The greatest strength of the referendum is the legitimacy it gives to political decisions. An increasing problem in modern democracies is the lack of legitimacy of many political decisions. Thus, transferring more political

---

* Turnout in recent elections was around 50 percent, thus, on the average, somewhat higher than for referenda.

responsibility from politicians and bureaucrats to the people has advantages. If the outcomes of a decision are mostly negative, the voters must share at least part of the blame.

GREAT BRITAIN

While the Swiss stress that democracy is above all else government *by* the people, the British see the ideal of democracy best fulfilled in government *of* and *for* the people. At the core of this notion is the belief that Parliament can better speak for the people than the people themselves. Parliament is *of* the people in the sense that its members are elected by the citizenry, but once elected, Parliament is sovereign and has not only the right but the duty to make decisions *for* the people. According to British political thinking, Parliament cannot delegate this duty to anyone else—not to the courts, and not even to the people.

How do the British justify the idea that decisions are best made in Parliament? There is a certain sacred mystique about the British House of Commons, located in Westminster palace on the Thames River in the heart of London. Westminster is considered the birthplace of modern Parliament, and there, generation after generation, the people have spoken out through their representatives. In the British view, the crucial point is that the voice of the people is not only heard but debated. In this process of debate, the people's true needs are expected to be clarified and to emerge in a "purified" form. Thus, the "sum" of the people's will expressed in the decisions of the House of Commons is more than the mere addition of what all individual citizens desire. Arguments are judged not simply according to the frequency with which they are expressed but also according to their logic and plausibility. Parliamentary debate also takes account of the intensity with which a position is held. The British doctrine is that in a referendum the voice of the people is expressed in raw form, whereas in parliamentary debate these manifold voices are integrated through negotiation into a more coherent overall will. The members of parliament are able to exercise a strong leadership role with this doctrine. They are not simply messengers for the demands of the voters; their task is, rather, to put those demands into the larger context of the common good and thus establish the best possible legislation.

As might be expected, the reality of the House of Commons does not correspond to this idealistic doctrine. Debates are often partisan and rancorous and sometimes deteriorate into shouting matches. But, as an ideal norm, this doctrine still helps to justify the belief that a true democracy should be of a representative, not a direct, nature. In their long history, the British have held only a single national referendum: in 1975, over Britain's continued membership in the European Community (see Chapter 16). Two years earlier, when the Conservatives were in power, Britain had joined the European Community. Labour was badly split on the issue, and they saw no other way to resolve their internal conflict when they came to power than to organize a national referendum. The notion that Parliament is sovereign was not formally overthrown with the referendum, because it was explicitly stated that the referendum was to be advisory only. The governing Labour party followed the advice of the people, who according to the referendum wished to remain in the European Community. The 1975 referendum may have set an important precedent that factually, but not formally, violated the principle that Parliament alone is sovereign in the British system of government. Thus, it can be argued that, if a British government ever wishes to withdraw from the European Community, it will first have to obtain the assent of the voters in a referendum. If so, other important decisions—such as withdrawal from NATO or abolishment of the House of Lords—may also require a referendum. Another precedent was set at the local level when the referendum was used to ask the voters of Scotland and Wales whether they wished more political autonomy (see Chapter 11). It remains to be seen whether Great Britain will use the referendum more frequently in the future.

_____ INCREASED IMPORTANCE OF THE REFERENDUM _____

The other European democracies have less of a tradition of parliamentary sovereignty than Great Britain. As a consequence, these countries are generally more open to demands that voters be allowed not only to elect representatives but also to decide substantive matters via the referendum. These demands have been made more frequently in recent years, especially by younger voters who feel that they are qualified to speak for themselves. They reject the idea that all decisions should be made by professional politicians, whom they tend to view with little respect anyway. Many recent scandals— such as the acceptance of illegal campaign contributions by leading members of the West German parliament, and the membership of Italian deputies in a secret and powerful lodge—have further eroded public respect for politicians. Today, many European citizens have begun to ask why such politicians should be thought to know what the people need better than the people themselves.

A push for referenda also comes from a development described in Chapter 11, namely, that party labels have little meaning when it comes to new issues like protection of the environment. Voters often have no idea which party to vote for in order to do something about the dying forests, for example. Would it be better in such cases to let the voters speak for themselves in a referendum?

Even when party labels still do have meaning, many European voters feel that important decisions are made not by the parties but by powerful interest groups and state bureaucracies. A vote for a particular party may not have any great impact in certain cases, and interest groups and bureaucracies are almost immune to election results. Here again, voters may wish to exercise their influence, not only in elections, but also in referenda.

Two political scientists, David Butler and Austin Ranney, state that referenda "are almost certain to increase in number and importance in the years ahead."[32] Both Sweden and Austria settled the tricky issue of nuclear power in referenda. In Italy, the divorce issue was very controversial for many years and was finally submitted to a referendum. Spain held a referendum on its membership in NATO.

The United States has a long tradition of referenda at the state and local level—influenced, incidentally, by the Swiss experience. Should Americans introduce the referendum at the national level? Could a world superpower leave key decisions of foreign policy—such as ratification of a disarmament treaty—to the people?

A REFERENDUM IN HUNGARY

The first truly free and unrestricted vote of the people in a Communist Eastern European country took place in Hungary on November 26, 1989. To be sure, as we have seen in Chapter 2, a few months earlier there were multiparty elections in Poland, but the Communists had reserved two-thirds of the seats for themselves, so that only one-third of the parliamentary seats were truly contested.

In Hungary, by contrast, the will of the people could be expressed in an unrestricted way. Interestingly enough, this first free vote was on a referendum. The question submitted to the people was when presidential elections should take place. Parliament, which at the time was still controlled by the Communists, had decided that presidential elections should be held on January 7, 1990. Four opposition parties—the Free Democrats, the Young Democrats, the Independent Smallholders Party, and the Social Democrats—objected to this plan. They argued that parliamentary elections, scheduled for later in the year, should be held first. The four opposition parties feared that early presidential elections would give an undue advantage to the Communist candidate. They considered it to be undemocratic to choose so important an official while the Communists still controlled all essential offices and such vital political advantages as access to state-run television and most of the press.

The four parties collected signatures in order to challenge the decision of parliament about the date of presidential elections. As we have seen, such challenges are possible in Switzerland, where 50,000 signatures are needed. In Hungary, 100,000 signatures are required for a decision of parliament to be submitted to a referendum. The four opposition parties had no difficulties in attaining this limit, and they even reached more than double the needed number of signatures.

In the referendum campaign, the fronts took a rather complicated shape, because another opposition party, the Democratic Forum, supported the Communists' desire for early presidential elections. The proposed Communist candidate, Imre Pozsgay, was a moderate, and the Democratic Forum expected that it could work with him.

Thus, it was not easy for the Hungarian voter to decide which way to vote. The choice was not simply to support or to oppose the ruling Communist party. As we have seen, in Switzerland too, the questions submitted to a popular referendum are often of great complexity. As a consequence, voter turnout is often quite low.

It was feared that in the first Hungarian referendum voter turnout would be low, too, which would have been a bad start for democratization in Eastern Europe. Fortunately, nearly 60 percent of the voters turned up at the ballot boxes, despite bad weather and a severe snowstorm that set in during the evening. A 50-percent voter turnout was required for the referendum to be valid. If it fell below this threshold, the referendum would fail, whatever the outcome. The four opposition parties could celebrate a double victory: Not only would the referendum be valid, but also the outcome would bring a decision, although a close one, to delay presidential elections until after parliamentary elections (see Box 7.2). Such close results would be in sharp contrast with the normal Communist pattern, in which almost 100 percent of the voters are forced to support the official party line. The referendum of November 26, 1989 was highly contested until all the votes were counted—a historical first in an Eastern bloc country!

The Communists accepted the outcome, and Pozsgay wisely said:

> While in eastern and central Europe hundreds of thousands of people are marching in the streets to express their opinions. Hungarians are going to the ballot box to express their political will.[33]

The Associated Press quoted a voter as saying: "We wanted to take into our own hands the possibility to decide on the people's future."[34]

It may be a good sign that the first free vote in an Eastern bloc country was on a referendum. When in the summer of 1989 I traveled in Hungary and explained to political science colleagues and ordinary citizens the working of the Swiss referendum, I encountered great interest. Transition to a democratic regime presupposes that the new rulers of the game are commonly accepted. The old rulers can, of course, not be trusted to establish fair new

---

_____ **BOX 7.2** _____

HUNGARIANS REJECT ELECTION TIMETABLE
OF THE RULING PARTY

BUDAPEST—Voters rejected the election timetable of the ruling party by the narrowest of margins in a referendum on Sunday, forcing it to abandon its plan to elect the first President of the republic while it retained full control of the Government.

In today's counting in Hungary's first free national vote since World War II, a narrow Government lead wilted steadily until Minister of State Imre Pozsgay conceded that the opposition proposal to delay the presidential voting had carried the day.

Source: New York Times, November 28, 1989.

rules. In Hungary, I have seen great mistrust toward the Communist leaders and also toward the reformers among them. This mistrust even spills over toward the leaders of the opposition parties. Having been misled and abused by politicians for so many years, it is understandable that Hungarians have become distrustful of any politician.

Under these circumstances, it seems wise to let the people themselves decide in referenda under what exact rules they wish to operate their newly formed democracy. In this way, the rules can assume the necessary legitimacy. In deciding for itself when presidential elections should be held, the Hungarian people have given to these elections great legitimacy. Whoever is elected does not have to face the challenge that the date of the election will be manipulated in his or her favor.

I hope that the Hungarians and the other Eastern bloc countries will often use the referendum to decide by what rules the democratic game should be played. It will also be useful if not only procedural but also substantive questions are decided in referenda. This will be particularly true for the hard economic times ahead for these countries. If tough austerity measures have to be taken, for example, to reduce the foreign debt, referenda decisions will be much more accepted by the people than decisions made by politicians. There is a lesson to be learned from the case of Switzerland, where the citizens can blame only themselves if they make the wrong decisions. If it turns out, for example, that not joining the United Nations has brought severe disadvantages to the country, the people can only blame themselves, because they decided against the recommendations of cabinet and parliament. There are, of course, problems with the referendum, such as the often low turnout and the influence of organizations with money. Eastern European countries would do well to study the Swiss case carefully in order to minimize these problems. They may, for example, put limits on the amount of money to be spent in a referendum campaign—a measure that the Swiss have not yet adopted.

A CANCELED REFERENDUM IN ROMANIA

The potential danger of the referendum was revealed in a bizarre five-day episode in Romania in January 1990. In the preceding month, Communist dictator Nicolae Ceausescu had been overthrown in a bloody revolution (page 33–34). On December 25, 1989, he and his wife had been sentenced to death by a secret military tribunal and immediately executed. On the following day, the so-called Council of National Salvation, which had grown out of the revolution, had abolished the death penalty. But many Romanians wished that some of the close collaborators of Ceausescu would also be put to death. On January 12, 1990, a huge crowd assembled in front of the headquarters of the Council of National Salvation shouting "Death to Communists." Three members of the Council emerged from the headquarters, and under the pressure of the crowd, promised that on January 28 a national referendum would be held on the reintroduction of the death penalty. As an immediate measure, they also announced the banning of the Communist party.

The following day, the 11-member executive board of the Council of National Salvation recalled the decision to ban the Communist party and decided instead that this issue would also be put to a national referendum. Four days later, on January 14, in a full session of its 145 members, the Council of National Salvation canceled both referenda. The cancellation was justified by the fact that the decision to hold the referendum was made "under the pressure of the crowd."[35] It is also important for us to know that there was foreign pressure not to reintroduce the death penalty. Such pressure came, in particular, from the Foreign Ministers of West Germany and Sweden, who were visiting Bucharest during those days.

Would holding the referendum not have been a crucial step for Romania's transition to democracy? Is not letting the people decide on political issues the most democratic means to settle them? Was the Council of National Salvation suddenly afraid of the power of the people? There were at least three problems with holding a referendum on banning the Communist party and on the reintroduction of the death penalty:

1. The calling of a referendum would have to be done in an orderly fashion, like in Hungary, where the citizens collected the necessary number of signatures. In Romania, it was indeed the pressure of the crowd that brought about the initial decision to have a referendum. Following this path could easily lead to the mob's ruling the situation: Who shouts the most has the most influence.
2. To hold a referendum within about two weeks would not allow enough time for reflection and cool deliberation. A referendum should not simply be an outlet for mass emotions. In a referendum, citizens become decision makers themselves, thereby assuming all the ensuing responsibilities. They have to inform themselves and to consider all the consequences of their decisions.
3. At the beginning of a transition to democracy, it would not be wise to have the first referendum on very emotional issues. As we have seen, Switzerland too sometimes decides on very emotional issues in a referendum, for example, whether to expell a large number of foreign workers or to abolish the army. In such cases, there is always the danger that emotions will become too high and that strain will be put on the country. But the Swiss people went through a long process in which they learned how to handle such situations, so that occasionally such referenda can be tolerated without threatening the stability of the country. In a transition to democracy, it would be more appropriate, like in Hungary, to begin with a procedural decision, such as determining the date of an election.

I conclude that it was a good decision of the Council of National Salvation to cancel the referendum; otherwise, the Council could easily have been discredited as a democratic institution.

8

CODETERMINATION AT THE WORKPLACE

Many Europeans argue that democracy cannot be practiced only in the political arena but also must be practiced in the economic arena. According to this view, people should have a voice at their workplace because it is there that they spend most of their time. A discussion of democracy at the workplace raises the question of how democratic a country really is if the principle of democracy is applied only to the political, not to the economic, field. Opinions differ widely on this issue among Europeans.

FEDERAL REPUBLIC OF GERMANY

The most prominent example of worker participation in corporate decision making is the West German concept of codetermination. According to West German law, business must, within certain limits, share power with labor.

This concept of codetermination is all but unknown in the United States. To be sure, American workers often have the option of purchasing shares of stock in their company. There have even been a few well-publicized cases— in the steel industry, for example—in which workers took over a troubled company by buying up all the outstanding shares of stock. The workers' decision-making power in these cases, however, is in their new role as shareholders, not as labor. In some sense, the workers become capitalists themselves and exert power like any other capitalists. It is also not codetermination in the West German sense if the president of the United Automobile Workers serves on the board of directors of Chrysler Corporation, because he is appointed as an individual, and the union as such has no right to the position. In West Germany, in contrast, labor has a legal right to sit on boards of directors. Since the early 1950s the country had experimented already with the concept of codetermination, in particular in the coal and steel industries.

The current law on codetermination was enacted by the West German parliament in 1976, and it applies only to companies with more than 2,000 employees. Thus, the owner of a small business, such as a bakery, is not legally required to let employees participate in business decisions. In companies to which the law does apply, the number of people serving on the board of directors depends on the size of the company. If a company employs more than 20,000 people, the board of directors must have 20 members.

In such large companies, how are the 20 board members elected, and how do they make decisions? At first glance, it seems that the principle of parity between the shareholders and labor is applied in a strict form, because each side elects 10 members to the board. In fine print, however, the law is tilted in favor of the shareholders. The most important provision in this regard is that tie votes are to be broken by the chairperson, and no chairperson can be elected against the wishes of the shareholders' representatives. The board elects a chairperson from among its members, and a candidate must get two-thirds of the vote in order to be elected on the first ballot. If nobody wins, a second ballot takes place in which only shareholders have the right to vote. Thus, shareholders have a clear veto over who becomes chairperson. The law diminishes the power of labor in two additional ways. First, one of the labor representatives must be a top manager, who, because of his or her position in the company, is likely to vote frequently with the shareholders. Second, labor is not allowed to have more than three union officials from outside the company among its representation. This limitation works against labor, because full-time union officials tend to have special skills in representing the interests of labor, whereas rank-and-file workers may lack such skills.

Despite these restrictions on labor, the law was challenged in court on the grounds that it infringed on the constitution's guarantees concerning property rights. The Federal Constitutional Court upheld the constitutionality of the law, in part because the law did not grant real parity to labor but left ultimate control with the shareholders. The court also found that there was no evidence of labor's using destructive tactics to the detriment of companies; on the contrary, the court found that labor had demonstrated a spirit of loyalty and cooperation in board deliberations (see Box 8.1).

The law on codetermination was seen by the West German labor movement as an important step toward a democratic restructuring of the economy and society. In a resolution, labor stated that "the economic crisis has clearly shown that jobs and trainee opportunities and other employee interests are endangered when economic and social development is subordinated to the profit motives of the firms." Labor argued that codetermination is necessary "for guarding the rights of employees, supervising investment, protecting employees in cases of rationalization, increasing job safety, improving working conditions."[36] West German labor is indeed dissatisfied that the law did not bring true parity but for the time being tolerates it as an acceptable compromise.

In other countries—France, Great Britain, and Italy, in particular—labor is strongly opposed to the West German model of codetermination, which it sees as a means of pacifying the unions. By participating in the decision making of large business companies, labor is said to have been co-opted by the capitalist class. As a consequence, workers lose their class consciousness, an argument encountered earlier in discussing current Marxist thinking in Europe (Chapter 1). In this view, as long as a society has a capitalist structure, the strategy of labor should be to fight the capitalists rather than to cooperate with them.

—————————————— **BOX 8.1** ——————————————

WEST GERMAN COURT CASE ABOUT CO-DETERMINATION

Appeals by Employers
On 29 June 1977, nine firms and 29 employers' associations lodged an appeal with the Federal Constitutional Court on constitutional grounds against the main provisions of the Co-determination Act.

The employers motivated their constitutional appeal as follows:

The Co-determination Act contains a provision on the right of employees to an equal say in the supervisory board and this will lead sooner or later to an equal number of employees' and shareholders' representatives in management. . . .

[T]he Co-determination Act infringes the property guarantee contained in Article 14 of the Basic Law. Shareholders' property is fundamentally affected both in the substance of members' rights as well as in that of their pecuniary rights.

The Co-determination Act contains elements of an enforced amalgamation between shareholders and employees and thus infringes the free right to form associations and societies pursuant to Article 9, para 1 of the Basic Law.

Furthermore, the Act infringes entrepreneurial freedom as part of the right freely to choose one's trade, occupation or profession (Article 12 of the Basic Law).

Ruling by Court
The Federal Constitutional Court gave its ruling on 1 March 1979. It rejected the constitutional appeals and held that the contested provisions of the Co-determination Act are consistent with the Basic Law. . . .

When reaching its decision, the Court proceeded from the assumption in agreement with the Federal Government that co-management by workers pursuant to the Co-determination Act will remain at less than parity, since the shareholders enjoy a slight preponderance. . . . They benefit in the supervisory board from the chairman's casting vote and, moreover, the group of employees in the supervisory board (due in part to the guaranteed seats for senior executives) is less compact than that of the shareholders. . . . Admitedly, the powers of the shareholders as members of the supervisory board have been reduced—though not by half—inasmuch as the shareholders as a whole retain their decisive influence in the undertaking. However, this restriction remains within the ambit of the commitments of property-owners to society in general.

Source: Co-determination in the Federal Republic of Germany (Bonn: Federal Minister of Labour and Social Affairs, 1980), pp. 23–26, 42.

SWEDEN

Sweden since 1984 has been experimenting with a model of codetermination that takes account of the complaints about the West German model. In this Swedish model, profits are shared between shareholders and labor, but not in the common sense of profit sharing in which individual workers receive bonuses in their paychecks. Instead, the profits go to special Employee Investment Funds. These funds are administered by management boards, each comprising nine members. Board members are appointed by the government, with the stipulation that at least five members have to represent employees. The other members are public interest representatives. The Employee Investment Funds use their capital to buy shares in Swedish companies, which gives the Funds voting rights at the companies' annual general meetings. In one of its publications, the Swedish Trade Union Confederation characterizes the Employee Investment Funds as "a step forward in the struggle for economic democracy."[37] As might be expected, there is also much resistance to the scheme, particularly in the business community, but also among many workers who would prefer to share profits individually rather than collectively.

EUROPEAN UNIVERSITIES

Student readers will be interested to learn that the principle of codetermination is also applied to many European universities. The argument is made that the university is the students' workplace and therefore students should have a right to participate in its decision making; a right granted to factory workers should also be granted to university students. The farthest-reaching model is for students to have one-third of the voting power in university bodies, such as faculty recruitment committees, departmental meetings, and so forth. Another third of the voting power goes to the junior faculty, and the remaining third goes to the senior faculty.

When this model of third-based parity is applied, coalitions are often formed between students and junior faculty against senior faculty. Such coalitions are justified by the argument that they allow new ideas to be implemented in the old university structures. From this perspective, the senior faculty is mainly viewed as defending old, established privileges. To end these privileges is seen in a broader political context, and students and junior faculty often argue in Marxist terms. The senior faculty are said to represent capitalist class interests by helping to train useful tools, such as tax lawyers and nuclear engineers, for the capitalist system. According to the Marxist argument, the main task of the university should be to unmask the unjust class structure and come to the help of all those suffering from exploitation. Decisions about curricula, hiring, and firing thus quickly become fierce debates about the nature of science and its purpose in society.

The counterposition is that the situation of students is not at all comparable to factory workers' because the university is not the students' permanent workplace but merely the institution where they receive training for later jobs. Because they are still in the learning process, students do not have the same expertise in university matters as factory workers are likely to have in their special fields. While an automobile worker may have acquired a good knowledge of how a car's brakes should be built through long experience, students do not yet have any special knowledge of how a long-term research project should be organized. They are at the university precisely to learn about such matters. Therefore, university decisions should be left to the faculty, who alone have the necessary competence to make responsible decisions for the long-term good of the institution. This argument does not necessarily exclude students from all decision making. They may be consulted, and it is even compatible with the logic of the argument to let senior students have a voice in certain votes for which they have gained the necessary knowledge, for example, concerning the curriculum for beginning students.

University life in Europe is strongly characterized by the struggle between these two positions. To take a middle position is often difficult and unpleasant, because professors and students who do so are treated as untrustworthy by both sides.

9

ECONOMIC INTEREST GROUPS

Having expanded the concept of democracy to include codetermination at the workplace in the last chapter, we now have seen how trade unions can be important political actors. In this chapter, I wish to deal more generally with economic interest groups. They are often said to defend special interests. What is the relationship between special interests and the common good?

SPECIAL INTERESTS AND THE COMMON GOOD

In the United States, many economic interest groups are active in the political process. Farmers, teachers, bankers, truckers, miners, and others are politically organized. For Americans, to represent special interests has mostly a negative connotation. The impression evoked is that a special interest group seeks privileges detrimental to the common good. In American political thinking, the influence of such groups should ideally be as limited as possible. Many people believe, for example, that members of Congress should be unencumbered by such special interests and instead should strive to make decisions for a higher common good. In this view, special interest groups should be kept to the lobbies of the Capitol, and it is from this perspective that interest groups are called lobbies in the United States.

The term *lobby* makes less sense in a European context. An official of an economic interest group often may also be a prominent member of a political party and as such, may sit in the national parliament. There he or she may speak not only for his or her party but also for his or her interest group. Thus, interest groups are heard, not only at hearings and in the lobbies, but in parliament itself. In Europe, possible discrepancies between the common good and special interests are stressed less than in the United States. In European political thinking, the common good is often seen simply as the outcome of fair and honest negotiations among the various interests. This perspective gives interest groups in Europe a greater legitimacy and more public visibility than in the United States. This does not mean, however, that European interest groups are necessarily more influential than their American counterparts.

Why do Americans tend to believe more than Europeans do in a common good that is more than the outcome of a particular interest group configuration? A first explanation can be derived from a certain European cynicism. Many Europeans consider it naive and unsophisticated to believe in a common good mysteriously located above all special interests. After all, politics is a battle, and the best one can hope for is that all interests be fairly represented.

To refer to a greater cynicism in Europe than in America is, of course, only begging the question. Why do Americans have more of a tendency to believe, idealistically perhaps, in a common good distinct from and superior to all special interests? Possibly, it is because they seem to share common national values to a greater extent, making it easier to agree on a common good. One such common national value is the wisdom of the American Founding Fathers. If it is possible to demonstrate that a political solution corresponds to their wisdom, Americans tend to accept it as serving the common good. Most European countries, however, do not have a readily recognizable set of founders. On the contrary, who a country's real founders were is often a topic for heated debate. The French, for example, disagree strongly over whether they should look more to the Bourbon kings, the leaders of the French Revolution, or perhaps Napoléon Bonaparte. Given such disagreements about the "spiritual" origin of the country, it is difficult to refer to the wisdom of the founders in defining the common good.

The situation is even more complex in Germany. Konrad Adenauer and other founders of the Federal Republic of Germany in 1949 are too recent and partisan to be revered as wise founding fathers. Adolf Hitler, founder of the Third Reich in 1933, is, of course, a negative symbol. There are also problems with militaristic Prussians like Otto von Bismarck, who founded the Second Reich in 1870–1871. The many emperors of the Holy Roman Empire of the German Nation are so distant and their connections to the current Germany tenuous that they can hardly be considered founding fathers. (For German unification, see Chapter 16.)

Great Britain and some of the smaller European countries like Switzerland and the Netherlands have fewer difficulties in identifying their founders. But even in these countries, there is less agreement than in America on who the founders were and what guidance they provide the current generation.

Besides the Founding Fathers, many Americans have a deep religious faith as a source from which to derive the common good of the country. Religious people of whatever faith are probably more open to the possibility that a common good can transcend individual interests. In Europe the situation is quite different, with widespread religious apathy (see Chapter 10). Therefore, religiosity is a weak basis on which to justify the higher common good.

As still another source for the justification of the common good, Americans often use the writings of free market philosophers. The idea of these philosophers that the invisible hand of the market contributes to the common good is deeply embedded in American thinking, although not always in practice. In European thinking, on the other hand, there is much less agreement on the beneficial effects of market mechanisms.

Thus, our conclusion so far is that economic interest groups occupy a more visible and legitimate position in the political process in Europe than in the United States because of a greater European cynicism about the feasibility of defining a common good above various special interests. Second, a long European tradition supports the legitimacy of economic interest group participation in political decision making. This tradition goes back to the medieval guild system in which bakers, butchers, and similar occupational groups were tightly organized in European towns. These guilds not only regulated their internal affairs but also played an important role in the political life of the community. Although the guild system has since been dissolved, the doctrine that occupational groups should have a central place in politics persists. It is a sign of this continuity that in many European cities guilds still flourish, although in a new form—as prestigious private clubs with important social functions. In Zurich, for example, the guilds organize a popular parade through the streets of the city every spring. Most members of these modern-day guilds no longer belong to the respective occupational groups but come from high-status professions such as law, medicine, business, and so forth. Memories of the guilds are also kept alive in the names of streets and fashionable restaurants. With this historical background, it is understandable that in European politics economic interest groups are not relegated to the lobbies of parliament but are allowed entry to parliament itself. This raises the question of the relations between political parties and economic interest groups.

POLITICAL PARTIES AND ECONOMIC INTEREST GROUPS

Although membership fees are, as a general rule, much higher in an economic interest group than in a political party (pages 63–64), many more Europeans join an economic interest group than a political party. It is seen as a more immediate personal advantage to belong to an economic interest group than to a political party. Usually more than half the work force of a particular economic sector is organized. Membership can even approach 100 percent when it is the precondition for receiving some essential service. Almost all farmers, for example, join a farmers' association because it offers access to advantageous insurance programs and many other services.

The combination of larger membership and higher membership fees means that economic interest groups tend to be much more affluent than the political parties. The unions, for example, are more affluent than the Socialist parties; the business associations, more affluent than the Conservative parties. These differences in financial resources are vividly seen in the headquarters, where it is not uncommon to find economic interest groups located in luxurious office buildings with huge staffs, while political parties have modest rooms and small staffs. In a few countries, notably Germany, the financial condition of the parties is somewhat better than elsewhere, as a result of government contributions.

Simultaneous membership in an economic interest group and a political party leads to a certain pattern of interaction between the two, but this pattern varies greatly from country to country. Such variation by country occurs clearly for the trade union movement. In Germany, Great Britain, and Sweden, for example, the trade unions have a single national organization, and most trade union leaders also belong to the Socialist party. In Great Britain, the trade unions even have a collective membership status in the Labour party. In other countries, including France, Italy, and Switzerland, the trade union movement is split into several separate national organizations, each having a special affiliation with a different party. Italy, for example, has three large trade union organizations, one close to the Communists, a second, to the Socialists, and a third, to the Christian Democrats.

Business associations, as might be expected, have a close affiliation with Conservatives and Liberal parties (remember that European Liberals are strong advocates of the free market). In some countries, farmers have developed their own agrarian parties: In Sweden, the Center party to a large extent represents farmers' interests. In countries without a special agrarian party, farmers mostly support parties of the political right, but some small farmers, mainly in Italy and France, are Socialists or even Communists. White-collar employees and their interest groups are usually not close to particular parties but pursue the strategy of having good relations with all the parties.

If leaders of an economic interest group also belong to a political party, they may or may not run for a parliamentary seat. The situation varies a great deal from country to country and from one interest group to another. German trade union officials, for example, are more likely than their French counterparts to run for parliament. To explain such variation between countries and interest groups would require detailed historical analysis. Important in the present context is the question whether, from the perspective of democratic theory, the leaders of economic interest groups *should* also sit in parliament. A negative response might arise from the fear that giving voice to special economic interests in parliament could decrease the chances that decisions will be made for the common good. But one could also argue that it is better to hear the representatives of economic interests in the open forum of parliamentary debates. In this way positions are made clearer to the general public than they are by interest group lobbying. Moreover, the responsibility of a parliamentary seat might lead to some moderation in the positions of interest group representatives.

POLICY PROGRAMS

Policy programs of the economic interest groups are not covered here as they were for the political parties. First, these programs are to a large extent self-explanatory and can be deduced from the group's name. Thus, it is easy to guess that teachers' associations fight for higher wages and better health insurance programs for their members.

At a more specific level, we come immediately to minute details. Do teachers' associations support merit pay, and, if so, how should a teacher's performance be measured? Should their health insurance programs cover psychoanalysis, and, if so, how many sessions should be covered per year? At this specific level, there is wide variation from country to country and even within countries, because many of these issues are dealt with more locally. Entire monographs have been published on the policy programs of teachers' associations in Europe. The same is true for medical associations, bankers' associations, trade unions, trade associations, and so on. More interesting than such detailed program descriptions is the question of how the demands of the various economic interest groups influence the political decision process and its outcome. This question will be addressed in Chapter 14 on corporatist decision making.

10

CHURCHES

A major difference between Europe and America lies in the place that religion occupies in the respective societies. In following the European news, Americans hear that Protestants and Catholics are engaged in a civil war in Northern Ireland, that many European political parties have names that include the term *Christian*, and that church and state are not separated in many European countries. One might, as a result, conclude that religion is very important in Europe today, but the opposite is true. Compared to the United States, there is pronounced religious apathy in Europe.

In order to understand the religious situation in Europe, we must first look back to history. In medieval times, the Catholic church competed with state authorities for worldly power. This was most vividly exemplified by the rivalry between the popes and the German emperors. Slowly, this battle was decided in favor of the state authorities. Protestant churches were placed from the beginning under the domination of state authorities. When the medieval period ended and modern nation-states began to develop in the sixteenth and seventeenth centuries, state authorities remained mostly in control of the churches. This gave the churches the advantage of state protection and financing. The states, on the other hand, were helped by the churches in guiding the behavior of the population. At that time, states attempted to regulate the lives of their subjects in minute detail, from the clothes that could be worn to the days and hours when dancing was allowed. The clergy greatly aided the implementation of these rules, for example, by announcing them during church services. State and church in fact had a close symbiosis, with their leaders often coming from the same families. One brother in a community could represent the state authorities and reside in the castle, while another brother stood for the church and lived in a splendid house next to it. The churches were always built in a central part of a village or town, as symbols of their importance. Traveling in Europe, one can still see these churches as impressive landmarks today.

Each state recognized only one church, the so-called state church. In a Catholic country like France, this was the Roman Catholic church. In Protestant countries, the situation varied, with the Lutheran church the state church in Sweden, for example, and the Anglican church the state church in Great Britain. Religious dissenters from the official state church had a hard time and often were persecuted, and many of them made their way to the United States to find religious freedom. Religious faith had to be very deep for people to take it as a reason to emigrate to a faraway continent. This emigration pattern from Europe to America is part of the explanation why religious faith is still so high in America.

The existence of state churches meant that national borders often were also religious borders and therefore all the more important. If a ruler could conquer a foreign territory, he or she could also gain the souls of its inhabitants—in part the motivation of many bloody religious wars from the sixteenth to the eighteenth centuries. In the nineteenth century, however, such religious wars ended, and today it is inconceivable that two European countries would fight a war over religion. The same is true for religious civil wars in countries like Germany, the Netherlands, and Switzerland, whose populations are composed of both Protestants and Catholics. Northern Ireland is no exception because, as we will see in Chapter 11, the civil strife there is really between two ethnic groups that happen to have different religious affiliations. To say that religious wars are impossible in Europe today does not exclude the possibility of lingering animosities between Protestants and Catholics. Most of the time, however, negative feelings remain below the surface.

In Europe today, states still have a special relationship with particular churches, but this relationship is fundamentally different from former times. There are countries such as France and Italy where the concept of an official state church has been formally abolished, but the change is more symbolic than real, because state churches effectively still exist. In France and Italy the Roman Catholic church still enjoys many privileges that are not given to other churches. The state, in particular, offers financial support to private Catholic schools and allows Catholic prayer in state schools.

Besides the formally or informally recognized state church, European countries today also tolerate other churches. Indeed, religious freedom is proclaimed, and there are practically no restrictions on any church concerning when and how it wishes to hold religious services. Thus, Jews can freely worship in synagogues and Mormons go from house to house to speak for their religion. Baptists, Methodists, and other denominations well known in the United States are not recognized as state churches anywhere in Europe, but they can now build their own churches. Numerically, the overwhelming majority of Europeans still belong to their respective state church. Even so, many minority churches today flourish, while their larger state counterparts are undergoing a severe crisis of spirit, at least partly as a result of their privileged position in the state. For members of a state church, the church is always there for special occasions like weddings and funerals. Since it is largely funded by the state, it requires no looking after by its members, for just as taxes are allocated for other state functions, they go to the state church. To belong to the state church is like belonging to your country, and just as many people have become apathetic citizens, so have they become apathetic members of the state church.

The attitude of many Europeans who belong to their state church only "on paper" is that membership in the church can be used if you wish, but no special effort is required to keep it up. If you do not use it at all, you could give it up by filling out a form somewhere in the state or church bureaucracy. But why bother, if continued membership has no importance one way or the other? Religious education in school does not prevent this attitude but, rather, contributes to it. Schoolchildren study religion like they study any other subject. Once they have completed a subject, they leave it; they complete religion courses like history or physics courses. For many young Europeans, the end of religious education in school is the end of any contact with church matters for a long time, sometimes forever. Surveys show that in some European countries less than 5 percent of young state church members regularly attend church services; in France, for example, 2.5 percent among young people below the age of 25.[38] Low attendance at church service does not mean, however, that most Europeans deny the existence of God. According to several surveys, all European countries have a clear majority believing in God. At the low end are Denmark and France, where about two-thirds of the population express a belief in God; at the high end is Ireland, where 97 percent of the people believe in God.

The state churches have lost many of the secular functions that they formerly performed for the state. In particular, they no longer help the state to any large extent in regulating the moral behavior of the population. There are three reasons for this: First, with the low attendance at church services, the clergy is simply unable to reach many people. Second, the state itself has largely given up any effort to tell people how to behave in moral terms. This is perhaps most visible in summer, when many young women sunbathe topless at Europe's beaches, lakes, and rivers. This behavior still runs contrary to many regulations, but it is increasingly tolerated by the state authorities. Third, the clergy itself is also less willing to render moral guidance, because many members prefer to maintain more distance between themselves and the state than their predecessors did.

This new distance between church and state needs some explanation. Only 25 or 30 years ago, the clergy was a prime symbol of state authority in society. Today, many members of the clergy see their main function as one of protest against this authority. This changed attitude is already visible in their dress. Formerly, members of the clergy stressed their dignity by wearing dark clothes and a tie; today, they are much less formal. More important than this exterior change is a substantive change in the church's message. The younger clergy, in particular, argue that Jesus Christ was a rebel in his time who challenged the strong in society and fought for the weak. According to this view, the Christian church should not have stood for centuries at the side of the powerful in politics and society. Its place should be at the side of the feeble and helpless.

With such beliefs, many clergy members find it necessary to extend their interests from narrow religious questions to the broad political issues of the world. They claim that, to be relevant, religion should deal with the totality of human existence, and this by necessity includes the political aspect. Thus, many clergy members have begun to express political positions in a variety of areas. (see Box 10.1 for the case of Sweden). With regard to the problems of the Third World, they no longer limit their activities to the organization of charitable work, such as sending food parcels to poor blacks in South Africa.

BOX 10.1

GOD WAS NOT REALLY DEAD IN SWEDEN, JUST SLEEPING

Astonishing as it seems, this most secularized of countries can still be stirred by religious controversy. It all started with a sermon by Stockholm's newly appointed bishop, Krister Stendahl. . . . The bishop did not unleash the controversy with some new version of the ontological proof of God's existence, but by riding one of Sweden's two hobby-horses: taxes. (The other hobby-horse in Sweden is alcohol.) Tax evasion could be a sin, the bishop declared. He did not mean only outright cheating on tax returns but also legal emigration with all one's belongings in order to enjoy a milder climate and less punitive taxes in Switzerland, Spain or England.

Those Swedes who emigrate are refusing to bear their social burden, the bishop maintained. In placing their own interests and those of their family before society's they are egoistic or, in short, sinners. He called on Christians to condemn this perfectly legal behavior of their brethren. The bishop's sermon predictably delighted the Social Democrats while the opposition, just as predictably, raised hell about religious functionaries meddling in politics.

The former Conservative Party leader, Gösta Bohman had, a few days before, fulminated against what he termed a politicized church. He demanded that the church respect Swedish law and abstain from encouraging, for example, the refusal to carry arms. The Swedish church, Mr. Bohman complained, weakens the national will to resist a possible future aggressor and went on: "Is it asking too much when I want the right not to have to see in my church posters with communist slogans painted by children?". . .

What the discussion comes down to is what role the state church should play in Sweden. Should it merely, as the conservative critics wish, tend to the spiritual needs of its members, or should it, as the more radical members want, also take an active political stance in questions such as aid to the Third World and the nuclear freeze? Does the fact that Sweden has a state church—the priests and the bishops are all paid by the government—in any way curtail what can be said in the pulpit?

Source: Carl Rudbeck, *International Herald Tribune,* 16–17, February, 1985.

They seek, instead, the political and social roots of problems and, in this case, for example, take up the political fight against the white regime in South Africa. This fight has made many of them aware of the strong connections between European banks and South Africa, which in turn has led them to a moral criticism of those banks. The clergy has also become very active in the peace movement. The justification in this case is that the survival of the human race is at stake and the church cannot and should not remain silent. No longer content to pray for peace in general terms, some clergy members choose to intervene in the political process by taking a public position in the Swiss referendum, for example, concerning the abolishment of the army (see Chapter 7) many clergy members supported the initiative, arguing their case with numerous quotes from the Bible (for example, Romans 5: "overpower evil with good").

It remains to be seen whether these political activities will bring new vigor to the state churches. Doubts are expressed not only outside but also inside churches when others, especially older clerics, do not favor mixing religion and politics. Further, a dilemma faced by politically active clergy members of state churches is that financially they depend on the very state whose authorities they so strongly criticize.

Finally, the political parties that include the term *Christian* in their names should be mentioned here. In Chapter 1, we noted that these are mostly Conservative parties, although in a few countries "Christian" parties pursue more centrist policies. Today, many politically active members of the clergy support Socialists, Greens, and even Communists. Yet for the voting behavior of the population at large, religious practice is still a good indicator of support for parties of the right. The clergy itself seems to have moved more to the left than ordinary churchgoers. It remains to be seen to what extent active church members will follow the clergy. If this indeed happens to a significant degree, the label "Christian" for Conservative parties would attain more historical than current significance.

11

SOCIAL MOVEMENTS

Besides political parties, economic interest groups, and the churches, there are still other actors in European politics: ethnic movements, the environmental movement, the peace movement, the women's movement, and the youth movement. We subsume all of these movements under the general term *social movements.* Generally, they have relatively loose organizations. Sometimes, for example, in the case of the youth movement, there is virtually no organization to speak of; and, although demonstrations occur, there are usually no permanent leaders to speak for the movement. This lack of organization justifies calling these groups *movements*, a term that evokes their transient nature.

Social movements may or may not be close to particular parties or economic interest groups. The women's movement, for example, is close to the Socialist parties and trade unions in most European democracies. The youth movement, on the other hand, tends to keep its distance from parties and economic interest groups. In other instances—the homosexual movement, for example—it is the parties and economic interest groups that do not wish to come too close. It can also happen that a social movement, or a part of it, tries to make the transition into a political party. We have already seen in Chapter 1 that, in many countries, supporters of the environmental and peace movements established the Green party.

ETHNIC MOVEMENTS

For Americans, ethnic groups are a familiar phenomenon. The term *ethnic groups* refers to immigrants from a particular country or region who retain an awareness of their common background. Polish Americans or Italian Americans are examples of ethnic groups. In the 1950s, some social scientists predicted that the importance of ethnic groups would steadily decrease. They argued that increased levels of communication, geographic mobility, and education would diminish the relevance of ethnic affiliations. These arguments have not been borne out by the developments of recent years. On the contrary, the United States has experienced a rebirth of ethnic identity, and many Americans identify more strongly with their ethnic affiliation today than in years past.

A similar development has occurred in Europe, where ethnic groups are not immigrants from other countries but descendants from a particular historical region. These descendants may still live in that region, or they may have moved elsewhere. A good example is the Scots. Scotland has its own long and rich history, in which it developed many traditions. Since the seventeenth century, Scotland has belonged to Great Britain, and in recent years, the Scots have once again become conscious of their separate historical roots. There has been a rebirth in the popularity of old Scottish songs and poems. Increased attention to Scottish origins, history, and culture in the mass media and an influx of tourists have made many Scots truly aware for the first time that they are different from the English. This heightened awareness is reinforced when Scots move to London, where their Scottish identity often increases rather than decreases. The rebirth of Scottish identity is not limited to the older generation but also occurs among young, highly educated people. Politically, the new Scottish nationalism has gained importance. Many Scots ask for more autonomy for their region, a demand that goes under the name *devolution*. There are even some calls for national independence. A Scottish National party has gained quite a bit of voter support and some seats in the House of Commons. To compete with this new party, the traditional parties had to adapt to many of the local demands in their campaigns in Scotland.

Within Great Britain, calls for more autonomy also come from Wales, which has its own traditions based on a Celtic background. Originally, the Welsh spoke a Celtic language very different from English. Today, there is a movement to reestablish Welsh as a language, and, when traveling in Wales, one can hear radio broadcasts in this ancient tongue. Welsh nationalists argue that English was imposed on them from outside and that every culture should have the right to its own language. From this perspective, language is not merely seen as a literal means of communication but as an expression of one's culture and history. Some extremist Welsh nationalists have expressed their hostility toward English domination by burning a few weekend houses belonging to English people.

The violence in Wales, of course, is very minor compared to the violence in Northern Ireland (see, for a tragic illustration, Box 11.1). In Northern Ireland, the problem appears on the surface to be a religious one, and the mass media usually speak of civil strife between Protestants and Catholics. But, below the surface, the battle is really between two ethnic groups, the British and the Irish (see Box 11.2.) The former happen to be Protestants and the latter, Catholics, but the conflict is not primarily about religious matters, although the purely religious dimension has some importance too. But essentially it is much more a struggle between two cultures unwilling to share the same territory. In medieval times, only Irish lived on the island, but in the sixteenth and seventeenth centuries, British settlers came to the northern part. Politically, the entire island eventually came under British domination, which was never fully accepted by the Irish. Even during the time when Great Britain had an impressive colonial empire, the Irish question occupied British leaders. Finally, following some bloody incidents at the end of World War I, Ireland got its independence from Great Britain. Dublin became the capital of the new Republic of Ireland, but Great Britain kept the island's northern

_____ **BOX 11.1** _____

I.R.A. KILLS MAN, CALLING HIM A PROTESTANT MILITIA TROOPER

BELFAST, Northern Ireland—Two gunmen fatally wounded a man several yards from a primary school in north Belfast today, and the Irish Republican Army claimed responsibility for the attack.

The I.R.A. statement to Belfast newspapers and television maintained the victim was a member of an unidentified Protestant paramilitary group.

The man was walking along a park in a mixed Protestant-Roman Catholic area when he was shot in the head and chest and collapsed in the street. . . .

Source: New York Times, October 5, 1989.

provinces. The majority of the population of Northern Ireland is British by ethnic background and Protestant by religion. But a substantial minority of Irish Catholics are also included in Northern Ireland. Protestants and Catholics live in the same cities and towns on separate streets. The British government made sure at independence that all Protestants lived within the borders of Northern Ireland and did not much care that this territory included an Irish Catholic minority.

What we have seen since in Northern Ireland are the difficulties British and Irish people have in trying to live together peacefully. The Irish want to make Northern Ireland part of the Republic of Ireland and consider the British as foreign invaders. The British, on the other hand, argue that Northern Ireland is their home, where they have lived for centuries. As the majority

_____ **BOX 11.2** _____

ETHNIC CONFLICT IN NORTHERN IRELAND

[E]thnic cleavages may superficially look like religious, ideological, or some other kind of divisions. The clearest case in point is Northern Ireland, where the groups in conflict are commonly referred to as Protestants and Catholics; the labels are religious, but the two communities are true ethnic groups. This does not mean that their religious differences are unimportant but, rather, that religion is only part of the distinctive set of characteristics that define the groups.

Source: Arend Lijphart, "The Power-Sharing Approach," in Joseph V. Montville, ed., *Conflict and Peacemaking in Multiethnic Societies* (Lexington: D. C. Health and Company, 1990), p. 491.

in Northern Ireland, they want to remain a part of Great Britain and object to the notion that a minority could impose its preference on a majority. The important point is that the Catholics do not have a primarily religious grievance. Their complaint is, rather, that they are forced as Irish people to remain part of Great Britain. In Chapter 13, on consociational decision making or power sharing, we will discuss possible solutions for the bloody conflict in Northern Ireland.

In older textbooks about European politics, Great Britain usually was described as a culturally homogeneous country. With the renewed cultural awareness of the Scots, the Welsh, and the Irish in Northern Ireland, this picture has changed markedly. The renewed importance of ethnic feeling can also be seen in most other European countries. Belgium, where the ethnic groups speak different languages—making the problem particularly difficult—is frequently in the news. In addition to a small German-speaking minority, the two major Belgian groups are French-speaking Walloons and Dutch-speaking Flemish. Relations between Walloons and Flemish are especially tense in Brussels and its suburbs, where the language border is often contested. There are endless debates and demonstrations about which language is to be spoken at a particular post office. To the outside world such incidents may seem ludicrous, but they are indicative of severe underlying tensions between the linguistic groups in Belgium. As in the case of Wales, here, too, the language question should not be seen as a mere problem of literal communication. If Flemish customers in a post office do not wish to be addressed in French, their main concern is with not being able to understand what the clerk says. Language stands for ethnic and cultural identity, and many Belgians consider it a violation of this identity if they are not allowed to use their own language.

Spain offers another example of the increased importance of ethnic identities. The Catalans increasingly stress their own culture based on a language that is not merely a Spanish dialect. The Basques have an ancient language unrelated in any way to Spanish and reside not only in Spain but also in France. Many Basques on both sides of the border claim to be neither French nor Spanish but members of their own group. In addition to the Basques, France has other ethnic groups, such as the Bretons and the Corsicans, who fight for greater cultural identity and less domination from Paris.

How is the apparent rebirth of ethnic identities to be explained? Perhaps the main explanation can be found in the anonymity of the modern world, where family and neighborhood ties have broken apart. In this situation, ethnic groups offer ties firmly rooted in the past. Nobody can take away the Scots' membership in the Scottish community; even if they move away from the region, they will remain Scots. As long as you live, you are one with the brothers and sisters of your ethnic affiliation. This belonging also links people with preceding generations and generations to follow, placing them in a historical perspective. This function can also be fulfilled by the nation-state, and for many Europeans it still is. But, in the daily life of its citizens, the nation-state appears more and more as a complex and distant bureaucracy whose computers send out tax bills and social security checks. This bureaucracy is often intimidating and threatening and does not fulfill many demands of the citizens, causing frustrations and aggressions. Under these circumstances, it is difficult for many people to identify with the nation-state. But ethnic groups are smaller in size than nation-states and do not appear in the form of bureaucracies. Indeed, they are often the source of joyful festivals and ceremonies.

Having tried to explain the rebirth of ethnic identities, both in America and Europe, we are faced with the question whether this rebirth should be applauded. Is it a reactionary trend reminiscent of medieval times, when groups counted more than individuals? This trend is particularly evident when ethnic groups press for quotas for their members. In this context, Switzerland is a good illustrative example. With a small population of 6 million, it has four official languages (see page 168). Language quotas are applied in practically all aspects of Swiss life. In the Swiss railway system and postal service, for example, the chief positions are distributed on a proportional basis among representatives of the language groups. This rule is not based on particular laws but on long traditions and customs. When a French speaker retires from a high position in the railway system, he or she is almost always replaced with another French speaker, even if there is a more qualified candidate from one of the other language groups. Thus, in this situation not only individuals but groups, too, have rights. Only in a second step do individuals in a group compete for the position. Such arrangements are characteristic of the Middle Ages, and it was considered a breakthrough when the Enlightenment brought the rights of individuals to the fore. Do language quotas in Switzerland violate the important modern principle that individuals should be judged on their own merits and not according to group affiliation? It certainly seems so, but one could argue that the preservation of relative peace among Swiss language groups more than counterbalances the damage to the cause of individualism.

What conclusions can be drawn from the Swiss case for other European countries and, for that matter, to the United States? Should ethnic groups have their own rights? In the United States, for example, this would mean recognizing rights of the Hispanic community. Following this argument, Hispanics should be encouraged to use Spanish in their daily lives so that they are able to express their authentic culture. In airports in New York and Chicago and in many public buildings throughout the country, signs are already written not only in English but also in Spanish. Should Americans go further and allow Hispanics to be taught in Spanish in school, not only in exceptional cases, but as a rule? Should Spanish be spoken in Congress or appear on the dollar bill? Should Hispanics have the right to proportional quotas in the federal bureaucracy, the universities, the railway system, the airlines? If such rights are given to the Hispanic community, should they not also be given to African Americans, Chinese Americans, Polish Americans, and so on? The problems appear immense. What are the alternatives? Is the old idea of America as a melting pot dominated by English-speaking whites still viable, or must new ways be found to satisfy the increasing demands of various ethnic groups?

Unfortunately, the Swiss success story cannot easily be repeated for the United States or, for that matter, for most other European countries. Switzerland has some very favorable conditions that allow a language quota system to work quite smoothly, although not always without problems. The first condition is the existence of relatively clear geographic borders between the languages. In the Geneva area, for example, French is the only official language. If a German-speaking family moves to the area, they have no other choice but to adapt to French, which means, in particular, sending their children to French-speaking schools. There is an old saying that good fences make good neighbors. This principle applies to the Swiss language situation in the sense that each group has its own territory where it can live without interference from other groups. In Belgium, the language situation is tense precisely because in Brussels there is no clear delimitation between the two major groups. A similar situation would exist in America if Spanish were to become a second official language. The Swiss experience suggests that a solution would be much easier if Hispanics were settled in their own distinct geographic regions. But in the United States such a situation would be labeled as "segregation," and as such would almost certainly be politically unacceptable.

A second favorable condition in Switzerland is the ease with which the members of the various linguistic groups can be identified. Few Swiss have any difficulty in identifying their first language. As a consequence, there are no ambiguities as to who qualifies to fill quotas for a particular language group. The situation is less clear with the Scots. How pure must a family's background be before it can be considered Scottish? The same difficulty arises in the United States for Hispanics and most other ethnic groups.

A third favorable condition for the application of the quota system in Switzerland is the approximate educational equality among the language groups. In individual cases, it can certainly happen that a less-qualified French speaker is preferred to a better-qualified German speaker because of the quota system. But in another case, it may be the other way around, and neither group feels permanently disadvantaged. In the United States, one of the great problems with a quota system is that, in general, whites in the ethnic majority are better educated than some of the ethnic minorities, so there would be frequent complaints of reverse discrimination against the majority.

A fourth favorable condition in Switzerland is the facility with which the Swiss converse in each other's languages. Especially important is the fact that the numerically dominant German speakers are willing to learn French, as it is the most important minority language. This willingness is aided by the fact that French is a language of high international prestige that can be used outside Switzerland. As a consequence of the general fluency of German speakers in French, no great problems of communication arise if a high-level job in Swiss society goes to a French speaker. With regard to Italian and, even more, Romansh, German speakers are less fluent, but the members of these two minority groups usually make a special effort to learn German or French, and sometimes both. The willingness to speak other languages is less prevalent in most other multilingual countries. This is a major problem in Belgium, for example, where French speakers are often unwilling to learn Dutch, a language that they feel has little international prestige and therefore little usefulness outside Belgium. The situation is even worse in Great Britain with regard to Welsh. Most English people would be unwilling to learn this ancient language because it is of no use outside Wales. A similar problem exists with regard to Spanish in the United States, but with the increased importance of international trade, English-speaking Americans may become more aware of the benefits of understanding and speaking Spanish.

A fifth favorable condition in Switzerland is the economic affluence of the country. When jobs are plentiful, it is less problematic to give quotas to minorities. Finally, Switzerland's small population may make it easier to arrange a functioning quota system.

Should we conclude that a quota system among ethnic groups only works if the favorable conditions found in Switzerland are present? This seems far too negative a conclusion; success may also be possible under less favorable conditions. But, in the final analysis, the introduction of a quota system is a normative question where a country must decide whether it wishes to give rights not only to individuals but also to groups.

ENVIRONMENTAL MOVEMENT

In Europe, as in the United States, there is an increasing concern about the environment. In Europe the concern may be even more immediate, because Europeans live in much more crowded conditions than Americans. The population density in Europe is about four times higher than in the United States. The environmental concern in Europe began in the 1960s, primarily with regard to water pollution. At that time, the problem was basically seen in technical terms. It was thought that sufficient know-how and financial resources could remedy the situation. This expectation was justified to a certain extent with regard to water pollution, and today some European rivers and lakes are cleaner than they were 20 years ago. Swimming is even allowed at a few places where it was prohibited only a short while ago, and salmon can be found today in London's Thames River.

In the 1970s, worries began to develop about the environmental impact of nuclear power, with the discussion taking a more fundamental turn. The question was raised whether there should be limits to economic growth in order to eliminate the need for provision of more and more energy. For many environmentalists, disposal of radioactive waste material became a symbol for technological development over which the experts had lost control. Fears were expressed about genetic damage to future generations.

In the 1980s, the environmental question assumed greater urgency when it began to be publicly reported that many of Europe's forests would die in this century because of air pollution (see Box 11.3 and photo on page 208). This brought home the problem to many who had not been particularly concerned before. Suddenly, warnings about catastrophic consequences to nature were relevant not merely to the indefinite future but to the present. There are certainly still "picture postcard" environments in Europe, such as the Matterhorn in Zermatt and peaceful Swedish lakes (see photos on page

―――――――――――――― BOX 11.3 ――――――――――――――

REPORT: ONLY 47 PERCENT OF FORESTS UNDAMAGED

Only 47 percent of the forests in the Federal Republic are currently undamaged, some 18 percent less than in 1983, according to a report on the condition of the forest made public by the federal cabinet last week in Bonn. The study found that 15.9 percent of the forest in the country had suffered medium or heavy damage—0.8 percent more than last year. Some 37 percent of the wooded areas were characterized as slightly damaged.

The parlimentary state secretary in the Agriculture Ministry, George Gallus, told the press that slightly damaged trees could still regain their health. . . .

Representatives of environmental organizations and the opposition Social Democratic and Green parties criticized the report, saying that the description of 37 percent of the trees as only "slightly damaged" was an attempt to play down and disguise the true degree of damage. The category "slightly damaged" includes trees with up to 25 percent damage to leaves or needles.

Source: The Week in Germany, German Information Center, New York, November 17, 1989.

210), but Europe increasingly looks like the photos on page 209 because there are so many sources of air pollution. The fight against air pollution became a prime political issue. But the task was much more difficult than that against water pollution: Dirty air cannot simply be cleaned mechanically like dirty water. The fight for clean air must begin at the sources of pollution, and many environmentalists believe that the fight cannot be won without basic changes in people's life-styles. Even more than in the 1970s, disagreements

Dying Trees Near Bonn, West Germany. (Courtesy German Information Center, New York.)

Environmental Concerns: *top*, Nuclear Power Plants (Courtesy Embassy of the Federal Republic of Germany, Bern, Switzerland); *center*, Industrial Pollution (Courtesy *Europe Magazine*); and, *left*, Automobile Pollution (Courtesy Embassy of the Federal Republic of Germany, Bern, Switzerland).

Picture Postcard Environments: *above*,
Swedish Lakes (Courtesy Swedish Em-
bassy, Bern, Switzerland); *right*, The
Matterhorn,   Zermatt,   Switzerland
(Courtesy Swiss National Tourist Office).

about the costs of economic affluence have appeared in European societies.
The environmental movement advocates a much simpler life-style, so that
the natural environment of the human race and, ultimately, the human race
itself can be saved from destruction. (Concerning the question of a simpler
life-style, see also the discussion on page 59).

Some steps have already been taken to change the life-style of Europeans
in a more environmentally sound direction. Strong efforts have been made,
for example, to curtail private transportation and to bring about a shift
toward using more public transportation. A good illustration are the measures taken by the West German state of Saarland, described in Box 11.4.
In spite of the increased demand for automobile use, the Saarland
is not enlarging roads, but, on the contrary, narrowing them. Thus, by
reducing the supply of space needed for automobiles, the demand for their
use is also forced down. As alternatives, foot and bicycle paths are being
built. Another good example of a change to a more environmentally sound
life-style is a program aimed at gardeners and farmers so that they will stop
using poisonous chemicals and use organic ones instead (see Box 11.5)
(more on farm changes in Europe in Chapter 16).

Organizationally, the environmental movement has anything but a unified
structure, attributable to its multilayered historical development. Associations for the beautification of nature existed long before the general public
became concerned about the environment. Traditionally, these associations
promoted such causes as the protection of rare plants and animals and the
building of foot trails. Mostly organized in an old-fashioned way, they reacted rather slowly when environmental questions became politically explosive issues. Most of these older associations eventually adapted their organizational structures to the new political situation, and today many of them
play an important role in the environmental movement.

_____ **BOX 11.4** _____

SAARLAND TO "BUILD BACK" SOME ROADS

The state of Saarland will embark on a program to "build back" major highways through some towns to stem the traffic flow, Jo Leinen, the state's environment minister, announced recently. Following an already well-established program for reducing traffic on side streets, a similar program for major thoroughfares is being introduced to improve the quality of life and to renew the ecology of cities and towns, according to Leinen. By narrowing the roadways, constructing foot and bicycle paths and adding green space, the state intends to reduce noise and dust pollution, and improve the microclimate and thus "reclaim" lost living quality, Leinen said. The state has targeted sites which Leinen characterized as "racetracks" with high accident rates.

Source: The Week in Germany, German Information Center, New York, September 18, 1987.

A second layer of environmental groups arose more or less spontaneously from specific local issues. These groups became known under the name of _citizen initiatives._ When a town or a neighborhood was threatened with some danger, like toxic waste or the establishment of a nuclear power plant, and no political parties or other organizations were willing to help, ordinary citizens often took the initiative and organized to defend their interests. Because their fights sometimes continued for many years, these groups tended after a while to take on a more formal organization. They often directed their attention to other issues and stayed together even when the original issue had been settled. There were also efforts to organize these local groups on a regional and even a national level.

_____ **BOX 11.5** _____

GARDENERS URGED TO GO ORGANIC

More than 60,000 metric tons of pesticides are sprayed annually on farmland and gardens in the Federal Republic, and traces of the poisonous chemicals can be found in foods and in ground and rain water, the Association for the Protection of the Environment and Nature in Germany (BUND), reported last week in Bonn. BUND Chairman Hubert Weinzierl called on the up to 15 million people in the country who cultivate backyard gardens or small plots to take part in a two-year campaign called "Garden without Poison," turning their flowerbeds and vegetable patches into "chemical-free zones."

Source: The Week in Germany, German Information Center, New York, March 24, 1989.

A third layer appeared when environmentalists began to organize their own political party. In Chapter 1, the development of the Greens as a special environmental party was described. However, the Green party does not speak for the entire environmental movement. Many environmentalists prefer to stay outside a party framework, while others try to work within the older parties—a fourth layer of the environmental movement. Most of the political parties have recently turned their attention to environmental concerns. This is particularly true of the Socialists but true also of the Conservatives. The latter play word games by arguing that "conservation" of nature has always been a key point in Conservative thinking. Environmentalists active in these older parties may have less public visibility but all the more political influence.

PEACE MOVEMENT

Many environmentalists are also active in peace work. They see a nuclear holocaust as the ultimate destruction of nature, so that work for the peace movement appears to be a logical continuation of activities in the environmental movement. This connection between the two movements is particularly strong in the Green party.

The peace movement became an important actor on the European political scene in the early 1980s. The movement, however, is not new. Peace was already a crucial issue for the student movement of the 1960s, especially in connection with the Vietnam War, which inspired many antiwar demonstrations in Europe. The 1950s saw mass protests against nuclear armaments, especially in Great Britain and West Germany. In the 1920s, after the catastrophe of World War I, pacifists sought complete disarmament so that no other war would ever occur. Peace through disarmament has a long tradition in Europe.

The European peace movement in the early and mid-1980s had a strong anti-American orientation. American nuclear missiles in Europe were the prime target of most peace activists, many of whom wished to abolish the entire American military presence in Europe. The professed goal of the peace movement was to distance Europe from the tensions between the Soviets and the Americans. In this context, neutrality, neutralism, or nonalignment were often mentioned.

In the meantime, of course, the military situation in Europe has drastically changed. In December 1987, Ronald Reagan and Mikhail Gorbachev signed a treaty to withdraw medium- and short-range missiles from Europe. And in the fall of 1989 the Berlin Wall came down and many changes in Eastern Europe occurred, which we described in Chapter 1. All of a sudden, the danger of a nuclear war between the superpowers on European soil lessened and perhaps virtually disappeared. What was the role of the peace movement in all of this? Did the mass demonstrations of the early and mid-1980s pay off? This is certainly what the peace movement claims. But there is another interpretation that says that it was the initial deployment of the American missiles in Europe that ultimately helped the cause of peace. Only when the Soviets saw that the Americans were willing to continue to defend Europe did they agree to negotiate about the missiles. According to this interpretation, the peace movement was not a help but, rather, an obstacle to peace. If its mass demonstrations had been successful in preventing the deployment of the American missiles, the danger of adventurous actions by the Soviet Union would have greatly increased.

Which interpretation is correct? An objective answer is difficult to give, perhaps even impossible. Both sides will continue for years to insist on their own interpretation. What is definite is that the peace movement has been severely weakened. Its core supporters insist that there is still a mission for the peace movement. But, as the reporter of the *New York Times* correctly asks in Box 11.6, "If missiles go, will rebels be without a cause?"

To show how dramatically the scene has changed in the last few years, I reprint here a quote from the first edition of a book by the French philosopher André Glucksmann, who in 1984 warned: "Where the Russians have walked in, freedom has never blossomed again. . . . The missiles are a shield to prevent a possible extension of the Soviet empire."[39] This quote shows with what kind of critique the peace movement was confronted, not only from military people, but also from intellectuals.

Who were the people active in the peace movement? As one may expect, many people of the Left, Socialists, Greens, and Communists. But it is noteworthy that many participated out of Christian faith, as we have already described in detail in the previous chapter. We can add here some interesting differences between the Roman Catholic and the Protestant churches. The pope and most other dignitaries in the Catholic church offered little support for the European peace movement. However, this negative attitude of the Catholic church hierarchy did not prevent many young priests from participating in the peace movement, even though such actions may have caused them difficulties within their church. And there were exceptions to the negative attitude of the Catholic church hierarchy, particularly in the Netherlands, where bishops were supportive of the ideas of the peace movement. In this sense, there were strong similarities at the time between Dutch and American bishops, who also spoke up against increased nuclear armaments.

Protestant churches are less hierarchically organized than the Catholic church, which may explain why they were much more active in the European peace movement. Indeed, there was a striking correlation between the strength of the peace movement and the size of the Protestant population in a country. The movement was relatively weak in Catholic countries, such as France and Italy, and strong in Protestant countries, such as Sweden, Denmark, and Great Britain. It was also strong in religiously mixed countries, such as West Germany and the Netherlands.

In the early and mid-1980s, many Americans believed that Moscow controlled the peace movement in Europe, using Communist and Socialist activists to weaken the military defense of the Western European democracies. There is indeed little doubt that the Soviets made some financial contributions to the European peace movement. But such contributions did not necessarily mean that the peace movement took its orders from Moscow.

_____ BOX 11.6 _____

IF MISSILES GO, WILL REBELS BE WITHOUT A CAUSE?

KASTELLAUN, West Germany—Sweeping her hand over the frozen, wind-swept field, Beate Ronnefeldt tried to evoke the moment almost four years earlier when a quarter of a million people gathered there with signs and songs, united in passionate opposition to the new cruise missiles being deployed behind the forest line and barbed wire.

Mrs. Ronnefeldt spoke almost wistfully of that rally and the other huge demonstrations held all across West Germany in 1983 and 1984. Thousands of groups from all walks of German life were joined in opposition to the new American cruise and Pershing 2 missiles. . . .

But now the cruise and Pershing missiles deployed amid such fury are to be quietly scrapped under the treaty signed in Washington by President Reagan and Mikhail S. Gorbachev, handing the movement both a major victory and stripping it of its prime rallying point. . . .

For Mrs. Ronnefeldt, the target is not only the missiles, but all of the American military. . . .

[T]he question is whether the public can be roused again as it was when snarling superpowers brandished frightening new weapons at each other over German soil.

Source: New York Times, January 21, 1988.

With regard to the social background and the basic values of the supporters of the peace movement, much research has been done. Although not limited to this group, the peace movement received its greatest support from the highly educated young. With regard to its values, political scientist

_____ BOX 11.7 _____

PEACE MOVEMENT AS A POSTMATERIALIST PHENOMENON

The peace movement that has recently emerged in Western Europe and to a lesser extent in the United States is in large part a Postmaterialist phenomenon. . . .

[Postmaterialists] give top priority to values that are fundamentally different from the Materialist emphasis on economic growth and domestic order that has long prevailed in industrial society. Instead, they place greater emphasis on the quality of life, social solidarity, and opportunities for self-expression. . . .

Source: Ronald Inglehart, "Generational Change and the Future of the Atlantic Alliance," *PS* 17 (Summer 1984), pp. 530–532.

Ronald Inglehart interprets the peace movement as a postmaterial phenomenon, with an emphasis on quality of life values (see Box 11.7).

WOMEN'S MOVEMENT

For an American, the women's movement in Europe is relatively easy to understand, because it raises, although with some delay, many of the same issues that the women's movement in the United States has raised. In this respect, there is indeed a strong American influence in Europe. American feminist authors, such as Betty Friedan and Marilyn French, have been widely read.

In many ways, the women's movement has had a more difficult time in Europe, because individualism is less emphasized there than in the United States. We will encounter this difference also in Chapter 14 on corporatism. In Europe the notion that not only individuals but also groups have basic rights is much more common than in the United States. In Europe it is important that the family be often treated as the crucial economic unit. The argument is that the important point for each family is to have a decent income. Increasingly, both wife and husband work outside the home. But where some families have no breadwinner at all, it is often argued that families with two breadwinners should give up one job to families with none. In practical terms, this nearly always means that a woman has to give up her job in favor of a man. It is precisely against this role for women that the growing women's movement protests and argues that women as individuals should have their own inalienable rights. They should be able to pursue their careers and their personal goals, regardless of their marital status. This is presented as a basic human right that women should be able to enjoy, just as men do.

The belief that women are not the equal of men has deep roots in European history. Popular culture has had a profound effect on how women should behave. Under the influence of the women's movement, studies have been done about eighteenth- and nineteenth-century books on marriage for young women, which were widely read at the time. The basic message was that wives should be subservient to their husbands. Fulfillment in their lives would come from providing their husbands with a pleasant home where they could find peace and tranquillity from the struggles of the outside world. According to these books, it was the duty of a wife to discover the wishes of her husband and to make every attempt to fulfill those wishes. If the husband was in a bad mood and complained loudly, it was recommended that the wife keep her calm. Interestingly, there were no such guidance books on the subject of marriage for men. Their task was to earn a living. In return, they had the right to be spoiled by their wives.

It was not only in popular but also in high culture that women were put in a subservient role. The women's movement points to many sexist remarks in the long history of European philosophers, poets, and writers. An extreme example is the often quoted statement by the nineteenth-century German philosopher, Friedrich Nietzsche, in which he said that men should take the whip when they go to a woman.

Such writings in both popular and high culture had a strong influence on the desirable behavior for women. It was the women themselves who tried to follow the set standards of behavior. As in Marxist literature (Chapter 1), we can speak here of a false consciousness. Just as many proletarians did not rebel against their exploited status, so many women gladly accepted their inferior position. The feminist literature writes of the exploitation of women and their treatment as serfs.

In this context it is noteworthy that many women fought against the introduction of women's suffrage. They were socialized in such a way that they prefered to depend on the power of men. Politics was considered to be something dirty, from which women should be kept out in their own best interest.

In legal terms, the situation for European women has dramatically improved. Everywhere women's suffrage has been introduced. Switzerland was the last country to do so by means of a popular referendum in 1971 (see Chapter 7).

Although the legal discrimination of women has largely been remedied all over Europe, much has still to be done in practical terms. In the universities, for example, there are still very few women who have attained the rank of professor (see Box 11.8). As in the United States, the argument is made that female students need female teachers as role models. Special women's days are organized at many universities to draw attention to these demands. Student newspapers have special issues devoted to women's issues. Research projects are launched to study the discrimination of women. In order to increase the number of female professors, various quota systems are discussed. Thus, the University of Geneva has a long-range plan to increase the number of female professors step by step.

The push for more opportunities for women may be strongest and most visible in the universities, but there are also efforts to increase leadership positions for women in political parties (see Box 11.9), churches (see Box

---

_____ **BOX 11.8** _____

WOMEN IN ACADEME REMAIN A TINY MINORITY

Despite improved educational opportunities, women who attain a doctoral degree remain a tiny minority in the Federal Republic, according to recent figures released by the Federal Bureau of Statistics. The figures show that only 91 of the 1,050 doctoral degrees successfully completed in 1988 were awarded to women. This low number, corresponding to 8.7 percent, has remained fairly constant in recent years.

Source:L The Week in Germany, German Information Center, New York, October 6, 1989.

_____ BOX 11.9 _____

BREMEN SPD SETS QUOTA FOR PARTICIPATION BY WOMEN

The Social Democrats in Bremen passed a resolution recently at their local party convention providing for a 40% quota for women. The decision, which passed by a large majority, means that at least 40% of all positions within the party and at least 40% of all candidates for parliamentary elections must be women, effective immediately. With this decision, the Bremen Social Democrats have gone far beyond provisions made by the national Social Democratic party organization, which call for the gradual introduction of a quota system between now and 1998.

Source: The Week in Germany, German Information Center, New York, December 15, 1989.

11.10), and other areas of society. For the women's movement, this push has not only a quantitative but also a qualitative aspect. The goal is not merely to increase the number of women in leadership positions but also to define in a new way the role expectations for women leaders. Women should not simply try to imitate the role patterns of men in leadership positions. For this reason, Margaret Thatcher is not appreciated very much by the women's movement, because she displays a masculine behavior, outdoing men on their own turf.

What should be the proper behavior of women in leadership positions? This issue is hotly debated among feminists, and many different opinions are articulated. The necessity of a special women's culture is stressed, but it is not altogether clear what the key characteristics of this culture should be. A common theme is that female leaders would think in less compartmentalized terms than male leaders. They would tend to see political issues in more global terms. Thus, female leaders would be more sensitive to how

_____ BOX 11.10 _____

CHURCH SETS QUOTA FOR WOMEN IN LEADING POSITIONS

At the annual meeting of the Seventh Synod of the Protestant Church in Germany . . . church leaders pledged to promote women during the next ten years to positions of responsibility in order to achieve a 40% level of involvement by 1999. The decision followed several days of heated discussion on "The Community of Men and Women in the Church," which had been chosen as the main topic for the meeting. . . .

Source: The Week in Germany, German Information Center, New York, November 17, 1989.

economic growth may negatively influence the quality of life of ordinary people. This would be the application of a broader principle of rationality, whereas male leaders would tend to be rational in a narrower sense, concentrating, for example, on how a particular decision would influence profit levels but forgetting the impact it would have on the environment. Thus, the argument is not at all that male leaders would be more rational and female leaders, more emotional. Rather, the difference would be that women would include more elements in their decision making than men would.

That leaders can be both men and women should be expressed more clearly in our everyday language. The women's movement is very concerned about language. The specific words that we use determine how we see the world. If language refers to leadership positions only in masculine form, we tend to think of leaders only as men. In languages such as German and French, this problem is even more acute than in English, because in these languages the article has both a masculine and a feminine form. Whereas in English the article *the* can refer to either a man or a woman, in German *der* refers to a man and *die* to a woman. The same difference exists in French with *le* and *la*. In addition, nouns, too, usually have masculine and feminine forms. The English *director* is *Direktor* in German and *directeur* in French in the case of a man, and *Direktorin* and *directrice* in the case of a woman. The women's movement insists that in such cases the feminine form should be used as often as the masculine form so that the language properly expresses that directors may be both men and women. Some professions have traditionally been so dominated by men that a feminine form does not even exist. Thus, in French there is only a masculine form for *professor*, namely *professeur*. Should the feminine form *professeuse* be introduced, or should a female professor be called *madame le professeur*? Some critics consider such issues to be trivial, but many people in the women's movement argue that equal status for women will never be achieved if our language is not changed properly.

Besides the broad issues of quotas for women and changes in the structure of language, the women's movement has many specific projects, in particular:

- Rape centers
- Houses for battered women
- Hotels exclusively for women
- Taxis for women
- Bookstores for women
- Discos for women
- Self-defense courses for women
- Music for women
- Theater for women
- Self-actualization groups for women

As in the other social movements described in this chapter, there is also a strong element of group solidarity in the women's movement. In the anonymous world of today, sisterhood gives to many women an emotional and natural bond. To be and to work with other women gives them a feeling of satisfaction. For some time, there was a close alliance between the women's and Marxist movements, both of which were fighting for those who are exploited in society. But many women found among Marxists the same male chauvinism that appears in society at large and decided to stay among themselves. The hope is that in the women's movement a feeling of togetherness will develop and that every woman will have the same status and the same say. As the Green party, the women's movement, too, has the ambition to practice internally a decision-making style of fundamental democratization and thus to serve as an example for the entire society.

YOUTH MOVEMENT

If we compare the younger generation in America and Europe, we will see that the most striking difference seems to be a more critical and pessimistic attitude toward the future among young Europeans. In order to understand the situation of their peers in Europe, young Americans must understand the very different educational system in Europe. Education is organized somewhat differently from one European country to another; but, despite such national variations, we can speak of a general European pattern, which can be contrasted with an American pattern.

Until about the mid-1960s, the European educational system was geared toward a small elite, which alone was eligible for higher education. Since then, Europe has changed to a pattern of mass education, with a larger portion of young people going to a university. This change was not completely smooth and caused many problems.

Under the earlier system, which existed through the mid-1960s, selection for higher education occurred very early, in most places at around the age of 11 or 12. On the basis of strict exams, a small number of students—usually not more than 5 percent of the age group involved—was accepted into university preparatory schools. These schools had different names; in Germany, for example, they were known as *Gymnasien* and in France as *lycées* (see the photo on page 220). The curriculum was very demanding; it might include, for example, six hours of Latin per week. At the age of about 18 or 19, students were required to take an extensive final exam. If they passed, they were eligible to enter any university and any field. The name of this exam again varied from country to country; the term *Matura*, as used, for example, in Switzerland, perhaps best expresses the nature of the exam. After a broad education, the student was considered "mature" enough to begin university studies. Unlike in America, no distinction was made between undergraduate and graduate studies in European universities. If students wished to study medicine, they enrolled in the faculty for medicine; if they wished to study law, in the faculty for law; and so forth. Usually only one degree was offered, a doctorate after five or six years of studies.

This system fostered a small, homogeneous, highly educated elite. If you did not belong to this elite, your educational options were limited. Mandatory education ended at the age of about 15. Afterward, you could immedi-

French Lycée Students. (Courtesy French Embassy, Bern, Switzerland.)

ately enter the work force or enter an apprenticeship for three or four years. As an apprentice, you could learn your trade in a practical way, working in a bakery or a bank, for example. Included in the apprenticeships were also a few hours of trade school per week.

This educational system had the big advantage of being financially cheap. But in the early 1960s, many Europeans began to wonder whether they needed a more expensive system. The U.S. model seemed particularly attractive, for at this time, Americans were economically very successful and much admired in Europe. Europeans were impressed by the broad-based American system of higher education that allowed a large portion of young Americans to continue their education beyond the secondary level. These educational opportunities were perceived as instrumental to American economic success, and most European reformers came to the conclusion that an expansion of higher education would be the key to the development of a stronger economy. From this perspective, the severe shortcomings of the old system were apparent. Early selection of university students was seen as giving an undue advantage to children from a milieu in which education was already important and as discriminating against others. It was feared that under this system Europe had lost many late-blooming talents.

So it was that, beginning in the mid-1960s, many profound changes were implemented in the European educational system, with some countries, such as the Netherlands and Sweden, moving much faster than others. A crucial change was made, so that the preparatory schools for university entrance now begin at a later age level. If students fail the initial selection process, they may still transfer to preparatory schools at a later date. As a

Table 19
Education at the Third Level (University, College, etc.): Number of Students per 100,000 Inhabitants (most recent year)

Austria	2,511	Luxembourg[1]	—
Belgium	2,566	Netherlands	2,749
Denmark	2,314	Norway	2,730
Finland	2,831	Portugal	1,020
France	2,395	Spain	2,542
Federal Republic of Germany	2,592	Sweden	2,209
Greece	1,987	Switzerland	1,874
Ireland	1,979	United Kingdom	1,880
Italy	1,995	United States	5,142

Source: UNESCO, *Statistical Yearbook 1989* (Paris: UNESCO, 1989), pp. 3-227-231.

[1] In Luxembourg, the majority of students at this level of education pursue their studies abroad.

result of these reforms, the number of students in preparatory schools increased dramatically. In many countries, it has become increasingly common for 20 percent or even 30 percent of an age cohort to go to a preparatory school, a rate that begins to resemble American high schools. This expansion naturally led to a strong increase in the number of university students. The number of students at the third level in different countries is compared in Table 19. The United States still has the most students in universities and colleges. But some European countries are now approaching the American situation. Among the European democracies, Finland, the Netherlands, and Norway have the highest number of students in relation to the population. At the other extreme is economically poor Portugal.

Important changes also took place with regard to apprenticeship, in which the emphasis has shifted from practical work to formal schooling. Many apprentices today have 2 or 2½ days per week of full-time classes. Opportunities also have been opened for continuing education after the apprenticeship. Such further schooling can even lead to transfer to a university without attending preparatory school.

In many respects, the reforms have not fulfilled their promise. This is probably due less to the basic idea of the reforms than to their often hasty implementation. Further, from the mid-1970s on, general economic conditions worsened in Europe, and this had a negative impact, because less money was available for reforms. Today there is much confusion—even crisis—in the European educational system. Universities are overenrolled because staff and buildings could not be adapted to the large increase in the number of students. Where formerly professors and students could interact in small groups, there are now large lecture classes and a sense of anonymity. Job prospects after graduation are much worse than under the old university system, when jobs were plentiful for the small number of graduates. Most European families still expect that children with a university education should achieve a high-status position in society. This creates frustration when only relatively low-level positions or, sometimes, no jobs at all are available. Even medical doctors have difficulties in finding work, and countries like Spain and Italy have thousands of unemployed physicians. Under these unsatisfactory conditions, it is no wonder that pessimism prevails in Europe's universities.

At the apprentice level, the situation is no better. In the past, obtaining a university education was so unrealistic for most young Europeans that they felt proud and privileged to earn an apprenticeship. Today many parents are almost embarrassed to say that their child is "only" an apprentice, because this implies that their child is not smart enough to make it to a university. And, as with university graduates, job prospects for apprentices are bleak, partly because many positions that formerly were reserved for candidates with an apprenticeship are now taken by university graduates.

This overview of the European educational system is important to an understanding of the youth movement. First, we must note that those who belong to the youth movement are far from all of the young people in Europe. There is indeed a very large number of young Europeans who are politically passive and never participate in demonstrations or other political action. The most recent trends seem to indicate that this group is increasing. Then there are the punks and other dropouts, who are very visible on the streets but who are few in number and should not be counted as part of the youth movement because they do not articulate politically relevant demands. For the sake of conceptual clarity, it is better to use the term *youth movement* only when political activities are involved. Even defined in this narrower sense, the European youth movement is a very heterogeneous phenomenon with fluid boundaries. The movement appears mostly at the local level without any firm organizational pattern.

The youth movement of the 1980s and 1990s has very different goals from the student movement of the 1960s, and it would not be accurate to see the former simply as a continuation of the latter. The student leaders of the 1960s developed grand designs for large-scale changes to society. Underlying their protests were hope and optimism for the future. The basic tone of the current youth movement is quite different. The hope of changing society in any fundamental way has been given up; the main goal is to be left alone. Demands are made for special youth centers where young people can lead their own lives, play music, dance, discuss, paint, and so forth. Where political authorities have granted such demands and established youth centers, however, controversies about the legality of the activities inside have arisen, especially in connection with drug use. Young people insist that they have the right to set their own rules. The key word is "autonomy," and much graffiti all over Europe features the letter *A*, standing for this demand. The letter *A* also stands for *amore*, "love," and expresses the need of these young people to live in communities of their own that are more humane than the cold, anonymous world outside. The demand for the autonomy and self-rule of youth centers is generally not well received by the general public, which is unwilling to allow ordinary laws not to be applied to these centers.

The question of legality becomes even more of an issue when young people occupy empty apartment buildings to establish their own youth centers. These buildings are usually scheduled to be torn down and replaced with expensive office complexes. The young people justify this type of occupation by citing a general housing shortage and the immorality of construction speculation. The political authorities are then confronted with the dilemma of either negotiating with the squatters or using police to clear the buildings. If they do the latter, pictures of police brutality on TV news may raise sympathy for the squatters among other young people, which in turn may lead to demonstrations with the risk of violent incidents. In cities like Amsterdam, Berlin, and Zurich, the question of how to deal with squatters has become a hot political issue.

In addition to demands for autonomous youth centers, the youth movement is also active in the environmental and peace movements. This activity grows out of a fear that the leaders of the older generation may cause the destruction of nature and, ultimately, the human race. Here again, the question of legality comes up when young people try to occupy, for example, construction sites of nuclear plants. Such illegal acts are justified as elementary self-defense. In this context, many members of the clergy try to play a mediating role. The increasing concern of the churches with the environment, the cause of world peace, and the troubles of youth has already been mentioned in Chapter 10. Youth work has become particularly important for the churches. Many members of the clergy are involved in helping drug addicts, and there they learn about the many problems of young people. Such an involvement, of course, also brings a certain responsibility for what happens in the youth centers where the clergy work, and church officials and clergy often become targets of public criticism for tolerating or even encouraging the breaking of the law by young people. Complaints are also raised that youth centers are outside the proper domain of the churches, which should concentrate on their genuine religious mission. Clergy who are active in the youth movement hope that, ultimately, they will be successful in leading many young people to a religious life. In their view, this goal necessitates seeking contact with young people in their centers and participating with them when they demonstrate for peace and the environment.

Often the political authorities, too, stretch out a helping hand to young people in distress. A good example is the liberal drug policy in the city of Zurich, described in Box 11.11. Despite all efforts and goodwill on the part of both the authorities and young people, there are many incidents of unrest and even rioting and rampaging (see Boxes 11.12, 11.13, 11.14, and 11.15. In this context, we must also refer back to the problem of soccer rowdies covered on page 56–57.

When we compare the situation of young people in Europe and America, we see that the lessons seem to go from the new to the old continent. The educational system in the United States, although much criticized at home, is, again, increasingly being used as a model by European educators. They realize that they learned only half the American lesson when they expanded higher education in Europe. The neglected other half of the lesson is to differentiate educational opportunities as the Americans do. Young Europeans still have only two basic options for further education after mandatory schooling: university studies or apprenticeship. European universities

_____ **BOX 11.11** _____

LIBERAL DRUG POLICY IN ZURICH

Zurich, Switzerland's biggest city, decided two years ago to tolerate a thriving drug scene in a park behind the central railroad station. Every day hundreds of drug addicts buy and use heroin and cocaine openly in the park, known as the Platzspitz, undisturbed by the police.

A federally financed health center in the park distributed 6,000 syringes in exchange for used ones each day in an attempt to prevent the spread of AIDS.

Zurich's policy has critics, and even supporters are uneasy with the bazaar-like attraction the open drug scene in the Platzspitz may have on the young. . . . [But the policy] represent[s] a decision by the authorities that arresting or harassing drug users and small-time dealers is counterproductive. Those approaches lead to more petty crime by pushing prices up, officials said, and hinder efforts to reach addicts with social services like AIDS prevention. . . .

Swiss officials do not suggest that decriminalization is a solution to their large drug problem. But many said it would stop the Swiss police and the courts from wasting their energies going after small fry. . . .

Source: New York Times, December 1, 1989.

_____ **BOX 11.12** _____

YOUTH GANGS GO ON RAMPAGE IN BRITISH CITY

LONDON (UPI)—Gangs of youths rampaged through the city of Leicester late Wednesday, smashing windows, looting shops and pelting police with rocks and firebombs. Several police officers were slightly injured and at least five people were arrested, a police spokesman said.

The street fighting, which raged in scattered areas into the early morning hours, broke out after a soccer match in the city, 75 miles north of London.

There were few immediate details of the violence.

The outbreak of violence in Leicester follows a series of riots in London, Liverpool and Birmingham in the past month and coincided with the annual convention in Blackpool of Prime Minister Margaret R. Thatcher's ruling Conservative Party.

Earlier this week, in the predominantly black, north London district of Tottenham an estimated 500 youths battled unarmed police for 10 hours. About 230 police officers and 20 civilians were injured and one policeman was hacked to death by a mob armed with machetes and knives.

Source: News and Observer (Raleigh, N.C.), October 10, 1985.

_____ **BOX 11.13** _____

RIOTING ERUPTS FOR 4TH NIGHT IN GERMANY

BONN—Groups of masked youths smashed store windows and set fires in downtown Frankfurt tonight in a fourth straight night of violence.

Authorities here agreed that the protests were the worst in West Germany since violent demonstrations to protest the stationing of American medium-range nuclear missiles here in 1983.

On Saturday, a man was run over and killed by a police vehicle in a battle between marchers and policemen.

Fighting and vandalism spread to about 16 cities Sunday night. In Frankfurt, where detained youths wrecked a detention center, damage to stores and automobiles was estimated at nearly $1 million.

On Monday, marchers in Berlin fought the police, set fires and overturned cars in the downtown area. In Hamburg, demonstrators set fires at banks, police stations, department stores, and other buildings. . . .

There seemed to be no overriding political cause for the violence, although the demonstration in Frankfurt on Saturday was to protest a meeting by the National Democratic Party, a neo-Nazi group. The group, which had fleeting electoral successes in the 1960's, is the regular target of leftist protests when its members gather.

According to the police, a demonstrator, Günther Sare, 36 years old, was crushed when a police water cannon truck inadvertently ran over him. But demonstrators accused the truck's crew of intentionally killing the man, and the Hesse State Interior Ministry has ordered an investigation.

The battles, according to the police, have been led by anarchist groups, specialists in street fighting, that are on the fringe of radical terrorist groups such as the Red Army Faction. That organization has been responsible in recent months for numerous attacks on United States military bases, including one in August in which two people were killed.

Source: New York Times, October 2, 1985.

are not ranked according to quality like American universities, for this was not necessary when they served a small elite. Equal ranking of all universities even offered certain advantages, such as easy transfers, and allowed students to study consecutively at several universities, perhaps, for example, going from Heidelberg to Bologna and finally to Paris for final exams. But today, with the large masses of students, the failure to rank universities systematically is a big disadvantage. As a consequence, brilliant students must take the same classes as average ones, lowering the overall level of education. In America, access to the top universities is limited to the very best students, who can be pushed to their intellectual limits. But the weaker students also have their opportunities, at intellectually less demanding universities and colleges, where they can be educated according to their capabilities. There is currently much discussion in Europe as to how its higher education could

BOX 11.14

CAMPUS UNREST IN ITALY

ROME—From Palermo to Turin, and on more than a dozen campuses in between, Italian universities are being rocked by student protests that had all but disappeared in the passive, self-absorbed 1980's.

The principal issue is the quality of academic life, or, more commonly, the lack of it in a system that is universally denounced as obsolete, overcrowded, inefficient and at times dehumanizing.

Over the last few weeks thousands of students have demonstrated in at least 17 cities, forcing the wholesale cancellation of classes in many departments.

At La Sapienza, the main campus of the University of Rome, protesters have occupied eight buildings, denouncing the Government and demanding the ouster of the university rector. . . . The litany of complaints is long, tending to focus on shabby equipment and overcrowding.

La Sapienza, Italy's largest campus, has 180,000 students, or 100,000 more than it should. . . . If not for the fact that fewer than 30 percent show up for classes, the rector said, "this place would look like a soccer stadium." Even so, an engineering major here says he must arrive an hour early for one of his courses to get a seat in the lecture hall.

Source: New York Times, January 24, 1990.

BOX 11.15

RIOT IN LONDON: ANGERED AND ALIENATED, YOUTH FIND TARGET IN A HATED TAX

Brimming with anger and despair, a growing number of alienated young Britons who feel passed over by the Thatcher era seem to have found a target for their rage in an unpopular new Government tax.

Their hostility erupted in rioting on Saturday after a rally in Trafalgar Square against the new local tax, which took effect on Sunday. Officials on both sides of the tax issue, including those who organized Saturday's rally, quickly disassociated themselves from the rioters.

Sociologists, experts on public order and politicians now say the violence was largely the work of a small group of unemployed young men who are generally homeless and penniless.

Whether operating as revolutionary groups or on their own, they are viewed as part of an embittered class of young people with little stake in the new Britain. Of the 339 people arrested in the disturbances, the police say, 70 percent are between 17 and 25 years of age and a third are unemployed.

Source: New York Times, April 4, 1990.

achieve this flexibility. For Americans, on the other hand, the moral of the story may well be to maintain the many different levels of their current system of higher education.

CITIZEN PARTICIPATION IN COLLECTIVE ACTIONS

The conventional way in which European citizens participate in politics is to vote in elections and to become a member of a political party. We have dealt with these two aspects of citizen participation at the end of Chapter 1 and Chapter 2. There are less conventional ways in which citizens can take part in politics, such as demonstrations, strikes, sit-ins, and collecting signatures. These forms of participation are often called *collective actions*. Social movements rely to a large extent on collective actions, although collective actions may also be undertaken by political parties and economic interest groups.

There are legal and illegal forms of collective actions, with often only a fine line drawn between the two forms. To occupy buildings, as we have seen in the section on the youth movement, is clearly breaking the law. To engage in battles with the police is certainly illegal. But to participate in a permitted demonstration is a perfectly legal act. Such a demonstration, however, may become illegal if it takes a detour that was not permitted by the authorities. Sometimes it is unclear what exactly the authorities permit and what they do not.

Why do social movements rely so heavily on collective actions? Often this is the only way in which they can draw attention to their grievances. In contrast to political parties, they are not represented in parliaments. They also do not have the privilege that most economic interest groups do of being regularly consulted by the government, although sometimes social movements, too, are included in the consultation process.

The often spontaneous nature of collective actions also corresponds well to the typical supporters of social movements. As already mentioned earlier in this chapter, young, highly educated people are the core supporters of social movements. In this final section of the chapter, it is important for us to note that there is a strong overlap between the various social movements. I have already mentioned the close connection between the environmental and peace movements. But those who are active in these two movements may also be active in an ethnic movement, the women's movement, or the youth movement. The different social movements have so much in common that it is quite possible to generalize about these movements at large. This is certainly true for the social background and the values of the key supporters. Political scientist Hanspeter Kriesi studied the Netherlands in-depth to see who among the young, highly educated are most likely to participate in social movements. He could identify an interesting subcategory, which he calls "the young specialists in social and cultural services." By this he means mainly "medical services, teaching, social work, arts and journalism."[40] What these professionals have in common is that their jobs do not directly depend on profit maximization. This contrasts with other young, highly educated people whose jobs depend on efficiency and profits, such as managers in private enterprises and computer experts. Kriesi also included in this latter category managers of public bureaucracies. Although they do not have to look out for profit maximization, efficiency is at the core of their job description. The work of Kriesi helps to explain why not all young, highly educated people participate in social movements. He sees a split that "separates the social and cultural specialists from the technocrats."

Another stream of research asks what motivates a supporter of a social movement to participate in a particular collective action, such as a demonstration. Someone may completely agree with the goals of a social movement, but why shouldn't he or she let others do the job? After all, participating in a demonstration incurs all kinds of costs, such as loss of time, perhaps braving bad weather, perhaps risking a confrontation with police. On the other hand, adding another "warm body" to the demonstration will have a minimal effect. One person more or less will be negligible. Would not a rational calculation be to stay at home and to watch the demonstration on television? To answer this question, Steven E. Finkel, Edward N. Muller, and Karl-Dieter Opp have done interesting research in the Federal Republic of Germany.[41] In addition to taking a national sample, they interviewed people from two local samples, one in Frankfurt, where there were many student activists, and a rural Bavarian community, where there was a great deal of antinuclear protest. They investigated what motivates people to overcome their fear of getting involved. They discovered one important thing: The group had to be seen as having a good likelihood of success. It is difficult to motivate people to fight for a losing cause. They found also that many people actually think that their personal participation will make a difference and that everyone has to take part if the group is to succeed. Such a belief clearly contrasts with the assumptions of the conventional rational-choice model. But beliefs are sometimes not logical. A rational-choice theorist may very well argue that adding another person to a demonstration will make no difference. However, if a person truly believes that his or her presence will make a difference, a good explanation has to take account of this belief, however illogical it may seem.

The results of Finkel, Muller, and Opp deal still another blow to the conventional rational-choice model in documenting the importance of moral obligations and feelings of duty. Many of the participants in collective actions agreed with this item in the interview: "If a citizen is dissatisfied with the policy of the government, he or she has a duty to do something about it."[42]

I find it rewarding that many citizens do not act only out of pure self-interest but also out of moral responsibility. Political scientists render a disservice to democratic politics if they insist on explaining the political world exclusively according to the conventional rational-choice model. As I have argued elsewhere, students may be influenced by their political science professors to act selfishly in their role as citizens.[43] But there is a broader collective rationality. I will come back to this rationality in Chapter 13 on power sharing and in Chapter 14 on corporatist decision making.

12

THE STATE AS A
POLITICAL ACTOR

The concept of the state has a different meaning in Europe than it does in the United States. For Americans, the term refers primarily to the 50 states of the union. It is also used to refer to important political figures—"statesmen." In Europe, the distinction is made between *state* and *politics;* in German, for example, between *Staat und Politik.* One of the difficulties of comparative politics is translating certain key concepts from one language into another. The English term *state* has a quite different connotation from the German *Staat* or the French *état.*

In Europe, the concept of the state grew out of a very different historical context than it did in America. No American leader has declared, "The state is me" ("L'état, ćest moi") as did the French king Louis XIV. In France, prior to the Revolution of 1789, the term *state* referred to the governmental institutions built by the kings of the Bourbon dynasty over several centuries. This royal family considered it a personal accomplishment to have given France a governmental structure; the French state was, in a way, its private possession. The Bourbon kings used "their" state to rule the territory of France. In order to give legitimacy to this rule, the kings claimed to act in the name of God. Thus, they had a higher mission to fulfill. It was God's will that they rule the country, and the instrument of this rule was the state, which took on a sacred character. A doctrine evolved that the state had its own interests above the interests of the contemporary population, because the state had to function for coming generations.

The state bureaucrats, in turn, were socialized to believe that they were obligated to serve the interests of the king and his state. This was particularly true during the period of French absolutism in the seventeenth and eighteenth centuries. Absolutist regimes prevailed during this time in many other European countries; in Prussia, for example, where the same doctrine of a higher state interest developed.

This discussion leads to clarification of the term *statesman.* In the words of the *Oxford English Dictionary,* a statesman is "farsighted," which means that he or she has the long-term interests of the state in mind. In the United States, we would speak in this context of the long-term interests of the nation or the country. The idea that the state—in the sense of the government—has its own interests runs against American tradition, but this concept is still very much alive in Europe. The state's interests are said to be above everyday politics. From this perspective we can see what is implied by the above-mentioned distinction between state and politics. In German, *Politik* refers to the competition among political parties and other societal groups, whereas considerations of the *Staat* are at a higher, more dignified level.

In contemporary Europe, the notion of a higher state interest is perhaps most pronounced in France. French history in the last 200 years was characterized by many upheavals, and today the French are already living under their Fifth Republic. But, through all the crises, the state bureaucracy has continued to work and has looked after the interests of the state. Top bureaucrats enjoy very high social status in France. Future state bureaucrats are rigorously trained at special postgraduate schools. Admission to these schools is extremely competitive, and the students who are accepted are immediately treated as the elite of their country. They form a special, distinguished class, with its own norms and values, whose goal is to excel in the service of the French state. A lifelong career with the state is considered to be more attractive and prestigious than a career in the private sector. High political offices are often filled by top bureaucrats; a case in point is Valéry Giscard d'Estaing, French president from 1974 to 1981.

Knowledge of the high social status of French bureaucrats sheds new light on the important role of the state in the French economy. Feeling as though they are the elite of the country, state bureaucrats have always been empowered to make important economic decisions. Thus, long before almost all banks were nationalized under François Mitterrand, the state played an important role in the French banking system, and many banks already belonged to the state. One can certainly object on the basis of free market principles to crucial investment decisions in a country being left to state bureaucrats. But, with regard to France, state bureaucrats can be highly competent from a professional perspective. Without question, they play an important part in political and economic issues and must be included among the key actors of the political game in France.

The French bureaucracy exemplifies in a particularly pronounced form the general characteristics of the state bureaucracies in Europe. The British civil service, for example, is also well known for its high professional standards and independence. To understand the Italian government, it is important to know that the state bureaucracies continue to function whenever one of Italy's frequent cabinet crises occurs.

Given the important role of state bureaucrats, we must ask exactly what such bureaucrats mean when they claim to represent the higher interest of the state. How do they know what is in the long-range interest of the state? As we saw in Chapter 1, Marxists argue that state bureaucrats in Western democracies simply help to maintain the capitalist system, and when bureaucrats speak of the interests of the state, they really mean the interests of the capitalist class. According to this Marxist view, the main function of the state is to preserve order and thus prevent any uprisings of the proletariat.

Another critical view of the role of state bureaucrats is that they mainly defend their own narrow career interests. When they refer to the interests of the state, they primarily mean the interests of the state bureaucracy itself. Thus, they try to get larger and plusher buildings, larger staffs, higher salaries, more travel money, and so on. An extensive literature addresses the validity of both these criticisms, with widely differing opinions. Of course, many bureaucrats honestly believe that they work for the higher interest of the state. But it is possible that they also serve other interests, perhaps unconsciously. We will return to this question in Chapter 14 on corporatism.

For a long time, when American political scientists studied European politics, many of them neglected the phenomenon of the state acting as an independent player in the political game. They looked at Europe through a particular theoretical framework that had grown out of the American context but was not adapted to the European scene. This input/output framework is closely linked with the work of the political theorist David Easton.[44] The framework is depicted in its most simple form in Figure 9.

This framework begins with the *inputs* that the political system gets from its societal environment. These inputs consist of *demands* aggregated and articulated by political parties, economic interest gorups, and social movements—the three sets of actors discussed in previous chapters. These demands are then converted by the political system into *decisions* and *actions*, or *outputs*, which may or may not satisfy the original demands. If the demands are satisfied, the political system receives an input of support from the affected societal groups.

This framework stems from the American tradition that the political system should serve society. Free citizens organize in groups and articulate their demands. The political system is the place where these demands compete and winners and losers are sorted out. Looking at reality through this framework, the political system appears to have no demands of its own—it is merely the neutral arena where societal groups compete with each other. But Easton could not deny that some demands originate with the state authorities. In order to account for this possibility, he introduced the concept of *withinput*, meaning inputs that come from within the political system itself.

Many European scholars have severely criticized the application of the input/output framework to the analysis of European democracies. They argue that the concept of withinput is not sufficient for a thorough analysis

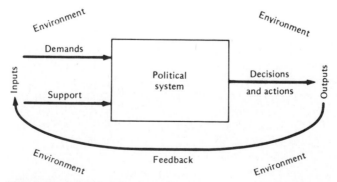

Figure 9. Input/Output Framework. SOURCE: David Easton, *A Systems Analysis of Political Life* (New York: Wiley, 1965), p. 32.

of the state as an independent actor. In order to understand European politics, one must recognize that state bureaucrats have their own specific interests that tend to be overlooked by an input/output framework. In this context, it is important to note that political appointees are much rarer in Europe than in the United States. With a new American administration, the top echelons of the bureaucracy in Washington, D.C., are usually replaced with supporters of the new president. In Europe, such replacements occur less frequently. The normal pattern is that most high-ranking civil servants, including ambassadors, for example, stay on the job. In this way, there is much more continuity, which contributes to the emergence of the state bureaucracy as an independent actor in the political game.

Profiting from analyses of European democracies, many political scientists have taken a second look at the usefulness of the input/output framework for the study of United States itself. Despite more frequent replacements in the top bureaucratic positions, there is much evidence that Washington bureaucrats, too, have become important political actors in their own right. Often, they do not simply implement decisions made by the president and Congress but are themselves decision makers.

13

CONSOCIATIONAL DECISION MAKING (POWER SHARING)

DEVELOPMENT OF THE CONSOCIATIONAL THEORY

The term *consociational* is rarely used in everyday language, but it has become very prominent in political science.* Consociational democracies are in contrast to competitive majoritarian democracies. This distinction was first made by Arend Lijphart and Gerhard Lehmbruch at the 1967 World Congress of the International Political Science Association in Brussels.[45] Their contributions opened an interesting discussion that continues up to the present. In recent years the term *power sharing* has been frequently used as a synonym for *consociational*. Lijphart and Lehmbruch coined the term *consociational democracy* to draw attention to some smaller European democracies that were neglected in prior theorizing. In the 1950s and early 1960s, the thinking of political scientists about democratic regimes was primarily influenced by the experiences of the United States, Great Britain, France, Germany, and Italy. The first two countries seemed to have long traditions of democratic stability, whereas the latter three were plagued by periods of instability. This comparison raised the question of what factors might account for the level of democratic stability. A very influential hypothesis was formulated in 1956 by Gabriel A. Almond, who identified the political culture of a country as a crucial factor.[46] He postulated that a homogeneous political culture, like that of the two Anglo-American countries, is conducive to democratic stability, whereas a fragmented political culture, as in the large continental European countries, tends to lead to democratic instability.

However, Austria, Belgium, the Netherlands, and Switzerland seemed to contradict Almond's hypothesis because they appeared culturally fragmented yet democratically stable. Lijphart and Lehmbruch explained this deviation by observing that these countries practiced a consociational, rather than a competitive, mode of decision making. From this line of theoretical reasoning, a more optimistic view emerged than that contained in Almond's hypothesis: Culturally fragmented countries could hope to attain democratic stability if they used consociational, rather than competitive, decision making. In the meantime, attempts have been made to apply this

---

* The term is derived from Johannes Althusius's concept of *"consociatio"* in his *Politica Methodice Digesta* (1603), reprinted, with introduction by Carl Joachim Friedrich (Cambridge, Mass.: Harvard University Press, 1932).

consociational theory to divided countries such as Lebanon, South Africa, and Northern Ireland. We will discuss the practical applications of consociational theory in the last section of this chapter.

Before we do, however, we must clarify three crucial concepts of the theory. First, we must define what is meant by a culturally fragmented society and how it is different from a culturally homogeneous society. Second, consociational decision making must be clearly distinguished from competitive decision making. Third, we must establish what is meant by democratic stability and instability. Only with these clarifications will it become apparent what Lijphart and Lehmbruch had in mind.

For a country to be culturally fragmented, its citizens must differ in such attributes as race, language, religion, and ethnicity. Such attributes are known as *ascriptive* attributes—having been present from birth, they are virtually permanent. Ascriptive attributes may be contrasted with *achieved* attributes, such as occupation and education, which are the result of individual achievement and can be changed relatively easily during a lifetime. Differences in ascriptive attributes are a necessary, but not sufficient, condition for cultural fragmentation. For a country to be culturally fragmented, its people, sharing the same ascriptive attribute, must also develop a common identity and express it in a politically relevant way. If these additional conditions are fulfilled, specific subcultures can be distinguished; for example, a Catholic and a Protestant subculture. These subcultures then become crucial elements in a country's political life. People feel an identity as either Protestants or Catholics and are politically active in Protestant and Catholic organizations.

What exactly do Lijphart and Lehmbruch mean when they say that the decision process among subcultures is consociational rather than competitive? An initial characteristic is that executive cabinets contain representatives from all of the subcultures. If a country is divided between a Catholic and a Protestant subculture, for example, consociational cabinet formation means that both subcultures share power in the cabinet. Such encompassing coalitions are called *grand* coalitions. Besides the cabinet, grand coalitions may also form in other bodies, such as advisory commissions. A second feature of consociational decision making is a veto power for each subculture on matters involving its essential interests. If Catholics are a minority, parliamentary rules would require that changes in abortion laws, which are so important to Catholics, could not be enacted without the consent of the Catholic minority. A third characteristic is that parliamentary elections, the appointment of public officials, and the distribution of public funds among the subcultures is guided by the principle of proportionality. If Catholics make up 20 percent of the population, they should receive 20 percent of the top positions in the armed forces. In other words, each subculture should receive its quota. Finally, consociational decision making means that the individual subcultures have a great deal of autonomy in regulating their own affairs—having control over educational matters, for example.

These consociational principles are very distinct from the principles of majoritarian decision making. If the majority principle is applied in resolving conflicts among subcultures in a fragmented society, the results will more or less correspond to a national census, because the size of the individual subcultures is a given. If Protestants, for example, comprise two-thirds of the population and Catholics one-third, the former would, obviously, always win with a majoritarian pattern of decision making. With consociational decision making, however, minorities also have a chance to influence policy outcome.

The crucial point in Lijphart and Lehmbruch's argument is that consociational decision making increases the probability of democratic stability in culturally fragmented societies. By democratic stability, they mean essentially that a country has a low level of civil violence and disorder, both actually and potentially. Why does one fragmented country make use of consociationalism and another does not? The answer most commonly given is that much depends on the wisdom and foresight of the subcultures' leaders. If they are sufficiently aware of the centrifugal tendencies in their society, they may choose to attempt to counterbalance these tendencies via consociationalism. This is not to say that leaders are always free to adopt a consociational approach to decision making. Certain conditions may prevent consociational decision making, even if the leaders wish to use it. Consociational decision making is facilitated if at least some of the following conditions are present:

- None of the subcultures has a hegemonic position, dominating all other subcultures numerically and/or economically.
- The subcultures have clear boundaries and can therefore easily be identified.
- Each subculture has preeminent leaders who are internally respected and can speak for the interests of their subculture.
- There is some overarching loyalty across all subcultures to the country as a whole, whose very existence is not questioned.
- The country is under international pressure that is seen by all subcultures in the same light.
- The country has some tradition of accommodation and compromise.
- The overall load of unresolved problems on the country (unemployment, inflation, etc.) is not very great.

In Austria, Belgium, the Netherlands, and Switzerland, these conditions were mostly favorable, which allowed their leaders to practice consociational decision making. This practice was so successful that all four countries can now again afford to introduce more competitive elements into their decision making. This move away from consociational decision making is also explained by the theory. If, as a result of consociational decision making, relations among subcultures remain peaceful for some time, cultural fragmentation begins to lose some of its importance, so that consociationalism is no longer necessary to preserve harmonious relations. You could say that successful consociationalism makes itself superfluous.

The Austrian case can be used to illustrate the dynamic workings of the consociational theory. After its defeat in World War I and the demise of the Hapsburg empire, Austria made an initial attempt at a democratic form of government in the 1920s and 1930s. At that time, Austria was a very fragmented society with two subcultures, the so-called red and black camps (*Lager*). That the military term *camp* was used to designate the two subcultures indicates just how deeply divided Austrian society was. The blacks were the middle-class bourgeois Conservative Catholics; the reds were the working-class anticlerical Socialists. The two camps were very segregated from each other, and Austrians spent most of their daily lives with members of their own camp. Politics was played according to the majority principle; as predicted by Almond's hypothesis, the result was instability, civil strife, and even a brief civil war. Austria then became easy prey for annexation by Hitler in 1938. After the atrocities of World War II and the concentration camps, surviving leaders of the two camps decided in 1945 to form a grand coalition of the two large parties. For about 20 years, blacks and reds ruled the country together according to the four consociational devices. Relations between the two subcultures became much more harmonious, and the subcultures themselves lost much of their importance. Marriage across subcultural lines, for example, was no longer uncommon. In 1966, its leaders felt that the grand coalition had fulfilled its purpose, so first the blacks and then the reds ruled alone. In 1987, however, the Conservatives and the Socialists once again entered a grand coalition.

In the Netherlands, Belgium, and Switzerland the story is much the same. The Netherlands was deeply divided between Catholics, Calvinists, and a secular group; the latter was further divided along class lines between Socialists and Liberals. As suggested by consociational theory, the politics of accommodation initiated in 1917 brought increasing stability, which in turn—particularly in the 1960s—decreased the importance of the subcultural rifts. Today, Dutch politics is played according to competitive rules. In Switzerland and Belgium, the significance of consociation was strong with respect to the language question; in Switzerland, also for relations between Catholics and Protestants; in Belgium, for relations between clerical and anticlerical Catholics.

———— CRITIQUE OF THE CONSOCIATIONAL THEORY ————

How good is the consociational theory? Has its "medicine" been tested sufficiently to ensure that it has the desired effect? Less metaphorically: Does consociation or power sharing really increase the probability of democratic stability? Do Austria, Belgium, the Netherlands, and Switzerland convincingly support the causality postulated by the consociational theory?[47] Here we encounter a difficult methodological problem common to all research in comparative politics: the small number of cases and their great complexity. Four countries obviously constitute a very narrow empirical basis. Even 10 or 20 countries would be too small a number of cases to allow for the use of sophisticated statistical analyses. Contributing further to this difficulty is the great complexity of the individual cases, which often prevents unambiguous identification of the causality of a single factor. If a country changed from competitive to consociational decision making and all other variables remained constant, the independent effect of the change in decision mode could be determined. In reality, such experimental situations do not exist. We refer first to the Austrian example to illustrate this difficulty.

As described earlier, the decision-making style in Austria's First Republic was majoritarian before civil war broke out in the early 1930s and an autocratic regime was established. By contrast, the Second Republic in the years after World War II practiced consociationalism, and democratic stability prevailed. If nothing save the decision mode had changed, we could safely conclude that that change caused an increase in democratic stability. But, because the Austrian situation changed in many other aspects as well, other plausible explanations for increased democratic stability are available. You could argue, for example, that economic conditions after 1945 were much better than in the 1920s and early 1930s and that this improvement in the economic situation allowed democratic stability to blossom. Advocates of consociationalism might reply that the economic boom after World War II was itself the result of the grand coalition. But, in other European countries, such as West Germany and France, economic recovery occurred under a majoritarian form of government. Thus, the Austrian economy might also have boomed without the grand coalition.

Increased democratic stability in Austria could also be explained by changes in the religious life of the country. In the years after 1945, religious devotion declined rapidly, so that the old rift between clericalists and anticlericalists lost much of its importance. With the decreased prominence of religion, the division between blacks and reds became less divisive, thereby allowing a more stable democracy. In addition, the social stratification of Austrian society changed noticeably during this period. The simple dichotomy between the bourgeois middle class and the working class, corresponding to an earlier phase of industrial development, was increasingly replaced with a more diversified structure. Both the middle class and the working class became more heterogeneous, blurring class distinctions. Less class distinction meant less fragmentation between blacks and reds, providing yet another explanation for the higher level of democratic stability.

We can thus identify at least five variables that had different values in the First Republic and the beginning years of the Second Republic: decision mode, democratic stability, economic affluence, religious practice, and social stratification. How can we sort out possible causalities among these and perhaps still more variables? Truly convincing conclusions could only be reached if we could manipulate the variables in an experimental way. Because that is not possible, conclusions can only be more or less plausible. The alternative explanations to consociational theory do not mean that power sharing in the grand coalition was not a factor contributing to democratic stability. It may even have been the most important factor, but that can never be proven. It is also possible that power sharing played only a minor role compared with the causal impact of the other factors.

The data for Belgium, the Netherlands, and Switzerland also allow for interpretations that conflict with the assumptions of consociational theory. Do these ambiguities mean that the theory should not be applied to countries like Northern Ireland, Lebanon, and South Africa? Certainly not. It is in the nature of comparative politics that the causal effect of a variable can never be laboratory tested. To require such tests would mean postponing practical applications forever and would make comparative politics irrelevant in crisis situations. Yet crisis situations exist in many parts of the world and they cry out for solutions. Political scientists have the moral obligation to offer help. They must only be sure that their advice is given with the proper care and caution.

A precondition for testing a theory is the ability to measure its variables in a reliable, valid way. Here we encounter additional difficulties with the consociational theory. If the theory says that consociational decision making increases the probability of democratic stability in culturally fragmented societies, all three of the variables contained in this hypothesis should be measurable. What indicators can we use to tell us how fragmented a society is, how much its political leaders use the consociational method of decision making, and how democratically stable its political system is? The Swiss case illustrates the problems inherent in answering these questions. There is a lively debate in the literature about the values of all three variables in that country.

With regard to fragmentation, it is often stated that consociational theory is applicable to Switzerland because of its linguistic fragmentation into German, French, Italian, and Romansh. Other researchers argue, however, that Swiss society is quite homogeneous, despite the existence of four languages, so that consociational theory is not applicable to the Swiss case. We must distinguish carefully between linguistic diversity and linguistic fragmentation. Here, the former means that two or more languages are spoken in a country. Linguistic diversity is a necessary, but not sufficient, condition for linguistic fragmentation. People speaking the same language may or may not develop a common and politically relevant identity. How is linguistic identity measured, for example, for French speakers in Switzerland? When asked how they usually think of themselves, 30 percent say that they think of themselves as French speakers; 40 percent, as Swiss; and 30 percent, as members of their canton (e.g., Geneva).[48] How do we interpret these survey results?

The task is not easy, because the picture is mixed. Linguistic identity is of prime importance for some French speakers and not for others. Also, consider that the relative importance of a person's identities may change from one life situation to another. In this context, the experiences of two students from the University of Geneva, who studied for a year at the University of North Carolina, are relevant. During their stay in the United States, they felt primarily Swiss. On arriving back at the airport of German-speaking Zurich, they felt that their primary identity was French. When they returned by train to the French-speaking region, still another change in identity took place; each now identified primarily with a canton—Geneva, for one student, and Jura, for the other. This story illustrates the dynamic perspective of identities. A person's primary identity may change from one situation to another. It is difficult to capture such a fast-changing picture with survey techniques. Be aware, also, that surveys are conducted at the attitudinal level, and it is a well-known phenomenon that attitudes do not always translate easily into behavior.

Hence, we must also look at behavioral data. How does the behavior of French speakers in Switzerland indicate their linguistic group identity? Do they marry, for example, primarily within their language group? Considering only marriages among Swiss nationals, statistics tell us that 82 percent of French speakers marry other French speakers, whereas 18 percent marry German, Italian, or Romansh speakers.[49] Again, the data are difficult to interpret. Because French speakers are concentrated in one region of the country, it is not surprising that most of them choose partners who live close by—other French speakers. Under these conditions, is it significant that 18 out of 100 marry someone with a different primary language? Some researchers think so and conclude that this figure indicates a low level of identity among French speakers. But does a French speaker marrying outside his or her linguistic group necessarily have a low identity with other French speakers? Perhaps marriage to a spouse who speaks another language actually increases a person's linguistic identity, even if that person uses the spouse's language in daily life. Take the example of a woman from Geneva who is married to a German-speaking man and living in Zurich. Even if she speaks German with her husband and otherwise, she may develop a stronger French-speaking identity in her new situation than when she lived back home in Geneva. She may become much more aware that as a French speaker she has different values from German speakers. Of course, it is also possible that in many cases marriages between linguistic groups indeed indicate a low level of linguistic identities. This discussion again shows the difficulty of interpreting data to measure cultural fragmentation.

Although surveys and intermarriage data may speak to the strength of subcultural identity, additional data are necessary to determine how a subcultural identity is expressed in a politically relevant way. To be politically relevant, a subcultural identity must find some form of organizational expression. Do French speakers in Switzerland have their own political party? No, and all attempts to establish such a party have failed. Does this mean that French speakers do not operate as an organized force in Swiss politics? Not quite. Looking at the Swiss party system in more detail, we see that French speakers often form a coherent subgroup in the large parties. Thus, linguistic identities are expressed not among but within parties. Also, there are always some issues in the national parliament on which French speakers vote more or less as a bloc.

We must also determine to what extent the three other linguistic groups have identities that they express in a politically relevant way. Based on all the data, we could then make a judgment about how linguistically fragmented Switzerland is. Such a judgment is obviously much more difficult than measuring the annual snowfall in a country. Meteorologists have commonly accepted yardsticks, but there are none to measure linguistic fragmentation; rather, there is constant debate in the literature about how best to measure the level of fragmentation. Because there is no agreement on this, it is not surprising that some authors classify Switzerland as linguistically quite homogeneous while others see it as relatively fragmented. Thus, there is also no agreement on exactly what the Swiss case tells us about the test of consociational theory. If a researcher comes to the conclusion that Switzerland is linguistically homogeneous, he or she argues that the consociational theory cannot be tested because there is no centrifugal fragmentation to be overcome by consociational decision making. The classification of Switzerland as a fragmented country, on the other hand, makes it a valid test for the theory.

Such difficulties of classification also emerge for other countries. To be sure, there is general agreement that Northern Ireland is highly fragmented and Denmark is homogeneous. But what about the linguistic cleavage in Canada or the racial cleavage in the United States? Are these rifts so deep that the two countries qualify as test cases for consociational theory? Is the racial cleavage in the United States deeper than the linguistic cleavage in Switzerland? How are cleavages compared if they are based on different attributes, such as language and race? Does a marriage across linguistic lines have the same meaning as one across racial lines? Such questions indicate once again the difficulty in measuring fragmentation.

Similar difficulties appear in trying to determine the prevailing political decision mode within a country. Again, the language situation in Switzerland serves as a good illustration. If we begin with the composition of the executive cabinet—the Federal Council—as an indicator, decision making among the language groups seems to be consociational. Although German speakers comprise 70 percent of the population, they never have more than five seats, and sometimes only four, in the seven-member Federal Council. Two or three seats always go to the linguistic minorities. This rule is not based on a constitutional article or a law but on custom and tradition, which guide the members of parliament when they elect the federal councillors. The principle that linguistic minorities get a proportionate share is applied to virtually all government positions. In the Swiss army, for example, there are seven men in the highest rank of three-star general; at present these positions are held by four German speakers, two French speakers, and one Italian speaker, which even gives some overrepresentation to the minorities. Federalism, another consociational device, is also strongly developed in Switzerland (as seen in Chapter 6).

Are these indicators sufficient for classifying decision making among Swiss language groups as clearly consociational? Many researchers think so, but perhaps we should look more closely at how decisions are actually made. The linguistic minorities may have two or three representatives in the Federal Council, but they can still lose if the Council makes its decisions in a majoritarian way. Decision making in the Federal Council is, in principle, treated as confidential, but occasionally there are leaks about how a particular decision was made. It seems that majority decisions are occasionally made, but it remains unclear how often and exactly who is on which side of such votes. The picture is clearer for parliament, where deliberations are open to the public. In many cases the Swiss parliament makes unanimous or near-unanimous decisions. Such cases have often been studied by consociational authors, who use them as illustrations to support their theory. But, in many other often-neglected cases, Swiss parliament takes close votes, and such votes sometimes pit a German-speaking majority against the linguistic minorities. In Chapter 6, on federalism, we mentioned a case in which a bloc of German speakers reduced subsidies for Geneva's airport. How frequent are such cases? Do they involve essential or only marginal issues for the linguistic minorities? If such votes occur, are some concessions nevertheless made to the minorities, or are they simply outvoted? These questions show that it is not a simple matter to measure the degree of consociational and majoritarian decision making.

The problem is further complicated because decision making takes place in other arenas of Swiss politics in addition to parliament; the so-called expert committees, where most legislation is prepared, are a good example. Interviews with committee members have revealed that, in this pre-parliamentary phase, consensual and majoritarian decision making are used with about equal frequency.[50] But, here again, how many of the majority votes are taken along linguistic lines? How important were the issues, and were concessions made to the minorities despite the application of the majority principle? These questions have not yet been studied in detail. Even if they had been, scholars would probably disagree on the exact interpretation of the data. There would most likely be disagreement over how to determine the importance of an issue for a language group or over how to measure the number of concessions a winning majority makes to the minorities, given that each side's original position was perhaps exaggerated for tactical reasons.

The study on expert committees has revealed further that consensual and majoritarian decision making are not the only alternatives. I identified a third decision-making mode, which I call *decision by interpretation*.[51] This mode is an interesting mixture of the two other modes. In the Swiss expert committees, decision by interpretation is used with about the same frequency as the other two modes. In a decision by interpretation, no explicit consensus is reached, but neither is the voting mechanism used to separate a majority from a minority. Rather, the chair sums up the sense of the meeting, and the other members go tacitly along with the summary. It remains unclear how much consensus has actually been reached. Some members may still dissent, but they prefer not to challenge the summary of the president. Sometimes such summary interpretations are only made in the minutes.

Decision by interpretation seems to be common, for example, in the British cabinet, as we have seen in Chapter 3. The existence of decision by interpretation, in addition to consensual and majoritarian decision making, reinforces the argument of how difficult it is to determine the prevailing decision-making pattern in a country. As in the case of cultural fragmentation, I do not wish to argue that measurement is impossible; I only wish to draw attention to the difficulties present in such measurement. As a consequence, we should not expect to be able to rank countries on a precise scale from consociational to competitive. Decision making among Swiss linguistic groups is certainly more consociational than decision making is among religious groups in Northern Ireland. But, if we compare the level of consociationalism in Switzerland and Austria, the judgment is much more difficult. In the United States, how consociational are relations between whites and blacks? Is it significant that blacks are represented on the Supreme Court and usually hold at least one cabinet position?

Of all the variables contained in consociational theory, the degree of democratic stability is the most problematic to measure. Switzerland, for example, seems democratically very stable. Very little civil violence and disorder arises from the language question,* which seems to indicate that all language groups accept the democratic legitimacy of the political order. In the consociational literature, it is commonly accepted without much further inquiry that Switzerland is a stable democracy. But another literature, inspired by a Marxist view, ranks the democratic quality of Switzerland much lower. Its basic argument is that consociational arrangements are merely a ruse to cover up the real power structure. The most extreme formulation of this argument stems from sociologist and left-wing Socialist Jean Ziegler, who claims that essential power in Switzerland rests with the bankers in Zurich.[52] Ziegler speaks of structural violence against the working class and the linguistic minorities, by which he means that these groups are repressed in such a subtle way that they are not even aware of it. In this view, consociational devices help to legitimate the existing repressive order in the eyes of the large masses of the people. (For the Marxist argument, in general, see Box 13.1.)

Without going as far as Ziegler, other critics complain that economic power is increasingly concentrated in German-speaking Zurich. Consequently, many consociational devices would lose at least some of their importance. Thus, Federal Council representation of the linguistic minorities could become somewhat symbolic if these minorities lose their say in the corporate headquarters. Federalism could become an empty shell if most important economic decisions are made in Zurich. Do such critiques indicate an increasing dissatisfaction among the linguistic minorities, perhaps even a potential for future unrest? Is Swiss democracy not as stable after all as it appears to the consociational authors? Again, no agreement can be found in the literature.

Is the fact that they cannot agree on how to measure the key variables of their theories discouraging for scholars of comparative politics? Physicists had no difficulty in agreeing on the definition of a meter or a kilogram. But, in physics, the observer and the object of observation are clearly separated, unlike the social sciences, in which both observer and observed are human beings. When social scientists publish their results, those results may be read by the objects of the study. Social scientists in this way become actors in the world they observe. To take the example of consociational theory, when Ziegler teaches and writes that Switzerland is characterized by subtle repression, his students and readers may begin to perceive Swiss reality in this light. Similarly, perceptions may be influenced by descriptions of Switzerland as a stable democracy. How to define and measure a political variable is influenced by the political values of the researcher. For all researchers to have the same values is not a desirable goal. With a pluralism of values, of course, researchers will arrive at different results. For some, Switzerland is linguistically fragmented and only remains a stable democracy thanks to the practice of power sharing. For others, Switzerland is relatively homogeneous, and consociational arrangements serve only to legitimize the power of a small elite cartel. Such different interpretations are not due merely to

---

* An exception occurred for the Jura question.

_____ **BOX 13.1** _____

A MARXIST CRITIQUE OF CONSOCIATIONAL DEMOCRACY

The state's need to maintain and consolidate the existing social relations of production, then, determined the general form of its economic and social policies, while the relative weakness of the working class determined its specific form.

Even though the working class was weak politically during this period, it still needs to be explained why its representatives so willingly facilitated and implemented a set of policies hardly favorable to its constituency. The underlying assumption of the accommodationist argument is, of course, that the various group and bloc elites not only speak for their membership but embody their general interest as well. It would never occur to the accommodationists that in placing primacy on the attempt to reconcile irreconcilable interests (labor vs. capital), the group or bloc leaders progressively subordinate the pursuit of membership interests to what has become the overriding concern for accommodation, even if it means, as it did in Holland, the restabilization of capitalist relations of production. What must be explained, then, is this increasing disjuncture between the interests pursued by the labor leadership and the interests of the rank and file.

. . . the leadership of the working class had been systematically co-opted directly into the state apparatus itself. In so doing, it came to adopt the interests of the state as its own, that is, the stabilization and maintenance of the capitalist relations of production. It thus came to perform a dual role. On the one hand, it served as the representative of its rank-and-file membership, while, on the other, it acted as a disciplining agent of the working class. In fact, the reconstruction of capitalism in Holland could not have been achieved without the labor leadership's ability to keep its members under control.

Source: Ronald A. Kieve, "Pillars of Sand: A Marxist Critique of Consociational Democracy in the Netherlands," *Comparative Politics* 13 (April 1981): 329–330.

errors of technical measurement but to fundamental differences in the value premises on which the research is based, as well. It is healthy that such fundamental differences are aired in the scholarly debate, and it speaks well for the consociational theory that it has led to heated but interesting and enlightening discussion.

_____ APPLICATIONS OF THE CONSOCIATIONAL THEORY _____

Among all theories recently developed in political science, consociational theory is perhaps the one most widely applied to trouble spots all over the world. Arend Lijphart has served on several occasions as an influential consultant to politicians in deeply divided countries. In the media, the term *power sharing* is often used to express the idea of consociational decision making. What are the chances of power sharing in such troubled countries as Northern Ireland, Lebanon, and South Africa?

None of the authors of consociational theory, of course, is so naive as to think that it would be a simple matter for such countries to adopt the consociational solution and that everything would then be fine. The theory explicitly recognizes that some countries are so deeply fragmented that there is no hope for power sharing to work. In such cases, the result is often civil war among the subcultures or the establishment, or both, of an authoritarian regime by one of the subcultures. If fragmentation is not extreme but still very high, power sharing may provide a glimmer of hope, and, as the consociational authors argue, probably the only hope. Considering this reasoning, the outlook for countries like Northern Ireland, Lebanon, and South Africa is not very optimistic. But any hope must be based on the notion of power sharing. These countries are so deeply divided that a majoritarian form of democracy is not a realistic option. The hatred between the subcultures is so great that none would accept an electoral defeat, fearing that the victor would unduly exploit its victory. Power sharing, on the other hand, would allow each subculture to maintain some control over the country's decision making. As Lijphart formulates it, the realistic choice for many fragmented societies "is not between the British normative model of democracy and the consociational model, but between consociational democracy and no democracy at all."[53]

Given this choice, Lijphart advocates power sharing as a normative model

for multiethnic societies because it is the optimal—indeed, usually the only—solution, regardless of whether the background conditions are favorable or unfavorable. To aspiring power-sharers who find themselves in an unfavorable situation, it does not say: "Give up." Instead, it counsels: "Be aware of the obstacles you face, and try extra hard."[54]

Lijphart becomes impatient with people who are overly pessimistic about power sharing, and he warns them, as we can see in Box 13.2, that, if nobody tries power sharing, it will certainly not be adopted.

─────────────── **BOX 13.2** ───────────────

AGAINST PESSIMISM WITH REGARD TO POWER SHARING

If everyone is convinced that power sharing cannot be applied, nobody will even try to introduce it, and consequently it will certainly not be adopted. Or if it is introduced in a particular multiethnic society, the conviction that it is bound to fail will kill any effort to make it succeed—and that will surely cause it to fail. It is vastly preferable to think of success and failure in terms of probabilities rather than absolutes.

Source: Arend Lijphart, "The Power-Sharing Approach," in Joseph V. Montville, ed., *Conflict and Peacemaking in Multiethnic Societies* (Lexington, MA: D.C. Heath, 1990), p. 497.

In this section, we will look more closely at the chances of power sharing in Northern Ireland. Given the great changes in Eastern Europe, it is also of interest to see to what extent power sharing can help with the democratic development of these countries. Of particular interest are the cases of Czechoslovakia and Yugoslavia, both ethnically diverse countries.

Northern Ireland

The society of Northern Ireland is deeply divided into two groups: British Protestants and Irish Catholics (on the ethnic nature of these two groups, see Chapter 11). When the Republic of Ireland obtained its independence in 1921 and Northern Ireland remained British, a parliament (Stormont) with extensive powers was established in Belfast, the capital of Northern Ireland. Protestants held a two-to-one majority in this parliament, and they practiced democracy in the traditional British way—by applying the majority principle. Not surprisingly, the Protestants won one parliamentary election after another and exercised all the governmental power. The local prime minister and all his cabinet members always belonged to the Protestant subculture, while the Catholics remained politically impotent. Over the years, this led to increasing dissatisfaction and frustration among the Catholic population, and in 1968 to the outbreak of widespread violence. Ultimately, British troops intervened, and in 1972 the Belfast parliament was dissolved and direct rule by London was imposed.

Partly inspired by the successful Swiss experience, the British tried to restore calm in Northern Ireland through a form of consociational power sharing. A local cabinet of moderate Protestants and Catholics was established, but within a few months a general strike of Protestant workers brought this experiment to a halt. The large majority of Protestants was obviously not willing to change from a majoritarian to a consociational pattern of decision making. The Catholics, for their part, reacted with further civil strife.

Why has power sharing not succeeded in Northern Ireland, and is there any hope that it may fare better in the future? Looking at the list of facilitating conditions in the first section of this chapter, we can conclude that there is no overarching loyalty between Catholics and Protestants to Northern Ireland as a political unit. The Protestants wish to remain British, whereas the Catholics would like to join the Republic of Ireland. There is no loyalty to a common land. In this respect, the situation is different from that in Switzerland, where Catholics and Protestants, German, French, Italian, and Romansh speakers have always felt like members of one political community despite all their differences.

Power sharing might still work if other factors were favorable, but they are not. Power sharing in Northern Ireland would be facilitated if Protestants and Catholics each had a comparable numerical strength, as the blacks and reds in Austria did when they formed their grand coalition in 1945. An even more favorable condition would be if there were more than two subcultures and none was a majority; this was the situation in the Netherlands when power sharing was introduced successfully.

The fact that no clear territorial boundaries exist in Northern Ireland between Protestants and Catholics is also unfavorable. The two groups live interspersed in the same cities, towns, and villages: One street is Protestant, another street, Catholic. This territorial proximity facilitates the outbreak of daily violence; it does not allow the consociational device of subcultural autonomy, in which the subcultures themselves regulate much of their own internal affairs. In this context, a comparison can be made to Belgium, where relations between Flemish and Walloons are most problematic in Brussels, the city in which the two communities have no clear boundaries. The old saying that "good fences make good neighbors" seems to have some validity.

A further negative factor in Northern Ireland is the internal rivalry and quarrels within both the Catholic and Protestant leadership. Neither group has uncontested leaders who can speak authoritatively for it. Therefore, neither subculture has representatives who can make deals that are also binding on their own members. An attempt by a political leader to negotiate a compromise with the other side is likely to be that leader's kiss of political death within his or her own group, because competing leaders would exploit such a step as weakness. The result is a tendency for leaders of each side to outbid each other for the most extreme position.

The international position of Northern Ireland is also not conducive to power sharing. The Republic of Ireland claims the territory, but, while Protestants perceive this claim as an external threat, Catholics see it as liberation. This situation is fundamentally different from that of the Netherlands, which introduced power sharing during World War I when the country's neutrality was militarily threatened by Germany, a development perceived by all Dutch groups as a grave external threat. Nor do British troops provide a rallying point for internal solidarity in Northern Ireland, for Protestants see their function as keeping the province within the United Kingdom, while Catholics consider them occupying forces. Still another obstacle to power sharing in Northern Ireland is the region's many unresolved problems, especially a desperate economic situation characterized by an extremely high rate of unemployment.

What is the solution for this troubled land? A seemingly easy way out would be a territorial separation, with Protestants remaining in the United Kingdom and Catholics joining the Republic of Ireland. Unfortunately, this solution is not feasible because the communities of Catholics and Protestants are so highly interspersed. Massive resettlements—impossible from a practical perspective and morally repugnant—would be required. Another solution is for Great Britain to share some of the governmental responsibilities for Northern Ireland with the Republic of Ireland. When the British and Irish governments made a tentative first step in this direction in 1985, the Protestants of Northern Ireland protested vehemently, fearing that they might ultimately be abandoned by London and integrated into the Republic of Ireland. Given this resistance, shared governmental responsibility does not seem to have much chance of success.

Power sharing still seems to be the best hope for restoring peace in Northern Ireland. As our discussion has shown, however, preconditions for this form of government are not at all favorable. The violence may even

_____ **BOX 13.3** _____

A GRIM VIEW ON NORTHERN IRELAND

Northern Ireland is a challenge to the comforting belief that describing a situation as a problem guarantees the existence of a solution. In this strife-torn land where the United Kingdom meets the Republic of Ireland, there is no solution—if a solution is defined as a form of government that is consensual, legitimate, and stable.

Source: Richard Rose, "Northern Ireland: The Irreducible Conflict," in Joseph V. Montville ed., _Conflict and Peacemaking in Multiethnic Societies_ (Lexington, MA: D.C. Heath, 1990), p. 133.

worsen before Protestant and Catholic leaders come to their senses and agree to make decisions in a consociational way. (For an even grimmer outlook, see what political scientist Richard Rose has to say in Box 13.3.)

Yugoslavia and Czechoslovakia

Eastern and Central Europe [for these terms see page 1] offer new opportunities for consociational scholars. The countries in Eastern and Central Europe have the advantage that they were not considered when the consociational theory was originally developed because under Communist rule neither power sharing nor competition were options. As a consequence, we have a good test situation for the theory. This test situation is all the better because the Eastern and Central European countries are quite comparable to the original countries from which the theory was developed. A study of Yugoslavia and Czechoslovakia seems to be a good beginning point, because ethnic unrest in Yugoslavia is much stronger than in Czechoslovakia. Thus, we have real variation to be explained. As one may expect, the data sources are quite bad, because Communist regimes have notoriously not been interested in allowing data collection on ethnic conflicts.[56]

One may object that Czechoslovakia is culturally homogeneous, so there is no potential for unrest. The consociational theory would not be applicable under these conditions. It could be that to be Czech or Slovak is a trivial attribute without political significance. But this is not the case. Thus, the Slovak minority demanded that the name of the country be hyphenated into Czecho-Slovakia in order to emphasize that there are two distinct cultures in the country. As one Slovak deputy said, "The hyphen is important because we want to anchor the Slovak name in the name of the country." Another Slovak deputy complained: "When you are abroad, you always hear Czech, Czech, Czech. Slovakia is always left out."[57] Finally, the solution was to call the country the Czech and Slovak Federative Republic; a cumbersome name, but it expresses that the country has two cultures. As we have seen in Chapter 2, ethnicity played also a large role in the first free election in June

1990. The conclusion is that in Czechoslovakia there are indeed cultural identities that matter in a political sense. Therefore, the consociational theory is applicable because there is potential for ethnic unrest, and the question is why there is so little unrest in Czechoslovakia and so much unrest in Yugoslavia.

I do not have to elaborate very much on my assertion that ethnic unrest is lower in Czechoslovakia than in Yugoslavia. Whatever indicator we take, we come to the same conclusion. In Yugoslavia, there are instances of violence between ethnic groups, for example, in the autonomous province of Kosovo between Albanians and Serbs. There is no violence reported between Czechs and Slovaks. Another indicator is trade boycotts between ethnic groups. Serbs, for example, boycotted merchandise from Slovenia in the spring of 1990. There are no such boycotts in Czechoslovakia.

It is equally clear that power sharing between ethnic groups is practiced more in Czechoslovakia than in Yugoslavia. When Václav Havel, a Czech, was made president, great care was taken that a Slovak would also get an important position (page 30–33). There were certainly also other reasons why Alexander Dubcek became president of parliament, but it was also important that he is Slovak so that the election of Havel could be balanced. It should be noted that this solution was worked out in a true consociational spirit of cooperation between the two ethnic groups. The election of Havel and Dubcek in a one-package deal is only one example of power sharing between Czechs and Slovaks since the so-called velvet revolution of 1989. Another example is the balanced cabinet formation between Czechs and Slovaks after the June 1990 election (see page 146–147). In Yugoslavia, many arrangements of power sharing have been attempted, but they have all failed, more or less. The country is now confronted with the danger of disintegration.

At first sight, the consociational theory seems to fail. To explain why power sharing succeeds better in Czechoslovakia than in Yugoslavia, the most obvious factor to consider is the number of ethnic groups and their respective numerical strength. Considering this, Yugoslavia seems to have more favorable conditions for power sharing than Czechslovakia. In Yugoslavia, there are seven major ethnic groups (see Figure 10 on page 249). Serbs (36 percent), Croats (20 percent), Slovenes (8 percent), Albanians (8 percent), Macedonians (6 percent), and Montenegrins (3 percent). 9 percent declare themselves as Muslims. The remaining 10 percent of the population see themselves either simply as Yugoslavs or as members of some tiny minority, such as Hungarians or Turks. According to the consociational theory, Yugoslavia, because it has seven ethnic groups, none of which are in a majority position, seems ideally fitted to practice successful power sharing. The number of ethnic groups does not have to be exactly seven, but close to that number, which is justified by Lijphart in the following way: With a much larger number of groups, the political game would become unwieldy. If the number of groups was much smaller—two or three—the game would not have enough flexibility and a stalemate could easily develop. With about six or seven groups, however, a fluid multiple balance of power with changing coalitions could develop. No group would be permanently left out; none would always win. This is said to be an ideal situation in which a pattern of power sharing could develop.

Figure 10. Yugoslavia.

Czechoslovakia, by contrast, has only two major ethnic groups—Czechs and Slovaks—with the former totaling about two-thirds of the population and the latter, one-third. According to the consociational theory, this is the worst possible situation, because the minority is at the mercy of the majority, which has no incentive to share power. This is usually the main argument used for explaining the unrest between the two-thirds Protestants and the one-third Catholics in Northern Ireland.

Although the first factor is disappointing for the consociational theory, other factors work much better. This is true for the boundaries between the ethnic groups. The consociational theory is based on the old saying that "good fences make good neighbors." In Belgium, for example, relations between Flemings and Walloons are quite trouble-free, with the exception of Brussels, where there are no clear boundaries separating the two communities. In Czechoslovakia there are clear boundaries between Czechs and Slovaks. In the Czech Republic, there are only 3.8 percent Slovaks; in the Slovak Republic, merely 1.1 percent Czechs. As a consequence—this is at least the argument of the theory—there is little potential for conflict in everyday life, which facilitates power sharing at the elite level. In Yugoslavia there are six republics: Serbia, Croatia, Slovenia, Macedonia, Montenegro, and Bosnia/Herzegovina. At first glance, it seems that here, too, each ethnic group has its own republic, but the situation is more complicated. Comparing the list of republics with the earlier list of group identities, we see that Muslims and Albanians do not have their own republics. Muslims have a stronghold in Bosnia/Herzegovina, but with 39 percent they do not form a majority in this ethnically diverse republic. Albanians are concentrated in a corner of the Republic of Serbia, where they have their own autonomous province, Kosovo. However, this province does not have the same status as a proper republic.

The ethnic groups that do have their own republics are rather strongly interspersed with other ethnic groups. The most ethnically homogeneous republic is Slovenia, but even here only 90 percent are Slovenes. In Serbia proper (without the two autonomous provinces of Kosovo and Vojvodina), only 85 percent are Serbs. The other republics are even more heterogeneous. In Croatia, only 75 percent are Croats; in Montenegro, 69 percent are Montenegrins; and, in Macedonia, 67 percent are Macedonians. The most heterogeneous republic is Bosnia/Herzegovina: Besides the 39 percent Muslims already mentioned, there are 32 percent Serbs, 18 percent Croats, and the remaining 11 percent dispersed among all other ethnic groups. Overall, Yugoslavia has quite fluid boundaries among its ethnic groups, which, according to consociational theory, makes power sharing difficult: There is too much potential for daily conflict. Furthermore, it is not easy to identify the groups, and thus there is no good basis to determine how the costs and benefits of government should be split among them. If subsidies go, for example, to Croatia, not only Croats benefit but also the 12 percent Serbs living in Croatia. In this respect, the situation is much better in Czechoslovakia: Subsidies to the Czech Republic, for example, benefit nearly exclusively Czechs. As a consequence, it is much easier to determine who gets what.

Another factor that makes power sharing more favorable in Czechoslovakia than in Yugoslavia is the religious composition of the country. In Czechoslovakia, the vast majority of the people who indicate a religious affiliation are Roman Catholic, with only about 15 percent declaring themselves Protestant. This religious homogeneity holds the country together across ethnic lines. It also helps that the Protestant minority is not concentrated in one ethnic group but is about equally strong in both groups. Yugoslavia is religiously much more diverse, and religious cleavages do not cut across ethnic cleavages but rather reinforce them. The two main groups are Christian Orthodox and Roman Catholics, with the former being slightly larger than the latter (exact figures are difficult to find). In addition, as we have already seen, there are nearly 10 percent Muslims. What makes the religious situation in Yugoslavia particularly difficult for power sharing is that Roman Catholics are concentrated in Slovenia and Croatia, and Christian Orthodox, in Serbia, Macedonia, and Montenegro. Thus, religious cleavages are superimposed on ethnic cleavages, which is a much more explosive situation than if the two cleavage lines would cross-cut each other. In

Yugoslavia, religious conflicts can easily spill over into ethnic conflicts, and vice-versa. To make matters worse, there is, in addition, a language cleavage superimposed on the two other cleavages: Slovenes and Croats use the Roman alphabet; the other ethnic groups use the cyrillic script. Thus, how people write gives already a good indication as to what religious and ethnic groups they belong to.

Besides the boundaries between ethnic groups and the nature of the groups, there is a third factor that is more favorable for power sharing in Czechoslovakia than in Yugoslavia, namely, the relative economic equality among the ethnic groups. To be sure, Slovaks were, in the past, economically less developed than the Czechs. In 1970, the Slovaks had still 20.4 percent in agriculture; the Czechs had only 14.8 percent. In the meantime, the gap has narrowed. According to the most recent figures, the Slovaks employ 15.3 percent in agriculture, and the Czechs, 11.5 percent. The gap has also narrowed for per capita income. In the Slovak Republic, the per capita income is now about 86 percent of the figure in the Czech Republic. For power sharing, it would be better if there were no economic gap at all between the two ethnic groups, a situation that Switzerland, for example, enjoys among its linguistic groups. But Czechoslovakia is certainly much better off than Yugoslavia, which suffers from a huge gap between the north and the south. Again, accurate data are difficult to find, but Slovenia on the Austrian border has a per capita income that is about seven times higher than that in the autonomous province of Kosovo and about three times higher than that in Macedonia and Montenegro. It is therefore no surprise that violence occurred in 1990 in Kosovo, whose mainly Albanian population is not only poor but, as we have seen, does not have the privilege of belonging to its own republic. Interestingly enough, there is also unrest in Slovenia, not in the form of violence, but as general dissatisfaction. The Slovenes have the feeling that, as the most prosperous republic, they carry too much of the burden of the country. As Roman Catholics, using the Roman alphabet, and living close to the center of Europe, many Slovenes do not feel that they have much in common with people in southern parts of Yugoslavia. This example shows that power sharing may sometimes be endangered, not only by the poorest group, but also by the most affluent group. Such a group may arrive at the conclusion that it would be better if it kept its economic power for itself rather than share it with the poorer inhabitants of the country.

This discussion brings us naturally to the next factor, namely, the presence or absence of overarching loyalty to a country. Here again, Czechoslovakia is better off than Yugoslavia. Both countries are relatively new independent political entities, both having been created after World War I. But Yugoslavia was put together out of much more disparate parts than Czechoslovakia. Both Czechs and Slovaks belonged to the Austro-Hungarian Empire and, after its demise, gained independence as a single unit. Thus, they had a certain common history. This is not at all the case with the parts out of which Yugoslavia was put together. Slovenia, Croatia, and Bosnia/Herzegovina were also remnants of the Austro-Hungarian Empire. If Yugoslavia had been limited to these three groups, the situation would have been similar to Czechoslovakia, but Yugoslavia was expanded to include also the kingdom of Serbia, the kingdom of Montenegro, and parts of the Turkish Empire. This was a nation with very little common history. It was therefore difficult to develop overarching loyalties to the country as a whole and all the more so because Yugoslav history was tension-ridden from the very beginning. The king of Serbia tried to dominate the country and established an autocratic regime, which led to severe rivalries, in particular with Croatia, the second largest group. In 1934, the Serbian king was assassinated in Paris by Croatian extremists. During this interwar period, Czechoslovakia, on the other hand, practiced a quite successful democratic regime. The rivalries between Serbia and Croatia continued during World War II, when Serbians were at the forefront of the resistance against the Nazis, whereas quite a few Croats collaborated with Hitler. It is clear that such a history did not contribute much to the building of common national feelings.

The consociational theory links the position of a country in the international system with the pattern of its domestic decision making. The specific hypothesis is that a common threat from abroad increases the likelihood of power sharing. An often mentioned example is the Soviet occupation troops in Austria from 1945 to 1955, which are said to have contributed to the Austrian power-sharing arrangement during this time. The hypothesis also helps to explain the difference in the success of power sharing in Czechoslovakia and Yugoslavia. Whereas Yugoslavia, under the leadership of Tito, could liberate itself in 1948 from the threat of Soviet domination, Czechoslovakia continued in a satellite status, having Soviet troops on its territory. Given this pressure from the Soviets, which was perceived in all of Czechoslovakia in the same negative light, internal differences between Czechs and Slovaks lost some of their importance, so that after the "velvet" revolution power sharing was made easier.

With regard to a last factor—the load on the political system—conditions for power sharing are once again better in Czechoslovakia than in Yugoslavia. Czechoslovakia has a somewhat smaller population than Yugoslavia: 16 million versus 24 million people, respectively. According to the consociational theory, a smaller population is loading a political system with fewer problems. This is said to facilitate power sharing, which is often a very time-consuming mechanism, because so many actors have to be included in the decision-making process. The classical cases of consociationalism consist of small countries that can better afford a relatively slow decision-making process.

Although Czechoslovakia has a somewhat smaller population than Yugoslavia, this is not the decisive factor concerning the difference in the political load on the two systems. More important is that Yugoslavia is much poorer than Czechoslovakia. Again, the data are not very good, but whatever indicator we use, the contrast between the two countries is overwhelming. Measured by per capita income, Czechoslovakia is nearly twice as wealthy as Yugoslavia. Czechoslovakia has only about half the people in agriculture that Yugoslavia has. The poor economic situation of Yugoslavia is also expressed in such indicators as high infant mortality (25 deaths per 1,000 living births in Yugoslavia, compared with 13 deaths per 1,000 living births in Czechoslovakia). The poor economic situation in Yugoslavia makes power sharing very difficult. In Czechoslovakia, by contrast, power sharing is made easier because of the better economic situation.

It is encouraging to see how well the consociational theory serves to explain why power sharing among ethnic groups is more successful in Czechoslovakia than in Yugoslavia. In the past, the consociational debate had become somewhat sterile, because the same few cases, such as Switzerland, Belgium, and South Africa, were constantly debated. Now there is new excitement in the consociational debate. With democratization in the Eastern and Central European countries—and for that matter in the Soviet Union—a whole new research field has opened up. With the end of the Cold War, ethnic conflicts will come very much to the forefront of world attention. If further developed, the consociational theory may contribute much to the understanding of these conflicts.

14

CORPORATIST
DECISION MAKING

Like consociationalism, the term *corporatism* is not often used in everyday language, but it has become very popular in the political science literature, and it is essential for an understanding of the current debate about decision making in European democracies. Like consociational decision making, corporatist decision making refers to a consensual form of government. The delimitation of the two concepts is somewhat ambiguous. They are often used synonymously, but at other times they have two distinct meanings.

HISTORY OF CORPORATISM

The notion of corporatism as a form of government has deep roots in European history, ranging back to medieval times. In our present era of individualism, it is difficult to imagine how in medieval times the lives of individuals were embedded and subordinated to the groups to which they belonged. Membership in these groups was not voluntary but compulsory. A baker in a medieval town had no choice as to whether to join the professional bakers' organization; all bakers had to belong to their guild. These guilds were hierarchical. At the bottom were apprentices, who trained to become journeymen and later, perhaps, masters of their craft. The guild established rules specifying how many journeymen and apprentices a master could employ. Standards were also set as to how much could be produced (for example, how many breads a baker could bake). In addition to guilds, there were other "corporations," for example, universities, whose internal differentiation was primarily between professors and students. In Latin, *university* is *universitas magistrorum studentiumque*, "corporation of professors and students."

The corporations played a crucial role in the government of a medieval town. Together with town officials, they managed public affairs. Decision making was characterized by mutual accommodation and bargaining; the ideological basis was a harmonious model of society. Each corporation was seen as a part of a living body, and the parts had to cooperate for the entire body to stay healthy. The main function of the individual in this organic view of society was his or her contribution to the whole.

It was only during the Enlightenment that philosophers began to place the individual at center stage. They proclaimed that individuals had natural rights independent of the groups to which they belonged, a notion alien to medieval thinkers. The French philosopher René Descartes made the influential statement, *"cogito, ergo sum"* ("I think, therefore I am"), indicating that the potential to think is the crucial element in human existence. The capacity of thought makes the individual free and gives him or her inalienable rights—among others, the right of free association. Individuals should be able to choose freely the groups to which they belong. Based on this right, political parties were founded, bringing together people of similar ideological orientations. This was the beginning of modern democracy, first put in practice in the United States and shortly thereafter, in France. The old harmonious model was replaced with the notion of competition. The emerging political parties competed for members and votes. Decisions increasingly were made with the device of the majority principle. The building blocks of society were no longer organic groups but individuals free to choose for themselves.

But notions of democracy based on individualism and competition led in nineteenth-century Europe to much turmoil, unrest, and bloody revolutions. As a result, there was a backlash, accompanied by nostalgic longing for the old order of cooperation and harmony, and a view of modern democracy as divisive and contrary to the laws of nature. Motivated by such views, in 1922 Mussolini overthrew the frail Italian democracy and established fascism based on a corporate form of government. Although similar forms of government were established in other countries, Mussolini was most explicit in the implementation of corporatist ideas: The will of the people should be represented not by political parties but by the natural economic forces of society. A national assembly should bring together the interests of farmers, businesses, workers, and so forth. Because everyone belongs to an economic sector of society, everyone would be represented. Interests would not be antagonistic but would complement each other for the good of the entire country. It would only be necessary for the *Duce* ("leader")—Mussolini himself—to give clear directions in which way the country should go. The result would be the reestablishment of order and strength for the Italian state. In fact, the outcome was dictatorship, an alliance with Germany, and military defeat in World War II. Because of its negative association with fascism, the concept of corporatism was discredited for many years in Europe (for a discussion of fascism, see also Chapter 1).

It has only been since the 1970s that some political scientists have once again begun to use the term *corporatism*. In order to distinguish their idea of corporatism from Mussolini's, these political scientists speak of neocorporatism, liberal corporatism, societal corporatism, or democratic corporatism. Whatever term they use, they claim that some European democracies have a corporatist form of government. The example cited most often is Austria, where laws have established chambers of business, labor, and agriculture. Membership in these chambers is compulsory. Representatives of the chambers meet regularly under the chairmanship of the federal chancellor to hammer out crucial economic decisions. In Austria, this form of decision making is called *social partnership.* Other countries frequently characterized as corporatist are Norway, Sweden, and the Netherlands.

CORPORATISM AND CONSOCIATIONALISM

We will begin this discussion with the narrow definition of corporatism, in which its meaning is clearly separate from consociationalism. At its core, corporatism in a modern democracy deals with the interactions among organized business, organized labor, and the state bureaucracy. These three actors cooperate at the national level in the pursuit of what they see as the public good. It is important for this definition that negotiations are not merely bilateral—between business and labor—but trilateral—including the state bureaucracy. The participation of the state bureaucracy as an independent actor in its own right is a crucial element of corporatism. (At this point, we can refer to Chapter 12, where the strong role played by the state bureaucracy in most European democracies is described.) The state bureaucracy's representatives meet around the same table with the representatives of the major business and labor organizations. These economic interest groups are not merely consulted but are themselves active decision makers. The style of decision making is characterized by bargaining. The interests of the three actors in corporatist decision making are usually quite divergent in the initial phases, but the three share a common belief that a solution optimal for the public good exists.

The representatives from all three sides are usually professional economists who are proficient in the same technical language, the consequence of which is that problems are usually addressed professionally. To determine an optimal wage settlement, for example, a huge amount of data is brought into play concerning inflation, unemployment, balance of payments, money supplies, budgets, and so on. The negotiators generally expect that a careful analysis of all the data will allow them to determine the optimal wage level for the long-term interests of the country. In these negotiations, state bureaucrats are not only mediators between business and labor but defenders of the interests of the state as a special entity. If corporatist decision making is successful, the final outcome is acceptable to all three sides, although it will most likely not correspond precisely to the initial demands of any one of the partners.

Besides wage settlements, other economic issues may be dealt with in a corporatist way; for example, public work programs or measures to help exporters. The range of issues may be even broader, including questions of old-age pensions, taxes and budgets. (For a West German illustration, see Box 14.1.) Through such an extension of corporatist decision making, political parties and parliament may lose many of their essential functions. To be sure, decisions reached in a corporatist way must still pass the parliamentary procedure. But this can amount to pure formality if the proposals submitted to parliament have already been accepted by the corporatist actors.

BOX 14.1

CORPORATIST EXAMPLE OF DECISION MAKING
IN WEST GERMANY

At the behest of Chancellor Helmut Kohl, representatives of the government, of employers, and of labor unions met in Bonn (September 5, 1985) to discuss solutions to the country's unemployment problem. Although unemployment figures for August dipped slightly from the level in July, at 8.9 percent, unemployment last month was still at the same level as August 1984. The committee, which met for six hours until well past midnight, agreed on a three-pronged approach to battling unemployment, according to Labor Minister Norbert Blüm, including training for unskilled workers, lengthening unemployment insurance eligibility for workers who have been jobless for a long period, and considering the reduction of overtime in public sector jobs. Future meetings will hammer out details of the strategy and address unresolved issues.

Source: The Week in Germany: Newsletter of the German Information Center, New York, September 13, 1985.

While classical corporatism is trilateral, that is, between business, labor, and the state bureaucracy, other actors, such as farmers, bankers, and consumers, can be added. Whether corporatism still exists when political parties are involved is a hotly debated definitional issue. For some authors, it is precisely a characteristic of corporatism that political parties do *not* participate. But, in some countries, political parties exist in close symbiosis with economic interest groups, so that a clear distinction cannot be made. In Austria, for example, the leaders of the Socialist party also tend to have leadership positions in organized labor, and the leaders of the Conservative party, in organized business. Therefore, in Austria participants in corporatist decision making are also party leaders, who will later defend the prearranged solution in parliament. Because of this symbiosis between political parties and economic interest groups, Austrian decision making is sometimes called consociational and sometimes corporatist. The two terms are also used alternatively to describe the historic compromise in Italy from 1976 until 1979 (see Chapter 3). This consensual phase in Italian politics involved not only Christian Democrats and Communists but also key economic interest groups of business and labor.

Let us now compare more carefully the meanings of consociationalism and corporatism. Recall that the former term emerged from the analysis of decision making in culturally fragmented societies and that the subcultures of these societies are based on ascriptive attributes—race, language, religion, ethnicity. Corporatist decision making, on the other hand, involves functional groups based on economic interests. But, in Austrian history, functional economic interests found organizational expression in two sharply differentiated subcultures—the red camp and the black camp (page 235)—

whose membership was ascriptive in nature. Therefore, the concepts of both consociationalism and corporatism applied in the Austrian case. This was also the situation in Italy under the historic compromise, when the labels Christian Democrat and Communist stood not only for two political parties but also for two distinctive subcultures. In summary, there are empirical cases in which corporatist and consociational decision making overlap.

While consociational decision making is usually contrasted with majoritarian decision making, corporatism tends to be seen as the polar opposite of pluralism. In a pluralist system of government, economic interest groups stand outside the institutional framework of government. Their representatives are not appointed to official governmental commissions; they therefore do not act as decision makers, as they do in corporatism. Their role is, rather, to influence government actions from the outside, mainly through lobbying elected officials and state bureaucrats. In these lobbying efforts, business, labor, and other economic interest groups are in competition with each other, and each group exercises as much pressure as possible.

THE THEORY OF CORPORATISM

If countries differ in the degree to which their decision making is corporatist, these differences must be explained theoretically. The corporatist literature offers several explanatory factors. The vulnerability of a country to international market forces is said to be of prime importance for the emergence of corporatist decision making. This factor would explain why corporatism is particularly prominent in smaller countries that depend heavily on imports and exports because of their size. The name of the game here is not so much internal competition between business and labor as it is survival of the country in the world market. Under such circumstances, labor would be very much aware that the country's products must remain competitive in international markets to prevent high domestic unemployment. Business, on the other hand, knows that it needs a satisfied and productive labor force in order to stay internationally competitive. Because both labor and business realize how much they depend on each other, they are willing to engage in corporatist decision making.

A second factor identified by theorists of corporatism as contributing to corporatist decision making is a strong labor movement. For a labor movement to be strong, membership must be high and a single, centralized organization must exist. Under these conditions, business is confronted with an adversary that it cannot easily ignore and one that has the further advantage of being able to negotiate settlements that will be upheld by the entire labor force. In contrast, if the unions are weak, business has little assurance that a settlement negotiated with union leaders will also be accepted by the rank and file. Thus, it is hypothesized that strong unions facilitate corporatist decision making. Some corporatist authors argue, however, that this hypothesis is valid only if still another factor comes into play, namely, a Socialist government. Under this additional condition, the unions are interested in helping their "friends" in government stabilize the economy. The Socialists, in turn, use their governmental power to guarantee that the settlement reached in corporatist decision making is actually implemented. Thus, the unions will not fear being left in the cold by a hostile government. If, on the other hand, strong unions face a Conservative government, chances for corporatist decision making decrease. The unions may be reluctant to help the government and thus to increase its electoral chances. The unions may also be afraid of being betrayed by a Conservative government.

At a more general and speculative level, some theorists argue that corporatism is a result of advanced capitalism, which is characterized by increased organizational concentration. Major interest groups and some individual corporations become so large and powerful that they have a virtual veto power in many economic areas. State authorities therefore have no choice but to assemble these interests around a common table if anything is to be accomplished.

What are the consequences of corporatist decision making? Here, too, we find interesting hypotheses. The effects of corporatism on the economy are seen by most corporatist theorists as positive. They hypothesize that corporatist decision making allows for a more flexible response to changes in the international market because internal domestic compensation is possible. If a sector of the economy is threatened by changing international factors, corporatist decision making allows the system to come to its aid. A good illustration is the crisis in the Swiss watch industry in the 1970s, a result of competition from the Far East. The Swiss government took the position that this crisis had implications for the entire country and called for joint meetings of all the important interests, especially business, labor, and the banks. A package was worked out to restructure the watch industry on a smaller scale. This package involved union concessions, bank credits, and government welfare measures. The recent upswing in the Swiss watch industry seems to indicate that the rescue operation worked. Free market purists may argue, of course, that in the long run Switzerland will be haunted by this rescue operation, because it was undertaken against the verdict of market forces. Economist Manfred E. Streit speaks in this context of the danger of "institutional sclerosis."[58] He warns that the participants in corporatist decision making are less able to solve the problem of incomplete information than the free market system (see Box 14.2). But supporters of corporatism reply that human and material costs are sometimes too high if market forces alone are allowed to predominate, so that joint steering by the state and the major economic interest groups is needed.

In another respect, corporatism is seen in a still more negative light. It is argued that successful corporatist negotiations presuppose a subservient trade union membership, so that labor leaders have sufficient leeway for striking deals. If rank-and-file members criticize such deals, their criticism must be repressed for corporatist decision making to continue. In other words, corporatism is not compatible with true internal democracy in the trade unions. As a consequence of the lack of internal democracy, labor leaders may begin to look out more for their own personal interests than for the interests of their members. They may also be tempted to accommodate

_____ **BOX 14.2** _____

THE INFORMATION PROBLEM OF CORPORATISM

Neo-corporatism as a concept does not provide reasons to believe that the lack of reliable steering-knowledge which at present contributes to the difficulties of policy conduct will not also hamper corporatist policy making. On the contrary, the difficulties are likely to increase since the market system and its built-in information process no longer appear to play an important rôle. But how the information problem of corporatist economic planning is to be solved remains in the dark.

Source: Manfred E. Streit, "Market Order and Welfare Politics: The Mirage of Neo-Corporatism," Research Unit for Societal Developments, University of Mannheim, Working Papers, No. 3, 1987.

business leaders and even to adopt their life-style. Manfred E. Streit speaks in this context of "the feudal barons of our time."[59] Eventually, ordinary members of the unions will realize that their needs have been forgotten, and they will revolt against the decisions reached in a corporatist way. As political scientist Gary Marks states in Box 14.3, ordinary union members will ask for greater individual participation. This argument leads to the conclusion that corporatist decision making is ultimately unstable because of its elitism, which eventually causes dissatisfaction and disruption at the rank-and-file level of the working class.

The discussion about the consequences of corporatist decision making shows that there is basic disagreement in the literature over whether corporatism helps with the "governability" of highly industrialized countries. This disagreement can also be seen in the public debate in the United States, where corporatism is better known as "industrial policy." The bailout of the

_____ **BOX 14.3** _____

MORE PARTICIPATION IN UNIONS

There are signs that the organizational bases of consensual incomes policy may be weakening. First, there has been a well-documented populist movement in several Western industrialized societies for greater individual participation and "self-actualization." In the sphere of industrial relations this movement has been manifested in demands for greater decentralization of decision-making within unions.

Source: Gary Marks, "Neocorporatism and Incomes Policy in Western Europe and North America," *Comparative Politics*, 18 (April 1986), p. 269.

Chrysler Corporation was a typical case of industrial policy, in which the federal government, labor, and the corporation owners mutually worked out a deal. Whether the government and labor should be involved in such business decisions is still hotly debated. Generally, the attitude toward corporatism or industrial policy is more critical in the United States than in Europe.

EMPIRICAL APPLICATIONS
OF CORPORATIST THEORY

The theory of corporatism has many of the same strengths and weaknesses as that of consociationalism. Both theories tend to use entire countries as the units of analysis, and they try to identify a prevailing decision mode. Corporatist authors encounter the same classification problems as consociational authors. Manfred Schmidt, one of the foremost experts in the field, at one time classified the degree of corporatism in the European democracies and the United States as follows:

Strong corporatism: Austria, Norway, Sweden, Switzerland

Medium corporatism: Belgium, Denmark, Federal Republic of Germany, Finland, Luxembourg, Netherlands

Weak corporatism: France, Greece, Ireland, Italy, Portugal, Spain, United Kingdom, United States[60]

In a later publication, Manfred Schmidt reclassifies some countries.[61] Switzerland, for example, is no longer classified under "strong corporatism"; rather, Schmidt coins a new term and puts Switzerland under the classification "national social partnership." Interestingly enough, in the very same publication, Franz Lehner classifies Switzerland under "medium corporatism."[62] France is another country for which classifications vary a great deal. After a careful review of the literature, Frank L. Wilson concludes that "some observers have claimed to find strong evidence of corporatism in France. . . . Others see France as having only a very low level of corporatism and as characterized by traditional pluralist interest group patterns."[63]

Such disagreements point to a major difficulty in classifying countries on a scale from corporatist to pluralist. Such classifications should certainly be treated with the necessary caution.

The classification of the degree of corporatism in a country is usually based in a first approximation on the presence or absence of particular institutions. One particular indicator of corporatism is the existence of a permanent institution such as an economic and social council, where the representatives of the state bureaucracy and the major economic interest groups meet on a regular basis. However, such institutions are sometimes merely symbolic shells without much substance. In such cases, the original classification is then modified. France, for example, possesses an Economic and Social Council, whose existence seems to indicate a high degree of corporatism. Some authors argue, however, that this council has little political importance. Wilson, for example, made a survey of French interest group leaders, of whom 59 percent saw the Economic and Social Council "as having very little or no effect on policy . . . most group spokesmen, including those who served personally on the Council, admitted that neither the government nor the parliament paid much heed to its work."[64] On the basis of this finding, Wilson challenges the claim of other authors that France is strongly corporatist. (See also Wilson's more general critique of corporatist studies, Box 14.4.)

For Switzerland, the problem is in a way reversed. Switzerland has no economic and social council or any other similar permanent institution, so that corporatism seems weak; yet some authors classify Switzerland as strongly corporatist. Peter Katzenstein, for example, detects among the representatives of the major economic interest groups and the state bureaucracy in Switzerland a spirit of cooperation manifest in many ad hoc ways; for instance, in expert committees preparing parliamentary bills.[65]

For the Netherlands, some classifications have shifted over time. On the one hand, the Dutch have a Social and Economic Council, but, on the other hand, this council seems to have lost much of its importance since its heyday in the 1950s. Some authors therefore classify the Netherlands for the present time as no longer under "strong corporatism" but under "medium corporatism," whereas other authors stick with the old classification.

Given that the existence of a permanent economic and social council is sometimes not a valid indicator of the presence of corporatism, some au-

_____ BOX 14.4 _____

CRITIQUE OF CORPORATIST STUDIES

Curiously, many of the neo-corporatist studies reflect a preoccupation with formal political institutions. Corporatism is ascribed to those countries where certain institutional forms emerge and flourish: tripartite committees or boards, concerted action bodies, economic and social councils, and/or government-sanctioned chambers. Little effort is made to study the actual operation of their bodies, many of which have only paper existences, and even less attention is paid to the evaluation of the political impact of their actions. For example, the Dutch Social and Economic Council is often cited as an important indication of the corporatist tendencies in the Netherlands. A closer look as this body's actual influence suggests that it thrived in the immediate postwar era but in recent years has lost much of its prestige and authority. Similarly, in nearly every account of French interest groups, reference is made to the thousands of committees and councils bringing together interest group spokesmen and government bureaucrats which have been created since the Second World War. Few go on to acknowledge that many of these bodies meet rarely or not at all and that none has much influence over major policy options.

Source: Frank L. Wilson, "Interest Groups and Politics in Western Europe: The Neo-corporatist Approach," *Comparative Politics* 16 (October 1983): 118–119.

thors study in depth how particular decisions are actually made, whether in a more corporatist or pluralist fashion. Katzenstein, in particular, has researched many decision cases in both Austria and Switzerland. The Austrian example illustrates his method of classification. In accordance with many other scholars, Katzenstein classifies Austria as strongly corporatist. He concludes from his case studies that

> the interest groups have been growing in prominence in matters of policy since their power to regulate the behavior of prices and wages was first institutionalized, informally, in the late 1950s. In the 1960s the groups' role in policy implementation was successively broadened to incorporate, among other issues, economic forecasting and advice, and labor-market policy (including the allocation of quotas for foreign workers), as well as agricultural, social, industrial, regional, and commercial policy. The role of the economic partners is less central but still important in areas such as research and development, the media, taxes, and transportation.[66]

Katzenstein also found cases that were not decided in a corporatist way. He compares these deviant cases to his general conclusion:

> Arguing that the scope of Austria's social corporatism is broad is, however, not the same as arguing that it is unlimited. Political conflict between the partners is sufficiently intense to prevent, for example, overarching economic planning, tax, or social policies. . . . issues such as family, abortion, education, and cultural affairs more generally, have not lent themselves to an accommodative style of policy making. The question of nuclear energy highlights these limitations with particular clarity. On an issue that had originally cut right through Austria's entrenched partisan alignments, and after prolonged political struggles, the Austrian government was forced to resort . . . to . . . the referendum.[67]

This list of exceptions to the assumed overall corporatist pattern seems rather long and also politically quite significant. It then becomes a question of judgment as to how to classify the country as a whole. It would certainly not be impossible to interpret Katzenstein's data differently and to conclude that the degree of corporatism in Austria is not strong but perhaps only medium. If such a debate is possible for Austria, which appears in the literature as a case that is particularly easy to classify, imagine the controversies developing over other countries. J. T. S. Keeler found so much variation in France's decision style from one issue area to another that he despaired of classifying the country in its entirety. He suggests that "rather than attempting to situate France in an undifferentiated manner on the pluralism-corporatism continuum, it appears advisable to acknowledge the variance across sectors."[68]

This variance across sectors is also stressed by Frank Baumgartner in Box 14.5. He goes a step further in his critique of corporatist studies in arguing that the two categories of pluralism and corporatism are too crude to take account of the complexities of political reality. In the box, he mentions

BOX 14.5

FRENCH INTEREST GROUPS AND
THE PLURALISM-CORPORATISM DEBATE

The paradox in France lies in the fact that despite governmental efforts, the interest group structure remains weak and divided. While there are areas of strength, the general picture is one of ideological hostility and competition. This precludes corporatist patterns of decision making from developing in all but a few areas of French politics. In those areas where dominant groups exist, such as agriculture or primary school education, the corporatist model of decision making may be relatively accurate. In other areas, however, including most areas of policy making in France, the interest group structure is too weak and/or divided to allow this to occur. The policy making process in most areas of French society cannot be described as corporatist. Does this mean that it is pluralist? Not necessarily. Pluralism implies an aloof state rather than an active one. This pluralist ideal type is certainly not met when the state is involved in massive subsidy programs as is the case in France. Pluralism is not simply the absence of corporatism. Rather than conceiving of only these two policy making styles, political scientists need to have a broader conception of the process. In some areas of policy making within a given country, a single dominant interest group may be closely involved with the state in making and administering policies. In other areas, many groups may coexist and compete with each other, with the state arbitrating between them, siding sometimes with one and sometimes with another. In other areas, there may be an organizational vacuum, with the state acting in the absence of well organized groups. Even in the presence of groups, the state is not required to engage in extensive consultations, and may make policies without their input. Without listing every possible situation, it is clear that the policy making process includes much more variation than is implied in the simple pluralism-corporatism dichotomy.

Source: Frank Baumgartner, "French Interest Groups and the Pluralism-Corporatism Debate," Paper delivered at the 1985 annual meeting of the American Political Science Association, New Orleans, 29 August–1 September 1985, pp. 21–22.

several cases that do not fit at all into the two broad categories of pluralism and corporatism.

I agree with the critiques of corporatist studies expressed by Wilson, Keeler, and Baumgartner. As I have said in great detail elsewhere, I see that the solution is in building a cross-national data bank of a large number of specific decision cases.[69] In this way, comparisons can be made, not only between, but also within, countries. The data can be collected in a uniform way so that they are much more comparable. Specific decision cases are certainly much easier to classify than entire countries. Thanks to the large number of cases that exist, it is also possible to use sophisticated statistical techniques. Research in this direction should allow researchers to test in a much more rigorous way the hypotheses discussed in this chapter and, incidentally, the consociational hypotheses discussed in the previous chapter.

15
POLICY OUTCOMES

Even with the casual view of a tourist, it is easy to discover differences in policy outcomes from one European country to another. Trains, for example, are more punctual in Switzerland than in Italy. And, since trains are mostly government run, their punctuality can be considered a governmental policy outcome. One might ask why the Italian government is less able than the Swiss government to make its trains run on time.

If tourists become ill on a European vacation, they can compare the quality of health care in the various European countries. Parents moving from one country to another can see where their children get the best education. There are literally thousands of criteria according to which one can evaluate the policy outcomes of a country. A specialist in education may wish to know on a cross-national basis how well students learn to read, whether there is sex discrimination in an educational system, what the social status of teachers is, and so on. An expert in criminology will have a similar multitude of questions regarding crime.

It is not possible to detail the various policy areas in the present context. I will, rather, concentrate on some broad questions, such as levels of economic growth and the amount of taxes raised by a government. I will also show how satisfied Europeans are with their governments' policy outcomes.

VARIATION IN POLICY OUTCOMES

It is always difficult to get truly comparable data for a large number of countries. Fortunately, the Organization for Economic Cooperation and Development (OECD) produces on a regular basis a variety of outcome data for all Western European democracies. For our purpose, it is beneficial that these data also include the United States so that in this chapter, too, we can engage in cross-Atlantic comparisons. The OECD data do not include, however, the Eastern European countries.

First, let us look at economic growth data. Usually, the assumption is made that the higher the economic growth of a country, the better it is. We have seen in Chapter 1, however, that some European Socialists, and especially Greens, challenge this assumption on the basis of a postmaterial value premise. Whatever the judgment on economic growth, it is certainly an important factor to be considered. Table 20 gives the average annual change in the Gross Domestic Product (GDP) for the period 1982–1987, and in

Table 20
Gross Domestic Product: Average Annual
Volume Change, in Percentages

Country	1982–1987	1987–1988
Austria	1.8	3.4
Belgium	1.5	3.3
Denmark	2.7	−0.3
Finland	3.2	4.6
France	1.6	3.2
Federal Republic of Germany	2.1	3.4
Greece	1.4	3.3
Ireland	1.8	1.7
Italy	2.6	4.0
Luxembourg	4.0	2.9
Netherlands	2.1	3.1
Norway	4.1	1.0
Portugal	2.1	4.5
Spain	2.9	4.9
Sweden	2.4	2.8
Switzerland	2.3	3.0
United Kingdom	3.2	4.2
United States	4.3	3.9

Source: Supplement to the OECD Observer, No. 158, June/July 1989.

addition, for the period 1987–1988. Compared with the European countries, the United States in recent years had a very high growth rate. In Europe, Norway and Luxembourg are at the upper end; Greece, Belgium, France, and Ireland are at the lower end. In this section, we simply register such a variation. Possible explanations of the variation will be addressed in the next section.

Besides the economic growth of their country, citizens are always interested in how much taxes the government imposes on them. Table 21 gives the total tax (including local taxes) as a percentage of the Gross Domestic Product. Compared with the European countries, the United States has the lowest tax rate. Within Europe, Sweden has the highest tax rate and Spain, the lowest.

What are governments doing with their taxes? Table 22 shows how much they spend, for example, for health services. Sweden spends the most; Greece, the least. Up to now, we have only given dollar figures. What ultimately counts, however, is the quality of life in a country. Thus, it is important to see how health expenditures are translated into quality of health care. For this, the infant mortality rate of a country is a good indicator. As Table 23 reveals, the United States, together with Greece and Portugal, have the highest infant mortality rates of children in their first year. For Sweden, the high government expenditures for health seem to pay off, because it has, together with Finland, the lowest infant mortality rate.

Table 21
Total Tax Receipts as Percentage of Gross Domestic Product (1987)

Austria	42.6
Belgium	45.4
Denmark	50.6
Finland	38.4
France	44.2
Federal Republic of Germany	37.5
Greece	36.7
Ireland	40.2
Italy	35.9
Luxembourg	42.4
Netherlands	45.5
Norway	49.8
Portugal	32.4
Spain	30.4
Sweden	53.5
Switzerland	32.6
United Kingdom	39.0
United States	28.9

Source: Supplement to the OECD Observer, No. 158, June/July 1989.

Table 22
Government Health Expenditure as Percentage of Gross Domestic Product (1986)

Austria	5.3
Belgium	5.5
Denmark	5.2
Finland	5.8
France	6.7
Federal Republic of Germany	6.3
Greece	3.7
Ireland	7.0
Italy	5.2
Luxembourg	6.2
Netherlands	6.6
Norway	6.6
Portugal	4.0
Spain	4.3
Sweden	8.3
Switzerland	5.2
United Kingdom	5.3
United States	4.5

Source: Supplement to the OECD Observer, No. 158, June/July 1989.

Table 23
Infant Mortality in First Year, Percentage of
Live Births (Most Recent Available Year)

Austria	0.98
Belgium	0.97
Denmark	0.84
Finland	0.58
France	0.76
Federal Republic of Germany	0.83
Greece	1.13
Ireland	0.91
Italy	0.96
Luxembourg	0.93
Netherlands	0.64
Norway	0.78
Portugal	1.16
Spain	0.87
Sweden	0.61
Switzerland	0.68
United Kingdom	0.91
United States	1.00

Source: Supplement to the OECD Observer, No. 158,
June/July 1989.

The OECD has many more interesting outcome data, for example, on number of calories consumed per person, life expectancy, unemployment, inflation, trade balance, savings ratio, purchasing power parities, energy consumption, public transportation, education, and air pollution. To save space, I refer the reader to the corresponding publications, in particular to the yearly supplement to the *OECD Observer.*

Besides objective indicators of policy outcomes, people's subjective perceptions of these outcomes are also important. Here, one has to rely on interview data, for which cross-national comparability may also be quite tricky. Fortunately, for this aspect, too, an excellent source is available—the so-called Eurobarometer. The only problem with using Eurobarometer in the present context is that, being organized by the Commission of the European Community, it is limited to the 12 member countries of the Community (see Chapter 16). As with the OECD data, I encourage interested readers to consult the original data, which can be ordered from the headquarters of the European Commission in Brussels. To give a feeling for the survey data, I give the results for two broad questions. Table 24 shows how satisfied with their lives people are. The least satisfaction we find in Greece, the highest in Denmark. The variation among the twelve countries is quite strong.

The question about life satisfaction may measure a primarily private mood. In order to tap a more public mood, Eurobarometer also asks the following: "On the whole, are you very satisfied, fairly satisfied, not very

Table 24

Eurobarometer Survey on Satisfaction with Life, November 1987 (in Percentages)

Country	Very Satisfied	Fairly Satisfied	Not Very Satisfied	Not at All Satisfied	Don't Know/ No Answer
Belgium	23.4	55.6	16.2	3.6	1.3
Denmark	48.3	46.8	3.8	0.7	0.6
Federal Republic of Germany	14.7	67.8	14.1	2.1	1.4
France	11.3	57.7	22.6	7.8	0.6
Greece	14.9	37.4	28.9	18.4	0.4
Ireland	20.8	53.3	16.0	9.1	0.8
Italy	11.0	53.7	24.2	10.7	0.4
Luxembourg	37.1	53.3	3.6	3.6	2.3
Netherlands	35.4	55.8	5.9	1.8	1.1
Portugal	7.6	67.1	19.0	5.1	1.2
Spain	24.3	48.1	23.3	3.8	0.5
United Kingdom	32.6	52.9	10.2	3.8	0.7

Source: Jacques-René Rabier, Helene Riffault, Ronald Inglehart, *Euro-Barometer 28: Relations with Third World Countries and Energy Problems* (Ann Arbor, MI: Inter-university Consortium for Political and Social Research, Fall 1989), p. 10.

Table 25

Eurobarometer Survey on Satisfaction with the Way Democracy Works in One's Country, November 1987 (in Percentages)

Country	Very Satisfied	Fairly Satisfied	Not Very Satisfied	Not at All Satisfied	Don't Know/ No Answer
Belgium	6.5	39.0	29.7	17.4	7.5
Denmark	16.3	53.1	23.4	4.8	2.2
Federal Republic of Germany	6.2	62.5	24.7	3.9	2.7
France	3.0	39.5	34.5	14.5	8.5
Greece	11.4	37.9	23.4	20.5	6.8
Ireland	6.0	39.9	26.5	21.4	6.2
Italy	1.9	23.8	46.6	25.6	2.0
Luxembourg	17.5	50.3	19.4	3.3	9.6
Netherlands	7.9	49.0	30.7	7.6	4.7
Portugal	8.1	61.9	18.7	3.9	7.4
Spain	15.9	39.3	26.9	10.9	6.9
United Kingdom	11.0	45.0	27.1	13.2	3.7

Source: Jacques-René Rabier, Helene Riffault, Ronald Inglehart, *Euro-Barometer 28: Relations with Third World Countries and Energy Problems* (Ann Arbor, MI: Inter-university Consortium for Political and Social Research, Fall 1989), p. 11.

satisfied, or not satisfied at all with the way democracy works in [name of your country]?"

A comparison of tables 24 and 25 shows that the private mood of Europeans is better than their public mood. They are generally more satisfied with their personal life than with the way democracy works in their country. The ranking of the countries in Table 25 is roughly the same as in Table 24.

THEORETICAL EXPLANATIONS

How can we explain differences in policy outcomes? In the previous chapters, we encountered many factors that may help us with such explanations. Does the rate of economic growth, for example, depend on the strength of the various political parties, on the pattern of cabinet formation, or on the level of government centralization?

At this point, readers may engage in some theorizing of their own. Having learned about the various aspects of European politics, they may relate this knowledge to explanations of policy outcomes. Students may do this for their term papers. They can take data for a particular policy outcome, for example, the rate of infant mortality. The task would be to identify factors that could explain variations in infant mortality rates. Students can then test to what extent their theoretical models explain the variations among the European countries and also in the United States. In this way, they can learn through their own efforts how complex theorizing is. For Italy, for example, it may seem plausible that its high cabinet instability is a major cause of the poor policy outcome. Or, students may argue for Great Britain that the great influence of the trade unions has a lot to do with the bad economic performance. The explanations in journalistic accounts are usually of such an ad hoc nature. The problem with such explanations is that what seems plausible to one observer may seem implausible to another. How can we prove convincingly that cabinet instability in Italy leads to a poor policy outcome if Great Britain, with an equally poor outcome, is characterized by high cabinet stability?

We need theories that apply to more than one country, in our case to all European, or even to all, democracies if possible. Thus, we should know in a general way whether cabinet instability, or for that matter, great trade union strength, has the tendency to worsen the policy outcome.

If we look at a single variable in an isolated way, the results are usually not very satisfactory. In most cases, the specific effect of a variable depends on the presence or absence of other variables. As a consequence, the best explanations operate in general with entire clusters of variables.

There are many theories in political science literature claiming to explain policy outcomes. Presenting some of these theories may stimulate the readers to develop their own theories. It is important to recognize that there is not simply one true theory to explain a phenomenon. Political science, and for that matter, science in general must be seen as a permanent battle between conflicting theories.

I wish to illustrate this point with theories that try to explain economic performance. The big issue is whether a government's being controlled by parties of the Left or parties of the Right makes a difference for economic performance. Manfred G. Schmidt summarizes the literature in the following way:

> Contrary to what many political scientists and politicians believe, and contrary to many findings in studies on policy making in the 1960's and early 1970's, there is no clear-cut relationship between the partisan composition of government and our indicators of social and economic performance. In other words, there is not much support for the view that countries under Social-Democratic rule produced policies that were consistently different from those with bourgeois governments.[70]

For Schmidt, these findings do not mean, however, that the party composition of a government does not have an effect on the policy outcome. But the effects are more complicated and depend on the presence or absence of third variables. A Social Democratic government, for example, pursues different policies depending on whether the trade unions are strong or weak and whether the bourgeois opposition is united or fragmented. Schmidt postulates that a complex interaction effect must be examined among the following variables: distribution of power between capital and labor and between competing political parties; the degree to which corporatist arrangements have been characteristic of modes of conflict regulation; the degree of coordination of policies across policy areas; and the dominant type of political ideology that constrains the decision-making process.

With such complex models, we are far from offering single-variable, monocausal explanations. Political reality does not lend itself to simplistic explanations of the sort that variable A has the effect X. We need more complex explanations in the sense that we can say, for example, that variable A in combination with variable B leads to X but in combination with variable C, to Y. Schmidt adds still another complication to his theorizing with the concept of *equifunctionality*, which means that different roads may lead to the same results. Using the above symbols, this would mean that not only the combination of variables A and B leads to X but also the combination of, say, variables P and Q.

Schmidt comes to the concept of equifunctionality in comparing the countries that he found to have the best policy performance: Japan, Austria, and Norway. What do these countries have in common that could explain their good policy outcome? Schmidt concludes that there are no real common characteristics that could serve as an explanation. He argues, rather, that there are two roads to a relatively successful reconciliation of a dynamic capitalist market economy and the maintenance or extension of welfare state efforts and higher levels of employment. For Schmidt, one road consists of a strategy in which a dynamic market economy has been successfully amalgamated with the pattern of a paternalistic capitalism and a creative conservatism on the part of a state-interventionist government. He sees Japan as the major example of this type of approach to macroeconomic policy.

The other road to relatively successful crisis management for Schmidt is based on a political structure that is completely different in character. Here, a strong labor movement, corporatist modes of conflict resolution, a powerful state-interventionist bureaucracy, and a high degree of cooperation across policy areas are the major preconditions of successful macroeconomic management. In Schmidt's view, Norway and, to a lesser extent, Austria correspond to this explanation.

Geoffrey Garrett and Peter Lange do not look at economic performance in general but more narrowly at economic growth. They had a fierce exchange with Alexander Hicks and Robert Jackman, in which the latter two argued that the party composition of the government has no influence on economic growth. In contrast, Garrett and Lange argued that a difference exists, but, like Schmidt, they insist that interaction effects have to be considered. Their

---

BOX 15.1

DETERMINANTS OF ECONOMIC PERFORMANCE

The best performance strategy of the left requires that potential inflationary pressures—that might be generated by sustained low unemployment and extensive welfare provision—be contained through the labor movement's restraint of its potential militancy (and support for government policies intended to induce investment by capital). This restraint is more likely where left governments are allied with encompassing unions. The "virtuous circle" of evolving cooperation then closes as the success of these policies reinforces the confidence of government, labor and capital in each other. These dynamics are indicative of "corporatist" political economies.

The interaction between right governments and much weaker labor movements ("weak labor" political economies) is hypothesized to generate similar levels of economic performance, although this interaction is very different from the above "virtuous circle." Right governments can be expected simultaneously to achieve their policy goals and to preside over desirable macroeconomic outcomes where labor is sufficiently weak to prevent it from using its organizational strength to impede the effective implementation of market-oriented policies. If such conditions exist, sustained economic growth can be promoted with low inflation. Furthermore, while these policies may sometimes lead to large job losses in the short term, beneficial outcomes—including low unemployment—are expected over time as economic actors adjust their expectations to the new market conditions.

In more "incoherent" systems—in which left governments meet decentralized labor movements or right governments encounter well-organized ones—we expect growth (and inflation and unemployment) performance to be poorer than in either of the preceding cases.

Source: Geoffrey Garrett and Peter Lange, "Government Partisanship and Economic Performance: When and How Does 'Who Governs' Matter?" *Journal of Politics* 51(August 1989): pp. 683–684.

complex argument, summarized Box 15.1 states that strong economic growth is most likely to occur under either of the following two conditions: (1) government of the Left and strong labor unions or (2) government of the Right and weak labor unions. Weak economic growth, on the other hand, is most likely to occur under either of the following two conditions: (1) government of the Left and weak labor unions or (2) government of the Right and strong labor unions.

Another example of a complex outcome analysis is the study by Hans Keman on the relationship of expenditures for "guns and butter." What are the government expenditures for military defense and welfare? The latter category includes not only welfare measures in a narrow sense but also health and education. Keman is interested in establishing whether a trade-off between defense and welfare is necessary. Does an increase in defense expenditures mean that expenditures for welfare decrease, and vice versa? Or is it possible for a government to circumvent this dilemma and have *both* guns and butter? Keman calls the latter strategy a "pay-off": The respective supporters of defense and welfare expansion pay each other off to secure their own programs.

Keman begins his analysis with the year 1962. The percentage of Gross

Table 26
Expenditures for Defense and Welfare
as Percentage of GDP, 1962

Country	Defense	Welfare
Australia	2.51	10.9
Austria	1.08	19.0
Belgium	3.33	19.3
Canada	4.17	13.1
Denmark	3.05	15.0
Finland	2.37	16.2
France	6.14	19.4
Federal Republic of Germany	4.77	20.7
Ireland	1.40	12.4
Italy	2.97	17.6
Japan	0.98	10.3
Netherlands	4.37	18.6
Norway	3.53	13.7
Sweden	4.11	16.0
Switzerland	2.61	8.8
United Kingdom	6.36	14.8
United States	9.30	11.8
Average	3.71	15.2

Source: Hans Keman, "Welfare and Warfare: Critical Options and Conscious Choice in Public Policy," in Francis Castles, Franz Lehner, Manfred G. Schmidt, eds., *Managing Mixed Economies* (Berlin and New York: Walter de Gruyter, 1988), pp. 135–136.

Domestic Product (GDP) that the individual countries spent for defense and welfare that year is shown in Table 26. (Besides the European democracies and the United States, Keman covers Australia, Canada, and Japan.) A comparison of the two columns in Table 26 reveals that, for all countries, welfare expenditures are higher than defense expenditures. The United States was the country that spent by far the highest percentage of its GDP for defense. Other high defense spenders were the United Kingdom and France. The highest welfare spender was the Federal Republic of Germany.

The figures for 1973 and the changes from 1962 to 1973 are shown in Table 27. The period from 1962 to 1973 is characterized by a clear reorientation in policies. All countries decreased the percentage of GDP spent for defense and at the same time increased the corresponding figure for welfare. This was a period of international détente and economic prosperity. Policymakers in the Western democracies used this situation to trade lower

Table 27
Expenditures for Defense and Welfare as Percentage
of GDP, 1973, and Change from 1962 to 1973

	Defense		Welfare	
Country	Level 1973	Change 1962–1973	Level 1973	Change 1962–1973
Australia	2.50	−0.01	13.7	2.8
Austria	0.93	−0.15	21.7	2.7
Belgium	2.79	−0.54	27.8	8.5
Canada	1.93	−2.24	19.5	6.4
Denmark	2.04	−1.01	27.4	12.4
Finland	1.31	−1.06	21.3	5.1
France	3.61	−2.53	23.3	3.9
Federal Republic of Germany	3.48	−1.29	26.4	5.7
Ireland	1.30	−0.10	18.8	6.4
Italy	2.67	−0.30	24.2	6.6
Japan	0.81	−0.17	10.7	0.4
Netherlands	3.09	−1.28	31.8	13.2
Norway	3.13	−0.40	25.7	12.0
Sweden	3.28	−0.83	24.2	8.4
Switzerland	1.92	−0.69	15.9	7.1
United Kingdom	4.81	−1.55	19.3	4.5
United States	5.97	−3.33	17.3	5.5
Average	2.68	−1.03	21.7	6.6

Source: Hans Keman, "Welfare and Warfare: Critical Options and Conscious Choice in Public Policy," in Francis Castles, Franz Lehner, Manfred G. Schmidt, eds., *Managing Mixed Economies* (Berlin and New York: Walter de Gruyter, 1988), pp. 135–136.

defense efforts for higher expenditures for welfare. The most dramatic reorientation in priorities can be seen for the Netherlands, which decreased its defense expenditures from 4.37 percent to 3.09 percent of its GDP and increased its welfare effort from 18.6 percent to 31.8 percent of its GDP.

Nineteen seventy-three was the year of the first oil crisis and was followed by worsening economic conditions. Détente also came to an end, and international tensions increased again. These developments led once more to a reorientation of policy priorities, as indicated in Table 28.

Keman interprets Table 28 as a relationship of payoffs between defense and welfare expenditures. In most countries, policymakers reversed the trend of the earlier period and increased the share of GDP spent for defense. But, instead of trading the increase in defense for a decrease in welfare, efforts in the latter area were increased too. As a consequence, these countries were hit by a fiscal crisis of huge budget deficits.

Table 28

Expenditures for Defense and Welfare as Percentage
of GDP, 1982, and Change from 1973 to 1982

Country	Defense		Welfare	
	Level 1982	Change 1973–1982	Level 1982	Change 1973–1982
Australia	2.80	0.30	19.4	8.5
Austria	1.20	0.27	27.8	8.8
Belgium	3.40	0.61	39.5	20.2
Canada	2.10	0.17	21.5	8.4
Denmark	2.50	0.46	34.7	19.7
Finland	1.60	0.29	27.1	10.9
France	4.20	0.59	31.1	11.7
Federal Republic of Germany	3.40	−0.08	32.1	11.4
Ireland	2.00	0.70	29.5	17.1
Italy	2.60	−0.07	30.0	12.3
Japan	1.00	0.19	14.5	4.2
Netherlands	3.30	0.21	36.7	18.1
Norway	3.00	−0.13	28.5	14.8
Sweden	3.30	0.02	34.6	18.6
Switzerland	2.00	0.08	19.4	10.6
United Kingdom	5.10	0.29	24.1	9.2
United States	6.50	0.53	21.3	9.5
Average	2.94	0.26	27.9	6.1

Source: Hans Keman, "Welfare and Warfare: Critical Options and Conscious Choice in Public Policy," in Francis Castles, Franz Lehner, Manfred G. Schmidt, eds., *Managing Mixed Economies* (Berlin and New York: Walter de Gruyter, 1988), pp. 135–136.

Now, with the end of the Cold War, defense expenditures may decrease once again. It will be interesting to see whether welfare expenditures will increase as they did in the period from 1962 to 1973 or whether the possible savings in defense will be used to decrease the huge budget deficits that were built up after 1973.

16

THE EUROPEAN COMMUNITY

More than 200 years ago, the 13 American states were joined together in a single political system—the United States of America. Today, there is a movement toward European integration. Will there be a United States of Europe similar in form to the United States of America in the foreseeable future? Probably not. The historical circumstances are so obviously different that Europe cannot simply copy the American model. The European countries have far older historical traditions than the American states had when the United States of America was founded.

Nonetheless, European integration is already a reality to a certain extent. In 1989, for the third time, European voters participated in elections for the European Parliament. There are also a European Council, a European Commission, and a European Court. What are the functions of these institutions, and how much power do they have? What is the relationship between these European institutions and the various countries' national institutions of the same type? These questions are very important for American students of international business. With regard to business dealings with Europe, the main responsibilities in many areas are no longer in the national capitals but in Brussels, the capital not only of Belgium but also of Europe. To export oranges from Florida to the European countries, the paperwork must be handled by European bureaucrats in Brussels. If an American company wants to sell kitchen tools in France or Spain, it must be aware of the safety standards that are set by European authorities.

THE HISTORY OF EUROPEAN INTEGRATION

European countries warred for many centuries. A serious effort to stop the seemingly endless European wars once and for all was made after World War I. In 1914, European leaders had sent their countries' youths to war fired with enthusiasm. Each side expected a quick and heroic victory. The eventual Allied victory, however, came only after four years of trench warfare and tremendous losses on both sides. After the war, many well-meaning people became active in the so-called Pan-European movement, which demanded the unification of Europe so that war could never again break out. Members of this movement urged Europeans to recognize their common cultural heritage. But the time for this movement was not yet ripe. Mussolini's Fascist party had taken over Italy by 1922. In 1929, the Great Depression began. In

1933, Hitler became dictator of Germany, and, in 1939, another world war began.

World War II was, if possible, even more dreadful than World War I. Aerial bombardment increasingly spread the suffering directly to the civilian population. After the war, the idea of European unification was quickly brought up again. In a famous speech at Zurich in 1946, Winston Churchill called for the construction of a "kind of United States of Europe." The Council of Europe was founded in Strasbourg, France, in 1949. However, the council required no surrender of national authority, because its decisions were based on unanimous, not majority, votes. Under British influence, the council, whose members were drawn from respective national parliaments, had merely consultative functions. The Council of Europe still exists and has 21 members today. It meets regularly in Strasbourg and does useful work in the areas of culture, education, and human rights, in particular.

A European initiative with a more limited number of participants—the European Coal and Steel Community—was founded in 1951 by France, West Germany, Italy, Belgium, Luxembourg, and the Netherlands. Its goal was to pool coal and steel production of the six countries. This initiative was made successful through such leaders as Jean Monnet and Robert Schuman of France, Alicide de Gasperi of Italy, and Paul-Henri Spaak of Belgium. Their names are linked with the birth of European integration.

In 1954, European integration suffered a painful setback. The six member countries of the European Coal and Steel Community had planned to extend their collaboration to the establishment of a European Defense Community. Five countries had already ratified the corresponding treaty when the French National Assembly voted against it, not wishing to have French troops under a common European command.

After this setback in defense affairs, the economic route to European integration was pursued further. A common market for coal and steel having been established, the six member countries of the community extended their economic collaboration to other areas. In 1957, they signed the crucial Treaty of Rome, establishing the European Economic Community, also called the Common Market. The name is now abbreviated to European Community (EC).

It is particularly significant that both France and Germany were members of the new organization, because the two countries had gone to war with each other three times in the preceding 100 years: 1870–1871, 1914–1918, and 1939–1945. The hope was that integrating the French and the German economies would make the two countries so dependent on each other that future wars would be unthinkable.

Despite Churchill's Zurich speech, Great Britain was not a founding member of the European Community. Even by 1957, the British still did not really feel that they were a part of Europe. For the British, Europe was the Continent, and when the British crossed the English Channel, they considered that they were "going to Europe." Britain finally joined the EC in 1973, mainly out of economic necessity. To this day, many British citizens still have strong emotional reservations about their membership in the European Community.

Denmark and the Republic of Ireland also joined the EC in 1973, increasing its membership from six to nine. With the entry of Greece in 1981, and of Spain and Portugal in 1986, one speaks now of the "Europe of the twelve" (see Box 16.1).

The European Community has signed treaties of association with a large number of countries within and outside of Europe. Switzerland, for example, is party to such a treaty of association because, as a neutral country, it does not wish to become a full member of the EC. Norway has a treaty of association because its voters rejected full membership in a referendum. The EC also has special treaties with developing countries, in particular, in Africa and the Caribbean. As a result of these treaties, the borders of the EC are somewhat fluid, with associate members participating in various activities of the community depending on the specifics of their treaties. With such broad yet heterogeneous membership, the EC has a different character from traditional nations like the United States and the Soviet Union. As we will see later in this chapter, the EC could be the beginning of a new world order in which national borders would lose much of their importance. But there is also a risk that ultimately the EC will fail, because its borders are so loosely defined.

BOX 16.1

COMMON MARKET GOES TO 12

Big decisions rarely come easy when the 10 members of the European Economic Community meet. Last week, they sat for 16 hours, including an all-night session, and in the end they agreed to become 12.

After six years of bargaining, Spain and Portugal accepted terms set down by the Common Market and, assuming the treaties are ratified in all 12 countries, will formally accede to one of the world's most powerful economic blocs next January. Late yesterday, a threatened veto by Greece was averted when it was accorded $1.5 billion in special aid for its poor rural areas.

The agreement was an important step for the Iberian Peninsula, which 10 years ago lived under dictatorships politically isolated from democratic Western Europe. "We can now get behind us this great frustration, this inferiority complex in international affairs," said Fernando Morán López, Spain's Foreign Minister. It was also a major step for the community, which, far from fostering the unity of Europe, has projected a picture of bickering and paralysis recently.

Much of the frustration in the long negotiation with Spain and Portugal arose from the fact that they compete directly with France, Italy and Greece in farming and fishing. On the other hand, Iberian industries are relatively weak and need to adjust to the competition of their more powerful partners. Transition periods will cover both the industrial and nonindustrial sectors.

Source: New York Times, March 31, 1985.

———— INSTITUTIONS OF THE EUROPEAN COMMUNITY ————

Institutionally, the European Community is a hybrid of international and supranational organization. In an international organization, each nation keeps its independence, whereas in a supranational organization, nations yield their sovereignty to the common organization. The hybrid character of the EC is best seen in its institutional structure. Its most powerful institution, the European Council (not to be confused with the Council of Europe), tends to act as if the community were merely an international organization. On the other hand, the behavior of the European Commission, which is also quite a powerful body, corresponds to a large extent to a supranational organization.

The European Council

The European Council is a meeting place for the chief executives of the 12 full member countries. These executives are the prime ministers of Belgium, Denmark, Great Britain, Greece, Ireland, Italy, Luxembourg, the Netherlands, Portugal, and Spain; the chancellor of the Federal Republic of Germany; and the president of France. Thus, this gathering brings together the most prominent political leaders in Europe: Margaret Thatcher, François Mitterrand, Helmut Kohl, and so forth. They meet about three or four times a year for short sessions of a couple of days. The chair for these meetings rotates among all the member countries every six months. Rotation also occurs with regard to the meeting site, which is not always in the European capital of Brussels.

Compared with the United States, the European Council corresponds closely to the Governors' Conference. Imagine if the Governors' Conference were the most powerful political body in the United States! Each governor would probably feel primarily responsible to the interests of his or her own state. This is indeed the situation in the European Council. Thatcher is first of all prime minister of Britain, and Mitterrand, president of France. The power base for each participant is in his or her own respective country. In order to survive politically, the members of the European Council must first of all win elections at home. If they lose those elections, they are also out of the European Council. Thus, the members of the council naturally view a problem first from their own national perspective and not from an overall European view. Therefore, important decisions can only be reached if all national interests are more or less accommodated. In principle, majority voting is allowed, but, in practice, it is most difficult to enforce a decision against a dissenter, especially if it is a large country and its vital interests are involved. Meetings of the European Council often resemble a game of chicken in which each participant tries to wait out all others before making concessions. This leads to hectic, late-night sessions in which some bargain is finally struck out of exhaustion. Quite often, however, such late-night agreements tend to obscure real differences, so that the issue must be taken up again at a later council meeting. Observers have grown accustomed to an atmosphere of crisis at European Council meetings. But somehow the council muddles through to keep the community going. After all, the participants know that the demise of the European Community would leave every country worse off. Thus, a solution of some kind is always found, even if it is only to study the problem further.

The European Commission

The institution that brings continuity to the operations of the European Community is the European Commission (see photo below). In contrast to the members of the European Council, commissioners work full time for the EC. There are 17 commissioners: two each from the five larger countries (France, Great Britain, Italy, Spain, and Germany) and one each from the smaller countries. The members of the commission are appointed by their respective national governments. The commission is headed by a president, who is chosen by agreement of the member states from among the 17 commissioners. The president of the European Commission, who occasionally visits Washington, D.C., is sometimes labeled by the American media as the European president. Pictures are published entitled "Two Presidents," showing the American and European Commission presidents standing side by side. The power of the two offices, however, is quite different.

In assessing the nature of the presidency of the European Commission, we see that there is an intriguing chicken-and-egg problem: What comes first, a powerful office or a powerful officeholder? Must the office be made powerful to attract powerful leaders, or is the first step appointing a powerful leader who can lend power to the office? The current president of the commission

European Commission. (Courtesy Delegation of the European Community, Washington, D.C.)

is Frenchman Jacques Delors (see photo below). Delors is a prominent Socialist who served Mitterrand as an influential economic minister but had no immediate prospect of becoming either president or prime minister in France. Hence, he was willing to move to Brussels to head the commission. His predecessor was Gaston Thorn, a former prime minister of Luxembourg who considered it a promotion to move from chief executive of his tiny country to head the European Commission. Before Thorn, the commission was headed by Roy Jenkins, foreign minister of a British Labour government. As Labour moved to the left, Jenkins, who is a moderate, lost any chance of moving up to the prime ministership and decided to move to Brussels as president of the commission.

These three career paths illustrate well the current status of the commission presidency. The basic job requirement is to be a leading politician in a member country. The really top people, however, such as Thatcher, Mitterrand, and Kohl, would rather remain chief executives of their own countries than preside over the commission. Exceptions to this rule may occur for some of the small countries, as Thorn's case illustrates.

It is even more difficult to recruit leading politicians to serve as ordinary commissioners. The public visibility of this position is so low that many ambitious leaders fear dead-ending their careers in Brussels and prefer to stay in their national capitals. The key for the future power of the commission will be in how much attraction it holds for the most prominent European politicians.

The European Commission directs a large bureaucracy at the headquarters in Brussels (see photo on page 285). The commission meets at least once

Jacques Delors. (Courtesy Delegation of the European Community, Washington, D.C.)

Headquarters of the European Commission, Brussels, Belgium. (Courtesy *Europe Magazine*.)

a week. Each commissioner is responsible for specific policy areas, such as external relations, agriculture, social affairs, energy, and transport. Compared to the European Council, deliberations of the commission are guided much more by European considerations, although national biases are not absent. The commission has complete charge of the EC's routine day-to-day operations. Sensitive political decisions involving the vital interests of one of the member countries, however, are dealt with by the European Council. The commission prepares the decision and oversees its implementation, but the crucial elements of the decision itself will be ironed out by the chief executives of the 12 member countries.

The European Parliament

The European Parliament, which is located in Strasbourg, France, has the same problem as the European Commission in the sense that it is unclear whether a powerful office or powerful officeholders come first. When voters were called to participate in European parliamentary elections for the first time in 1979, some eminent leaders, such as Willy Brandt and François Mitterrand, were running and were elected. But it soon turned out that, for many, their participation was mostly a symbolic gesture of goodwill. Brandt and Mitterrand, for example, gave up their seats in the European Parliament in order to continue their careers in Bonn and Paris. When the European Parliament was elected for the second time in 1984, relatively few prominent leaders entered the race. They considered a seat in the European Parliament an insufficiently powerful position. This has not greatly changed with the

1989 election, although former French President Giscard d'Estaing is now a member of the European Parliament.

How powerful is the European Parliament? A historic analysis of the development of national parliaments suggests that the crucial step has been gaining control over the budget. In this respect, the European Parliament is still lacking. The revenues of the European Community are determined not by the European Parliament but by the powerful European Council. These revenues come mainly from the EC's common external tariff and a share of a sales tax levied by the member states, the value-added tax (VAT). The European Parliament has some power to determine how these revenues are spent. It can, in particular, reject the budget prepared by the commission, something that has already happened. But, even after such a rejection, the parliament lacks the power to enact its own budget. Its only power is to continue to reject the commission's budget, which ultimately would not be very constructive. All in all, the budgetary powers of the European Parliament are still very limited. The power of the European Parliament ultimately will be determined in the battle over these very budget questions. If parliament can obtain significant control over both revenues and expenditures, this will be the crucial step in transforming the European Community into a truly supranational organization: Essential sovereign power will have been transferred from the member nations to the European level. But many politicians and voters, especially in Great Britain, fear such a development and will resist any effort to expand the European Parliament's budgetary power. In their view, European integration is only acceptable insofar as it benefits one's own nation but does not endanger national sovereignty. Seen in this broader context, quarrels over the budgetary rights of the European Parliament are not at all technical in nature but go to the heart of the question of European integration.

In the parliamentary system of government to which Europeans are accustomed, it is crucial that parliament exercise power in another area besides the budget; namely, in the selection of the executive cabinet. The European Parliament does not yet have this power, and it is not even clear who the executive really is—the council or the commission. If the EC were a full-fledged supranational organization, the commission, with full-time members, would function as an executive cabinet. But, as things stand, the main executive power lies with the council, whose members are primarily oriented to the interests of their respective countries. As their countries' chief executives, council members depend exclusively on their national parliaments for their political survival, not on the European Parliament.

The European Parliament, in principle, has the power to dismiss the European Commission with a vote of no confidence. This power has not yet been used, partly because the parliament lacks the power to appoint a new commission. New commissioners would, instead, be appointed again by the national governments, and nothing would prevent the reappointment of the same commissioners. The European Parliament's power to dismiss the commission thus carries little effective weight.

Given its lack of real power with regard to the budget and the executive, the European Parliament is in danger of becoming a mere debating club. Although such a function might, in fact, be quite useful, it is not sufficient to induce prominent political leaders to seek a career in the European Parliament. There is also the danger that the voters will lose interest in it. In the 1979 European Parliament elections, voter turnout was 62.5 percent, which was lower than usual in national elections; voter turnout dropped further in 1984 to 59.0 percent and in 1989, to 57.2 percent. This apathy shows that the European Parliament has not yet been able to develop into a voice for the European people.

On a hopeful note, it should be registered here that, in the future, new members to the European Community have to be approved by the European Parliament. As we will see later in this chapter, the further expansion of the European Community will be quite an issue in the coming years, so that the new stipulation may help to strengthen the role of the European Parliament.

Another hopeful sign for the European Parliament, to which we already referred in Chapter 1, is that its members are not organized by nations, but by political parties. This should strengthen cross-national cooperation and, ultimately, perhaps parliament itself.

The European Court

The European Community has a judicial branch, headed by the European Court of Justice in Luxembourg. Its 13 judges, like the members of the commission, are appointed by their respective national governments.

In many fields, such as most areas of criminal law, national law is still supreme. But, in other fields, like patents and trademarks, EC law takes precedence over national law. Thus, some transfer of legal sovereignty from the member states to the EC has taken place. For Italy, political scientist Mary L. Volcansek has studied this transfer, and she concludes that "[i]n the space of three decades, the Italian Constitutional Court accorded supremacy to European Community law in the Italian legal system."[71] Businesspeople, in particular, must be aware of laws enacted by the EC; otherwise, they may encounter difficulties with the European Court, which has the authority to enforce these laws.

The European Court functions relatively smoothly and efficiently when individual firms or citizens are involved. (For a case involving a French student, see Box 16.2). Although the EC has no police force, it can depend on police forces of the member nations to collect fines or to put someone in jail. But, if an EC law is broken by a national government, it is more difficult to enforce a ruling of the European Court. In 1979, for example, the French government imposed import restrictions on lamb from Great Britain in order to protect its dissatisfied sheep farmers. The European Court declared these restrictions illegal, but the French government disregarded the court's judgment, arguing that it was acting in its own vital national interest. If a governor in the United States were to disregard a Supreme Court ruling in a similar way, the federal government could, for example, use the state's National Guard to make him or her comply. Lacking an enforcement agency of their own, authorities of the EC are unable to exercise such power.

This comparison perhaps best illustrates how the European Community

_____ BOX 16.2 _____

EUROPEAN COURT RULES ON EQUAL TREATMENT
FOR STUDENTS

An E.C. member state cannot subject students from other member states to requirements different from those to which it subjects its own nationals, according to the Court of Justice of the European Communities. The ruling, which applies to all students, resulted from a recent case involving a French art student who wanted to study cartoon drawing at the Liège art college in Belgium.

When Françoise Gravier signed up for the course in 1982, the Belgian authorities asked for a special fee charged to all students who do not come from either Belgium or Luxembourg. She refused to pay on the grounds that, as an E.C. citizen, she was entitled to the same treatment as Belgians in the course.

The Belgian authorities refused to accept her argument, and Gravier was refused both an extension of her resident's permit and permission to reregister for courses the next year. She took her case to court in Liège, where it was referred to the Court of Justice. The Court asked for clarification on two issues: Did the ban on discrimination on grounds of nationality contained in the E.C. treaties extend to students studying in other member states? And did it apply to cartoonists?

The Court ruled in Gravier's favor on both counts.

Source: Europe Magazine, May/June 1985, pp. 49–50.

is still very different from the United States. The American states are clearly subordinate to federal laws, whereas the EC member states still have some leeway when it comes to obeying community laws. Under these circumstances, the European Court usually prefers to stay out of conflicts between member countries in the hope that a solution can be found through political bargaining. This discussion of the power of the European Court again shows the hybrid character of the EC, combining elements of supranational and international organization. The European Court has less power than it would in a truly supranational organization but more than the International Court of Justice at The Hague, which serves the United Nations—a classic international organization.

European Bureaucracy

Perhaps the best guarantee of the European Community's continued existence is the many thousands of bureaucrats it employs. These "Eurocrats," as they are often called, have an obvious career interest in the continuation of EC operations. In addition, many lobbyists working in Brussels have a personal professional interest in the survival of the community. Over the years, all of these people, working directly or indirectly for the EC, have developed some elements of a common cosmopolitan European culture. They tend to live in the same neighborhoods in Brussels; they attend the same parties and share the same gossip. When the Eurocrats went on strike one day, without regard to nationality, it was said only half-jokingly that this was the best sign yet that the EC was alive and well. A drawback to the development of this huge bureaucracy in Brussels is that ordinary European citizens increasingly see the community as a giant, anonymous organization over which they have no control. And yet, they sense that this distant bureaucracy has an important impact on their daily lives.

POLICIES OF THE EUROPEAN COMMUNITY

The first major policy goal of the European Community was to establish a common market for its member countries. The importance of this goal is such that the EC is often called the Common Market. To what extent has the goal of a common European market been achieved?

Common Market for Goods

All trade tariffs have been abolished among the member countries of the European Community, and the EC levies a common external tariff against other countries. Yet moving goods from one EC country to another is not the same thing as between American states.

As we will see later in this chapter, each European country still has its own currency. Furthermore, custom officials continue to check goods at border crossings. The reason for this is that national laws have not yet been sufficiently harmonized. For example, one country may have stricter health standards than other countries, so it will want to check meat products that cross its borders.

But such nontariff trade barriers should all be eliminated by December 31, 1992. This was decided in the Single European Act of 1985, the first major revision of the Treaty of Rome. The goal is that all requirements which individual products have to meet with regard to health, safety, and the environment be harmonized within the EC. This is a tremendous task, since it involves products ranging from children's toys to medical equipment. This process of harmonization is on its way, and for many products harmonization has already been achieved. Thus, 1992 will not be a turning point but, rather, a target date in a long process of integration (see Box 16.3).

Generally, the work toward the goals of 1992 is going quite smoothly, but there are also tricky issues that have to be resolved. One example is the "pasta war" between Italy and West Germany, which had to be settled by the European Court of Justice (see Box 16.4). The ruling was that Italy's pasta-purity law was an illegal restraint of trade. In two other cases involving beer and sausage, the European Court ruled against German purity laws (see Box 16.5). These cases show that progress toward harmonization is indeed possible, even if fierce national interests are involved. If necessary, the European

_____ BOX 16.3 _____

1992: RECASTING THE EUROPEAN BARGAIN

Under the banner of "1992," the European Communities are putting in place a series of political and business bargains that will recast, if not unify, the European market. This initiative is a disjunction, a dramatic new start, rather than the fulfillment of the original effort to construct Europe. It is not merely the culmination of the integration begun in the 1950s, the "completion" of the internal market. The removal of all barriers to the movement of persons, capital, and goods among the twelve member states (the formal goal of the 1992 process) is expected to increase economies of scale and decrease transaction costs. But these one-time economic benefits do not capture the full range of purposes and consequences of 1992. Dynamic effects will emerge in the form of restructured competition and changed expectations. Nineteen ninety-two is a vision as much as a program—a vision of Europe's place in the world. The vision is already producing a new awareness of European strengths and a seemingly sudden assertion of the will to exploit these strengths in competition with the United States and Japan. It is affecting companies as well as governments.

Source: Wayne Sandholtz and John Zysman, "1992: Recasting the European Bargain," *World Politics*, 42(October 1989): p. 95.

Court has to step in, which shows its increased importance among the European institutions. As a footnote, we may register that the powerful process of European integration may hurt once-flourishing border towns, as illustrated in Box 16.6, by the fate of Modane at the French border to Italy.

_____ BOX 16.4 _____

ITALY LOSES BATTLE ON PASTA IMPORTS

FRANKFURT—The spaghetti war between the two nations is over. . . .

The war, which began with an attempt by a West German company to ship 100 kilograms of egg noodles into Italy in 1985, ended Thursday with a decision by the European Court of Justice that overturned Italy's pasta-purity law as an illegal restraint of trade and opened the door for pasta imports.

The court ruled that Italian law No. 580 of 1967, which declared that pasta could be made only from hard wheat and water, violated the European Community's policy on the free movement of goods.

Source: International Herald Tribune, July 15, 1988.

―――――――――――――――――― BOX 16.5 ――――――――――――――――――

ATTACK ON "PURITY LAW": FIRST BEER, NOW SAUSAGE

Having barely recovered from the successful European Community assault on its centuries-old "purity law" for beer, the Federal Republic finds itself defending against an attack initiated by French and Belgian paté producers on a similar law regulating the content of meat products, primarily sausage. The West German law, which the EC Commission views as an inadmissible trade barrier, forbids the import and sale of meat products containing such ingredients as milk and eggs as well as vegetable proteins and starches.

In oral argument before the European Court in Luxembourg Wednesday (November 16), the Federal Republic based its defense on health and consumer protection grounds, saying the law is there to insure "that the population is provided with a sufficient amount of the important nutrients contained in meat," especially protein. The commission countered that the health of West Germans would not be endangered by a "slight change in the composition of meat products." Because of the country's high meat consumption, West German protein intake already exceeds "internationally recommended amounts," Brussels' representatives argued, adding that furthermore sausages in particular contained considerable amounts of harmful substances like cholesterol, while the healthy qualities of vegetable protein were generally recognized. [February 2, 1989, the Court ruled against the Federal Republic.]

Source: The Week in Germany, German Information Center, New York, November 18, 1988.

Common Market for Services

The common market for services was long lagging behind the common market for goods. With the Single European Act of 1985, a great push was given toward integration in the service sector. Banks, insurance companies, securities firms, and other service businesses would get unrestricted access to the entire EC. This, too, requires much, and often very technical, work of harmonization among the member countries. For the securities sector, for example, rules for insider dealings or regulations of investment advisors must be harmonized. For banking, harmonization of supervision is a big issue. Although for the service sector, too, 1992 is set as a target date, much will probably still have to be accomplished after that date.

Common Market for Labor

Much also still needs to be done for a common market of labor, and here, too, many measures probably have to wait until after 1992. Many problems exist, in particular, for professionals, such as lawyers, doctors, teachers, and engineers. The issue is the mutual recognition among the member countries of diplomas and proficiency certificates. This is more easily accomplished for some professions, like doctors, than for others, like lawyers. To treat patients

—————————— **BOX 16.6** ——————————

'92 SCARES EUROPEAN BORDER TOWNS

MODANE, France—In this never-never-land setting of soaring mountains and burbling streams, Modane's 7,000 people have a fairy-tale wish: that 1992 never come.

With its hundreds of border police officers, customs agents and freight forwarders, this isolated Alpine town on the Italian frontier owes its existence to the border. But townspeople worry that if the European Community eliminates the barriers between community countries by Dec. 31, 1992, as planned, it will eliminate Modane's raison d'être as well.

A Government report estimates that the 1992 process will eliminate 800 jobs here—one fourth of Modane's work force. All told, 1,000 people have jobs directly tied to the border: . . .

"No one knows for sure what will fall on our heads," said Alexandre Vasina, chairman of Socatrom, a freight-forwarding company. "But people are worried that the town will be hit by a disaster."

Source: New York Times, September 11, 1989.

is pretty much the same all over Europe, but to practice law presupposes familiarity with local laws. Here, a solution is sought in the requirement of some adjustment courses. With such adjustment courses, a German lawyer, for example, should get the right to practice, let us say, in Spain or Italy.

If no special diplomas or proficiency certificates are required for particular jobs, a free labor market has already existed for many years. This market was mainly used by unskilled workers from Italy, Spain, Greece, and Portugal who were looking for work in the economically more affluent northern countries. They are called *foreign workers*, or more politely, *guest workers.* But, whatever they are called, unfortunately they encounter much hatred and negative prejudice. I discussed this sad phenomenon already in Chapter 1 when I discussed the Neofascists. Foreign workers tend to be the last hired and the first fired. In much the same fashion as minorities in the United States, they face discrimination when they are trying to obtain housing, so that they often live in segregated ghettos. With the establishment of the EC free labor market, Europeans have learned that it is indeed not easy for people from different cultural backgrounds to live in harmony. The original hope of the European Community was that national prejudices would decrease if Europeans had more contact with one another in their daily work. As we have seen, this hope has been justified for the highly educated and professionally trained Eurocrats who converse easily with each other, no matter what their nationality. Business executives whose companies operate branches in the various EC countries also have few problems. The problem of prejudice exists for poor unskilled laborers who come from faraway countries and are resented by their indigenous co-workers.

The European Monetary System

If a German car dealer wishes to import Italian Fiats, the value of the Italian lira can increase between the time the cars are ordered and the time they are delivered, making the cars more expensive than anticipated. Of course, this is a common problem in world trade, for which businesses have found a variety of solutions. But the purpose of a common market is precisely to make business transactions easier than in ordinary world trade. The EC's effort to stabilize exchange rates among its member states should be viewed in this light. If the German car dealer and the Italian Fiat producer know that the exchange rate between the deutsche mark and the lira will remain stable, their business transactions will be less risky.

Considerable knowledge of banking is necessary in order to understand fully all the technical details of the European Community's efforts to maintain relatively stable exchange rates. The basic principle, however, is quite simple. In what is called the European Monetary System (EMS), the central banks of the individual member countries intervene in the financial markets to stabilize exchange rates among the various national currencies. If a particular currency begins to rise against the other currencies, the central banks sell this currency on the financial markets until the resulting increase in supply lowers its value. On the other hand, if a currency begins to drop against the other currencies, the central banks will buy this currency, thus reducing its supply in an effort to make its value rise again. To finance these interventions, the central banks have established a common fund—the European Monetary Fund. Attaining absolute stability in the exchange rates is not possible, however, and a certain margin of error is tolerated. To determine this margin of error, a baseline—the European Currency Unit (ECU)—is used. The ECU corresponds to a weighted average of the national currencies. An exchange rate for each currency is fixed against the ECU; for example, it is determined that a set number of French francs should correspond to one ECU. From this relationship, a margin of error of 2.25 percent in either direction is allowed. As long as the French franc stays within this margin, the central banks do not intervene, but if it rises above the margin or falls below it, the central banks sell or buy the French currency.

Thus, the overall policy objective is to maintain relatively fixed exchange rates among the EC member states. Because exchange rates float internationally according to market forces, it could be said that the EC is trying to float the currencies of its member states together on the world market. This means, for example, that, if one EC currency rises or drops against the U.S. dollar, all other EC currencies should do the same.

How well has the European Monetary System worked so far? The system works fairly well, although occasional rate adjustments are necessary. Such adjustments are made when a currency is consistently too strong or too weak, so that it is no longer feasible for the central banks to keep it within the tolerated margin of error. Under these circumstances, a new relationship is set between that currency and the ECU. If the value of a currency is raised, it is *revalued;* in the opposite case, *devalued.*

Because such revaluations and devaluations still occur, the European Community is far from having stable exchange rates among all of its members. The basic problem is that the national governments pursue different policies with regard to inflation, unemployment, money supply, budgets, taxes, balance of payment, and so on. Such policy differences have an impact on the value of the national currencies. For example, if one country has consistently higher inflation rates than another, its currency is bound to weaken—perhaps not in the short run but certainly in the long run.

Given this situation, it is understandable why the EC encourages its member countries to pursue similar economic, fiscal, and monetary policies. Based on the Single European Act of 1985, efforts are made, for example, to harmonize the tax systems and to set similar rates of taxation.

If one day economic, fiscal, and monetary policies were sufficiently coordinated, the step could be made to a single European currency, under the control of a European Central Bank. Such a goal is postulated by many European leaders but still fiercely opposed by British Prime Minister Margaret Thatcher. She argues that giving up the British pound in favor of a European currency would damage in an irreparable way British sovereignty. Thatcher is right, of course, that the introduction of a European currency would mean that the member countries would have to give up part of their sovereignty. The question is whether this is desirable or not. Thatcher thinks not, but even within Great Britain this is becoming a minority position.

Although the European Community does not yet have a minted currency, the ECU as a basket of the national currencies already has some importance. You may call it an artificial currency, but already in this form one can have a checking account in ECU and can pay one's bills in ECU. In the business section of any newspaper, the exchange rates for the ECU are given and one can check its value against the dollar.

Common Agricultural Policy

When the European Community was founded in 1957, there was great enthusiasm about the idealism of its goals. Today, many Europeans are disappointed that so many of the EC debates deal with mundane matters such as olives, wine, lamb, and butter. Indeed, agricultural problems are central to the activities of the EC, which spends nearly 60 percent of its money on farm subsidies.

The supply side of farming depends very much on unpredictable weather conditions. In most countries it is therefore considered the government's responsibility to help balance the relationship between supply and demand. The U.S. government, too, is heavily involved in regulating the farm sector. European governments have always had a strong hand in agriculture, and with the founding of the EC, these governmental functions were to a large extent transferred from the national to the European level. Farmers are guaranteed an income comparable to the wages of an industrial worker. As the agricultural policy of the EC has taken shape, farmers have been able to produce pretty much what they wish. If supply exceeds demand, the surplus is purchased by the EC. This system has resulted in increasing surpluses, and people have begun to speak of "butter mountains" and "wine lakes."

In due course, agricultural overproduction emerged as perhaps the EC's most severe problem, overloading the bureaucracy in Brussels. What do bureaucrats do with a "mountain" of butter? The case of the "butter mountain" is a good illustration of the kind of bureaucratic nightmares caused by the common agricultural policy. Some of this butter was sold at heavily subsidized prices to Communist countries in the East, which created a controversy over why EC consumers were not entitled to the same low prices. Things were made worse for the bureaucracy in Brussels when some of this butter found its way back to markets in the EC countries, with someone obviously having turned a quick profit. In another effort to solve the butter problem, the EC bureaucracy encouraged dairy farmers to produce powdered milk instead. But what do you do with an excess of powdered milk? Some of it was used to feed livestock, which in turn helped lead to an oversupply of meat.

These agricultural surpluses lead not only to bureaucratic hassles but also to severe political conflicts among the member countries. It was noted earlier how France placed illegal import restrictions on British lamb. The British reacted by arresting some French fishermen, and the crisis became so severe that it had to be managed at the highest levels of government of the two countries. The importation of Italian wine to France caused such a severe dispute that people spoke of a "wine war." To understand the severity of

---

BOX 16.7

AGRICULTURE NOT JUST "BUSINESS"

[West German] Agriculture Minister Ignaz Kiechle said Monday (Sept. 18) in Washington, at the start of his one-week visit to the United States, that he feels there to be greater awareness in Europe than in the U.S. of the need to achieve a balance between economy and ecology and of the fact that agriculture is not only "business." Speaking at a reception in the West German embassy after his first day of talks with senior American government officials, he suggested that such heightened awareness might be due to the high degree of industrialization and population density in Europe.

The minister said that "the strain currently being placed on the soil and ground water in the Federal Republic must not be allowed to continue." He predicted that the efforts of West German farmers to develop alternative farming methods would eventually gain recognition. In order to preserve the natural environment, industrial nations need a healthy agricultural sector, he continued, and should be willing to provide financial assistance toward that end.

Source: The Week in Germany, German Information Center, New York, September 22, 1989.

these agricultural crises, you must know that European farmers have a lot of political clout.

The EC's overall financial crisis has become so acute that some efforts are now underway to curtail the huge farm subsidies. It remains to be seen to what extent the major farm-producing countries will continue to support the EC when subsidies for their farmers begin to dwindle. Conversely, the net importers of farm products—Great Britain, in particular—are no longer willing to support the expensive EC farm program at current levels.

A way out of the farm crisis may be a complete reorientation of the agricultural policy of the EC. As the West German Agriculture Minister, Ignaz Kiechle, argues in Box 16.7, agriculture is more than just a business, and a balance has to be achieved between economy and ecology. If a change were undertaken from intensive to extensive farming, the oversupply of farm products could be reduced and the environment would be helped. Extensive farming means less reliance on chemical products and more usage of organic methods. It may even mean going back to the medieval farming method, in which a field was left fallow every third year. We have seen in Chapter 1 that, among Europeans with a postmaterial value orientation, there is much support for such a radical change in agricultural policy.

Part of the job description of the farmer would be to act as protector of the environment, for which he or she would need a thorough professional training. As we will see in the next section, such a reorientation would also have advantages for foreign policy, especially for relations between the EC and the United States and Third World countries.

Foreign Policy

With regard to foreign policy, the EC countries try to speak with a single voice in world affairs. Sometimes this is possible, sometimes not (for a negative example see Box 16.8). The status of the European Community as an international actor is still unclear. In Washington, D.C., for example, each EC country has its own embassy, but there is also diplomatic representation of the European Community. Thus, both the individual member nations and the EC are active in international affairs. This can also be observed at the yearly economic summit meetings of the large industrialized countries, which bring together the chief executives of Canada, the Federal Republic of Germany, France, Great Britain, Italy, Japan, the United States, and—in addition—the president of the European Commission. Europe is therefore represented at two levels: national and EC. To evaluate the importance of the two levels, it is important to know that the president of the commission does not act as "captain" of the European "team"; rather, he or she remains in the background. This is clearly revealed in the conference group pictures: National leaders like Margaret Thatcher are in the center forefront, while the commission's president tends to stand toward the back or may not be pictured at all.

Generally speaking, the EC member countries are still sovereign in their foreign affairs, but they try to coordinate their policies within the EC. For instance, the individual countries have membership status in the United Nations. The EC, however, does have observer status, so that offices of the EC, too, are located in the UN building in New York City. There, EC members try to coordinate their positions in order to speak with a single voice. Such coordination also takes place within many other international organizations.

Will the European Community develop internationally into a superpower like the United States, the Soviet Union, and China? Given its population and economic wealth, it has the potential. But it remains unclear whether the European nations will ever be willing to subsume the right to make their own foreign policies under the EC. With regard to the foreign policy of the European Community, the relationship that the EC will have with the Third World, the countries of Eastern Europe, and the United States will be important.

At the beginning of this chapter, we mentioned that the EC has special treaties with many developing countries, particularly in Africa and the Caribbean. These poor countries hope to expand their treaties with the EC, which would allow them to export more of their products, especially agricultural products, to European markets. Such a collaboration would be helped if European farmers indeed changed from intensive to extensive farm methods. Thus, agricultural policy of the EC is closely linked to its foreign-policy relations with the Third World. In this context, a word has to be said

---

BOX 16.8

BRITAIN BREAKS EUROPEAN RANKS TO EASE SOUTH AFRICA SANCTIONS

LONDON—Britain broke ranks with the other members of the European Community today and ended its ban on new investments in South Africa.

Foreign Secretary Douglas Hurd announced the move at a community meeting in Dublin. . . .

As the Foreign Ministers were meeting in Dublin, Prime Minister Margaret Thatcher of Britain repeated her stand in the House of Commons. "We believe it is right, step by step, to lift some of the sanctions, in particular the voluntary ones," said Mrs. Thatcher, one of South Africa's milder critics in recent years. "We are not suggesting lifting those sanctions which are in force by order."

Britain's intention to break the investment ban drew criticism within the community and at home.

"It will destroy political cooperation within the European community as it has been up to now," said Foreign Minister Gerry Collins of Ireland, whose Government now holds the community presidency.

Source: New York Times, February 21, 1990.

about the shipping of farm products from Europe to Third World countries. Such shipments have to be applauded in the case of emergencies, like famines resulting from war or natural catastrophes. To distribute, however, free or heavily subsidized food to the Third World may actually hurt developing countries, because it discourages the development of the indigenous agriculture. Thus, it is no solution for the EC to give away for free or at strongly reduced prices oversupplies of oranges and grapes to North African countries. What these countries need are European markets for their farm products.

How closely should Third World countries be integrated into the EC? Turkey has already applied for full membership in the EC. Geographically, Turkey is not located in Europe, but, although it is poor, it is not a classic Third World country. If Turkey is accepted, however, what prevents North African countries, such as Morocco or Tunisia, from one day applying for membership? Where should the line be drawn? For the time being, the EC is not willing to consider the membership application of Turkey. The justification is that the internal integration steps for 1992 have to be accomplished before new members can be considered. Then there are still questions about the democratic status of Turkey, and it should be remembered that only full-fledged democracies are allowed to become full members of the EC.

Some of the neutral European countries would probably be considered for membership before Turkey. Austria has already submitted its membership request. It remains to be seen how its status of international neutrality can be made compatible with full membership. If negotiations with Austria turn out to be positive, neutral Sweden may be next. In the cases of Finland and Switzerland, neutrality is interpreted in a much broader sense, so that for these two countries full membership in the EC will not come soon, if ever.

A special case is Norway, a member of NATO, whose membership was acceptable to the EC but failed in 1973 because the Norwegian people decided against it in a national referendum. Norway may soon reconsider this negative decision, and it should have no major difficulty entering the EC.

This discussion shows that after 1992 the EC will be busy with new applications, not even considering the Eastern and Central European countries. In this direction, the task is even more formidable. The authorities of the EC have already expressed a willingness in principle to consider these countries. After all, Eastern and Central Europe is certainly a traditional part of Europe; Prague, Budapest, Warsaw, Bucharest, and Sofia are old European cities. With the ongoing democratization in these countries, they fulfill the prime preconditions for membership. The big problem will be the poor economic situation of all Eastern and Central European countries. The EC is already burdened with poor regions, in particular, in Southern Italy, Greece, Portugal, major parts of Spain, Ireland, and Scotland. Could it digest and handle the problems of the Eastern and Central European countries? Let us hope so! There is no real alternative. In the medium or long range, these countries have to be integrated; otherwise, the EC will have failed as a truly European institution.

The EC already took up the challenge when Spain, Portugal, and Greece democratized in the mid-1970s, and it is inconceivable that one day the EC will not grant to the Eastern and Central European countries what it granted to the Southern European countries. To become part of the EC will be the best safeguard for the democratic stability and economic well-being of the Eastern and Central European countries.

A puzzling question is how far to the East the EC should go. Gorbachev often speaks of the common European house. Does this imply a Soviet interest in participating in the EC, perhaps as an associate member? Would this not completely change the nature of the EC, leading to possible domination by the Soviets? What if the Soviet empire should dissolve? Would the EC be open to the Baltic communities of Lithuania, Latvia, and Estonia? How about Moldavia, Georgia, and the Ukraine? Charles de Gaulle always spoke of a Europe from the Atlantic to the Ukraine. The French Nobel prize winner in economics, Maurice Allais, rejects such ideas.[72] He suggests that the Soviet republics should build a democratically organized federation similar to the EC. Allais envisions three entities from the East to the West: (1) the Soviet Republics; (2) the European Community; and (3) the United States and Canada.

With German unification accomplished, East Germany, the former German Democratic Republic, already has become a part of the European community. Will such an expanded Germany not be too dominant in the EC? The German question is so complex that I will deal with it in a special section at the end of this chapter.

There remain the transatlantic relations between the EC and the United States, or, in the perspective of Maurice Allais, between the EC and North America. All EC countries, except the Republic of Ireland, are military partners of the United States and Canada in NATO. Yet economic relations across the Atlantic are quite stormy. The United States is particularly angered by the protectionism of the EC. High tariffs and the imposition of quotas make it very difficult for American farm products to penetrate the European market. Americans also complain that, with heavily subsidized farm products, Europeans compete unfairly on world markets. But Europeans express dissatisfaction with American trade policies, too; for example, U.S. restrictions imposed on steel imports from Europe.

Despite all of the problems, some kind of solution is always hammered out as a result of these transatlantic disagreements. A good illustration is the end of a 20-year-old disagreement about European soybean subsidies, which is described in Box 16.9. Trade relations between the United States and the EC would become easier if the EC and, for that matter, the United States would reduce their food production by changing from intensive to extensive farm methods. Hopes in this respect are currently higher for the EC than for the United States.

The United States and Europe must ask themselves whether it is possible to be military allies and fierce economic competitors at the same time. Should cooperation be extended from the military to the economic arena? Full membership for the United States in the European Community is certainly out of the question, but more cooperation may be feasible; in the areas of research and development, for example. Further steps, such as the extension of the free labor market to both sides of the Atlantic, would probably

--- BOX 16.9 ---

VICTORY FOR THE U.S. IN A 20-YEAR BATTLE
WITH EUROPEAN BLOC

WASHINGTON—The United States has won a 20-year fight with the European Community over European soybean subsidies, the United States trade representative, Carla A. Hills, said today. American farmers have complained that the subsidies cost them hundreds of millions of dollars a year in lost exports.

Under the settlement, the European Community has agreed to pass legislation before the end of next year that would eliminate the subsidies. The agreement removes an immediate threat of American retaliation. Had there been no settlement, the Bush Administration faced a Jan. 31 statutory deadline for reprisal.

Source: New York Times, December 21, 1989.

encounter insurmountable resistance within both Europe and America. A radically different alternative would be to loosen existing military ties and let Europeans handle defense matters themselves. This could be done, at least initially, within the NATO framework. Indeed, European defense ministers have already met together without their U.S. counterpart to define a specific European position in the areas of disarmament and weapons procurement policy. Here, again, questions with broad implications for world affairs arise, particularly after the end of the Cold War.

EUROPEAN SYMBOLS

The EC has introduced a certain number of European symbols that are noticeable in everyday life. The most noticeable symbol is a common passport for all member countries (see Box 16.10 and photo on page 301). Another noticeable symbol appears in airports: EC citizens have special entry gates where they are processed more quickly. For me, as a Swiss citizen, this is perhaps the most visible sign in everyday life that Switzerland is not a full member of the EC.

The EC has also its own flag, which has a blue background with 12 stars, which represent the 12 member countries. If the reader is traveling in Europe, he or she might find it interesting to check how often the EC flag can be seen. Usually it is flown less often than national and local flags. The EC has even its own anthem, adapted for this purpose from Beethoven's Ninth Symphony.

How important is it that European children be made aware of such symbols? This depends on what kind of entity the EC wishes to become—a new

_____ **BOX 16.10** _____

EUROPEAN PASSPORT IS INTRODUCED

Citizens from a number of E. C. Member States can now move freely about the globe on a new E. C. passport, a document being introduced this year that will gradually replace national passports. Since January 1st, the passport has been issued in Denmark, Ireland and Luxembourg. It will be introduced very shortly in France and Italy and from mid-1985 in Greece, Belgium and the Netherlands. For technical reasons, the Federal Republic of Germany and the United Kingdom have delayed introduction until late 1986. In the German case, to permit them to be read electronically.

The passports, burgundy-colored with the title "European Community" above the name of the issuing member state, have the same legal status as national passports and can be used under the same conditions for travel anywhere in the world. In the initial stages, the new passport encountered some difficulties. Spanish and Czechoslovakian customs officials at border crossings claimed they had not been informed of the new document. The few bugs in the system now appear to have been ironed out.

Source: Europe Magazine, March/April 1985, p. 49.

world superpower with clear and well-defined borders or the beginning of a new world order with fluid borders reaching out to the Third World, the Soviet Union, and North America. In the latter case, the emotions of symbols will be less important. I think the development of a European nationalism

Italian Version of the European Passport. (Courtesy *Europe Magazine.*)

would be rather dangerous. We probably need a new world order in which national borders become less important. For issues like the environment or the fight against AIDS, even a greatly enlarged EC would be too small. For other issues, such as cultural questions, the EC and even the traditional nations are too big. Here, more autonomy should be given to regional and local units. With such a vision, we would end up with a multilayered world order in which each layer has specific functions to fulfill.

THE EUROPEAN COMMUNITY
AND GERMAN UNIFICATION

Within such a multilayered world order, it would also be easier to find a solution for the tricky question of German unification. If more power were given, on the one hand, to the EC and, for that matter, to world organizations such as the United Nations, and, on the other hand, to regional and local units, the question of German unity would lose much of its importance. This is also the position advocated by Roderick MacFarquhar, a former British Member of Parliament and now a professor of government at Harvard. He wishes to "regionalize, and centralize, Europe" at the same time. This would "bind the Germans into a stronger and more integrated European Community [and] a further devolution of power to the *laender* in a future unified Germany could diminish fears of an 80-million strong mega-state in Central Europe."[73]

Before we proceed further with a discussion of German unification, some German history is needed. In medieval times, there was the Holy Roman Empire of the German Nation. It stretched from Southern Italy to the Netherlands and was thus far too big to be governed in an efficient way. This First Empire was further weakened by the fact that to be emperor was not a hereditary position; each new emperor, rather, had to be elected by electors, such as powerful kings, bishops, and so on. It also worked against the emperor that the pope was a mighty rival who headed a special church state in Rome and its vicinity. By the sixteenth and seventeenth centuries, the Holy Roman Empire of the German Nation had lost practically all of its power, and it was formally dissolved during the time of Napoleon I at the turn from the eighteenth to the nineteenth century.

The weakness, and then the absence, of a central political authority meant that a wide range of independent political entities developed on German soil, for example, the Kingdom of Bavaria, the Kingdom of Prussia, and the Free Hanseatic City of Hamburg. During these times, Germans were known as rather peaceful people. Henry Ashby Turner, historian at Yale University, notes correctly that "[i]n the middle of the 19th century, the Germans were widely considered a quaint, impractical 'nation of poets and thinkers,' whereas the French were feared as Europe's most bellicose nation."[74] The image of Germans only changed when Prussia, under the leadership of Chancellor Otto von Bismarck, united Germany in 1870–1871 into a Second Empire. In order to achieve this goal, Bismarck first launched a sucessful war against Austria and then another successful war against France. These events, however, have to be seen in a broader context. The latter part of the nineteenth century was a time of worldwide imperialism and colonialism. In the battle to get a place in the sun, Germany was a latecomer, with other nation-states, such as Great Britain and France, already way ahead. Most of the colonies were divided up when Germany, too, tried to get some pieces. When Germany began to build up a navy, Great Britain accelerated its own plans. The goal of Great Britain at that time was that its navy should be at least twice as strong as the second largest navy in the world. No wonder a ferocious arms race set in that led directly to the catastrophe of World War I. Certainly, Germany was to be blamed too, but so were the other participants in the war. The question of guilt was far less clear for World War I than for World War II. If we look at German history up to World War I, there were no signs that Germans were predisposed to aggressive or even criminal behavior. I agree with Henry Ashby Turner that "[h]istory abounds with examples of nations whose behavior has altered. . . . Surely, no one conversant with the record of humanity can seriously entertain the hackneyed notion of indelible national character."

If Germans are not by nature bad people, how do we explain their submission to Hitler and the brutal and criminal atrocities of his Third Reich? Possible explanations are shame and humiliation as a result of losing World War I, the hugh reparation costs imposed on the Germans by the Peace Treaty of Versailles, and the misery of the Great Depression that resulted in millions of unemployed people in Germany. But weren't the atrocities of the concentration camps so terrible that any attempt at explanation takes away from these acts? Wasn't the evil so great that it is simply inexplicable? Some historians have attempted to compare the crimes of the Nazis with other crimes committed in world history, such as the crimes committed by the Soviets in their own concentration camps or the genocide committed by Turks against millions of Armenians. There are strong objections by other historians against such comparisons, because they are said to take away from the uniqueness of the Nazi crimes.

What are the consequences for the Germans who were only children during Hitler's time or who were born afterward? Do they have to carry a collective guilt into eternity? In Boxes 16.11 to 16.15, five positions on this question are presented. The well-known German writer Günter Grass states that "Auschwitz belongs to us, is branded into our history." A. M. Rosenthal, a commentator for the *New York Times*, fears "that 10 or 12 years from now, if the Germans want to cut out for some political or economic expansionism," they will simply do it, whatever their treaty obligations are, the implication being that Germans will always be expansionists. Chancellor Helmut Kohl, in a letter to an American rabbi, outlines the great changes that have taken place in Germany since the end of World War II and expresses "deep disappointment at how little many opponents of German unity take note." President Richard von Weizsäcker knows "how important it is during this process of German unification not to give our neighbors a reason for harboring fears." Finally, I reprint a thoughtful letter of Renate Lasker-Harpprecht, a survivor of the concentration camps who now lives in France. She has not forgotten or

_____ BOX 16.11 _____

WRITER GÜNTER GRASS ON GERMAN UNIFICATION

Auschwitz speaks against even a right of self-determination that is enjoyed by all other peoples, because one of the preconditions for the horror, besides other, older urges, was a strong, united Germany. Not Prussia, not Bavaria, not even Austria, alone, could have developed and carried out the will and the method for organized genocide; it required a united Germany.

We have every reason to be afraid of ourselves as a functioning unity. . . . We cannot get by Auschwitz. We shouldn't even try, as great as the temptation is, because Autschwitz belongs to us, is branded into our history and—to our benefit!—made possible an insight that could be summed up as: Now we finally know ourselves.

Source: New York Times, March 8, 1990.

forgiven the Germans who have committed the Nazi crimes, but she reminds us that two-thirds of the Germans who are living today were born after 1945 and she pointedly asks: "Are they collectively guilty by history? By race? This sounds only too familiar." The theme of Renate Lasker-Harpprecht that general anti-German feelings may be equated with anti-Semitism is also

_____ BOX 16.12 _____

FEARS OF GERMAN UNIFICATION

The Soviet Union and the West both tried once to appease Nazi Germany; both failed and paid the price. The West may be ready to slap its lederhosen in great good spirit, but in the Soviet Union memories of World War II are acutely alive, as is fear of a Germany resurgent.

Western leaders say don't worry, a united Germany will be "anchored" in NATO and restrained within the Western economic system.

Does anybody really believe that garbage—that 10 or 12 years from now, if the Germans want to cut out for some political or economic expansionism, they will submit to being "anchored" by an outdated alliance or restrained by Western economies that by then will be economically dependent on the new united Reich?

The goal is not to stop German unification forever. The goal is for all neighbors and victims of one united Germany to be heard on the timing and conditions for the creation of a new united Germany.

Source: A. M. Rosenthal, New York Times, February 8, 1990.

_____ BOX 16.13 _____

KOHL, WRITING TO RABBI, SAYS FEAR OF
FASCIST GERMANY IS UNJUSTIFIED

Washington—Chancellor Helmut Kohl of West Germany says he understands the anxieties of Holocaust survivors about the unification of Germany, but he insists that such fears are unjustified.

Fed up with Communism and its "distorted view of history," East Germans are "immune to any new totalitarian temptations," Mr. Kohl said in a philosophical letter discussing the Nazi era and the burden of German history. . . .

The letter, dated Feb. 28, was sent today to Rabbi Marvin Hier, dean of the Simon Wiesenthal Center for Holocaust studies in Los Angeles. Rabbi Hier sent a letter to Mr. Kohl three weeks ago asking how a united Germany would preserve the memory of Nazi crimes.

In his response, Mr. Kohl said West Germans had been fully informed of "the causes and consequences" of Nazi tyranny, through schools and universities, church groups and the press. He expressed "deep disappointment at how little many opponents of German unity take note" of that public information campaign.

Under West Germany's penal code, Mr. Kohl said, "crimes of hatred" are punishable with fines or prison sentences. Such crimes, he said, include the dissemination of neo-Nazi propaganda, "instigation of the people, incitement to racial hatred or defamation of National Socialist victims, especially by denial of the Holocaust."

"To my mind, there is no doubt that these provisions will also apply in a united Germany," Mr. Kohl wrote.

Source: New York Times, March 2, 1990.

_____ BOX 16.14 _____

RICHARD VON WEIZSÄCKER ON GERMAN UNIFICATION

We know very well how important it is during this process of German unification not to give our neighbors a reason for harboring fears, either old ones or new ones. How they perceive this process will continue to be something we take very seriously. We want to maintain close contact with the governments of our neighboring countries, in order both to reach agreement on the steps to be taken and to ensure that the people of these countries understand them. Through our words and deeds we want to convince people that German unity is not only a factor based on democratic legitimacy but also one that will promote peace in Europe.

Source: Speech in Prague, March 15, 1990. German Information Center, New York, *Statements and Speeches*, Vol. 13, March 21, 1990.

_____ BOX 16.15 _____

MUST GERMANS BE HELD GUILTY BY RACE?

To the Editor:

Before I respond to A. M. Rosenthal's reservations about German reunification, I should mention that I lost my parents and many relatives in the extermination camps of the Nazis; I myself survived Auschwitz-Birkenau and Bergen-Belsen. I share the relief of all well-meaning citizens of our Western civilization about the liberation of the Eastern European countries from the yoke of Stalinism.

I also share the anxiety of many about the renaissance of the suppressed spirit of nationalism: in the Soviet Union, in Poland, in Romania, in Bulgaria —yes, and in Germany. I wouldn't be surprised to see a reemergence of anti-Semitic resentments that were only hidden under the bell jar of authoritarian regimes, which were anti-fascist by confession and fascist in reality. I would feel easier if German unification were controlled by the European Community.

But why not praise the Germans for having freed themselves from a dictatorship—so far without bloodshed? Why the hysterical fear that they "will probably be the most powerful nation on earth"? (Do they have nuclear weapons—like the United States, the Soviet Union, Britain, France and perhaps Israel?)

The task of young Germans, Mr. Rosenthal writes, "should be to remove fears if they can, not to pretend they do not exist or are unworthy." Most do not pretend that our fears do not exist, and have tried hard to remove them for decades. Does Mr. Rosenthal expect them to assemble every morning for a roll call—as we did in Auschwitz—pounding their breasts and shouting, "We are guilty, guilty, guilty—forever!"

Germans have not shed responsibility for the unspeakable Nazi crimes, which are not forgotten and not forgiven. But two-thirds of the Germans of 1990 were born after 1945. Are they collectively guilty by history? By race? This sounds only too familiar.

[signed] Renate Lasker-Harpprecht La Croix-Valmer, France, Feb. 18, 1990

Source: New York Times, March 15, 1990.

taken up by Václav Havel, a playwright and former dissident, now president of Czechoslovakia (page 146–147). Addressing the visiting West German president Richard von Weizsäcker, Havel said: "To speak with disdain about the Germans is the same as to speak about the Vietnamese or the people of any other nation. To condemn them only because they are Germans, to be afraid of them only because of that, is the same as to be anti-Semitic."[75] I think that Havel and Lasker-Harpprecht are right and courageous in the current emotional atmosphere to express their views.

Before we discuss the details of German unification, we still have to describe what happened to Germany after its defeat in World War II. In the western part of Germany, the Americans, the British, and the French established occupation zones, and the Soviets did the same in the east. The part farthest east was taken over by Poland, which in turn lost its own eastern part to the Soviet Union. The former German capital, Berlin, located in the Soviet zone, was divided into American, British, French, and Soviet sectors. Immediately after the war, severe tensions began between the Soviets and the Western powers, and one result of these tensions is the fact that only an armistice, but no peace treaty, was concluded. In 1948, the Soviets cut off Berlin from the Western zones. The Americans reacted with the famous airlift into West Berlin that prevented the entire city from being taken over by the Soviets (see photo below). But Berlin remained very much a world trouble spot, and it was feared that the explosive situation in the former German capital could trigger World War III. Tensions increased even further when the Soviets built the Berlin Wall in 1961. It was after this event that President John F. Kennedy came to West Berlin to say, "Ich bin ein Berliner" ("I am a Berliner"), thereby expressing with this symbolic gesture the willingness of the United States to defend the freedom of West Berlin (see Box 16.16).

Politically, the Soviets established a Communist regime in their occupation zone, the German Democratic Republic, while the three Western powers organized a democratic regime in their zones, the Federal Republic of Germany, which began in 1949. This West German state claimed to be the sole legitimate German government. According to the West German constitution, the prime task of its government would be to unite Germany under one

U.S. Airlift to West Berlin, 1948. (Courtesy Embassy of the Federal Republic of Germany, Bern, Switzerland.)

_____ BOX 16.16 _____

PRESIDENT KENNEDY SPEAKS IN BERLIN, JUNE 26, 1963

You live in a defended island of freedom, but your life is part of the main. So let me ask you as I close to lift your eyes beyond the dangers of today to the hopes of tomorrow—beyond the freedom merely of this city of Berlin or your country of Germany to the advance of freedom everywhere, beyond the Wall to the day of peace with justice, beyond yourselves and ourselves to all mankind. Freedom is indivisible, and when one man is enslaved all are not free. When all are free then we can look forward to that day when this city will be joined as one, and this country, and this great continent of Europe in a peaceful and hopeful globe. When that day finally comes, as it will, the people of West Berlin can take sober satisfaction in the fact that they were in the front lines for almost two decades.

All free men, wherever they may live, are citizens of Berlin, and therefore as a free man, I take pride in the words: "Ich bin ein Berliner."

Source: Common Values, Common Cause: German Statesmen in the United States, American Statesmen in Germany, 1953–1983. Statements and Speeches (New York: German Information Center, 1983), p. 58.

democratic regime. With this policy, the Federal Republic refused to recognize the German Democratic Republic as another German state. West German politicians referred to the Communist regime in the east as the Soviet zone. With détente between the superpowers setting in toward the end of the 1960s, relations also relaxed between West and East Germany. A real turning point came in 1969, when Willy Brandt became the first Socialist chancellor of the Federal Republic. He inaugurated a new Eastern policy (*Ostpolitik*) that resulted in treaties with Poland and East Germany in 1972. The West Germans conceded the lands east of the rivers Oder and Neisse to Poland, the lands that the Poles had taken after World War II. In legal terms, however, the issue of these lands would be settled in a final way in a general peace treaty. The West German organizations of emigrants from this region insisted on this point.

The West Germans also recognized the existence of a second German state in the east, but this state was still supposed to be a part of one German nation. The legal construction was that two states existed within the same nation. West Germans insisted that for them to go to East Germany was not going abroad. This legal language preserved the option of a later unification. Willy Brandt's "opening to the East" did greatly reduce East-West tensions related to the German question. But the policy still failed at the time to remove the Iron Curtain between the two Germanies or the wall dividing East and West Berlin. Several measures were implemented, however, to facilitate communication between East and West Germans. The latter were allowed to travel to East Germany, although there were still many restrictions. Under some rare conditions, especially for family matters, travel was also possible in the opposite direction. Telephone lines were reestablished, most importantly between West and East Berlin. The East German government no longer intervened when its citizens watched West German television.

All these measures increased contact between West and East Germans. When, in the late 1970s and early 1980s, tensions increased again between the superpowers, relations remained remarkably good between the two Germanies. In West Germany, the new coalition of Christian Democrats and Free Democrats more or less continued the policy begun by Willy Brandt, including a continuation of substantial financial credits to East Germany, which in turn reacted with some further concessions in travel arrangements. But, as long as the Communists were in power in East Germany, all these small steps could not go beyond certain limits.

All this changed in a dramatic way in the fall of 1989. In the first two chapters, I described how on November 9, 1989, the Berlin Wall fell and how on March 18, 1990, free elections were held in East Germany (see pages 25–30; see also photo, page 310). After the Communists were swept from power, the push for unification was irresistible but not unproblematic. Many issues had to be resolved within Germany itself and at the international level. It was not even clear whether the process should be called unification or reunification, Karsten Voigt, a leading West German Social Democrat, opposed the term *reunification* with the following justification: "I don't like to speak about re-unification, because we are not talking about going back to an old state of affairs."[76] And it was precisely this old state of affairs, the Third Reich of Hitler, that worried many people both in Germany and abroad. Reunification had for many the connotation that Germany wanted to go back to the old "Grossdeutschland" (Greater Germany). It was in particular the Oder/Neisse line, the western border of Poland, that came again to the center stage of the discussion. The position of Helmut Kohl, the West German chancellor, was at first somewhat ambiguous. He insisted, on the one hand, that he recognized personally the Oder/Neisse line as the western border of Poland, but he stressed, on the other hand, that legally he could not make any commitments for a future united German state. Although, from a purely legal perspective, Kohl's position was certainly correct, it did not sufficiently take into account the political sensitivities involved. Kohl was seen as hedging the question, and criticism was expressed that electoral considerations were on his mind, in the sense that he did not dare to offend nationalistic voters. And there were indeed nationalistic forces in Germany demanding that the country should try to regain some of the territories lost in World War II, in particular, in Poland but perhaps also in Czechoslovakia.

With the question of national borders raised again, the issue of German unification received a strong international dimension. Already on December 6, 1989, during a visit to Kiev in the Soviet Union, French President François Mitterrand warned that "[w]e should not begin by talking about changing borders." In a clear reference to Germany, Mitterrand continued: "None of our countries, and especially one whose weight is so great and whose geographical position is such, can act without taking into account the balance of Europe."[77] The balance of Europe was indeed suddenly at stake. As

Berlin Wall is Open. (Courtesy Embassy of the Federal Republic of Germany, Washington, D.C.)

long as the Iron Curtain still existed, there was a balance of power in Europe, although a dangerous balance based on mutual deterrence. Now with the Iron Curtain gone, a great fluidity had developed, the main reason being the uncertain position of Germany in a future European order. Although the West German government of Helmut Kohl always took the position that a unified Germany should remain in NATO, there was also talk of German neutrality. What would such neutrality mean? Would it mainly mean that there would be no more checks on German foreign policy? Such questions began to worry Germany's neighbors. Even if Germany stayed in NATO, there were many puzzling questions: What would happen to the Soviet troops in East Germany? Could NATO also have troops on the territory that was formerly East Germany? Could soldiers be drafted who lived in East Germany?

————————————————— BOX 16.17 —————————————————

FORMER CHANCELLOR HELMUT SCHMIDT ON GERMAN UNIFICATION

Where I fault our political leaders is that they haven't taken the feelings of our European neighbors into account. German unification can only be legitimate if the French and the Poles agree to it. Both nations have existed for a thousand years—800 years longer than the Americans. There will always be a negative attitude in New York to German unification, but it doesn't matter. What really matters now is the soul of the Polish nation and the French nation. The Germans have not gone far enough to calm their concerns.

Source: New York Times, March 8, 1990.

In the beginning, Chancellor Kohl emphasized too much that German unification was an issue to be decided primarily by the German people. When he presented to the Bundestag on November 28, 1989, a "Ten-Point Program for Overcoming the Division of Germany and Europe," Kohl did not clear the text with his allies and partners in NATO and the European Community, which led to some irritation. In Box 16.17 former Chancellor Helmut Schmidt criticizes his successor for not having gone far enough to calm the concerns of crucial neighbors like France and Poland. On February 13, 1990, an East-West Conference held in Ottawa agreed on a two-plus-four formula

————————————————— BOX 16.18 —————————————————

GERMAN BUSINESSES RACING TOWARD UNITY

While politicians take the spotlight in the days leading up to East Germany's landmark elections Sunday, business executives have been working feverishly behind the scenes to build a united Germany, brick by brick, deal by deal.

West German executives are pressing to build factories, form joint ventures and market products. West German companies have announced so many deals recently that some people have dubbed German reunification "the world's biggest takeover."

"It's a potential new market," said Thomas Ruhnke, a spokesman for Siemens A.G., the West German electronics giant, which signed an agreement Monday to form a joint venture to make machine tools and robots in East Germany. "It's a market where we know the language. It's a market that's close to us. It's a market with huge demand."

Source: New York Times, March 15, 1990.

to deal with the question of German unification. The *two* in the formula refers to the two Germanies, which would first discuss the details for domestic unification. They would later be joined by the four Allies of World War II—the United States, Great Britain, France, and the Soviet Union—for a discussion of international security issues. Poland was granted participation when the discussion of its western border came up.

While these international negotiations were held, unification in the daily lives of Germans took place at a very rapid pace. As Box 16.18 aptly describes, German businesses were "racing toward unity." But the real breakthrough came with the election results of March 18, 1990. As already described in Chapter 2, the East German Christian Democrats were the clear winners, which was interpreted as a mandate for unity "as soon as possible," as shown in the headline of the *New York Times* the following day (see Box 16.19). The Christian Democrats formed a broad-based cabinet under Prime Minister Lothar de Maizière (Chapter 3). De Maizière was sworn in on April 12, 1990, the same day that the East German parliament took responsibility for the crimes committed by the Nazis and asked for forgiveness, in particular from the Jews. In addition, the parliament recognized solemnly the western border of Poland (see Box 16.20). The recognition of this border was stressed again in June 1990, when both the West and the East German parliaments voted for a resolution guaranteeing Poland's post-World War II border at the rivers Oder and Neisse. There were only a few deputies voting

---

BOX 16.19

MANDATE FOR UNITY 'AS SOON AS POSSIBLE'

EAST BERLIN—In their surprising endorsement of a conservative alliance led by the Christian Democrats, the East Germans declared loudly that, as a young voter named Susanna Frank put it, "We should get out of this mess as soon as possible."

The large vote for the Christian Democrats and more generally for West German-backed parties was in effect a death sentence for the German Democratic Republic and an endorsement of absorption, as quickly as possible, into big, rich West Germany.

Even those worried about their jobs and social benefits seemed to accept that unification was like an injection—painful, frightening, but unavoidable and so best gotten over with.

"Every day we waste not having reunification just makes matters worse," declared Miss Frank, a 25-year-old East Berliner who seemed to echo the sentiment of hundreds who flocked to a discotèque in the center of the city for an exuberant celebration by the Christian Democratic Union of a victory that no polls and no pundits had really anticipated.

Source: New York Times, March 19, 1990.

_____ **BOX 16.20** _____

STATEMENT BY NEWLY ELECTED EAST GERMAN PARLIAMENT

We, the first freely-elected parliamentarians of East Germany, admit our responsibility as Germans in East Germany for their history and their future and declare unanimously before the world:

Immeasurable suffering was inflicted on the peoples of the world by Germans during the time of National Socialism. Nationalism and racial madness led to genocide, particularly of the Jews in all European countries, of the people of the Soviet Union, the Polish people and the Gypsy people.

* * *

Parliament admits joint responsibility on behalf of the people for the humiliation, expulsion and murder of Jewish women, men and children. We feel sad and ashamed and acknowledge this burden of German history.

We ask the Jews of the world to forgive us. We ask the people of Israel to forgive us for the hypocrisy and hostility of official East German policies toward Israel and for the persecution and degradation of Jewish citizens also after 1945 in our country.

* * *

We declare solemnly once more our unequivocal recognition of the German borders with neighboring states that resulted from World War II.

The Polish people in particular should know that their right to live within safe borders will not be questioned by territorial claims from us Germans, either now or in the future.

We confirm the inviolability of the Oder-Neisse border with the Republic of Poland as a foundation for the peaceful co-existence of our peoples in a common European house.

Source: New York Times, April 13, 1990.

against the resolution or abstaining in both parliaments. The overwhelming support for the resolution was hailed in Poland, as seen in Box 16.21. The final step will be a border treaty between the unified Germany and Poland. As Box 16.21 indicates, Poland has given up its earlier demand that this border treaty be initialed by the two German states before their unification. Thus, a big stumbling block on the way to German unification was removed.

Negotiations between the two German governments focused at first on the establishment of a currency union. The problem was that the West German mark was much stronger than the East German mark. Because the East German currency did not float freely on the international markets, but was government-controlled, it was most difficult to determine the appropriate exchange rate. Some hints could be gained from how the East German mark did on the black market. The West Germans, however, were willing to offer a

_____ BOX 16.21 _____

POLAND HAILS BORDER VOTES

WARSAW—Poland welcomed the resolutions by both German parliaments guaranteeing its post-World War II frontiers with Germany and said it would no longer press the two states to initial a border treaty before unifying, Reuters reported from Warsaw.

"The government of the Republic of Poland accepts the resolutions of both German parliaments with satisfaction, recognizing them as a major step forward," Malgorzata Niezabitowska, a government spokesman, said at [a] news conference.

She said Poland would be satisfied with a border treaty, which would be signed once the Germanys were reunified, and that Warsaw would not press its earlier demand that Bonn and Berlin initial it separately.

Source: International Herald Tribune, June 23–24, 1990.

much better deal. At first, Chancellor Kohl spoke of an exchange rate of 1 : 1, 1 East German mark for 1 West German mark. But it was feared that this would be too expensive for West Germany, and a rate of 2 East German Marks against 1 West German Mark was thrown into the discussion. Finally, a complicated mix between the two rates was chosen. For old age pensions and small private savings, for example, the rate was 1 : 1, for larger savings and business holdings 2 : 1. A corresponding treaty between the two German governments was signed May 18, 1990 (see Box 16.22), and ratified by the two German parliaments in June 1990. July 1, 1990, Germany became a Currency, Economic, and Social Union.

After the West German DM was introduced in East Germany, the unification process speeded up further. On August 23, 1990, the East German parliament decided to join the Federal Republic, effective October 3, 1990. Internationally, the crucial step was made September 12, 1990, when the two-plus-four talks (see pages 311–312) came to a successful conclusion and the Treaty on the Final Settlement With Respect to Germany was signed (Box 16.23). The four wartime allies—the United States, Great Britain, France, and the Soviet Union—relinquished all their occupation rights over Germany. In return, the two German states agreed that their unified nation would reduce its armed forces and would not acquire nuclear, chemical, or biological weapons and that its territory would consist of what are now the areas of West and East Germany and nothing more. With regard to NATO membership of a unified Germany, the Soviet Union agreed that Germany can "belong to alliances with all the rights and responsibilities arising therefrom." This passage in the treaty allows Germany to stay in NATO. The Soviet troops in East Germany will leave by 1994. Germany will make a contribution of $7.5 billion to house and resettle these soldiers in the Soviet Union. Until 1994,

_____ BOX 16.22 _____

THE TWO GERMANYS SIGN FOR A SINGLE ECONOMY

BONN—The two Germanys on Friday took their first official step toward be-coming one country by agreeing on a treaty that scraps East Germany's Communist system and creates a single German economy.

In a festive ceremony at the desk of the first West German chancellor, Konrad Adenauer, the two German finance ministers signed a 114-page document that in many ways spells the end of East Germany's four decades of separate existence.

"What we are experiencing here is the birth of the free and united Germany," Chancellor Helmut Kohl said before adjourning to the terrace of Schaumberg Palace in Bonn to sip German sparkling wine with the East German prime minister, Lothar de Maizière.

The unification of the two German currencies, economies and social security systems—all of which is to happen July 1—makes the complete merger of the countries "irreversible," Mr. de Maizière said at the ceremony, which was televised in both Germanys.

The treaty details the legal changes involved when West Germany takes control of everything from banking to how much the East German government can spend.

East Germans will give up their nearly worthless currency in exchange for the Deutsche mark, their ticket to the consumer society. East Germans will pay West German taxes, get West German unemployment checks and buy largely West German goods.

Source: International Herald Tribune, May 19–20, 1990.

Germany is not allowed to station in East Germany any troops that are integrated into the NATO military structure. After 1994, German NATO troops, but not any foreign NATO troops, can be moved to East Germany.

Now it is up to the Germans to prove that the worries which linger among the people of many countries, especially the neighboring nations, are unfounded. The best way for Germany to do this will be to consistently conduct its foreign policy within the framework of the European Community. Of course, Germany will now be by far the strongest member of the Community, but it may very well fulfill this role with great responsibility and with solidarity with the interests of Europe at large.

With the formal unification of Germany on October 3, 1990, Helmut Kohl became chancellor of all Germans, East and West. Thus, after the opening of the Berlin Wall on November 9, 1989, it had taken less than a year to bring the unification process to a formal conclusion. Overall, this was a good performance. To be sure, there was much bickering among the politicians both in East and West Germany on how exactly to proceed with the details of the unification process. But given the enormous complexity of the task, such bickering had to be expected.

BOX 16.23

FOUR ALLIES GIVE UP RIGHTS IN GERMANY

MOSCOW—The four wartime Allies who defeated Nazi Germany 45 years ago signed a treaty with the two German nations Wednesday relinquishing all their occupation rights, leaving East Germany and West Germany finally free to reunite Oct. 3.

* * *

"The new Germany is here," U.S. Secretary of State James A. Baker III said. "Let our legacy be that after 45 years, we finally got the political arithmetic right. Two plus four adds up to one Germany in a Europe whole and free."

* * *

At the news conference Wednesday, Mr. Shevardnadze spoke eloquently about the implications of relinquishing control over the Germans.

"Let me dwell on a very important subject," Mr. Shevardnadze said. "It is no secret that the German issue, for well-known reasons, has been sensitive for the Soviet people and the people of Europe. There are widespread concerns that the new country will do damage to Soviet security and the security of Europe.

"We took that into account, and I believe that we have received all the necessary safeguards and guarantees. We cannot continue to live in the past. We have to think about the future. We are now dealing with a new Germany which has drawn its lessons from history."

Foreign Minister Hans-Dietrich Genscher of West Germany, who spoke in a very subdued manner, said: "In this hour, we remember the victims of the war and the totalitarian domination—not only the agony of the peoples represented here in Moscow. We are particularly thinking of the Jewish people. We would not want their agony to ever be repeated."

Source: New York Times, September 13, 1990.

Germany's formal unification does not mean, however, that conditions would now be basically the same in East and West Germany. On the contrary, the economic problems of unification have been far more severe than many optimists, including Chancellor Helmut Kohl, had expected at first. Forty years of Communism have left deep traces in the social and economic structure of East Germany and the mentality of its people. A planned economy could not be changed over night into a well-functioning market economy. Although East Germany's top communist leaders were all ousted, many old-guard Communists stay on in middle-level positions in the economy and the state bureaucracy. They can not easily be replaced, given the lack of people trained in market mechanisms. In addition, there is the tricky problem of the old secret state police and the uncertainty of how many of them still hold influential positions in politics and society.

The first elections to an all-German parliament are scheduled for December 2, 1990. This parliament will have to prove that, in a reasonable amount of time, it can solve the economic problems in East Germany so that its people will no more feel like second-class citizens in their own country.

Five states (*Laender*) have emerged in East Germany—for example, Saxony and Thuringia. They join the eleven existing states for a total of 16 German states. The new states from East Germany have to become full partners in the federal structure of the country. Real unification will have been achieved only if one speaks no more of East and West Germany but of individual states like Bavaria and Saxony. It must be stressed that the parts of the new Germany are not East and West Germany, but the 16 states.

EPILOGUE

When Americans look outside the North American continent, the European democracies seem in many respects closest to their own country. Europeans may perhaps appear to be not brothers and sisters but cousins. There are at least three reasons for this feeling of proximity. First are historical roots that for many Americans extend to Europe. To be sure, immigrants have come to America from all corners of the world. But the first settlers were Europeans, and the majority of Americans have a European background, even though the newest waves of immigrants have come increasingly from other parts of the world. In the long run, decreased immigration from Europe may weaken the special bonds across the North Atlantic. But, for the time being, these bonds still exist. Many Americans even have relatives in Europe, whom they may visit from time to time. Even for Americans who have lost track of their specific family roots, a trip to Europe can have the character of a reunion with a family heritage.

A second reason why many Americans feel close to Europe is the fact that the majority of stable democracies outside the United States are located in Europe. Arend Lijphart states correctly that worldwide "democracy is a recent and rare phenomenon." He defines democracy, in accordance with my own definition, by two criteria: "political rights, such as the right to participate in free and competitive elections, and civil liberties, such as freedom of speech and association."[78] Based on this definition, Lijphart finds that a mere 21 countries have been continously democratic since World War II; 14 of these are located in Europe. Outside Europe and the United States, Lijphart counts only 6 other stable democracies: Australia, Canada, Iceland, Israel, Japan, and New Zealand. Given this distribution of stable democracies in the world, it is natural for Americans to feel a close affinity to Europe. With the newly emerging democracies in Eastern Europe, this affinity many even increase.

A third reason for the affinity is the fact that, for ordinary Americans, NATO is the best-known military alliance in which their country participates. In U.S. military planning, the NATO partners indeed have a special and enduring significance for the defense of the free world. It remains to be seen how close this partnership will remain after the apparent end of the Cold War.

Given that America is so close to Western Europe with regard to family ties, a democratic form of government, and participation in an important military alliance, it is puzzling for Americans how different Europeans are after all. These differences may not be so apparent at first glance, but a closer look at Europe, such as this book tries to give, reveals major differences between the old and new continents. We have seen for example that Socialism is not a dirty word in Europe, while it has strong negative connotations in the United States. Several European countries have a monarchical form of government but are still full-fledged democracies. Compared to Americans, Europeans vote more for political parties than for individual candidates. In European parliaments, party discipline is much stricter than in the U.S. Congress. A European prime minister may be removed quite easily through a vote of no confidence, but it is very difficult to impeach an American president.

In many respects, Americans are equally puzzling to Europeans. Most Europeans have difficulty understanding the primary system by which Americans select their presidential candidates. They also find it hard to comprehend how initiatives of the U.S. president are often blocked in Congress, a system very different from the parliamentary system practiced in Europe. Most of all, perhaps, Europeans are surprised by questions of political style prevalent in the United States. For example, it is unusual for the spouses of European politicians to play such an important role, as is customary in the United States. Still, in terms of political style, Europeans tend to be amazed by the flag-waving, chanting, dancing, and general noise at American party conventions. Another good example of differences in style is the ways in which Ronald Reagan's and former French president Georges Pompidou's cancers were dealt with. While the public was informed about every detail of Reagan's illness, Pompidou was sick for a long time and finally died before the French people were told about his condition. Insiders in Paris, including many journalists, knew about his fight with cancer, but it was considered a personal matter that did not belong in public. Which case was handled better? An absolute answer seems impossible when dealing with questions of political style and taste that are judged differently in different countries.

As we have seen at several places in this book, relations between the United States and the European democracies are currently rather strained. To ameliorate the situation, the quality of information about each other must improve. Much remains to be done in this respect. The American media's reporting of European affairs is sparse; events with a sensational value, such as terrorist acts in Northern Ireland or of the Italian Red Brigade, are most often covered. By comparison, the European media pay much more attention to the United States, a fact easily explained by the size of the country and its importance as a superpower in world affairs. But the great quantity of American news in the European media does not necessarily mean that Europeans are well informed about the intricacies of life in America. Here too, sensational aspects, like the activities of the Mafia, are often overstressed. Moreover, the reporting tends to be condescending, and many aspects of politics in America are ridiculed. Thus, European journalists have taken many cheap shots at the fact that Ronald Reagan was once a movie star and Jimmy Carter, a peanut farmer. A favorite topic is also the supposedly poor quality of American schools. Here, self-critical American studies help to document the reports with negative quotes and statistics. Overall, the European media tend to convey the impression that life in America is not very sophisticated. The basis for this one-sided view is at least partly a reflection of the envy of formerly powerful countries for a newcomer who has replaced them as the dominant force in world affairs.

Many well-intentioned people on both sides of the Atlantic hope that mutual misperceptions can be remedied through more personal contacts. Here tourism could play a helpful function, but unfortunately its effects are often of a dubious value. Europeans who travel in three weeks to the Empire State Building in New York, the White House in Washington, D.C., the Golden Gate Bridge in San Francisco, and Yellowstone National Park can hardly get to know America. They receive no impression of how most Americans live. The same criticism holds true for many Americans traveling in Europe, in particular, for typical American students backpacking through Europe who tend to have one big party in Europe, meeting together at a few selected places like London, Paris, Amsterdam, Munich, Venice, Florence, Rome, and Athens. They have virtually no opportunity to get to know Europeans in anything but the most superficial way. American students would be better advised to leave the tourist track and take some back roads. Europe has many roads with light motor traffic and even roads reserved for bike riding. Moving at a slow pace from village to village, from farmhouse to farmhouse, allows a deep insight into the European countryside and its people.

If Americans and Europeans knew each other better, would they stop fighting with each other over farm exports, steel quotas, Central America, and so forth? Not necessarily. But they could approach their conflicts in a more rational way. The conflicts themselves would remain, because Europeans and Americans have necessarily different vital interests in world affairs because of their specific locations. Central America is in the backyard of the United States but not of Europe. It is therefore understandable that Communist infiltration in Central America is of greater concern to Americans than to Europeans. In economic matters, the United States and Europe are often natural competitors, both, for example, having large oversupplies of farm products and steel.

Such conflicts of interest must not be negated but, on the contrary, be openly recognized. Only on this basis is a rational bargaining process with mutual give and take possible. Ultimately, Europeans and Americans have so much in common that, as a rule, solutions should be possible that will leave both sides better off than if negotiations broke down. The United States and Europe do not need a love affair but, in their mutual interest, a businesslike partnership.

NOTES

1. Evelyne Pisier, Pierre Bouretz, "Camus et le marxism," *Revue française de science politique* 35(Décembre 1985): 1056.
2. Pauline M. Rosenau, "Philosophy, Methodology, and Research: Marxist Assumptions About Inquiry," *Comparative Political Studies* 20(January 1988): 423–454.
3. Jeane J. Kirkpatrick, *Dictatorships and Double Standards. Rationalism and Reason in Politics* (New York: Simon & Schuster, 1982), p. 51.
4. Kirkpatrick, *Dictatorships and Double Standards*, p. 125.
5. Kirkpatrick, *Dictatorships and Double Standards*, p. 16.
6. George Homans, *Social Behavior: Its Elementary Forms* (New York: Harcourt Brace Jovanovich, 1974).
7. Albert O. Hirschman, *Exit, Voice and Loyalty* (Cambridge, Mass.: Harvard University Press, 1970).
8. Václav Havel, *Letters to Olga* (New York: Knopf, 1988).
9. *Washington Post*, January 26, 1990.
10. Bertolt Brecht, *Threepenny Opera* (New York: Grove Press, 1949), pp. 66–67.
11. Klaus von Beyme, "Right-Wing Extremism in Post-War Europe," *West European Politics* 11(April 1988): pp. 15–16.
12. For the distinction between material and postmaterial value priorities, see Ronald Inglehart, *The Silent Revolution: Changing Values and Political Styles among Western Publics* (Princeton, N.J.: Princeton University Press, 1977).
13. Claude Longchamp, "Linke und Grüne an die Wand nageln und mit dem Flammenwerfer drüber! Die Autopartei unter der sozialwissenschaftlichen Lupe," Referat, gehalten an der Fachtagung Rechtspopulismus in Europa. *Wien*, Dezember 5, 1988.
14. Herbert Kitschelt, "Left-Libertarian Parties: Explaining Innovation in Competitive Party Systems," *World Politics* 40(January 1988): 194–234.
15. Ivor Crewe, "Why Labour Lost the British Election," *Public Opinion*, June/July 1983, p. 60.
16. Enid Lakeman, "The Case for Proportional Representation," in Arend Lijphart and Bernard Grofman, eds., *Choosing an Electoral System: Issues and Alternatives* (New York: Praeger, 1984), p. 49.
17. George H. Hallett, Jr., "Proportional Representation with the Single Transferable Vote: A Basic Requirement for Legislative Elections," in Lijphart and Grofman, *Choosing an Electoral System*, p. 125.
18. Domenico Fisichella, "The Double-Ballot System as a Weapon Against Anti-System Parties," in Lijphart and Grofman, *Choosing an Electoral System*, p. 183.
19. Max Kaase, "Personalized Proportional Representation: The 'Model' of the West German Electoral System," in Lijphart and Grofman, *Choosing an Electoral System*, p. 163.
20. Kaase, "Personalized Proportional Representation," pp. 163–164.
21. *The News and Observer*, Raleigh, N.C. The Associated Press, March 26, 1990.

22. Craig R. Whitney, "A Talk with Helmut Schmidt," *New York Times Magazine*, September 16, 1984, p. 118.
23. Patrick Gordon Walker, *The Cabinet* (London: Jonathan Cape, 1970), p. 151.
24. Richard Crossman, *Inside View* (London: Jonathan Cape, 1972), pp. 50–51.
25. For this argument, see the classical formulation of William H. Riker, *The Theory of Political Coalitions* (New Haven, Conn.: Yale University Press, 1962).
26. Paul Furlong, "The Constitutional Court in Italian Politics," *West European Politics*, 11(July 1988), pp. 21–22.
27. Alec Stone, "In the Shadow of the Constitutional Council: The 'Juridicisation' of the Legislative Process in France," *West European Politics*, 12(April 1989): 30.
28. Robert D. Putnam, "Explaining Institutional Success: The Case of Italian Regional Government," *American Political Science Review* 77(March 1983): 55–74.
29. Arend Lijphart, *Democracies. Patterns of Majoritarian and Consensus Government in Twenty-One Countries* (New Haven, Conn.: Yale University Press, 1984), pp. 169–186.
30. For the half cantons, see footnote on page 122.
31. For the period 1945–1980, see Lijphart, *Democracies*, p. 202.
32. David Butler and Austin Ranney, *Referendums: A Comparative Study of Practice and Theory* (Washington, D.C.: American Enterprise Institute, 1978), p. 226.
33. *New York Times*, November 28, 1989.
34. *New York Times*, November 27, 1989.
35. *New York Times*, January 18, 1990.
36. Carl-Christoph Schweitzer, Detlev Karsten, Robert Spencer, R. Taylor Cole, Donald Kommers, and Anthony Nicholls, eds., *Politics and Government in the Federal Republic of Germany: Basic Documents* (Leamington Spa, Great Britain: Berg Publishers, 1984), p. 278.
37. *Employee Investment Funds in Sweden in 1984*, (Stockholm: Swedish Trade Union Confederation, 1984).
38. *Le Figaro*, December 27, 1989, p. 10.
39. *Die Zeit*, July 27, 1984 (my translation).
40. Hanspeter Kriesi, "New Social Movements and the New Class in the Netherlands," *American Journal of Sociology* 94(March 1989): 1078–1116.
41. Steven E. Finkel, Edward N. Muller, and Karl-Dieter Opp, "Personal Influence, Collective Rationality, and Mass Political Action," *American Political Science Review* 83(September 1989): pp. 885–903.
42. Finkel, Muller, Opp, "Personal Influence, Collective Rationality, and Mass Political Action," p. 893.
43. Jürg Steiner, "Rational Choice Theories and Politics: A Research Agenda and a Moral Question," *PS: Political Science and Politics* 23(March 1990): 46–50.
44. David Easton, *A Systems Analysis of Political Life* (New York: Wiley, 1965), p. 32.
45. Arend Lijphart, "Consociational Democracy," *World Politics* 21(January 1969): 207–225; Gerhard Lehmbruch, "A Noncompetitive Pattern of Conflict Management in Liberal Democracies: The Case of Switzerland, Austria, and Lebanon," in Kenneth MacRae, ed., *Consociational Democracy: Political Accommodation in Segmented Societies* (Toronto: McClelland and Stewart, Carleton Library No. 79, 1974).
46. Gabriel A. Almond, "Comparative Political Systems," *Journal of Politics* 18(August 1956): 391–409.
47. For a more detailed critique of the consociational theory, see Jürg Steiner, "The Consociational Theory and Beyond," *Comparative Politics* 13(April 1981): 339–354.

48. Jürg Steiner, "Research Strategies Beyond Consociational Theory," *Journal of Politics* 43(November 1981): 1243–1244.
49. Steiner, "Research Strategies Beyond Consociational Theory," p. 1243.
50. Raimund E. Germann and Jürg Steiner, "Comparing Decision Modes at the Country Level: Some Methodological Considerations Using Swiss Data," *British Journal of Political Science* 16(January 1985): 123–126.
51. Jürg Steiner and Robert H. Dorff, *A Theory of Political Decision Modes. Intraparty Decision Making in Switzerland* (Chapel Hill: University of North Carolina Press, 1980).
52. Jean Ziegler, *Une Suisse au-dessus de tout soupçon* (Paris: Editions du Seuil, 1976).
53. Arend Lijphart, *Democracy in Plural Societies* (New Haven, Conn.: Yale University Press, 1977), p. 238.
54. Arend Lijphart, "The Power-Sharing Approach," in Joseph V. Montville, ed., *Conflict and Peacemaking in Multiethnic Societies*, p. 499.
55. Richard Rose, "Northern Ireland: The Irreducible Conflict," in Montville, *Conflict and Peacemaking in Multiethnic Societies*, p. 133.
56. In addition to various English publications of international organizations, such as the United Nations and UNESCO, I consulted also the statistical yearbooks of Yugoslavia and Czechoslovakia. For helping me with the translation of these yearbooks, I express my thanks to Joseph Anderle and Vasa Mihailovich, both colleagues at the University of North Carolina at Chapel Hill.
57. *New York Times*, March 28, 1990.
58. Manfred E. Streit, "Market Order and Welfare Politics: The Mirage of Neo-Corporatism," Research Unit for Societal Developments, University of Mannheim, Working Papers, No. 3, 1987, pp. 21–22.
59. Streit, "Market Order and Welfare Politics," p. 7.
60. Manfred G. Schmidt, "The Welfare State and the Economy in Periods of Economic Crisis: A Comparative Study of Twenty-three OECD Nations," *European Journal of Political Research* 11(1983): 20–21.
61. Manfred G. Schmidt, "The Politics of Labour Market Policy. Structural and Political Determinants of Rates of Unemployment in Industrial Nations," in Francis G. Castles, Franz Lehner, and Manfred G. Schmidt, eds., *Managing Mixed Economies* (Berlin and New York: Walter de Gruyter, 1988), p. 20.
62. Franz Lehner, "The Political Economy of Distributive Conflict," in Castles, Lehner, and Schmidt, *Managing Mixed Economies*, p. 70.
63. Frank L. Wilson, "French Interest Group Politics: Pluralist or Neocorporatist?" *American Political Science Review* 77(December 1983): 895.
64. Wilson, "French Interest Group Politics," p. 901.
65. Peter Katzenstein, *Corporatism and Change: Austria, Switzerland, and the Politics of Industry* (Ithaca, N.Y.: Cornell University Press, 1984).
66. Katzenstein, *Corporatism and Change*, p. 77.
67. Katzenstein, *Corporatism and Change*, p. 78.
68. J.T.S. Keeler, "Situating France on the Pluralism-Corporatism Continuum: A Critique of and Alternative to the Wilson Perspective," *Comparative Politics* 17(January 1985): 246.
69. Robert H. Dorff and Jürg Steiner: Decision Cases in Western Democracies: A Data Bank," *Comparative Political Studies* 20(July 1987): 160–173.
70. Manfred Schmidt, "The Welfare State and the Economy," Paper Presented at the Conference on the Future of Party Government, European University Institute, Fiesole, 1983.
71. Mary L. Volcansek, "Impact of Judicial Policies in the European Community: The

Italian Constitutional Court and European Community Law," *Western Political Quarterly* 42(December 1989): p. 580.

72. *Le Figaro*, December 27, 1989.
73. Roderick MacFarquhar, "Regionalize, and Centralize, Europe," *New York Times*, December 20, 1989.
74. Henry Ashby Turner, "Baseless Fears of a Unified Germany," *New York Times*, February 11, 1990.
75. *New York Times*, March 16, 1990.
76. *The New York Times Magazine*, February 25, 1990, p. 14.
77. *New York Times*, December 7, 1989.
78. Lijphart, *Democracies*, p. 37.

SUGGESTIONS FOR FURTHER READING

BOOKS

Ashford, Douglas E. *British Dogmatism and French Pragmatism: Central-Local Policymaking in the Welfare State.* London: Allen & Unwin, 1982.

Baylis, Thomas A. *Governing by Committee. Collegial Leadership in Advanced Societies.* Albany: State University of New York Press, 1989.

Bogdonor, Vernon, ed. *Coalition Government in Western Europe.* London: Heinemann Educational Books, 1983.

Browne, Eric C., and John Dreijmanis, eds. *Government Coalitions in Western Democracies.* New York: Longman, 1982.

Butler, David, Howard R. Penniman, and Austin Ranney, eds. *Democracy at the Polls: A Comparative Study of Competitive National Elections.* Washington, D.C.: American Enterprise Institute, 1981.

Castles, Francis G., Franz Lehner, Manfred G. Schmidt, eds. *Managing Mixed Economies.* Berlin and New York: Walter de Gruyter, 1988.

Daalder, Hans, and Peter Mair, eds. *Western European Party Systems: Continuity and Change.* Beverly Hills, Calif.: Sage, 1983.

Dyson, Kenneth. *The State Tradition in Western Europe.* Oxford, England: Martin Robertson, 1980.

Goldthorpe, John H., ed. *Order and Conflict in Contemporary Capitalism.* London: Oxford University Press, 1985.

Gourevitch, Peter, et al. *Unions and Economic Crisis: Britain, West Germany and Sweden.* Boston: Allen & Unwin, 1984.

Inglehart, Ronald. *The Silent Revolution: Changing Values and Political Styles Among Western Publics.* Princeton, N.J.: Princeton University Press, 1977.

Inglehart, Ronald. *Culture Shift in Advanced Industrial Society.* Princeton, N.J.: Princeton University Press, 1989.

Katzenstein, Peter J. *Corporatism and Change: Austria, Switzerland, and the Politics of Industry.* Ithaca, N.Y.: Cornell University Press, 1984.

Katzenstein, Peter J. *Small States and World Markets.* Ithaca, N.Y.: Cornell University Press, 1985.

Lange, Peter, George Ross, and Maurizio Vannicelli. *Unions, Change and Crisis: French and Italian Union Strategy and the Political Economy, 1945–1980.* Boston: Allen & Unwin, 1981.

Lawson, Kay, and Peter H. Merkl, eds. *When Parties Fail: Emerging Alternative Organizations.* Princeton: N.J.: Princeton University Press, 1988.

Lijphart, Arend. *Democracies: Patterns of Majoritarian and Consensus Government in Twenty-One Countries.* New Haven: Yale University Press, 1984.

Lijphart, Arend, and Bernard Grofman, eds. *Choosing an Electoral System: Issues and Alternatives.* New York: Praeger, 1984.

Logue, John. *Socialism and Abundance: Radical Socialism in the Danish Welfare State.* Minneapolis: University of Minnesota Press, 1982.

Marks, Gary. *Unions in Politics. Britain, Germany, and the United States in the Nineteenth and Early Twentieth Centuries.* Princeton, N.J.: Princeton University Press, 1989.

Miliband, Ralph. *Capitalist Democracy in Britain.* London: Oxford University Press, 1982.

Montville, Joseph V., ed. *Conflict and Peacemaking in Multiethnic Societies.* Lexington: D.C. Heath, 1989.

Powell, G. Bingham. *Contemporary Democracies: Participation, Stability and Violence.* Cambridge, Mass.: Harvard University Press, 1982.

Rose, Richard, and Ezra N. Suleiman, eds. *Presidents and Prime Ministers.* Washington, D.C.: American Enterprise Institute, 1980.

Tiryakian, Edward A., and Ronald Rogowski, eds. *New Nationalism of the Developed West.* Boston: Allen & Unwin, 1985.

Zysman, John. *Governments, Markets, and Growth: Financial Systems and the Politics of Industrial Change.* Ithaca, N.Y.: Cornell University Press, 1983.

PROFESSIONAL JOURNALS

British Journal of Political Science
Comparative Political Studies
Comparative Politics
European Journal of Political Research
Government and Opposition
Political Studies
Politische Vierteljahresschrift (Germany)
Revue Française de Science Politique (France)
Scandinavian Political Studies
West European Politics
World Politics

NEWSPAPERS

The Times (London)
Le Monde (Paris)
Frankfurter Allgemeine Zeitung (Frankfurt)
Neue Zürcher Zeitung (Zurich)

INDEX